EU CIVIL JUSTICE

This seventh volume in the Swedish Studies in European Law series brings together some of the most prominent scholars working within the fast-evolving field of EU civil justice. Civil justice has an impact on matters involving, inter alia, family relationships, consumers, entrepreneurs, employees, small and medium-sized businesses and large multinational corporations. It therefore has great power and potential. Over the past 15 years a wealth of EU measures have been enacted in this field. Issues arising from the implementation thereof and practice in relation to these measures are now emerging. Hence, this volume will explore the benefits as well as the challenges of these measures. The particular themes covered include forum shopping, alternative dispute resolution, simplified procedures and debt collection, family matters and collective redress. In addition, the deepening of the field that continues post-Lisbon has occasioned a new level of regulatory and policy challenges. These are discussed in the final part of the volume which focuses on mutual recognition also in the broader European law context of integration in the Area of Freedom, Security and Justice.

EU Civil Justice

Current Issues and Future Outlook

Swedish Studies in European Law
Volume 7

Edited by
Burkhard Hess
Maria Bergström
and
Eva Storskrubb

SVENSKA NÄTVERKET FÖR EUROPARÄTTSFORSKNING

Max Planck Institute LUXEMBOURG for Procedural Law

·HART·
PUBLISHING
OXFORD AND PORTLAND, OREGON
2016

Hart Publishing, 16C Worcester Place, Oxford, OX1 2JW
Telephone: +44 (0)1865 517530 Fax: +44 (0)1865 510710
E-mail: mail@hartpub.co.uk
Website: http://www.hartpub.co.uk

Published in North America (US and Canada) by
Hart Publishing
c/o International Specialized Book Services
920 NE 58th Avenue, Suite 300
Portland, OR 97213-3786
USA
Tel: +1 503 287 3093 or toll-free: (1) 800 944 6190
Fax: +1 503 280 8832
E-mail: orders@isbs.com
Website: http://www.isbs.com

British Library Cataloguing in Publication Data
Data Available

Library of Congress Cataloging-in-Publication Data

EU civil justice : current issues and future outlook/edited by Burkhard Hess, Maria Bergström and Eva Storskrubb.
pages cm. – (Swedish studies in European law; volume 7)

includes papers presented at the conference "Civil Justice in the EU: Growing and Teething" held in 2013 in Uppsala organised by the Swedish Network for European Legal Studies (SNELS) in collaboration with the Max Planck Institute in Luxembourg for International, European and Regulatory Procedural Law, and Uppsala University.—ECIP preface.

ISBN 978-1-84946-682-0 (hardback : alk. paper) 1. Justice, Administration of—European Union countries—Congresses. 2. Civil law—European Union countries—International unification—Congresses. I. Hess, Burkhard, editor. II. Bergström, Maria, 1969– editor. III. Storskrubb, Eva, editor.

KJE3655.E9 2015 349.24—dc23
2015033346

ISBN: 978-1-84946-682-0

Typeset by Compuscript Ltd, Shannon
Printed and bound in Great Britain by
CPI Group (UK) Ltd, Croydon CR0 4YY

Preface

Civil justice in the EU broadly impacts on civil matters involving, inter alia, family relationships, consumers, entrepreneurs, employees, small and medium-sized businesses and large multinational corporations. Therefore, it has great power and potential to contribute to the European project. Since 1999, a decade and a half of policies related to the political vision of an Area of Freedom, Security and Justice (AFSJ) have entailed a wealth of new and ever-deepening measures. The benefits and challenges created by implementing these measures formed the background to and framework for a conference in late 2013 organised by the Swedish Network for European Legal Studies (SNELS) in collaboration with the Max Planck Institute in Luxembourg for International, European and Regulatory Procedural Law, and Uppsala University. The papers in this collection were subsequently prepared based on the presentations given and the themes explored at the conference. We would like to thank all the speakers and participants at the conference for fruitful and engaging exchanges. We would also like to thank all the authors for their efforts and insightful contributions.

The title of the conference—'Civil Justice in the EU: Growing and Teething?'—played on the colloquial metaphor of civil justice as a baby or young child growing up happily and perhaps even prodigiously but equally experiencing certain growing or teething pains. Civil justice has been a prodigious area within the AFSJ, but unsurprisingly this rapid growth has not been entirely without problems and has raised certain issues both at the micro level of practical implementation and application and at the macro constitutional level of fundamental rights and freedoms. In particular, in the context of the reform of certain measures and of the deeper integration aims behind some of the more recently proposed measures, searching questions can be asked in relation to whether the professed aims of civil justice are being met. The aims of the conference were to capture recent developments, measures and debates with a focus on particular topics of civil justice, to identify current issues and upcoming challenges, and hopefully to understand emerging trends and provide a future outlook.

The keynote speech at the conference given by Burkhard Hess on the 'State of the Civil Justice Union', reproduced in chapter one, provides a panoramic view of the current state of affairs in the European judicial area. Hess picks up on several specific EU developments and measures that are delved into more extensively in subsequent chapters and he puts them in an overall context. He identifies different levels of procedural law-making in Europe: the domestic level, the cross-border level, and the supranational

EU level. Domestic procedural systems are touched by all of these levels and are, according to Hess, challenged by diverging performances, competition between each other, and pressures to communicate and cooperate. He finds that the regulatory approach of encouraging true cooperation is important and highly relevant in moulding the future of civil justice. He observes three parallel strands of regulatory development in the EU procedural landscape: the coordination of domestic systems, minimum standards, and self-standing procedures. Crucially, he notes that at present there is neither a master plan nor a comprehensive approach. Procedural science should, according to Hess, also address the broader perspective and ask: 'where will the civil justice system in Europe stand in ten years' time?' Many of the subsequent chapters rise to the challenge set by Hess and also seek to explore broader regulatory intersections albeit within the confines of a particular theme.

The first specific theme explored at the conference was forum shopping with the following introductory questions being asked: does the EU jurisdiction framework work in practice; what about third-country litigants and the EU legal order; and has case law added predictability? The recast of the Brussels I Regulation (Regulation (EU) 1215/2012), which has applied since 10 January 2015, formed the starting point for discussions. The contribution of Gilles Cuniberti in chapter two falls within this theme, specifically dealing with jurisdiction clauses, *lis pendens* and the 'Italian torpedo' problem. The strengthening of jurisdiction clauses by creating a special exception to the *lis pendens* rule was one of the most significant aims of the recast of the Regulation. Cuniberti, however, notes that there are several uncertainties surrounding the new rules and identifies in particular the issues of conflicting jurisdiction clauses and complex or asymmetric jurisdiction clauses. In dealing with the logic of the regime behind the Brussels I Regulation, he notes that there is a 'general philosophy of mutual trust'. Mutual trust is a central issue for the development of civil justice and it runs like a thread through the chapters in this volume, being raised both explicitly and implicitly in many contributions. Mutual trust also forms a part of the final specific theme, mutual recognition, which we return to in the final contributions.

Alternative dispute resolution (ADR), in particular the consumer perspective, formed the focal point of our second theme of enquiry where the context of the debate was the new sector-specific EU measures for consumers; the ADR Directive and the online dispute resolution (ODR) Regulation (Directive 2013/11/EU and Regulation (EU) 524/2013). Here, the underlying questions were, inter alia: is ADR the right approach; can mediation ensure access to justice; and is further and deeper regulation the way forward? The contribution of Jim Davies in chapter three raises the question of whether there is too much optimism behind the consumer ADR Directive and ODR Regulation that will apply from July 2015 and January 2016 respectively. In particular, he notes that the regulatory intersection of these measures is closely linked to substantive consumer law as well as the broader projects of the Internal Market such as the Digital Agenda for Europe. He questions whether the complexities of consumer behaviour and the diverse domestic structure into which the new framework is intended to fit as an 'idealised and sanitised model' have been sufficiently considered. The contribution of Cristina Mariottini in chapter four looks at ADR and consumer rights more broadly than in the EU civil justice context, dealing specifically with ICANN domain name registration and its associated international dispute resolution process. This process has been entirely detached from domestic and EU law although it addresses business activities with a strong impact on the Internal Market. In this context, Mariottini raises the difficult issue of consumer redress and access to a dispute resolution process and like Davies she also highlights regulatory challenges and weaknesses.

The next theme to be analysed at the conference was simplified procedures and debt collection, the context being the European Enforcement Order (EEO), Payment Order (EOP) and Small Claims (ESCP) Regulations (Regulations (EC) 805/2004, (EC) 1896/2006 and (EC) 861/2007). Given that these measures have been applicable for some years now, the underlying concern of our conference was 'much ado about nothing', ie, what impact if any have these measures had and have there been any problems with implementation? The introductory questions were set in the same vein: has an additional small claims mechanism added anything in practice; and has the removal of *exequatur* in enforcement and payment orders been successful? The contribution of Carla Crifò in chapter five demonstrates, from the UK and in particular the English viewpoint, both principled and practical challenges in the application and further development of these measures. From the practical perspective she identifies the difficulty of 'fitting' the European measures into the domestic legal framework, given the concomitant lack of information and lack of awareness. She perceives a legal uncertainty in the measures and a parallel lacklustre approach of negotiators and legislators to the measures. She observes that you cannot simply assume, as the Commission does, that mutual trust will magically ensure similar action at the domestic level, for example, in domestic courts.

In chapter six, Xandra Kramer first analyses empirical data and information from Dutch courts in relation to the EOP and ESCP Regulations. She finds that in general there has been a low uptake and insignificant growth over the reviewed years, partly due to a lack of awareness. She also finds that based on the limited cases so far, the procedures have worked fairly well. However, perhaps unsurprisingly, issues have arisen in relation to the international procedural aspects, such as language, jurisdiction and service abroad even for these simplified procedures. At the end of her chapter, she reviews the European Commission's proposal for amendments to the ESCP Regulation and notes in particular the proposal to regulate court fees that could, if successful, have a significant impact on domestic judicial policies and court financing. Like Crifò, she concludes that institutional idealism and economic rhetoric will not suffice as driving forces for civil justice and that an effort should be made to raise awareness as well as research and work on 'filling the gaps between European and domestic procedure in daily practice'. Cristian Oro Martinez also deals with the application and proposed reform of the ESCP Regulation in chapter seven. His analysis is significantly based on research of empirical data from a number of Member States. He identifies several issues relating to the scope of the Regulation and its interplay with both domestic laws and other EU civil justice instruments. He also highlights the 'severe consequences' of deferring many aspects of the functioning of the Regulation to domestic procedure, such as the possibility of appeal. Therefore, he finds that there is pressure towards further harmonisation beyond the current reform proposal.

The next conference theme was the family law field of civil justice, which has seen a number of significant measures recently enacted including the Rome III Regulation (Regulation (EU) 1259/2010) applicable from 21 June 2012 only for the Member States participating in the enhanced cooperation and the Succession Regulation (Regulation (EU) 650/2012) applicable from 17 August 2015. One issue that was raised was the consequence of the fragmentation caused by the Rome III Regulation being the first enhanced cooperation in civil justice. In her contribution in chapter eight, Maarit Jänterä-Jareborg provides an insight into the reasons why unanimity was not possible. She approaches the issue from a Nordic, and specifically Swedish and Finnish perspective, and notes that the position of these Member States may have been perceived as 'legal irritants' in the civil justice sphere of family law. She, however, sees that overall the development is far more unitary than immediately meets the eye. In addition, the Nordic dimension has even led to EU rules having an impact beyond the EU Member States. Another question for the family law theme was how the Succession Regulation will change the landscape of civil justice. Björn Laukemann in chapter nine deals with one particular and important novelty in the Succession Regulation, the European Certificate of Succession. He notes that 'every legislative innovation comes at a price' and finds that for the Succession Certificate, and its ancillary new legal concept of cross-border 'acceptance', this price is a lack of regulatory coherence. He identifies several open issues in particular in relation to real property and the interaction with transfer of ownership questions and the applicable law under the *lex rei sitae* principle.

Collective redress was the next theme discussed, with the context being the Commission's Communication and Recommendation, COM(2013) 401 and C(2013) 3539, published on 11 June 2013 following an extensive consultation process. Several levels of enquiry were addressed in relation to these soft law measures, the underlying questions being, inter alia: can collective redress provide additional guarantees for European consumers and other litigants; and how should such collective redress rules be modelled?

In chapter ten, Laura Ervo considers the Communication and Recommendation model as unsatisfactory as regards the choice between 'opt-in' and 'opt-out', ie, for constituting the claimant group in collective redress. Based on a comparative Nordic analysis, as well as on arguments related to the functions of civil proceedings in society and access to justice, she argues in favour of the opt-out model stating that 'Without courage and a bit of risk-taking there will be no progress'. Stefaan Voet, who deals with the funding and financing of collective redress proceedings in chapter eleven, is pleased that the Recommendation has not overlooked funding because 'the funding and financing issue is the crux of the matter, because it goes to the heart of the class action system'. However, there are several more detailed issues, policy choices and particular procedural aspects to take into account as highlighted in his comparative analysis and review of funding options. Rebecca Money-Kyrle's contribution in chapter twelve deals with legal standing in collective redress matters, juxtaposing various underlying approaches and perspectives, including the autonomy principles, social justice and economic analyses. She sees that there are tensions, unresolved confusion and 'vacillation' in the overall EU approach to standing and finds that it fails to fully acknowledge the social justice perspective. She notes that there are currently varying approaches in the Member States and that these may have an impact and create significant problems of discrimination, forum shopping and complexity in a cross-border context. She considers the lack of clarification in the Recommendation in these respects as a missed opportunity. Finally, she raises regulatory cohesion and integration of regulatory approaches, for example, between collective redress and ADR schemes, which she finds that the Recommendation also fails to build and integrate.

The final theme dealt with the quest for mutual recognition in EU civil justice asking questions such as: how are the national courts coping with mutual recognition; and is the complete abolition of *exequatur* possible? Marie Linton provides an overview in chapter thirteen of the various EU civil justice measures to simplify or remove *exequatur*. There is a patchwork of schemes and a fragmentation that may lead to confusion and complication for users, for parties, as well as for courts and other relevant authorities. In addition, she highlights that there is a tension between the abolition of *exequatur* and the protection of a defendant's rights. Further, there is a tension with national laws of execution that becomes more apparent with the recent reforms. In chapter fourteen, Marta Requejo Isidro also analyses the abolition of the *exequatur*, in particular in light of the *ordre public* exception. She contrasts the reform of the Brussels I Regulation with case law concerning recognition and enforcement under the Brussels II *bis* Regulation and fundamental rights. In particular she asks what level of discretion remains for Member States in their public policy review. In her conclusions she reverts to mutual trust and notes that differences in understanding between Member States on fundamental rights should 'come to light' and be 'addressed' in the interest of mutual trust. In chapter fifteen, Eva Storskrubb analyses the concept of mutual recognition from an overarching regulatory perspective. She notes that it has been described as a principle of tolerance, similar to multiculturalism, and that it embodies the idea of 'all different, all equal'. She questions whether the concept should be imported into civil justice without safeguards and asks if the civil justice understanding of what mutual recognition fully entails is 'coming late to the game'. Finally, in chapter sixteen, Maria Bergström identifies some of the benefits and shortcomings, which are inextricably linked to the principle of mutual recognition within criminal and civil justice and the broader context of the AFSJ. While drawing on the examples provided in this volume, her chapter emphasises the need for a methodological awareness and argues that transplanting not only the principle of mutual recognition, but also the methodological considerations so inextricably linked with this cornerstone of judicial cooperation in civil and criminal matters, might be beneficial.

All in all, the contributions in this volume demonstrate that recent developments in the European law of civil procedure have triggered a multitude of regulatory approaches, which were implemented in different instruments in a rather uncoordinated way. The experience of the last 15 years demonstrates that it is now time to evaluate and to streamline existing instruments and to improve the efficient and uniform application of the existing law. The political programme of the Juncker Commission has slowed down the respective legislative process. Nevertheless, there are still fields where EU law-making is needed in order to improve the current situation—one example relates to cross-border collective redress. However, the challenge for legal science today is to assist the ongoing review process in order to discuss the wider perspective of the future architecture of the EU civil justice system. The Uppsala conference of 2013 and this book have aimed to contribute to the ongoing political debate on the future procedural landscape in the AFSJ.

Burkhard Hess, Maria Bergström and Eva Storskrubb

Contents

Table of Cases

European Court of Human Rights

France

Germany

International Criminal Court

Italy

Netherlands

Spain

Sweden

United Kingdom

United States of America

Table of Legislation

European Union

Treaties

Directives

Other Instruments

Finland

France

Germany (Federal Republic)

Norway

Poland

Portugal

Spain

United States of America

Table of International Instruments

1

The State of the Civil Justice Union

BURKHARD HESS*

1. INTRODUCTION: EUROPEAN PROCEDURAL LAW: THE CURRENT STATE OF AFFAIRS

MORE THAN 50 years after the foundation of the European Union the procedural landscape in Europe has been transformed considerably. These developments become evident if you go back half a century: in the 1960s, the procedural systems of the EU Member States acted as self-contained regimes; cross-border litigation was managed using national norms and even then such cases were an exception. In academia comparative procedural law was not recognized as important, and scientific exchange and meetings of specialists of procedural law took place only on rare occasions.[1] Procedural law was considered as part of public law, and its application was dominated by national codes and procedural cultures. The procedural laws and the procedural legal science in Europe operated more or less as self-contained regimes.[2]

Today, the situation has changed considerably: the procedural systems of the EU Member States are coordinated and interlinked by various EU instruments. Important areas of procedural law have been harmonized, especially in international civil litigation. Since 1999, the European Union disposes of a genuine competence in private international and procedural law (*cf* Articles 67 and 81 of the Treaty on the Functioning of the European Union (TFEU)). At first sight, the list of the adopted instruments is impressive as it encompasses almost 20 different instruments.[3] Sometimes,

* Director, Max Planck Institute Luxembourg for International, European and Regulatory Procedural Law; Professor, Heidelberg University and University of Luxembourg.

[1] B Hess, 'Deutsches Zivilprozessrecht zwischen nationaler Selbständigkeit und europäischem Anpassungszwang' (2010) 27 *Ritsumeikan Law Review* 191, 199ff.

[2] However, there were some bilateral and (sometimes) multilateral conventions on specific issues of international legal assistance, which were seldom applied. H Schack, *Internationales Zivilverfahrensrecht*, 6th edn (Munich, CH Beck, 2014) paras 59ff.

[3] For an overview *cf* B Hess, 'The Brussels I Regulation: Recent Case Law of the CJEU and the Commission's Proposed Recast' (2012) 49 *Common Market Law Review* 1075ff; below (n 11).

the European law of civil procedure is assimilated into the instruments on cross-border litigation;[4] at other times, it is assimilated into European private international law.[5]

However, these approaches do not provide the whole picture, as there are additional areas where Union law strongly influences the civil procedures of the EU Member States. From the perspective of the European legislator, procedural law comes into the realm of law-making whenever the integrative processes of the Internal Market and the judicial area deserve specific legislative action.[6] Against this backdrop, it comes as no surprise that European law-making also addresses procedural law although the national civil procedures have not been a main focus of the EU legislator so far. Yet, recent legislative activity, especially with regard to consumer ADR, collective redress and the protection of IP rights, shows a growing influence of EU law on national civil procedures.[7] Although the European Court of Justice developed the principle of the procedural autonomy of EU Member States, this principle does not at all preclude all legislative activity in this area in order to implement EU law in an efficient way.[8] It must be noted that the competences of the Union with regard to procedural law are not confined to Article 81 TFEU (requiring cross-border implications) and—on the contrary—can also be based on the general competence provided in Article 114 TFEU, as well as on the more specific competences provided in Article 118 TFEU (on the protection of patents)[9] or Article 102 (addressing the enforcement of cartel law).[10]

2. DIFFERENT AREAS OF EUROPEAN LAW-MAKING

2.1 The Legal Framework for Cross-Border Litigation

As the task of this introductory chapter is to examine the European *acquis* in procedural law, a brief stocktaking of the existing legislation would seem to be necessary. At present, there are three areas where EU law influences national civil procedures: first, through the instruments on international civil litigation; second, by harmonizing domestic procedures and, third, by

[4] J Adolphsen, *Europäisches Zivilprozessrecht*, 2nd edn (Baden-Baden, Nomos, 2014).

[5] G Van Calster, *European Private International Law* (Oxford, Hart Publishing, 2013) 1–2; P Stone, *EU Private International Law*, 2nd edn (Cheltenham, Edward Elgar, 2012).

[6] B Hess, *Europäisches Zivilprozessrecht* (Heidelberg, CF Müller, 2010) § 3, paras 1ff.

[7] XE Kramer, 'Procedure Matters: Construction and Deconstructivism in European Civil Procedure' *Erasmus Law Lectures 33* (The Hague, Eleven International Publishing, 2013) 23ff.

[8] Hess, *Europäisches Zivilprozessrecht* (n 6) § 11, para 4.

[9] A recent example is the Directive on Consumer Mediation of 21 May 2013 [2013] OJ L165/63, see (n 37). This legal situation is not always appropriately assessed in the legal literature, especially in Germany where the principle of subsidiarity is often used as a vehicle for contesting any legitimacy of EU action.

[10] Hess, *Europäisches Zivilprozessrecht* (n 6) § 2, paras 43ff.

means of the considerable influence of the Court of Justice of the European Union (CJEU) and the European Court of Human Rights (ECtHR) on the judicial architecture of the Member States.

At first sight, the legislative agenda in international procedural law has been and still is impressive. During the last 15 years, the following Regulations have been adopted: Brussels I[11] (including the recast),[12] Brussels II *bis*,[13] the Evidence Regulation,[14] the Service Regulation (including a recast),[15] the Insolvency Regulation,[16] the Maintenance Regulation,[17] the European Enforcement Order (EEO) Regulation,[18] the European Small Claims (ESCP) Regulation,[19] the European Payment Order (EOP) Regulation,[20] and the Succession Regulation.[21] Two directives were adopted: on legal aid[22] and on mediation[23] in cross-border cases. In 2013, a regulation on mutual recognition of protection measures in civil matters was enacted—the purpose of this instrument is to protect victims of crime and violence.[24] Recently, the Regulation on the Attachment of Bank Accounts was published—the latter being the first European instrument which addresses cross-border

[11] Regulation (EC) No 44/2001 of 22 December 2000 on jurisdiction and the recognition and enforcement of judgments in civil and commercial matters [2001] OJ L12/1.

[12] Regulation (EC) No 1215/2012 of 12 December 2012 on jurisdiction and the recognition and enforcement of judgments in civil and commercial matters (recast) [2012] OJ L351/1; effective from 10 January 2015.

[13] Regulation (EC) No 2201/2003 of 27 November 2003 concerning jurisdiction and the recognition and enforcement of judgments in matrimonial matters and the matters of parental responsibility, repealing Regulation (EC) No 1347/2000 [2003] OJ L338/1.

[14] Regulation (EC) No 1206/2001 of 28 May 2001 on cooperation between the courts of the Member States in the taking of evidence in civil and commercial matters [2001] OJ L174/1.

[15] Regulation (EC) No 1393/2007 of 13 November 2007 on the service in the Member States of judicial and extrajudicial documents in civil or commercial matters and repealing Regulation (EC) No 1348/2000 of 29 May 2000 [2007] OJ L324/79.

[16] Regulation (EC) No 1346/2000 of 29 May 2000 on insolvency proceedings [2000] OJ L160/1.

[17] Regulation (EC) No 4/2009 of 18 December 2008 on jurisdiction, applicable law, recognition and enforcement of decisions and cooperation in matters relating to maintenance obligations [2009] OJ L7/1.

[18] Regulation (EC) No 805/2004 of 21 April 2004 creating a European Enforcement Order for uncontested claims [2004] OJ L143/15.

[19] Regulation (EC) No 861/2007 of 11 July 2007 establishing a European Small Claims Procedure [2007] OJ L199/1.

[20] Regulation (EC) No 1896/2006 of 12 December 2006 creating a European order for payment procedure [2006] OJ L399/1.

[21] Regulation (EU) No 650/2012 of 4 July 2012 on jurisdiction, applicable law, recognition and enforcement of decisions and acceptance and enforcement of authentic instruments in matters of succession and on the creation of a European Certificate of Succession [2012] OJ L201/107.

[22] Directive 2002/8/EC of 27 January 2003 to improve access to justice in cross-border disputes by establishing minimum common rules relating to legal aid for such disputes [2003] OJ L26/41.

[23] Directive 2008/52/EC of 21 May 2008 on certain aspects of mediation in civil and commercial matters [2008] OJ L136/3.

[24] Regulation (EU) No 606/2013 of 12 June 2013 on mutual recognition of protection measures in civil matters [2013] OJ L181/4.

enforcement.[25] All these instruments encompass in their scope a wide array of cross-border civil litigation; many of them address very specific areas; some of them overlap.[26] The Brussels I Regulation can be regarded as the backbone instrument of European civil procedural law as it provides the basic rules on jurisdiction, pendency and free movement of civil judgments. In addition, the Brussels I Regulation is often used as a term of reference for the parallel regulations on civil procedure.[27]

From the perspective of regulatory techniques applied, it is possible to distinguish several 'generations' of legal instruments. The first generation aimed at the coordination of the national procedures in cross-border situations by providing for common rules on jurisdiction, pendency and recognition, and enforcement. The Brussels I Regulation (2001), the Insolvency Regulation (2000) and the former Brussels II Regulation (2000) are pertinent examples.[28] The second generation aims at the abolition of *exequatur* proceedings and is based on the overarching principle of mutual recognition.[29] Since 2004, the European legislator has endorsed several sectoral instruments, which provide for procedural minimum standards and rules, and for an automatic recognition of judicial decisions in other Member States. These instruments focus on procedural law; the most prominent examples are the EEO Regulation (2004), the EOP Regulation (2006) and the ESCP Regulation (2007). The latter instrument provides for a self-standing European procedure in cross-border cases whose value does not exceed the amount of EUR 2,000.[30]

Since 2008, the regulatory approach of the European lawmaker has changed again: private international law (conflict of laws) became a priority, and the Rome II and Rome I Regulations on the applicable law to torts and contracts were adopted. Recent instruments openly combine international procedural law and private international law. The Regulations on Maintenance (2009) and Succession (2012) are the latest examples of this

[25] Regulation (EU) No 655/2014 of 15 May 2014 establishing a European Account Preservation Order procedure to facilitate cross-border debt recovery in civil and commercial matters [2014] OJ L189/59; B Hess and K Raffelsieper, 'Eckpunkte der Kontenpfändungsverordnung' in B Hess (ed), *Die Anerkennung im internationalen Zivilprozessrecht* (Bielefeld, Gieseking, 2014) 214f.

[26] The current, sometimes incoherent situation is criticized in the legal literature, *cf* T Rauscher, 'Der Wandel von Zustellungsstandards zu Zustellungsvorschriften im Europäischen Zivilprozessrecht' in D Baetge et al (eds), *Die richtige Ordnung Festschrift für Jan Kropholler* (Tübingen, Mohr Siebeck, 2008) 851.

[27] B Hess, T Pfeiffer and P Schlosser, *Heidelberg Report on the Brussels I Regulation* (Munich, CH Beck, 2008) para 1; Hess, 'The Brussels I Regulation' (n 3). eg, Conclusions AG Spunar, Case C-4/14 *Bohez v Wiertz*, EU:C:2015:233, paras 70ff (on the application of Art 49 of the Brussels I Regulation in the context of the Brussels II *bis* Regulation).

[28] Hess, *Europäisches Zivilprozessrecht* (n 6) § 3, paras 13ff.

[29] ibid, paras 24ff.

[30] The proposed reforms of the Regulation are addressed by C Oro Martinez in this volume, chapter 7.

'third generation'. However, the classification of different 'generations' of EU instruments does not imply that one type definitely out performs law-making according to the previous model. In the current practice, all the different types of law-making are applied simultaneously. In this respect, the recast of the Brussels I Regulation still appears to be an instrument of the first generation.[31] The difficulty in separating different generations or types of instruments also stems from the fact that the law-making process has slowed down during the last few years due to political resistance in the Member States and the European Parliament with regard to underlying regulatory concepts such as mutual trust, the abolition of the public policy clause and the growing empowerment of the CJEU as a consequence of the communitarization of procedural (and substantive) law.[32]

2.2 Domestic Procedures Influenced by European Law

The second area of EU law-making in procedural law relates to the domestic procedures of the Member States. Here, it should be noted at the outset that the core parts of the national procedural laws have remained untouched so far. However, there are specific areas where European law influences the civil procedures; the most prominent example is the Directive on the enforcement of IP rights.[33] This Directive provides for minimum standards with regard to the preservation and the disclosure of evidence, rights of information (to be obtained from the (presumed) infringer of IP rights as well as from third parties), and provisional measures.[34] As the IP Directive only addresses a specific area of law (infringement of IP rights) its implementation at the domestic level of the Member States has usually not affected general procedural law. In some Member States, as in Germany, the Directive influenced the application and interpretation of general procedural law, which is considered in the legal literature as old-fashioned and in need of legal reform.[35] However, a comprehensive reform of the provisions of the Code of Civil Procedure on the taking (and evaluation) of evidence has not yet taken place. It remains to be seen whether the implementation of the Directive

[31] Although *exequatur* proceedings were abolished, the grounds for non-recognition of a foreign enforcement title are maintained. In practice, the cross-border enforcement of judgments has become more difficult than under the 'old' Regulation, see (n 95) ff.

[32] The political dimensions of the latest developments, which are also strongly influenced by the financial crisis since 2008, have not yet been sufficiently explored.

[33] Directive 2004/48/EC of 29 April 2004 on the enforcement of intellectual property rights [2004] OJ L195/16, *cf* C Heinze, 'Die Durchsetzung geistigen Eigentums in Europa—Zur Umsetzung der Richtlinie 2004/48/EG in Deutschland, England und Frankreich' (2009) *Zeitschrift fur Europaisches Privatrecht* 282ff.

[34] Hess, *Europäisches Zivilprozessrecht* (n 6) § 11 II, paras 14ff.

[35] O Jauernig and B Hess, *Zivilprozessrecht*, 30th edn (Munich, CH Beck, 2011) § 26, paras 12ff.

on damage actions in cartel law[36] will entail a fundamental change: the adopted text mainly addresses issues of public enforcement. Again, the EU lawmaker made legislative changes in a very specific area of law.

However, in the field of consumer protection, the legislative perspective seems to be much more ambitious: the Directive on alternative dispute resolution (ADR) of consumer disputes of May 2013[37] enjoins Member States to set up a comprehensive institutional framework of consumer ADR which is aimed at complementing and substituting court proceedings. Member States must ensure that the new ADR procedures cover all areas of EU consumer contract law, and they must designate competent authorities for the accreditation and supervision of ADR bodies.[38] The procedures shall be free of charge for the consumers; representation by lawyers is not required. Several principles shall guarantee the quality of the system: they comprise the independence and impartiality of the ADR entities,[39] the transparency and effectiveness of the system (Articles 7 and 8) and the fairness of the proceedings (Article 9).[40] According to Article 11, Member States must ensure that the ADR proceedings do not deprive consumers of mandatory protection. Consequently, the ADR bodies must apply mandatory consumer law, at least when they propose a mandatory settlement.[41] By giving a binding

[36] Directive 2014/104/EU of 26 November 2014 on certain rules governing actions for damages under national law for infringements of the competition law provisions of the Member States and of the European Union [2014] OJ L349/1.

[37] Directive 2013/11/EU of 21 May 2013 on alternative dispute resolution for consumer disputes and amending Regulation (EC) No 2006/2004 and Directive 2009/22/EC [2013] OJ L165/63.

[38] The new framework shall comprise existing private and public ADR institutions, like ombudsmen, complaint boards and consumer mediation. However, Member States must introduce new ADR entities for areas of EU consumer law not covered by the existing bodies. *cf* H Roth, 'Bedeutungsverlust der Zivilgerichtsbarkeit durch Verbrauchermediation' (2013) *Juristenzeitung* 637ff; G Wagner, 'Private law enforcement through ADR: wonder drug or snake oil?' (2014) 51 *Common Market Law Review* 165ff.

[39] *cf* Art 6. As the ADR bodies shall be mainly financed by the businesses, the Regulation provides for safeguards aimed at avoiding undue influence of the businesses on the dispute resolution bodies.

[40] The Directive endorses guiding principles of consumer ADR which were contained in two Recommendations of the Commission of 1998 and 2001, see Hess, *Europäisches Zivilprozessrecht* (n 6) § 10, paras 107ff.

[41] It must be noted that this obligation distinguishes consumer dispute resolution from other forms of ADR; Wagner, 'Private law enforcement through ADR' (n 38) 165, 175ff, criticizes that the Directive does not impose a full application of the law and characterizes this approach as 'enforcement light'. However, Art 11 of the Directive should be implemented in such a way that a full application of mandatory law of consumer protection is required. According to G Rühl, 'Die Richtlinie über alternative Streitbeilegung: Handlungsperspektiven und Handlungsoptionen' (2014) 127 *Zeitschrift fur Zivilprozess* 61, 78f, Art 11 of the Directive requires a comparison between the results of the ADR procedure and the application of the law: the better result for the consumer shall prevail. See generally: B Hess and N Pelzer, 'Rechtsstaatlichkeit und Transparenz verbessern—Vorschläge zur Streitbeilegung in Verbraucherangelegenheiten' in K Gelinsky (ed), *Schlichten statt Richten?* (St Augustin, Konrad-Adenauer-Stiftung, 2015) 35ff.

effect to these principles, the Directive will create a level playing field for ADR and strengthen the confidence of both consumers and businesses in ADR procedures.

This instrument will considerably change the practice of dispute resolution in Europe. Its main objective is to introduce an institutional framework for ADR in the Member States, which shall complement the ('traditional') adjudication of consumer disputes by civil courts. Consumer ADR shall be less expensive and faster than court proceedings.[42] The use of information technology will further enhance the system. In the long run, the new system will not only supplement, but also substitute the civil litigation system and may remove consumer disputes from the realm of the civil judiciary—including the CJEU.[43] Unfortunately, the fundamental issue of the relationship (and balance) between dispute resolution by courts and by non-judicial bodies was not sufficiently discussed during the law-making process.[44] Furthermore, the application of fundamental procedural guarantees to consumer ADR has not been sufficiently debated.[45]

Another area of legislative activity in procedural law relates to collective redress. The initial ambition of the EU Commission was to harmonize the respective procedures in the EU Member States and to set up a level playing field by enacting a European collective redress procedure.[46] Although most of the Member States recently adopted legislation enabling and enlarging collective redress, there are still considerable differences between master proceedings, the involvement of ombudsmen, and settlement schemes.[47] Against this backdrop, the EU Commission has been working on the elaboration of a horizontal instrument on collective redress which should not only apply to specific sectors (as cartel damages or consumer protection), but rather should apply generally to the procedures of the Member States. However, the legislative initiatives of the Commission met much scepticism

[42] Roth (n 38) 637, 640ff; M Stürner, 'ADR and Adjudication by State Courts: Competitors or Complements?' (2014) 3 *European Union Private Law Review* 122, 127; Rühl (n 41) 61ff.

[43] According to Art 9(2) of the ADR Directive, parties are not bound by the suggested solution of the consumer ADR unless they agree to it. For a critical assessment, *cf* Roth (n 38) 637, 640ff.

[44] Lately, the Directive has become a topic of academic debate, *cf* C Meller-Hannich, C Höland and E Krausbeck, '"ADR" und "ODR": Kreationen der europäischen Rechtspolitik—Eine kritische Würdigung' (2014) *Zeitschrift fur Europaisches Privatrecht* 8ff; Stürner, 'ADR and Adjudication by State Courts' (n 42) 122ff; G Rühl (n 41) 61ff; Wagner, 'Private law enforcement through ADR' (n 38)165.

[45] B Hess, 'Prozessuale Mindestgarantien in der Verbraucherschlichtung' (2015) *Juristenzeitung* 548.

[46] A Stadler, 'Die Bündelung von gleichgerichteten Ansprüchen durch Inkassozession—Geschäftsmodelle zur Prozessfinanzierung auf dem Prüfstand' (2014) *Juristenzeitung* 613ff.

[47] C Hodges, 'Collective Redress: A Breakthrough or a Damp Squib?' (2014) 37 *Journal of Consumer Policy* 67, 79ff.

and resistance in the Council and in the European Parliament.[48] In the political debate, the US class action model was often quoted as a deterrent and abusive example (to be avoided).[49]

Against this backdrop, the Commission finally opted for a non-binding Recommendation (Article 292 TFEU), and refrained from proposing any mandatory mechanisms. The Recommendation on Collective Redress of 11 June 2013 provides for a set of common principles for injunctive and compensatory collective redress mechanisms.[50] These principles contain legislative guidelines for the Member States with regard to the enactment of collective redress procedures in their respective procedural systems. With regard to the content of the proposed instruments, the Recommendation is based on an understanding of collective redress, which shall mainly avoid the implementation of a litigation culture similar to the US class action.[51] Accordingly, the Recommendation strongly promotes the introduction of opt-in instruments,[52] limits the standing to representative actions brought by non-profit entities (and prohibits the standing of self-appointed law firms),[53] provides for a loser pays principle (with regard to the costs of the proceedings),[54] and sets clear limits regarding the funding of litigation by third parties. Last, the Recommendation proscribes punitive damages.[55] However, the Recommendation does not legally bind the Member States, which thus remain free to adopt legislation in this area of dispute resolution.[56] Nevertheless, the Recommendation provides for a review procedure of the Commission by 2017. Therefore, it is possible that the 'soft regulatory approach' will finally be replaced by a comprehensive directive.[57]

[48] European Parliament Resolution of 2 February 2012 on 'Towards a Coherent European Approach to Collective Redress' (2011/2089/INI). *cf* B Hess, 'Die Regulierung der privaten Rechtsdurchsetzung auf europäischer Ebene' in M Nietsch and M Weller (eds), *Private Enforcement* (Baden-Baden, Nomos, 2014) 33ff.

[49] H Buxbaum, 'Class Actions, Conflict and the Global Economy' in A Bruns et al (eds), *Festschrift für Rolf Stürner*, vol II (Tübingen, Mohr Siebeck, 2013) 1443ff.

[50] Recommendation (2013/396/EU) on Collective Redress [2013] OJ L201/60.

[51] Buxbaum (n 49) 1443ff.

[52] Recommendation (n 50) paras 21–24.

[53] ibid, paras 4–7; contingency fees shall be prohibited, paras 29 and 30.

[54] See, similarly, Art 10 ESCP. According to C Kern, 'Das euorpäische Verfahren für geringfügige Forderungen und die gemeineuropäischen Verfahrensgrundsätze' (2012) *Juristenzeitung* 389, 391, the 'loser pays' rule should be considered a general feature of the European civil procedures.

[55] Recommendation (n 50) para 31.

[56] B Hess, 'The Role of Procedural Law in the Governance of Enforcement in Europe' in H-W Micklitz (ed), *The Transformation of Enforcement* (2015—in print).

[57] A Stadler, 'Foreword' in E Lein et al (eds), *Collective Redress in Europe—Why and How?* (London, BIICL, 2015) XIX. As it was the case with regard to consumer dispute resolution, see above (n 38).

2.3 The Influence of the European Court of Justice on the National Justice Systems

Aside from direct law-making, there is an additional area of considerable influence, which should be mentioned here: the procedure of preliminary references according to Article 267 TFEU.[58] Although the preliminary references procedure does not directly intrude on the procedural structures of the Member States, its mere existence affects the national appeal systems. First, Article 267(2) TFEU empowers national judges (at all levels of the adjudicative systems) to refer questions of EU law directly to the European Court of Justice, without any recourse to the superior courts. As a result, instance judges in the Member States may elude the (binding) case law of the superior courts in their own jurisdiction when it comes to the application of EU law.[59]

The second implication of the preliminary references procedure refers to the second appeal proceedings in the Member States. Traditionally, the supreme courts of the Member States are the courts responsible for the interpretation and (progressive) development of their respective civil law regimes, and they decide as courts of last resort. However, Article 267(3) TFEU enjoins the highest courts of the Member States to refer preliminary questions on the interpretation of Union law to the Court of Justice. In the last few decades, the situation in private law has changed dramatically: as the European Union is harmonizing central areas of private law, the final (judicial) say no longer lies with the national supreme courts, but rather with the CJEU. In the near future, the respective role of the CJEU and the supreme national (civil) courts should be evaluated and discussed[60]—the future accession of the European Union to the European Convention on Human Rights will certainly complicate the judicial architecture within the EU further.[61] In addition, the Charter of Fundamental Rights has reinforced the constitutionalization of the national procedures by European law[62]—this development is also largely dominated by the case law of the ECtHR in Strasbourg. The future judicial framework will certainly reinforce this development, although the accession process of the EU to the Convention

[58] K Lenaerts, I Maselis and K Gutman, *EU Procedural Law* (Oxford, Oxford European Union Law Library, 2014) para 3.05.

[59] H Rösler, *Europäische Gerichtsbarkeit* (Tübingen, Mohr Siebeck, 2013); K Giannopoulos, *Der Einfluss der Rechtsprechung des EuGH auf das Zivilprozessrecht der Mitgliedstaaten* (Köln, Heymann, 2006) 67ff; C Kohler and J-C Puffer-Mariette, 'EuGH und Privatrecht—Ein Rückblick nach 60 Jahren' (2014) *Zeitschrift fur Europaisches Privatrecht* 696, 709ff.

[60] M Berger, *Organisation und Verfahren der ordentlichen Gerichtsbarkeit im Lichte der Rechtsprechung des EuGH* (Wien, Manz, 2013) 385ff.

[61] Since Opinion 2/2013 of the CJEU on the accession of the EU to the ECHR, the coordination of the two systems has become problematic and the future accession of the EU to the ECHR seems to be unpredictable.

[62] Berger (n 60) 200ff.

on Human Rights has come to a standstill as a result of the CJEU Opinion 2/13 of 18 December 2014.

3. THE BROADER PERSPECTIVE: THE CIVIL JUSTICE UNION

The growing importance of procedural law at the European level is also mirrored by the existence of a Commissioner for Justice within the European Commission. Since the entry into force of the Amsterdam Treaty, the Commissioner for Justice and Fundamental Rights implements a genuine law-making policy not only with regard to cross-border litigation under Article 81 TFEU, but also with regard to the supervision of the national judicial systems. Since 2013, the European Commission has published the 'EU Justice Scoreboard' which is aimed at the evaluation of the adjudicative systems of the Member States.[63] Although this Scoreboard does not provide for substantial new information (the data is largely borrowed from the Council of Europe—CEPEJ), the political ambition goes further: the Commission understands its mission in a comprehensive way covering all areas of dispute resolution, including the efficiency and the independence of the national court systems. In the present financial crisis, the Commission considers the efficiency of national judicial systems as a priority for the proper functioning of the economy in the Internal Market. Thus, the supervision of the judicial systems of Member States is part of the general policy of the Commission. In the context of the troika process, the Commission ensures the implementation of far-reaching reforms of the national procedural laws and courts systems of Member States.[64] The wider perspective is to build up a European Civil Justice Area where the national systems operate smoothly, and are efficiently supported by a European framework for the procedural laws and the adjudicative systems of the Member States.[65]

4. THE CHALLENGES AHEAD

4.1 The Diverging Performance of National Systems

According to the case law of the European Court of Justice, the national courts shall implement and enforce Union law as decentralized European

[63] Accessible at: ec.europa.eu/justice/effective-justice/scoreboard/index_en.htm.

[64] However, it must be noted that the legislative basis in the TFEU for these activities of the Commission is far from clear.

[65] V Reading, 'Strengthening mutual trust: Towards a true European Area of civil justice' lecture given at the MPI Luxembourg on 25 March 2014, available at: www.mpi.lu/fileadmin/mpi/medien/news/2014/4/Speech_VP_Reding.pdf.

courts.[66] This perspective implies a level playing field and a similar (and efficient) performance of the national systems. However, this situation is not mirrored by reality. The procedural systems of the Member States are very divergent with regard to the length of the proceedings, the accessibility of the courts, the qualifications of the judges, the costs of the proceedings, and the prospects of the enforcement of a judgment. As the comparative surveys of the CEPEJ demonstrate, obtaining a judgment in Greece or in Brussels takes a matter of years; the Italian torpedo is notorious, and enforcing a monetary judgment in Portugal is an even more difficult ordeal.[67]

Differences also relate to the organization of the court systems, especially to the empowerment of judges with regard to the organization of the proceedings and to settlement. For instance, the managerial powers of judges in England and Wales and the settling powers of Dutch judges are much wider than the corresponding powers of judges in France or Germany. Furthermore, the reputation of the judiciary varies considerably: it is low in Member States like Croatia or Italy while it is very high in England or Germany. In some Member States (Italy and Hungary) courts have been exposed to considerable political pressure. Thus, the cultural and political environment of the judicial systems, including the diverging funding of the courts, are still considerable impediments to an equal judicial protection throughout the European Judicial Area.

You might have expected that the case law of the ECtHR and the European Court of Justice on fundamental procedural guarantees like, for example, access to justice, efficiency and the right to obtain a judgment in a reasonable period of time would have helped to improve and to assimilate the level of judicial protection in the Member States.[68] However, the

[66] The preliminary reference procedure under Art 267 TFEU permits a direct contact between the national judge and the Court of Justice. On the concept of private enforcement in the context of the Brussels I Regulation, Conclusions AG Jääskinen in Case C-352/13 *CDC*, EU:C:2014:2443, paras 27ff.

[67] EU Justice Scoreboard (n 63) 8.

[68] eg, CJEU Case 222/84 *Johnston*, EU:C:1986:206, para 18, where the Court stated that principle of effective legal protection is recognized as a general principle of EU law, and enjoys the status of a fundamental right of the EU. This was reiterated in several cases: Case C-222/86 *Heylens*, EU:C:1987:442, para 14; Case C-424/99 *Commission v Austria*, EU:C:2001:642, para 45; Case C-50/00 *Unión de Pequeños Agricultores*, EU:C:2002:462, para 39; Case C-467/01 *Eribrand*, EU:C:2003:364, para 61. See also Case C-213/89 *Factortame I*, EU:C:1990:257 on the role of interim relief in order to ensure the full effectiveness of the judgment to be given on the existence of the rights claimed under EU law. See further ECtHR, *Bellet v France* App no 23805/94 where the Court ruled that the right of access to a court must be 'practical and effective'; *Cañete de Goñi v Spain* App no 55782/00, where the Court held that the rules governing the formal steps to be taken and the time limits to be complied with in lodging an appeal or an application for judicial review are aimed at ensuring a proper administration of justice and compliance, in particular, with the principle of legal certainty; *Melnyk v Ukraine* App no 23436/03, where the Court stated that the practical and effective nature of the right of access to a court may be impaired, for instance, by the time taken to hear an appeal leading to its being declared inadmissible.

practical influence of this case law on the application of national procedural law in practice seems to be limited—it is possible that the guidance coming from the case law of the European Court is still not sufficiently reflected by the legislators and the courts in the Member States.[69]

Against this backdrop, the recent legislative initiatives of the Commission in the area of civil justice seem to be justified. During the financial crisis, the Commission endorsed the keywords 'justice for growth' and developed a policy approach according to which efficient judicial systems and procedures in the Member States are necessary for economic welfare. This broader perspective triggered far-reaching legislative activity in the field of insolvency;[70] similar initiatives can be found in other areas of law such as consumer ADR or e-justice.

4.2 Competition Between National Procedural Systems

Another predominant development in the European Judicial Area is the growing competition between the national procedural systems.[71] As the European instruments on private international and procedural law do not only coordinate, but also open up national procedures, powerful stakeholders (often commercial litigants) use the open framework in order to file their lawsuits at the national courts where they expect the best services.[72] Similar to the situation in arbitration, specialized international law firms are able to coordinate and allocate litigation to the most promising judicial marketplaces.[73] These developments are mainly driven by national legislation, they relate to specific sectors like patent and IP litigation, cartel law, insolvency, and collective litigation. The most prominent keywords are: 'Paris, the home of arbitration'; 'London, the capital of divorce and of corporate restructuring'; and 'Amsterdam as a safe haven for collective settlements'. Düsseldorf is considered to be the most prominent place for IP litigation.[74]

[69] This assumption must be detailed with regard to different areas of law. In the context of the Brussels I Regulation, national lawmakers often adapted the legal environment to the case law of the CJEU, see K Lenaerts and M Stapper, 'Die Entwicklung der Brüssel I-Verordnung im Dialog des Europäischen Gerichtshofs mit dem Gesetzgeber' (2014) 78 *Rabels Zeitschrift für ausländisches und internationales Privatrecht* 252, 279ff.

[70] C Thole, 'Die Reform der Europäischen Insolvenzverordnung' (2014) *Zeitschrift fur Europaisches Privatrecht* 40 (on the proposed reform of the Insolvency Regulation).

[71] G Wagner, 'Dispute Resolution as a Product: Competition among Civil Justice Systems' in H Eidenmüller (ed), *Regulatory Competition in Contract Law and Dispute Resolution* (Munich, CH Beck, 2013) 337, 352ff.

[72] A wide array of accessible heads of jurisdiction encourages forum shopping in these cases.

[73] S Vogenauer, 'Regulatory Competition Through Choice of Contract Law and Choice of Forum in Europe: Theory and Evidence' in H Eidenmüller (ed), *Regulatory Competition in Contract Law and Dispute Resolution* (Munich, CH Beck, 2013) 227.

[74] Vogenauer (n 73) 227, 231, describes this development as a 'battle of brochures'; G-P Callies, *Der Richter im Zivilprozess, Sind ZPO und GVG noch zeitgemäß?, Gutachten für den Juristentag Hannover* (Munich, CH Beck, 2014).

From a regulatory point of view, you may wonder whether this development is healthy and should be welcomed. On the one hand, competition entails that the most efficient model prevails. Competition between judicial marketplaces may also raise the awareness of national governments providing an input to adequate investments in their adjudicative systems. On the other hand, civil litigation is not a commodity or a (simple) service where the best price prevails; it is about procedural fairness, the equality of the parties, the protection of the weaker party, the enforcement of law, and (maybe) justice.[75] Regulatory competition in procedural law entails the export of 'legal products' such as 'settlements based on opt out', 'schemes of arrangement'[76] and other hybrid instruments. Under the Brussels I Regulation, judgments and settlements are recognized automatically according to the principle of mutual trust.[77] Yet the original drafters of the Regulation did not foresee these developments, and the question remains as to whether the Regulation is the appropriate facilitator for a cross-border extension of these procedural devices. However, it is important to state that the framework of European procedural law encourages the growing competition between the national adjudicative systems.

4.3 Judicial Dialogue and Direct Communication Between Courts

A third development of European procedural law relates to cross-border cooperation between courts.[78] Modern procedural instruments encourage judges to communicate directly with their counterparts in other Member States. For instance, the judge seised in the main proceedings may contact the judge who ordered a provisional relief directly in order to discuss the case and to adapt the provisional measure to the needs of the main proceedings.[79] The most important areas of these developments are in family law, where the (immediate) return of abducted children may be supported by direct judicial communication and cooperation. The Brussels II *bis* Regulation aims to facilitate this direct cooperation; and the CJEU has urged national judges to communicate directly and to rely on the support of the European Judicial Network.[80] Recently, the ECtHR held that the

[75] *cf* H Eidenmüller, *Regulatory Competition in Contract Law and Dispute Resolution* (Munich, CH Beck, 2013) 1ff; H Genn, *Judging Civil Justice* (New York, Cambridge University Press, 2010).

[76] Bundesgerichtshof, 15 February 2012, *Neue Juristische Wochenschrift* 2012, 2113.

[77] Hess, *Europäisches Zivilprozessrecht* (n 6) § 3, paras 22ff.

[78] B Hess, 'Justizielle Kooperation/Judicial Cooperation' in B Hess and P Gottwald (eds), *Procedural Justice* (Bielefeld, Gieseking, 2014) 387ff.

[79] Example: Main proceedings are pending in Paris, a bank account is blocked in Luxembourg. Unfortunately, the Regulation on the attachment of bank accounts (n 25) does not provide for a direct dialogue.

[80] Case C-491/10 PPU *Joseba Andoni Aguirre Zarraga v Aguirre Pelz*, EU:C:2010:828, paras 42ff; the pertinent case law is analyzed by M Requejo Isidro in this volume, see chapter 14.

return mechanism of Articles 11 and 42 of the Brussels II *bis* Regulation complies with Article 8 ECHR.[81] Under Articles 42 and 56 of the recast of the Insolvency Regulation, the competent judges for the main insolvency proceedings shall communicate directly with the judge responsible for secondary insolvency proceedings. With regard to these developments, the use of modern information technology is key.[82] In November 2014, the proposal for a recast of the Insolvency Regulation was adopted by the Council and the European Parliament.[83] Finally (and hopefully), the old paradigm of international legal assistance between sovereign states will be replaced by a modern approach based on judicial activism and shared responsibility for decision-making. However, the legal framework for direct judicial communication still needs to be developed, and the most recent instruments on judicial cooperation do not provide sufficient guidance.[84] Nevertheless, the phenomenon of direct communication between judges demonstrates that the Civil Justice Union should be based on mutual trust, direct cooperation between the courts and the proper allocation of the cases among motivated and skilled judges.[85] In this respect, encouraging cooperation between the competent courts seems to me to be the better regulatory avenue than a laissez-faire approach, which finally entails forum shopping and open competition between judicial marketplaces in the Member States.

5. REGULATORY TECHNIQUES IN PROCEDURAL LAW

5.1 Coordinating the National Procedural Systems

Against these developments, the European lawmaker has different regulatory options and may apply different legislative techniques. Experience since 1999 shows that diverse approaches have been adopted—but that not all of them proved to be successful. From the perspective of the Member States, the less invasive regulatory choice of European law-making is to simply coordinate the national procedures. This approach was initially adopted with the Brussels Convention in 1968; it still prevails in the area of international civil litigation in civil matters and with regard to divorce proceedings. In this regard, the current regulatory objective of the European lawmaker is to simplify cross-border enforcement by abolishing *exequatur* proceedings.

[81] ECtHR *Povse v Austria* App no 3890/11, paras 77–79.

[82] Communication takes place via phone and video-conferencing, the exchange of emails and electronic documents.

[83] The most recent document is found in [2015] OJ C141/1.

[84] Example: Arts 6 and 7 of the Succession Regulation. This Regulation is explained by B Laukemann in this volume, see chapter 9.

[85] eg, in 2014, the Oberlandesgericht Karlsruhe transferred proceedings on the protection of a minor child to Scotland after an exchange of emails between the judges.

However, the recast of the Brussels I Regulation[86] demonstrates that a simple coordination of the national systems may prove to be insufficient. Under the former regime (Articles 38–40 of the Brussels I Regulation), foreign judgments are formally recognized in the Member State of enforcement by the judges of first instance. On the basis of a form, foreign judgments are declared enforceable in accelerated proceedings without any review of grounds for non-recognition (Articles 38–42). However, on the application of the debtor, grounds for non-recognition are reviewed by the Courts of Appeal in a procedure, which is mainly prescribed by the Regulation itself (Articles 43–46).[87] The recast aims at further simplifying the free circulation of civil judgments. According to its Articles 39 and 42, judgments no longer deserve any declaration of enforceability—they are enforced on the basis of a form filled out by the court of origin.[88] However, Article 45 of the recast maintains the possibility for the debtor to attack the judgment on grounds of non-recognition. Consequently, the Member States must provide for review proceedings (Articles 45–47 and 75 of the Brussels I recast Regulation).[89] Unfortunately, these proceedings are no longer addressed by the Regulation itself, since Article 47 of the recast simply refers to the enforcement laws of the Member States. Yet, the redress procedures in the national enforcement systems diverge considerably and often lack sufficient transparency.[90] As a result, it may turn out that the free movement of judgments under the Brussels I recast Regulation will be less efficient than under the current regime.[91] This example demonstrates that a (simple) coordination of the national procedures may not manage the practical impediments of cross-border litigation in an appropriate manner. European instruments should at least address the interfaces of the national procedures.

5.2 Establishing Minimum Procedural Standards

At present, European law does not provide for a set of minimum standards of domestic civil procedures. However, the pertinent standards are not found in EU instruments;[92] they were developed by the case law of

[86] See (n 12). The new instrument has been applicable since 10 January 2015.

[87] Hess, Pfeiffer and Schlosser (n 27) paras 568ff.

[88] P Schlosser and B Hess, *EU-Zivilprozessrecht*, 4th edn (Munich, CH Beck, 2015); Brussels I recast Regulation (n 12) Art 39, para 1.

[89] ibid, 2ff. The German Implementing Law addresses these proceedings in section 1115 of the Code of Civil Procedure (2015).

[90] This is especially the case in Germany, see B Hess, 'Rechtspolitische Perspektiven der Zwangsvollstreckung' (2010) *Juristenzeitung* 662ff.

[91] B Hess, 'Urteilsfreizügigkeit unter der VO Brüssel Ia: beschleunigt oder ausgebremst' in B Hess et al (eds), *Festschrift für Peter Gottwald* (Munich, CH Beck, 2014) 295ff.

[92] Minimum procedural standards are found in Arts 13–19 of Regulation (EC) No 805/2004: With regard to the EEO the Regulation provides for minimum norms on service and review proceedings. Member States are not directly bound by these norms but have to apply them when an Enforcement Order is issued.

the CJEU.[93] In this respect, several principles can be detected: first, Union law provides for procedural guarantees such as the principle of access to justice, fair trial and also mutual trust. These principles are derived from human rights law, which entails a growing constitutionalization of the procedural laws at the EU level (reinforced by the Charter of Fundamental Rights and the European Convention on Human Rights). Second, the principles of effectiveness and equivalence influence the national adjudication systems.[94] In practice, however, these principles are applied according to the circumstances of a specific case,[95] and it seems to be difficult to elaborate a comprehensive line in the case law. Nevertheless, it might be advisable to elaborate a set of common principles of European and of constitutional law to be applied in domestic proceedings.

5.3 Implementing Self-Standing Procedures

At present, two self-standing procedures are found at the EU level: on the one hand, the ESCP Regulation which was established in 2007;[96] on the other hand, a group of experts (mainly judges) is currently elaborating the procedures of the new Unified Patent Court.[97] In addition, the European Law Institute recently started a project on the elaboration of a set of rules of European civil procedure, which may eventually set a common model for a modern civil procedure in the European Judicial Area.

The first self-standing European civil procedure can be found in the ESCP Regulation. However, four years after its entry into force, the Regulation cannot be considered a successful instrument:[98] the procedure is not often used in legal practice and remains almost unknown in the Member States.[99] The failure of this ambitious legislative project may be traced back to two factors: first, the limitation to cross-border cases entailed that its

[93] For a critical assessment *cf* J Schmidt, *Rechtssicherheit im Europäischen Zivilverfahrensrecht* (Tübingen, Mohr Siebeck, 2015) 260ff.

[94] Hess, *Europäisches Zivilprozessrecht* (n 6) § 11, paras 4ff.

[95] Conclusion of AG Jääskinen in *CDC* (n 66) paras 119ff, on the restrictive interpretation of arbitration and jurisdiction clauses according to the principle of effectiveness in order to guarantee the efficient enforcement of EU cartel law.

[96] ESCP Regulation (n 19). See also C Oro Martinez in this volume, chapter 7.

[97] At: www.unified-patent-court.org.

[98] W Hau, 'Zur Fortentwicklung des europäischen Verfahrens für geringfügige Forderungen—die große Zukunft der kleinen Münze?' in B Hess et al (eds), *Festschrift für Peter Gottwald* (Munich, CH Beck, 2014) 255, 258ff.

[99] A recent survey on the application of the ESCP in the European Judicial Area, conducted by the MPI Luxembourg on the basis of national databases, revealed that the Regulation is only used regularly in the Netherlands (20 cases). Three cases were published in Spain, two were found in Germany, four in Austria and one in France; no published cases were found in Italy, Belgium, Bulgaria or Greece. In Germany, 332 small claim proceedings were initiated in the local courts in 2011 (the figure for 2010 is 187 proceedings). Note, however, that the overall number of civil proceedings in the local courts was 1.209.201, *cf* www.destatis.de.

practical importance remained limited; in the practice of the civil courts (with exception of the English High Court), cross-border cases are still rare exceptions.[100] Second, the Regulation does not address its application within the Member States—the designation of the competent court remains a matter of national legislation. Yet, many Member States have not endorsed any implementing legislation (since the Regulation as a self-standing and directly applicable legal instrument does not need any implementation). As a result, the competent local courts are not familiar with the European instrument.[101] The ESCP Regulation demonstrates that the adoption of self-standing procedures must be accompanied by implementing measures of the Member States, and a strong supervisory process of the Commission itself is necessary.[102]

However, there is an additional sector where a genuine European procedure is evolving. After many years of discussion, the European patent litigation system was finally adopted at the beginning of this year.[103] The new legislative framework provides for a self-standing litigation system of specialized European courts, which will apply their own autonomous procedures. The basic provisions on the structure of the court and the applicable procedure are found in the Agreement of the Patent Court.[104] The Court will have its seat in Paris, and additional sections will operate in London and Munich. The detailed future procedure of the European patent courts is currently being elaborated by a group of stakeholders (mainly judges and practitioners). In September 2013, a 'preliminary set of provisions for the Rules of Procedure of the Unified Patent Court' was published—it consists of more than 300 provisions (addressing proceedings in the first instance,[105] evidence,[106] appellate proceedings,[107] and general provisions).[108] Although the first draft still needs considerable improvement, the elaboration of a comprehensive procedure for patent litigation among private parties seems to be an important endeavour.[109] Compared with the ESCP, the new

[100] Art 3, which is also found in parallel instruments of European procedural law, appears to be too limited. It requires that one of the parties is not domiciled in the Member State where the ESCP is conducted.

[101] *cf* B Hess, 'The European Small Claims Procedure in the Context of the European Law of Civil Procedure' in *Le temps et le droit, Hommage au Professeur Closset-Marchal* (Brussels, Bruylant, 2013) 231ff.

[102] Note that supervision by the Commission in the context of a regulation is much more difficult than in the context of a directive.

[103] This system is not entirely integrated into the framework of European law: see Regulation (EU) No 1257/2012 of 17 December 2012 implementing enhanced cooperation in the area of the creation of unitary patent protection [2012] OJ L361/1 and the Agreement on a Unified Patent Court of 19 February 2013 entered into force on 1 January 2014.

[104] Arts 6–19 (institutional provisions); Arts 52ff (proceedings before the Court).

[105] Part 1, rules 10–157.

[106] Part 2, rules 170–213.

[107] Part 4, rules 220–54.

[108] ibid, rules 260–382.

[109] The 18th version of the procedure was discussed at an expert meeting in Trier in November 2014.

patent litigation system must be expected to work successfully as its legal framework addresses all pertinent issues—not only the procedure, but also the institutional framework.

The latest political initiative is found in the work programme of the European Law Institute. In 2013, it started a common project with Unidroit aimed at elaborating a set of uniform rules of a European civil procedure. In this context, the ALI-Unidroit principles of transnational civil procedure of 2003[110] will serve as a starting point for elaborating a kind of European model code of civil procedure. At present, several working groups are addressing different issues of civil proceedings. Although the final outcome of the project is currently not predictable, the underlying initiative demonstrates the need for a discussion on the future law-making activities of the European Justice Area.[111] Perhaps it is too early to decide whether an instrument on European rules of civil procedure should operate as a(n) (optional) twenty-ninth procedure in the Member States or rather as a model law for the reform of the national systems. Furthermore, the question remains whether this instrument should apply to all civil proceedings or only to cross-border cases. However, it seems eminently sensible to take stock of the recent and ongoing developments of civil procedures in Europe and to explore the avenues of future improvements of the current situation.

6. CONCLUSION: STRIVING FOR A COHERENT ARCHITECTURE IN THE CIVIL JUSTICE UNION

If you consider the development of European procedural law not from the number of instruments enacted so far, but from a systematic point of view, the balance appears less successful. Until now, the law-making of the Union has been mainly sectoral and the choices of legislative activities have not been comprehensive, but rather incidental. At present, there is no master plan, no roadmap; a comprehensive and systematic approach is lacking. All in all, a more systematic approach is needed, including a better coordination of the EU instruments at the horizontal and vertical levels.

Against the background of these developments, it seems necessary that procedural science in Europe adopts a more fundamental and structured approach: although it is important to discuss the different layers of European procedural law, the different instruments, the different regulatory techniques, the case law of the CJEU and the national courts, procedural science

[110] N Trocker, 'From ALI-Unidroit Principles to Common European Rules on Access to Information and Evidence? A Preliminary Outlook and Some Suggestions' (2014) 19 *Uniform Law Review* 239ff.

[111] M Stürner, 'Principles of European Civil Procedure or a European Model Code? Some Reflections on the Joint EIL-Unidroit Project' (2014) 19 *Uniform Law Review*, 322ff.

should also address the broader perspective. The current developments, especially the growing legislative process of the last decade and the expanding activities of the Commission in the area of the justice systems, give rise to the question about the future of the European law of civil procedure and the national and European justice systems. It seems that a discussion about the future architecture of the European law of civil procedure is needed, addressing its objectives (only efficiency, also justice?), its function, the relationship between the national courts, judicial networks, and the necessary communication between the courts, including national courts and the CJEU. The questions to be asked are the following: where will the civil justice system in Europe stand in ten years' time? What shall be achieved? What should be avoided? Which improvements are necessary? In this discussion, procedural science should play an active role in developing the future procedural landscape of Europe.

Part I

Avoiding 'Torpedoes' and Forum Shopping

2

Lis Pendens *and Jurisdiction Clauses: Open Issues*

GILLES CUNIBERTI*

1. INTRODUCTION

WHEN THE EUROPEAN Commission launched the process of revising the Brussels I Regulation in 2000,[1] it identified five main objectives, one of which was to strengthen jurisdiction clauses. Commentators have argued that the efficacy of jurisdiction clauses had been weakened by the decision of the Court of Justice of the European Union (CJEU) in *Gasser*[2] where the Court held that the *lis pendens* provisions of the Brussels I regime were to apply even when the jurisdiction of one of the competing adjudicators lay in a jurisdiction clause. As a result, if proceedings were initiated first before a court of a Member State other than the chosen one, any court seised subsequently, including the chosen court, had to stay proceedings until the court seised first would rule on its jurisdiction. While the courts of some Member States might be able to decide relatively quickly on their jurisdiction, others are notoriously slow. Proceedings initiated first in such jurisdictions could therefore significantly delay the resolution of the case, and hurt the party willing to argue the case before the agreed court.

This strategy, which came to be known as the Italian torpedo,[3] was denounced throughout Europe. It became one of the targets of the European lawmaker, and the Brussels I recast Regulation eventually addressed the issue. Article 31 of the new Regulation[4] introduces a remedy aimed at protecting

* Professor of Private International Law and Comparative Law, University of Luxembourg.

[1] Report from the Commission on the application of Regulation (EC) No 44/2001 on jurisdiction and the recognition and enforcement of judgments in civil and commercial matters COM(2009) 174 final, 6.

[2] Case C-16/02 *Erich Gasser GmbH v Misat Srl* [2004] ILPr 7.

[3] M Franzosi, 'Worldwide Patent Litigation and the Italian Torpedo' (1997) 19 *European Intellectual Property Review* 382, 384.

[4] Regulation (EU) No 1215/2012 of 12 December 2012 on jurisdiction and the recognition and enforcement of judgments in civil and commercial matters (recast) [2012] OJ L351/1.

jurisdiction clauses. The remedy is to create an exception to the application of the *lis pendens* doctrine when parallel proceedings are pending before a court designated by a jurisdiction clause and the court of another Member State. In such a case, priority is given to the chosen court by obliging any other court, whenever seised, to stay proceedings until the chosen court has ruled on its jurisdiction,[5] and to decline jurisdiction if the chosen court retains jurisdiction.[6] The newly introduced remedy will no doubt offer the required protection to choice-of-court agreements in most cases of parallel proceedings. There are, however, a few issues which are left open by the recast of Brussels I. The chapter will focus on two of them: conflicting jurisdiction clauses (section 2) and complex jurisdiction clauses (section 3).

2. CONFLICTING CLAUSES

2.1 Background

The remedy introduced by Articles 31(2) and 31(3) of the Brussels I recast Regulation is designed to protect jurisdiction clauses in cases where only one jurisdiction clause is at stake. It is not meant to apply in cases where several clauses might apply. In a number of case scenarios, the claims of the parties could indeed be argued to fall within the scope of several jurisdiction clauses which might provide for the jurisdiction of different courts. One could first think of the well-known case scenario of the battle of forms. The parties agreed on the essentials of the contract, and then sent to each other forms that possibly contained different jurisdiction clauses, typically in favour of the sender's court. But one could also think of cases where the parties concluded several contracts, which contained different jurisdiction clauses. For instance, the parties could have concluded a master contract and a number of contracts implementing it. Both the master agreement and the contracts implementing it could contain different jurisdiction clauses. In each of these case scenarios, each of the parties could argue that its claims fall within the scope of a different clause and thus initiate proceedings in a different court. The result would be parallel proceedings pending as a consequence of conflicting jurisdiction clauses.

Recital 22 of the Brussels I recast Regulation expressly excludes the situation of conflicting exclusive choice-of-court agreements from the scope of the new remedy. As a consequence, the general *lis pendens* rule applies. Recital 22 reads:

> This exception should not cover situations where the parties have entered into conflicting exclusive choice-of-court agreements or where a court designated in an

[5] Brussels I recast Regulation, Art 31(2).
[6] Brussels I recast Regulation, Art 31(3).

exclusive choice-of-court agreement has been seised first. In such cases, the general *lis pendens* rule of this Regulation should apply.

One important reason why the general *lis pendens* rule should apply in such situations is that the newly introduced remedy would simply not work in the presence of more than one chosen court. This is because the remedy consists of giving priority to the chosen court. Such a remedy only works if it has one beneficiary. Otherwise, several courts might claim that they should benefit from it, which would amount to saying that none of them would. The regime of conflicting clauses, however, still raises a number of issues.

2.2 Is there a Need for Defining the Concept of Conflicting Clauses?

Recital 22 explains that the general *lis pendens* rule applies in cases where the parties entered into conflicting jurisdiction clauses. The existence of conflicting clauses is thus one of the cases where the general rule applies. The existence of a jurisdiction clause is both a legal and a factual issue. Applicable legal rules define what the legal requirements are for such a clause to be considered as binding on the parties, and the facts, which are necessary for such requirements to be met, must be found by the competent adjudicator. The general *lis pendens* rule will apply and allow the court first seised to rule on its jurisdiction if two conflicting jurisdiction clauses are found to exist.

At first sight, there would thus appear to be a need for defining the concept of conflicting clauses and, possibly, for setting a special standard of proof of the existence of conflicting clauses. The main purpose of the recast with respect to jurisdiction clauses was to avoid situations where a party could delay the proceedings by merely alleging that the court that he had seised had jurisdiction on the matter. The fear was not so much that the court seised would eventually ignore the jurisdiction clause and retain jurisdiction, but rather that it would do so late, after considerably delaying the resolution of the dispute.

In practical terms, however, a defendant who would want to behave strategically and rely on recital 22 for that purpose would logically have seised his preferred court first. His goal would be to benefit from recital 22 for avoiding the court chosen in an otherwise enforceable jurisdiction clause. If the other party has already initiated proceedings before the chosen court, the defendant would not gain anything from seising another court and alleging that a conflicting jurisdiction clause exists. He would still have to go and litigate before the court first seised something he would have been attempting to avoid, as a consequence of the *lis pendens* rule.

The issue would thus be raised before the court first seised. The plaintiff would argue that this court need not decline jurisdiction in favour of the court second seised, despite the existence of a jurisdiction clause granting it jurisdiction, because of the existence of another clause granting jurisdiction to the court first seised. The logic of the *lis pendens* rule is to fully trust, and thus to rely on the court first seised to establish its jurisdiction. As a consequence, it seems unavoidable that the first court conducts a full analysis of the jurisdictional arguments of the parties. In *Gasser*, the CJEU held:

> 48. Moreover, the court second seised is never in a better position than the court first seised to determine whether the latter has jurisdiction. That jurisdiction is determined directly by the rules of the Brussels Convention, which are common to both courts and may be interpreted and applied with the same authority by each of them (see, to that effect, Overseas Union Insurance, paragraph 23).[7]

Although the intent of the European lawmaker was to overrule *Gasser*, it is submitted that this statement reveals the general philosophy underlying the Brussels regime and the principle of mutual trust in the application of European rules of jurisdiction. There is no doubt, therefore, that the court first seised should have the power to fully address the argument of the plaintiff that a competing clause exists and grants jurisdiction to the first court. If the court second seised was then compelled, in the meantime, to stay proceedings and wait for the decision of the first court, there would still be room for strategic behaviour in courts where getting a decision on jurisdiction takes a long time, such as in Italy.

Would this be an acceptable outcome? Under the conflicting clause exception, could a party argue, for instance, that an oral jurisdiction agreement was concluded in favour of the court first seised without offering any serious evidence, and thus delay proceedings in the other chosen court until the time the court first seised would rule that no evidence of the existence of this oral clause was brought, and that the formal requirements of Article 25 were not met in any case? One remedy against such delaying tactics would be to impose a certain standard of proof for the allegation of the existence of a jurisdiction clause to produce effect for the purpose of the *lis pendens* rule. The idea will be familiar to English lawyers, as specific standards of proof already apply to jurisdictional issues in England.[8] Unsurprisingly, the question of the compatibility of national standards of proof with the Brussels regime was referred to the CJEU by the House of Lords in *Shevill*.[9] The Court answered that, as the goal of the Brussels regime was not to unify the rules of procedure of Member States, the issue was to be settled by the application of the national law of the court seised.[10] An English court first seised would thus only retain jurisdiction if satisfied that the claimant arguing that

[7] Case C-16/02 *Erich Gasser GmbH v Misat Srl* [2003] ECR I-14693, EU:C:2003:657.

[8] A Briggs, *Agreements on Jurisdiction and Choice of Law* (Oxford, Oxford University Press, 2008) 283.

[9] Case C-68/93 *Fiona Shevill et al v Presse Alliance SA* [1995] ECR 415, EU:C:1995:61.

[10] At para 39.

an agreement grants jurisdiction to the English court has 'the much better argument'[11] than the other party.

As always with references to national law, the issue with the *Shevill* ruling on this point is that courts in other Member States will have different standards of proof. Indeed, in a number of European national systems, courts either are not allowed to, or in practice do not, rule separately on jurisdiction. The idea of a special standard of proof to be applied to the establishment of jurisdiction is unknown. In these Member States, courts will rule both on jurisdiction and the merits, rather later than sooner, irrespective of the strength of their jurisdiction.

In jurisdictions where no special standard of proof applies to the establishment of jurisdiction, the court first seised will simply assess whether the alleged choice-of-court agreement granting it jurisdiction exists and applies in the case at hand. A mere allegation of its existence will be enough to found the jurisdiction of the court to rule on its jurisdiction. In effect, there will be no need to define the concept of conflicting clauses allowing the court to make such an assessment. In slow jurisdictions, and in jurisdictions where a separate ruling on jurisdiction cannot be obtained, the result will be that the mere allegation of the existence of a conflicting clause will suffice to delay the resolution of the dispute in the court which was designated by a clear choice-of-court agreement.

One last issue is whether the court second seised would necessarily have to stay proceedings for the time needed for the court first seised to rule on its jurisdiction. The *lis pendens* rule directs it to do so.[12] But it is unclear whether it applies in a case where the existence of conflicting clauses is disputed. The court second seised could have a different view on the existence of a competing clause granting jurisdiction to the court first seised. It could consider that the alleged clause does not exist and that there is only one jurisdiction clause, which makes the court second seised the only chosen court. From the perspective of the court second seised, therefore, the case would fall within the scope of Article 31(2), and the general *lis pendens* rule would not apply. That court might therefore consider that it has no reason to wait for the ruling of the court first seised, as the purpose of the introduction of a new remedy was precisely to protect jurisdiction clauses in such a situation. The court second seised could thus consider that it may as well address the argument of the existence of a conflicting clause, whether under a lower standard of proof or not. The result would be that the introduction of the first proceedings would not delay proceedings before the chosen court, but that a risk of conflicting decisions would arise. The Brussels I recast Regulation does not expressly address the issue, but the CJEU has repeatedly

[11] Briggs (n 8) 284; L Collins et al (eds), *Dicey, Morris and Collins on the Conflict of Laws*, 15th edn (London, Sweet & Maxwell, 2012) paras 12–120.

[12] Brussels I recast Regulation, Art 29(1).

expressed its understanding that one of the most important objectives of the Brussels I Regime is to avoid conflicting decisions.[13] It seems, therefore, that the CJEU would probably summon the principle of mutual trust to resolve the issue and impose on the court second seised the appreciation of the first court on the existence of competing clauses. Reports of the death of the Italian torpedo might have been greatly exaggerated.

2.3 Conflicting Clauses in Separate Contracts

While recital 22 refers to conflicting exclusive choice-of-court agreements without any qualification, it must be kept in mind that the context is the operation of the *lis pendens* rule. *Lis pendens* exists 'where proceedings involving the same cause of action and between the same parties are brought in the courts of different Member States'.[14] The parties to the proceedings could each rely on different jurisdiction clauses, but that would be a useful move only if the other requirements for *lis pendens* were met. To start with, the parties should be the same in each proceeding. Most importantly, the proceedings should involve the same cause of action.

This last requirement could raise an issue if the parties were relying on jurisdiction clauses which were included in different contracts and narrowly drafted. In such a case, the parties would have to rely on different contracts not only from a jurisdictional perspective, but also from a substantive perspective. The result could be that, while the claims would arguably be related, they would not have the same cause of action, as they would each be grounded in a different contract, and indeed potentially in a different law.

Imagine that the parties concluded a master agreement and a number of contracts implementing it. The master agreement and implementation contracts contained different jurisdiction clauses which each provided that any dispute arising out of the present agreement/contract shall be litigated in the court of X/Y. The substantive claims of the parties could probably be analyzed as a breach of the substantive clauses of each contract. However, if the jurisdiction clauses were drafted narrowly, they would only encompass claims grounded in the contract that they would refer to. Each of the parties would thus have to rely on a separate contract both from a jurisdictional and a substantive perspective. The claims would therefore (to many thus) be grounded in separate contracts, and thus arguably have different causes of action.

In contrast, jurisdiction clauses drafted broadly to encompass all disputes arising out of, or in connection with, the relevant contract, would not raise

[13] See, eg, Case C-406/92 *The Tatry v The Maciej Ratja* [1994] ECR I-5439, EU:C:1994:400, para 32.

[14] Brussels I recast Regulation, Art 29(1).

the same issue, as they would allow parties relying on such a clause to make a claim based on the breach of another contract, as long as it was connected with the contract including the preferred jurisdiction clause. All encompassing jurisdiction clauses are certainly enforceable under the Brussels I recast Regulation, since Article 27 allows the parties to provide for the jurisdiction of courts to settle disputes/or a dispute in connection with 'a particular relationship', and not with a particular contract.[15]

The CJEU has not ruled on the specific issue of whether claims made pursuant to related contracts have different causes of action. However, in *Gubisch*, it stated in passing: 'the same cause of action, that is to say the same contractual relationship'.[16] In The *Ship Tatry*,[17] the Court accepted that an action brought by one group of cargo owners against a shipowner under separate but identical contracts, and another action brought by owners of another part of the cargo against the same shipowner under contracts which were separate from but identical to those between the first group and the shipowner, were related and thus governed by the related action rule of the 1968 Brussels Convention. It seems, therefore, that two claims made under two different contracts, whether related or not, would not be considered as having the same cause of action for the purpose of *lis pendens* under the Brussels regime.[18]

2.4 Chosen Courts and Non-Chosen Courts

The last issue is whether the remedy introduced by Article 31(2) of the Brussels I recast Regulation should only benefit courts designated by a jurisdiction clause, or whether it might benefit all courts. Recital 22 explains that the general *lis pendens* rule should apply in the presence of conflicting clauses. As already underscored, there is no doubt that the main objective is to clarify that parallel proceedings initiated in courts which were all chosen cannot possibly be regulated by giving them all priority to rule on their jurisdiction. But what about courts other than the courts designated by each of the conflicting jurisdiction clauses? A party could decide to argue that none of the jurisdiction clauses applies, and that the court of a third Member State has jurisdiction under Article 7(1) of the Brussels I recast Regulation. Should this action fall within the scope of the remedy introduced by Article 31(2), or within the scope of the general *lis pendens* rule?

[15] Briggs (n 8) 285.

[16] Case C-144/86 *Gubisch Maschinenfabrik KG v Giulio Palumbo* [1987] ECR 4861, EU:C:1987:528, para 15.

[17] Case C-406/92 *The Tatry* (n 13).

[18] See T Simons and L Carpaneto in T Simons, R Hausmann and I Queirolo (eds), *Regolamento 'Bruxelles I' Commento alla Regolamento (CE) 44/2001 e alla Convenzione di Lugano* (Munich, IPR Verlag, 2012) Art 27, para 38.

It could be argued that the rationale for reintroducing the general rule for cases of conflicting clauses was first and foremost that the new remedy would not work: priority could not be given to all competing adjudicators. If so, there would be no reason to apply the general rule to non-chosen courts. They could not benefit from the remedy, and it would be perfectly conceivable to direct them to stay proceedings until all chosen courts have declined jurisdiction.

3. COMPLEX CLAUSES

Another instance where the operation of the remedy introduced by Article 31(2) of the Brussels I recast Regulation will raise issues is complex clauses. Simple jurisdiction clauses provide for the exclusive jurisdiction of one single court, irrespective of which party initiates the proceedings. But more complex clauses are also conceivable. In particular, asymmetric clauses are common in certain industries such as the banking industry. Asymmetric clauses impose on one of the parties the obligation to sue in one single court, but give a range of options to the other party, who is thus entitled to initiate proceedings in different jurisdictions.

Complex jurisdiction clauses such as asymmetric clauses raise issues in the context of the *lis pendens* rule, because they grant jurisdiction to several courts. As already noted, the protection afforded by the newly introduced remedy is to grant priority to 'the' chosen court over all other courts. Such a remedy can only function if there is one chosen court to which priority can be given. If the clause grants jurisdiction to several courts, there is more than one chosen court. Granting priority to all chosen courts amounts to granting priority to none.

It is unclear, however, whether complex clauses are within the scope of the new remedy. This is because Article 31(2) limits its scope to jurisdiction clauses conferring exclusive jurisdiction on a court of a Member State. The Regulation does not define the concept of an exclusive jurisdiction clause, but a first interpretation could be that an exclusive jurisdiction clause must be a clause providing for the jurisdiction of a single court, and that any clause granting jurisdiction to more than one court cannot be regarded as exclusive.[19] The consequence of such an interpretation would be that Article 31(2) would not apply to jurisdiction clauses granting jurisdiction to more than one court. The general *lis pendens* rule would thus apply.

A second interpretation, however, could be that exclusivity should be defined from the perspective of each party taken in isolation from the other.

[19] In the words of A Briggs and P Rees, *Civil Jurisdiction and Judgments*, 5th edn (London, Informa Law, 2009) para 2.122: 'to give exclusive jurisdiction to two courts is inelegant, even self-contradictory ... a choice of concurrent exclusive jurisdictions may be taken as a case in which the parties have agreed that the jurisdiction should not be exclusive'.

A clause could grant exclusive jurisdiction to two different courts if each party was obliged to sue in one single court, though not the same as the court where the other party would be under the obligation to sue. In this view, clauses granting jurisdiction to the 'court of the defendant' could be exclusive despite the fact that the court would be different depending on who initiated the proceedings.[20] By contrast, asymmetric clauses such as those found in the banking industry, which give a range of options to the bank, would not be exclusive,[21] and would thus fall outside of the scope of Article 31(2).

A third interpretation could be that the meaning of exclusivity is merely that the choice-of-court agreement excludes the jurisdiction of some courts. In that view, the number of courts which are granted jurisdiction is irrelevant; what matters is only that their jurisdiction excludes the jurisdiction of another court, that is the court/courts which would have had jurisdiction pursuant to the default jurisdiction rules of the forum, for instance the default rules of the Brussels I recast Regulation.[22] Asymmetric clauses could thus be characterized as exclusive, including for the bank.[23] The application of Article 31(2) would not be excluded on the grounds that the clause did not grant exclusive jurisdiction.

For the purpose of this chapter, these distinctions might well be academic. If a jurisdiction clause falls outside the scope of Article 31(2), the general *lis pendens* rule will apply. The court first seised will thus have jurisdiction. If a clause falls within the scope of Article 31(2), however, recital 22 will lead to the same result. This is because recital 22 not only excludes the application of the priority rule in the case of conflicting clauses, but also 'where a court designated in an exclusive choice-of-court agreement has been seised first'. The purpose of this last exception might have been to underscore that there was no need to protect a chosen court from the dangers of the *lis pendens* rule when the chosen court was seised first. But a further consequence of the rule is that it implicitly provides for the application of the general rule to

[20] Such a clause was validated by the CJEU under Art 17 of the 1968 Brussels Convention, which only applied to exclusive jurisdiction clauses: see Case C-23/78 *Meeth v Glacetal* [1978] ECR 2133; EU:C:2005:716.

[21] Or would only be exclusive for one party. See T Hartley, *Choice-of-Court Agreements under the European and International Instruments* (Oxford, Oxford University Press, 2013) para 7.34: 'Such an agreement is in effect exclusive as regards one party and non-exclusive as regards the other'.

[22] See U Magnus in U Magnus and P Mankowski (eds), *Brussels I Regulation*, 2nd edn (Munich, Sellier, 2011) Art 23, paras 145–46; R Geimer and R Schütze, *Europäisches Zivilverfahrensrecht*, 3rd edn (Munich, CH Beck, 2010) Art 23, para 166.

[23] The only exception could be asymmetric clauses leaving all default options open to the bank. This would be the case, for instance, of a clause providing that the bank could sue in any court of competent jurisdiction, which would mean all courts having jurisdiction under default jurisdiction rules. Such a clause would not exclude the jurisdiction of any court, and thus could be characterized as exclusive even in this third view.

cases where an exclusive jurisdiction clause, or several exclusive jurisdiction clauses, grant jurisdiction to several courts. The court first seised will have jurisdiction.

However, if the court seised first is a non-designated court, the applicability of Article 31(2) will become essential. If the new remedy does not apply, the general *lis pendens* rule will apply. By contrast, if the new remedy applies, all non-designated courts will have to stay proceedings until any designated court that was seised of an action declined jurisdiction.

Part II

Alternative Dispute Resolution

3

ADR/ODR: Too Much Optimism in the Promotion of Cross-Border Trade?

JIM DAVIES*

1. INTRODUCTION

THE NEW RULES for consumer alternative dispute resolution (ADR) and online dispute resolution (ODR), the ADR Directive and the ODR Regulation,[1] were introduced with an optimistic narrative based on the consumers', and businesses', desire to engage in non-litigious redress actions. Expert, impartial and professional schemes will, as a consequence of the introduction of the new measures, provide new standards of access to justice, provide a cheap and speedy remedy for consumer disputes, improve market efficiency and reduce consumer detriment. In this chapter I consider the substance of this optimistic narrative: a narrative that heralded a new importance for the consumer as an influential actor in the process of developing the Internal Market, in particular in relation to cross-border consumer trade. The optimistic narrative is found in the documentation that accompanied the proposal for these measures and which appears to set out a dual rationale for their adoption. On the one hand the new measures are intended to increase access to non-litigious consumer dispute resolution, reduce consumer detriment, bring benefit to both consumer and trader, and deliver a significant economic benefit to the Internal Market. On the other hand, the documentation sets out a second or perhaps complementary rationale for the new measures based on an anticipated reduction of costs, complexity, and legal uncertainty that would stimulate cross-border trade and e-commerce in the Internal Market.

* Associate Professor, University of Northampton.

[1] Directive 2013/11/EU of 21 May 2013 on alternative dispute resolution for consumer disputes and amending Regulation (EC) No 2006/2004 and Directive 2009/22/EC (Directive on Consumer ADR) [2013] OJ L165/63; and Regulation (EU) No 524/2013 of 21 May 2013 on online dispute resolution for consumer disputes and amending Regulation (EC) No 2006/2004 and Directive 2009/22/EC (Regulation on Consumer ODR) [2013] OJ L165/1.

With some discussion of the relationship between these new measures, and other initiatives introduced as levers to help develop the cross-border dimension of the Internal Market, the central question this chapter sets out to address is whether or not this optimism is well founded. The rhetoric that accompanied the proposals for the new measures is reviewed and the scope of application of the measures briefly discussed, as are the enduring notions in EU policy of the average consumer and consumer empowerment. The discussion then takes on a more circumspect and critical analysis drawing, in particular, on Eurobarometer survey data that raises questions over the optimism surrounding the ADR and ODR legislation from a number of perspectives and invites discussion of the effectiveness of existing consumer ADR schemes, the consumer awareness of such schemes and barriers to consumer engagement with such schemes.

The empirical analysis of consumer behaviour and existing ADR schemes suggests that a counter perspective should be drawn between the introductory rhetoric and policy objectives that lauded the empowering opportunity for consumer engagement in non-litigious redress and what we may expect in practice. As the new measures come into force there already exists a complex and extensive landscape of ADR schemes that embrace arbitration, conciliation, mediation and negotiation mechanisms but that are fragmented, diverse and incomplete both between and within national and sectoral approaches. Adding to this complexity, individual engagement with consumer redress be it litigious or non-litigious, is subject to a variety of individual and cultural norms, to choice and capability dependencies, and to socio-economic factors. The discussion then highlights a complex of structural and behavioural barriers that suggest we should expect a much more limited effect from the new measures than the introductory rhetoric suggests.

Taking this observation as a point of departure, the final substantive section provides an alternative focus for the new ADR/ODR measures as complimentary additions to the broader procedural and private law developments at the EU level that are concerned with simplifying, enabling and encouraging cross-border trade and consumer sales in the Internal Market. In this context, the chapter goes on to discuss the general approach to achieving this objective that includes the introduction of optional EU measures that would coexist with, but not replace national law. Within this discussion the relationship between the new ADR/ODR measures, collective redress and the Common European Sales Law (CESL) initiative is considered.

2. ENFORCEMENT AND REMEDY: THE NEW ADR/ODR MEASURES

2.1 The Rationale behind the New Measures

The 2007 Commission Study on ADR identified that the policy context for ADR was one of increasing access to justice: that ADR provides opportunity for redress in the gap between 'a consumer (or business) deliberately deciding not to take any action and a consumer (or business) wishing to take action but refraining from doing so because of the perceived disadvantages of an ordinary court procedure'.[2] An opportunity, the study emphasises, that is not only about improving access to intermediate methods for redress, but is also related to a question of the preferred nature of European society and the role of the consumer.[3] In the context of this question the study enquired whether the EU would prefer a society where consumer claims could be enforced on the one hand privately by individual or collective groups of consumers, or on the other hand publicly by Member State consumer protection bodies; whether the EU would want to increase access for consumers who would normally remain passive; and where the proper balance should sit between consumer access to justice and certainty for business. However, the answers to these questions, the study acknowledges, involve important policy decisions that reflect a significant divergence in the approach of the Member States towards the regulatory environment for national ADR schemes. As each Member State has typically adopted a mix of self-regulating mediation/arbitration schemes, direct regulation of the dispute resolution mechanisms, and regulation of the processes that provide for access to ADR mechanisms, we are left with an ADR landscape in which there is a 'multitude of methods of consumer dispute resolution in 28 jurisdictions ... [that are rooted in] historic, legal, political, socio-economic, educational or cultural factors'.[4]

With this background of mixed national approaches, the 2007 study suggested that it did 'not seem that a particular method or mix of dispute resolution processes or techniques can or should be put forward as the best choice from a consumer perspective'.[5] Where the variable circumstances of the dispute and the monetary value involved define one dimension of complexity this is compounded by the variable capabilities and motivation of the consumer, and by the jurisdictional history of 'legal, political, socio-economic, educational or cultural factors' of the Member State.[6] Against this complex background the new ADR Directive and ODR Regulation have been introduced to improve the functioning of the Internal Market, and in particular the volume of consumer cross-border e-commerce transactions. An apparent rationale for these new measures can be developed in

[2] J Stuyck et al, *Commission Study on alternative means of consumer redress other than redress through ordinary judicial proceedings* (Catholic University of Leuven, 17 January 2007) 6 at: www.eurofinas.org/uploads/documents/policies/OTHER%20POLICY%20ISSUES/comparative_report_en.pdf.

[3] ibid.

[4] ibid, 37–38.

[5] ibid, 38.

[6] ibid.

part from the April 2011 Special Eurobarometer on consumer empowerment which suggests that:

> A thorough understanding of the **capacities, knowledge and assertiveness** of consumers will help policymakers to develop policies that take account of the actual behaviour of consumers ... [in order to] help to design 'smart' policies to identify and empower consumers who are disadvantaged and to highlight vulnerabilities in the European population

asserts that the

> survey constitutes a better empirical basis for robust estimation of the prevalence of overall consumer detriment in the EU and of consumer redress, in particular through Alternative Dispute Resolution (ADR)

and expresses the opinion that

> consumers' skills and capacities represent an intangible stock of capital, as empowered consumers contribute to boosting market competition and innovation, by forcing businesses to strive to deliver value, thus strongly influencing economic growth and sustainability.[7]

These are high ideals and the European consumer is thus elevated in his or her status as an economic actor based on the presumption that, at the level of the individual, he or she will be capable and motivated to pursue redress action. The new ADR Directive and ODR Regulation set out to define such a framework and underpin this elevation within a context of consumer protection and consumer information that anticipates a general procedural engagement as an aspect of European consumer citizenship practice.[8] As a mechanism for consumer protection the new legislation seeks to develop and increase the opportunity for individual access to effective redress mechanisms and to improve empowerment through the requirement for efficient non-litigious dispute resolution processes: the objective being to influence market competitiveness, innovation and value, and to help drive economic growth and sustainability, through individual consumer behaviour.

With some dependency on the degree to which the new ADR/ODR rules are promoted and explained, then the greater would be the proportion of European consumers who would attain the individual capability to do so.[9] From a motivational perspective, if the barriers of cost, time, complexity, uncertainty and the unfamiliarity of pursuing litigious redress can be avoided through ADR/ODR processes then individual self-interest may well

[7] Special Eurobarometer 342, Consumer Empowerment, 5 and 6, available at: ec.europa.eu/consumers/consumer_empowerment/docs/report_eurobarometer_342_en.pdf.

[8] See J Davies, *The European Consumer Citizen in Law and Policy* (Basingstoke, Palgrave Macmillan, 2011) 149 and associated text.

[9] ibid and see Special Eurobarometer 342 (n 7) which provides socio-demographic data identifying capability issues/barriers.

drive the use of ADR/ODR and influence market competitiveness. Certainly, the Impact Assessment accompanying the proposals for the ADR/ODR legislation was confident that 'consumers will get to know about ADR and how it works' such that

> ADR will become common knowledge for consumers and the levels of awareness will increase substantially. Better knowledge will inevitably lead to more frequent use of ADR for all kinds of problems and will encourage consumers to use ADR. The creation of a consumer-friendly EU web-based platform will enable consumers to solve their disputes by electronic means and consequently increase their confidence to buy goods and services online and cross-border.[10]

Such will be the impact of this initiative, according to the Impact Assessment, that its introduction will have 'a positive social impact', it will

> allow all consumers, including the vulnerable ones, to refer their disputes and be compensated. The recovered losses can then be reallocated in the internal market and contribute to growth. By offering effective means of online dispute resolution the willingness of businesses to offer goods and services online will increase. Consequently, consumers will have access to a wider range of goods and services, which will lead to more competitive markets with a likely reduction of prices.[11]

For businesses the overall impact of the ADR mechanisms is suggested by the Impact Assessment to be reasonable. Whilst they may be required to contribute to the setting up and funding of ADR schemes in sectors where they do not exist, and may need to adapt their contracts and commercial documents to include information on the relevant ADR, the Assessment suggests that

> businesses, including SMEs, will save on a yearly basis, if they use ADR instead of court proceedings, from EUR 1.7 billion to EUR 3 billion, while at the same time saving 258 days ... [and] enhance their reputation with consumers and to a significant extent address issues of reputational risk, by showing willingness to solve disputes in a non expensive and easily accessible way.[12]

Adherence to ADR schemes, suggested the Impact Assessment, 'will create a virtuous circle from which businesses which are reluctant to adhere will be excluded and bear a reputational risk' whilst those businesses adapting to full coverage of ADR/ODR schemes will 'avoid lengthy and costly in-court procedures and maintain their business reputation, whilst building good relations with their clients ... for all online, off-line, domestic and cross-border goods and services'.[13] Such is the optimism of the Impact Assessment

[10] Commission Staff Working Paper, 'Impact Assessment, Accompanying the document Proposal for a Directive on Alternative Dispute Resolution for consumer disputes (Directive on Consumer ADR) and Proposal for a Regulation on Online Dispute Resolution for consumer disputes (Regulation on Consumer ODR)' SEC(2011) 1408 final, 66.

[11] ibid, 67.

[12] ibid.

[13] ibid.

in relation to the development of ODR that it considered that the willingness of businesses to offer products and services via the Internet will increase and that '[a]s a result, consumers will have access to a wider range of products and competition within the internal market will increase'.[14]

This win-win model of consumer and trader self-interest leading to the common good, in a sufficiently competitive market, can be found in the mid-nineteenth century economic theories of Adam Smith:[15] but, perhaps importantly, Smith's analysis also claims that the accuracy of this model is dependent on the majority of people in society having internalised a general moral law as a guide for their behaviour. A dependency, that Wilber suggests, 'means that the efficiency claims that economists make for a competitive market system require that economic actors pursue their self-interest only in "fair" ways': 'fair' ways, where a behavioural requirement is placed on both suppliers and consumers to 'act on the basis of embodied moral values as well as from self-interest' and where market efficiency needs such ethical behaviour also to be efficient.[16] If we agree with the moral dependencies propounded by Smith and Wilber then resting on this moral and 'fair' engagement the rewards of such ethical efficiency could be significant. The size of consumer detriment across the EU, resulting from problems with purchased goods or services, is estimated at 0.4% of EU GDP (circa EUR 50 billion), a figure that includes the detriment suffered by European consumers in relation to cross-border shopping, which is estimated between EUR 500 million and EUR 1 billion.[17]

2.2 The Scope of the New Measures

The ADR Directive takes as its legal basis the establishment and functioning of the Internal Market pursuant to Article 114 TFEU; the consumer protection provisions of Article 169 TFEU; and Article 38 of the Charter of Fundamental Rights. It also emphasises, in the context of simple and low-cost dispute resolution, the provisions of Article 26(2) TFEU whereby the Internal Market is to comprise an area without internal frontiers.[18] In scope, the ADR Directive is applicable to contractual disputes between consumers and traders arising from the sale of goods or the provision of services, in all sectors, through the development of an alternative dispute resolution mechanism that, it suggests, is one of the 12 levers to boost growth and

[14] ibid.

[15] A Smith, *Theory of Moral Sentiments* (London, Henry Bohn, 1861).

[16] CK Wilber, 'Ethics And Economic Actors' (2003) 21 *Real-World Economics Review* (formerly—*Post-Autistic Economics Review*) at www.paecon.net/PAEReview/issue21/Wilber21.htm.

[17] SEC(2011) 1408 final, 20.

[18] ADR Directive (n 1) recitals 1 and 2.

strengthen confidence that were set out in the 2011 Single Market Act.[19] Under the title of 'consumer empowerment', the ADR legislation was identified as a key action designed to boost consumer confidence in their ability to obtain redress and reduce the consumer deficit estimate of 0.16 per cent of the EU's GDP and generate an additional EUR 2.5 billion of economic benefit through improved consumer confidence in cross-border electronic commerce.[20] This strengthening of consumer confidence was, according to the Single Market Act, to be linked with other 'practical steps' that included a proposal for the revision of the Directive on General Product Safety[21] and an assertion that the Commission would 'pursue its work on a European approach to [consumer] collective redress'.[22]

The scope of application of the ADR Directive, as set out in Article 2, extends the application of the procedures to traders 'established within the Union' and consumers 'resident in the Union' and inter alia precludes its application where the natural persons in charge of the dispute resolution process, or the complaint handling systems, are employed or operated by the trader. In Article 4, the Directive defines the consumer as 'any natural person who is acting for purposes which are outside his trade, business, craft or profession' and the trader as any natural or legal person 'irrespective of whether privately or publicly owned, who is acting, including through any person acting in his name or on his behalf, for purposes relating to his trade, business, craft or profession'. Set against this broad scope of application and the definitions of consumer and trader, the obligation the Directive places on Member States is to ensure that ADR entities, managing disputes falling within the scope of the Directive, would have a web-based process providing for the submission of complaints and information exchange online, for both domestic and cross-border disputes, in conformity with national legislation and giving effect to the Data Protection Directive.[23] The ADR Directive calls for guarantees of professional standards with regard to the expertise and impartiality of ADR entities and transparency with regard, inter alia, to the individuals in charge of the ADR entity and the circumstances of their appointment; the financing arrangements of the entity; the rules for dispute resolution employed by the entity; the costs, if any; the approximate length of the ADR procedure; and statistical information relating to the performance of the ADR process.[24] The ADR Directive requires this information

[19] Communication from the Commission, 'Single Market Act, Twelve levers to boost growth and strengthen confidence: Working together to create new growth' COM(2011) 206 final.

[20] ibid, 9–10.

[21] Directive 2001/95/EC of 3 December 2001 on general product safety [2002] OJ L11/4.

[22] COM(2011) 206 final, 10.

[23] ADR Directive (n 1) Art 5, with reference to Directive 95/46/EC of 24 October 1995 on the protection of individuals with regard to the processing of personal data and on the free movement of such data [1995] OJ L281/31.

[24] Arts 6 and 7.

to be publicly available but Article 7 limits the obligation for providing the information to the website of the ADR entity, by request, and 'by any other means' the Member State considers appropriate.

The ADR Directive provides for the effectiveness of ADR through requirements for easy accessibility by both parties to the process without any obligation for legal representation and for the procedure to be 'free of charge or available at a nominal fee for consumers'.[25] The consumer has a right to seek independent advice, legal or quasi legal, within an ADR process that addresses issues of fairness and allows the consumer the choice of whether or not to accept a solution proposed by the ADR entity.[26] In Article 13, the ADR Directive sets out to address the informational needs of the consumer by requiring traders to set out in 'a clear, comprehensible and easily accessible way on the traders' website, where one exists, and, if applicable, in the general terms and conditions of sales or service contracts' the ADR entities appropriate to that trader.

The ODR Regulation adopts, in contrast to the broad scope of the ADR Directive, a narrow focus, and is applicable only to disputes stemming from online sales or service contracts between a consumer resident in the EU and a trader established in the EU.[27] It was introduced as an essential complement to the ADR Directive, although that affiliation is questioned below, and with a rationale that was, in part, based on the premise that ODR offers a 'simple, efficient, fast and low-cost out-of-court solution to disputes arising from online transactions'.[28] It is the absence of such an ODR dispute resolution platform that the Regulation cites as leading to consumer detriment and that constitutes a barrier, 'in particular, to cross-border online transactions', and the creation of an uneven playing field for traders that 'hampers the overall development of online commerce'.[29] This is however too simplistic an analysis and, whilst the consumer has, in EU soft law and policy, developed citizenship-like attributes as a market actor, there is a much broader analysis of consumer detriment that will suggest the optimism of the narrative in the new ADR Directive and ODR Regulation is overstated.

3. EU POLICY AND CONSUMER EMPOWERMENT: A DISCONNECT?

3.1 Policy Developments and Consumer Categorisation

The role of the consumer has developed significantly since the 1975 Preliminary Programme for a Consumer Protection and Information Policy

[25] Art 8.
[26] Art 9.
[27] ODR Regulation (n 1) Art 2(1).
[28] ibid, recital 8.
[29] ibid.

of the EC. This initial policy statement characterised the consumer 'as a person concerned with the various facets of society which may affect him either directly or indirectly as a consumer' but who, as a consequence of the globalisation of markets had become 'merely a unit in a mass market, the target of advertising campaigns and of pressure by strongly organized production and distribution groups'.[30] The vulnerability, inherent in this characterisation of the consumer, was to be addressed through protection at the Community level by positive harmonisation and the introduction of basic rights, including the right of redress, the right to information and education, and the right to be heard.

Recognition of the potential vulnerability of the consumer soon led to the appearance of the notion of the average consumer,[31] and, some years later to the enduring benchmark notion of the 'the average consumer who is reasonably well informed and reasonably observant and circumspect'. First expressed by the CJEU in 1996 in *Gut Springenheide*,[32] a case concerning the potential for a printed statement on the inside of pre-packed egg cartons to mislead: at the time of writing the most recent use of the phrase appears in the July 2013 judgment in *Green Swan*,[33] that also concerns statements appearing on food packaging, this time in relation to nutrition and health claims.

Together with the benchmark average consumer, the notion of empowering consumers became both enduring and central to the Union's consumer policy strategy.[34] Empowering the consumer, through information and education, became recognised as having a dual objective: of providing consumers with the means to protect themselves and of utilising the behaviour of consumers as market agents to drive up the quality of goods and services, and to stimulate competition in the market. As such, consumer empowerment was explicitly linked to a healthier economy such that 'the rationale for consumer protection becomes in part the health of the economy'.[35] Such was the economic importance of the empowered consumers to the Internal Market that the Commission identified them as the 'lifeblood of the economy ... [adding the accolade that] [c]onfident, informed and

[30] Council (1975) Preliminary programme of the European Economic Community for a consumer protection and information policy. Brussels, 14 April 1975 [1975] OJ C92/2, item 6.

[31] Commission (1977) Relating to a proceeding under Article 85 of the EEC Treaty (IV/28.812 Theal/Watts) Brussels, 10 February 1977, Decision 77/129/EEC, OJ L39/19.

[32] Case C-210/96 *Gut Springenheide and Tusky v Oberkreisdirektor des Kreises Steinfurt* [1998] ECR I-4657, EU:C:1998:369, para 31.

[33] Case C-299/12 *Green—Swan Pharmaceuticals CR*, EU:C:2013:501.

[34] For a comprehensive analysis of the development of the notion of the consumer in both consumer law and policy, see Davies, *The European Consumer Citizen* (n 8).

[35] G Howells, 'The Potential and Limits of Consumer Empowerment by Information' (2005) 32 *Journal of Law and Society* 349, 350.

empowered consumers are the motor of economic change as their choices drive innovation and efficiency'.[36]

The optimism found in the rhetoric accompanying the new ADR/ODR measures is found mirrored in the Europe 2020 Strategy which identifies individual empowerment, in the form of a reinforced ability and confidence to buy goods and services across borders, as the mechanism through which citizens may be empowered to play a full role in the Single Market. It identifies consumer policy as an area that can make 'a telling contribution' in strengthening the Single Market and stimulating new sources of growth. Consumer empowerment as a strategy construct is construed as a composite of codified legal protection, identified as consumer rights, and the creation of

> an overall environment that enables consumers to make use of those rights and benefit from them. It means building a framework wherein consumers can rely on the basic premise that safety is assured and that tools are in place to detect failings in standards and practices and to address them effectively across Europe.[37]

The policy approach to building such an environment continues the traditional focus on consumer education, information and developed expertise to confidently engage with the EU Single Market, and the new ADR/ODR legislation represents the next strategic step in a legal framework which is promoted by the Commission as creating easy and affordable access to efficient redress procedures.[38]

EU policy has therefore come to acknowledge the economic and social importance of the role of the consumer in both a European and the global market context. In the present critique, the optimism associated with this policy position and the new ADR Directive and ODR Regulation is challenged, primarily on the basis of the Commission's own research. A Eurobarometer analysis of consumer behaviours and everyday experiences relating to both consumer information designed to promote consumer confidence, and to actual consumer detriment and redress experience, suggests a significant gap between the everyday practice and experience of European consumers and the optimistic claims that accompany the legislation and are reflected in developed policy. This is a gap defined by the transactional nature of both consumer choice decisions and the incidence of consumer detriment, where structural consumer deficit may be addressed in part through education, information and the new provisions for enforcement and redress, but where complex socio-economic issues and national traditions of consumer behaviour will limit the potential of the new legislation.

[36] Communication from the Commission, 'EU Consumer Policy Strategy 2007–2013—Empowering consumers, enhancing welfare, effectively protecting them' COM(2007) 99 final.

[37] Commission, 'Proposal for a Regulation on a Consumer Programme 2014–2020' COM(2011) 707 final, 2.

[38] ibid.

3.2 How Well Placed is the Optimism? A Counter Perspective[39]

Undoubtedly, the importance and status of the European consumer has reached new levels as an influential market actor in which we recall, the 'consumers' skills and capacities represent an intangible stock of capital, as empowered consumers contribute to boosting market competition and innovation, by forcing businesses to strive to deliver value, thus strongly influencing economic growth and sustainability'.[40] The rhetoric that accompanied the proposal for the new ADR/ODR legislation we have already noted is remarkably positive, asserting that 'consumers will get to know about ADR' with the inevitable result that its more frequent use will increase their confidence to buy goods and services online and cross-border.[41]

The enthusiasm of the Impact Assessment indicates that the new measures would have 'a positive social impact'; that they will allow all consumers, including the vulnerable consumers, to refer their disputes through ADR/ODR procedures and to be compensated for their losses. Reallocated in the Internal Market, these recovered losses would contribute to economic growth whilst the ODR platform is suggested to promote the willingness of businesses to offer goods and services across borders. The conclusions drawn from the analysis in the Impact Assessment suggest that businesses will be more willing to engage in e-commerce activities; consumers will have access to a wider range of goods and services; markets will become more competitive; and prices will fall. So effective will be the use of the new ADR/ODR schemes that the virtuous circle of low-cost dispute resolution, enhanced trader reputation, improved product and service quality, and reduced consumer detriment, presents a model of the consumer market based on a pursuit of self-interest tempered with behavioural fairness from both trader and consumer. A model in which, according to the Impact Assessment, consumers will be able 'to address all their disputes to an ADR scheme ... no matter the business channel of purchase or the country where the product or service was purchased from'.[42] Clearly, the prediction of such an economic nirvana is to be welcomed, but a more nuanced analysis at this point may also prove valuable.

Consumer redress is a complex area in which the effectiveness of the consumer outcomes is shaped by norms of consumer behaviour, influenced by tradition, individual competence and confidence, and shaped by social demographics as much as by market forces and the legislative *acquis*.[43]

[39] Much of the argument and content in this section is drawn or adapted from the author's earlier editorial commentary: J Davies, 'How well placed is the optimism surrounding the new ADR/ODR proposals?' (2012) 1(2) *Journal of European Consumer and Market Law* 63.

[40] Special Eurobarometer 342 (n 7) 5 and 6.

[41] SEC(2011) 1408 final, 66.

[42] ibid, 65.

[43] See Davies, *The European Consumer Citizen* (n 8) 144ff.

The European Parliament has warned, with good cause, that too many different ADR schemes may confuse the consumer and deliver mixed results, and yet the Impact Assessment draws attention to over 750 European ADR schemes that are already in existence but with little consumer, or business, awareness of their presence. The schemes are diverse, established by public authorities or by industry; they may be located in the public sector, industry or in consumer organisations; their funding may be private, or public or a combination of both; geographical coverage may be national or it may be provided at a regional or local level; schemes may be sector-specific or multi-sectoral; decisions may be made collegially or by individuals, and may be mere recommendations or may be binding.[44] Even where provisions exist at the EU level, for example, as public service obligations requiring the Member States to provide for ADR in the energy sector,[45] there remains a 'persistent' gap in coverage, a lack of awareness by consumers and businesses, and a failure to respect the core principles set out in two Commission Recommendations.[46] Whilst there may be shortcomings with the implementation of these sectoral schemes, they do require additional measures to protect vulnerable consumers, a distinction not drawn in the new ADR Directive and mentioned only in passing in the ODR Regulation, requiring only that the ODR platform be 'accessible and usable by all, including vulnerable users ... as far as possible'.[47]

Consumer behaviour may also serve to temper the optimism accompanying the new proposals: the preference to shop in person, out of loyalty to shops or merely out of habit. Around 40 per cent of consumer problems are satisfactorily resolved between consumer and trader, whilst in just under a quarter of cases consumers feel that the value of the detriment is too small to pursue redress. Even with over 750 schemes operating, 8 per cent of consumers do not know that ADR options exist and around 25 per cent suggest that they would not turn to ADR because it would be too much effort, too expensive or take too long.[48] Demographic analysis shows a significant variation in consumers' perceptions and behaviours towards ADR, both between Member States (cultural consumer tradition) and within Member

[44] SEC(2011) 1408 final, 10 and 16.

[45] Directive 2009/72/EC OF THE EUROPEAN PARLIAMENT AND OF THE COUNCIL of 13 July 2009 concerning common rules for the internal market in electricity and repealing Directive 2003/54/EC [2009] OJ L211/55, Art 3(13); and Directive 2009/73/EC OF THE EUROPEAN PARLIAMENT AND OF THE COUNCIL of 13 July 2009 concerning common rules for the internal market in natural gas and repealing Directive 2003/55/EC [2009] OJ L211/94, Art 3(9).

[46] Respectively, the Working Group Report on Alternative Dispute Resolution in the Energy Sector, 2, available at: ec.europa.eu/consumers/citizen/my_rights/docs/energy_adr_report_en.pdf; and Commission Recommendations 98/257/EC [1998] OJ L115/31 and 2001/310/EC [2001] OJ L109/56.

[47] ODR Regulation (n 1), Art 5(1).

[48] Special Eurobarometer 342 (n 7) 210.

States (socio-economic status). The most vulnerable of consumers, the oldest, the least well educated and particularly those who have never used a computer and who do not use the Internet are the least empowered, the most likely to suffer consumer detriment, and the most likely to say that they would never use ADR.[49]

The new provisions suggest a generic solution to reduce consumer detriment in a somewhat idealised and sanitised model of the consumer redress environment. Existing ADR schemes are so diverse, entrenched and potentially incomplete as to dilute any potential for conformity in the implementation of any residual scheme, or alternative, at Member State level and consumer behaviour indicates that the rhetorical optimism that accompanied the proposals for the new legislation is overstated. In the 2009 Civic Consulting report to DG SANCO this 'fragmentation of systems and jurisdictions governing ADR' was identified as potentially one of the most important of barriers to consumer use of ADR.[50]

3.3 Limitations of Consumer Agency: Why Consumers may not Engage

In addition to the fragmentation of available ADR systems the Civic Consulting report identified as '[t]wo of the more tangible barriers revealed by the research ... the lack of compliance by business and the lack of available ADR schemes'.[51] With regard to non-compliance, the report highlighted the problem of existing ADR procedures that often only result in a non-binding recommendation: where consumers who are successful with an ADR claim are left questioning the value of the ADR scheme when, perhaps after pursuing remedy for a damage over some months, the business concerned simply decides not to comply with an ADR decision. A similar situation, the report notes, to a situation where a 'business simply refuses to enter the [ADR] procedure'.[52] It is contingent with the fragmented nature of the ADR landscape that the report identified a lack of schemes as a barrier to consumer redress: whilst many schemes exist across the EU, and some individual schemes work very well, there are for many EU consumers both sectoral and geographical ADR 'black holes'.[53]

The empirical analysis of the Eurobarometer survey draws attention to behavioural issues of consumer economics, to issues of cultural tradition, and to aspects of consumer vulnerability. The understanding of consumer

[49] ibid, 225.

[50] F Alleweldt et al, *Final Report to DG SANCO—Study on the Use of Alternative Dispute Resolution in the EU*, Civic Consulting of the Consumer Policy Evaluation Consortium (2009), available at: ec.europa.eu/consumers/redress_cons/adr_study.pdf, 112.

[51] ibid, 115.

[52] ibid.

[53] ibid.

engagement with ADR/ODR, or indeed with litigation processes, is complex and involves the consideration of individual capability and motivation as well as the acknowledgement of any accessibility and informational issues. This is an area in which the European Parliament has recently expressed an interest, calling for a development of the 'widely used' concept of vulnerable consumers as an endogenous, heterogeneous, group 'comprised of persons who, on a permanent basis, are considered as such because of their mental, physical or psychological disability, age, credulity or gender', and suggesting that

> the concept of vulnerable consumers should also include consumers in a situation of vulnerability, meaning consumers who are placed in a state of temporary powerlessness resulting from a gap between their individual state and characteristics on the one hand, and their external environment on the other hand, taking into account criteria such as education, social and financial situation (for example over-indebtedness), access to the internet, etc.[54]

The European Parliament resolution, in particular, notes that for 'many consumers' vulnerability results from a lack of assertiveness; of comprehension of the information they receive; of the options available; 'or from their lack of awareness of the existing complaint and redress schemes, and that these barriers grow in the case of cross-border consumption and door-to-door sales, including online cross-border commerce'.[55]

The narrative of the European Parliament's resolution turns specifically to issues of consumer e-commerce and recognises the inherent vulnerability of consumers 'who, for various reasons, cannot access or use the Internet' and, unable to take advantage of the benefits of online commerce are excluded from a substantial part of the Internal Market.[56] It urges the Member States and the Commission to accelerate the delivery of the European Digital Agenda and, with regard to the ADR Directive and ODR Regulation, to 'make it possible for vulnerable consumers to have effective access ... either free of charge or at the lowest cost possible' whilst also calling on the Commission to ensure that vulnerable consumers' needs and rights are taken into account in the context of any collective redress scheme at EU level.[57]

Given the empirical analysis provided in the Eurobarometer survey, and the consideration by the European Parliament of a notion of consumer vulnerability that goes beyond any mere economic imbalance, we should question to what degree the ADR/ORD provisions should be assessed only from the perspective of consumer protection and an improved access to justice.

[54] European Parliament Resolution of 22 May 2012 on a strategy for strengthening the rights of vulnerable consumers (2011/2272(INI)) [2013] OJ C246 E/11, 13.

[55] ibid, 14.

[56] ibid, 17.

[57] ibid.

In associating the issues of effective consumer engagement with the new ADR/ODR provisions together with the broader initiatives of the European Digital Agenda and opportunities for collective redress, the European Parliament resolution provides for a point of departure in this discussion of the new provisions. Where, from the perspective of a consumer protection/remedy dimension, empirical analysis and other studies suggest that even with a growing online consumer market, only a small percentage of individuals will stand to benefit: when perceived as accessories to, or components of, the developments in European procedural law, a more rigorous logic for the ADR/ODR provisions can be developed.

4. MARKET DEVELOPMENT AND EUROPEANISATION OF PRIVATE AND PROCEDURAL LAW

4.1 Pragmatic Developments: From ODR and CESL to ODR and ADR to CESL and ODR/ADR

In his analysis of the need for ODR, Cortés suggests that the aim of EU consumer regulation is to obtain a higher level of uniformity across the Member States, with an approach that acknowledges that 'the internal market of itself does not and will not result in effective consumer protection'.[58] It is this, he suggests, that provides a rationale for the EU to develop both substantive and procedural consumer protection legislation and within which the ODR Regulation in particular is significant because it allows flexible, asynchronous communication at a distance that 'may be an alternative to lack of access to justice, rather than an alternative to courts'.[59] Undoubtedly, the role of technology is important and ODR, as an Internal Market tool of civil justice, complements the development of e-commerce and cross-border trade but the benefits of ODR, and ADR, as forces for the development of the Internal Market will be limited for some time to come. To his own rhetorical question of why online mediation is not more extensively used, Cortés suggests that the answer probably lies in the failure of mediation to attract disputants and that before 'online mediation can gain credibility, offline mediation must be better understood and valued by the public'.[60] Notwithstanding the difficulties in attracting disputants to ODR, Kaufmann-Kohler suggests that an increased use of ODR will be

[58] P Cortés, *Online Dispute Resolution for Consumers in the European Union* (Oxford, Routledge, 2010) 44.

[59] ibid, 85.

[60] ibid, 172, citing L Ponte, 'Throwing Bad Money after Bad: Can Online Dispute Resolution (ODR) Really Deliver the Goods for the Unhappy Internet Shopper?' (2001) 3 *Tulane Journal of Technology and Intellectual Property* 55, 91.

an inevitable consequence of an increasing e-commerce market and online retail turnover.[61]

Mak and Nemeth have previously discussed the (then proposed) ADR/ ODR provisions within the context of the EUs Digital Agenda and its objectives of boosting growth and jobs with 'sustainable economic and social benefits from a digital single market based on fast and ultra fast internet and interoperable applications'.[62] They draw attention to the ADR/ODR legislation as *having to be seen* as one part of a wider policy programme under the EUs 2020 flagship initiative, the 'Digital Agenda for Europe',[63] which is seen as one of the 'main levers for boosting growth and employment in the EU ... designed ultimately to bring the digital single market into being'.[64] It is within this economic focus that the importance of consumer confidence to the Single Market is linked to ADR/ODR, to collective redress initiatives,[65] and to the optional Common European Sales Law (CESL) initiative.[66] The 2011 'Single Market Act' communication from the Commission emphasised a need to facilitate easier and less costly cross-border business to consumer contracts by making progress towards a CESL,[67] and the Digital Agenda for Europe[68] also envisaged 'an optional instrument in European contract law to overcome the fragmentation of contract law and boost consumer confidence in e-commerce'.[69]

Viewed from the perspective of these separate but related initiatives, the ADR Directive and the ODR Regulation take on a greater coherence than when viewed through the somewhat extravagant consumer protection lens that was applied to the proposals and Impact Assessment that preceded the new provisions. In their assessment of the scope of the new ODR platform for the European Parliament, Micklitz and Sartor express some concern over what they describe as 'the problematic divide between ADR/ODR and

[61] G Kaufmann-Kohler, 'Online Dispute Resolution and its Significance for International Commercial Arbitration' (2005) *Global Reflections on International Law, Commerce and Dispute Resolution, Liber Amicorum in honour of Robert Briner*, ICC Publishing, Publication 693 at www.lk-k.com/data/document/online-dispute-resolution-and-its-significance-for-international-commercial-arbitration-global.pdf.

[62] V Mak and K Nemeth, 'The EU's Digital Agenda: New Proposals for Online and Offline Consumer Disputes, E-commerce and Card, Internet and Mobile Payments' (2012) 2 *Journal of European Consumer and Market Law* 112, 113 citing ec.europa.eu/europe2020/reaching-the-goals/flagship-initiatives/indwx_en.htm.

[63] See: ec.europa.eu/digital-agenda.

[64] COM(2011) 206 final, 13.

[65] ibid, 10.

[66] Commission, 'Proposal for a Regulation on a Common European Sales Law' COM(2011) 635 final.

[67] COM(2011) 206 final, 19.

[68] Communication from the Commission, 'A Digital Agenda for Europe' COM(2010) 245 final, 13.

[69] COM(2011) 635 final, 5.

domestic/transnational' within the context of the consumers' perspective of the separate provisions and their scope of application.[70] Whilst asserting their conviction that the EU has the competence to strengthen the links between ADR/ODR and domestic/cross-border application for consumers, the authors also draw attention to the deep connection between the ODR Regulation and the draft CESL: pointing out that the original intention was to publish the ODR and draft CESL Regulations together, and that it was only after the failure to achieve that that the proposal for the ODR Regulation became 'intertwined' with the proposal for the ADR Directive.[71]

Whilst the CESL was awaiting its first reading in the European Parliament,[72] the closeness of the relationship between the CESL and the ADR Directive was highlighted in the amendments prepared by the Committee on Legal Affairs and proposed by the Commission.[73] The first proposal acknowledges the lack of access to efficient and inexpensive redress mechanisms as an additional obstacle to cross-border trade and suggests a new recital be added to the preamble providing that

> a consumer and a trader concluding a contract on the basis of the Common European Sales Law should consider submitting disputes arising from that contract to an existing alternative dispute resolution entity ... entirely without prejudice to the possibility for the parties to initiate proceedings before the competent courts without first having recourse to alternative dispute resolution.[74]

This first proposal is then reflected in the proposal for a new Article 186(b) CESL that would provide for parties to be encouraged to consider submitting disputes arising from a business to consumer contract to an ADR entity.[75] In its commentary on the proposed CESL, the European Economic and Social Committee (EESC) drew attention to the Commission's data that indicated that one of the main obstacles preventing consumers from buying across borders in business to consumer transactions is the lack of effective means of redress, but also that other barriers to cross-border trade included 'differences in tax regulations, administrative requirements, difficulties in delivery, different language and culture, low level of broadband penetration,

[70] H Micklitz and G Sartor, 'Assessing the Scope of European Online Dispute Resolution Platform' available at: www.europarl.europa.eu/document/activities/cont/201204/20120417ATT43146/20120417ATT43146EN.pdf, 20.

[71] ibid.

[72] The optional Common European Sales Law for consumers and businesses (CESL) was adopted by legislative resolution in the European Parliament on 26 February 2014. The draft legislation remains subject to adoption by the Council of Ministers under the ordinary legislative procedure.

[73] European Parliament, 'Draft Legislative Resolution on the proposal for a regulation on a Common European Sales Law' COM(2011) 635, 2011/0284(COD).

[74] ibid, Amendment 19.

[75] ibid, Amendment 200.

data protection requirements, design, territorial limitations of intellectual property, payment facilities and differences in the legal framework'.[76]

Wallis also emphasises a need for a 'holistic approach' to ensure that the ADR Directive and the ODR Regulation are integrated with the CESL and vice versa. Such integration, she suggests is important within the context of the objectives of both the CESL and ADR/ODR measures in overcoming the historic barriers to the realisation of the full potential of the Internal Market that stem from traders wanting to keep disputes in their own national courts, thus depriving consumers in cross-border transactions of access to their own local courts.[77]

Returning to the EESC, its Opinion also drew attention to the need to 'boost consumer confidence in the Internal Market and to encourage consumers to make cross-border purchases by providing effective means of individual redress',[78] a position that the Committee subsequently extended to include 'collective redress'.[79] The Committee elaborated on this call for a provision on consumer collective redress acknowledging the ADR/ODR initiatives as an important step in addressing consumers' concerns over the lack of means for effective redress in cross-border transactions whilst expressing concern over the lack of a European judicial collective redress mechanism.[80]

4.2 Consumer Collective Redress and ADR/ODR

There have been a significant number of legislative initiatives associated with the Europe 2020 Strategy and the Single Market Act over recent years concerning matters of effective redress. At the EU level, horizontal procedural law solutions have been developing apace and once disparate topic areas are being forged into close relationships as the legislative initiative is informed by an approach that asks what is to be achieved and what options exist to achieve those ends.[81] It is in this context that non-judicial ADR/ODR solutions and the traditionally judicial collective redress solution are drawn together in a synthesis of the available options.[82] Hodges distinguishes

[76] OJ C/2012/181/75, citing the Consumer Market Scoreboard, 5th edn, March 2011, available at: ec.europa.eu/consumers/strategy/docs/5th_edition_scoreboard_en.pdf.

[77] D Wallis, *Common European Sales Law: A Practical View* (European Parliament Policy Department: Citizens' Rights and Constitutional Affairs), available at: www.europarl.europa.eu/RegData/etudes/note/join/2012/462474/IPOL-JURI_NT(2012)462474_EN.pdf, para 6,

[78] (n 76) para 4.13.

[79] ibid, Appendix, [2012] OJ C181/83.

[80] ibid, Appendix, Point 5.4.1.

[81] See C Hodges, 'Current Discussions on Consumer Redress: Collective Redress and ADR' (2012) 13 *ERA Forum* 11.

[82] ibid, 31. Hodges also draws attention to the relationship between ADR and the model rules for European private law drawn up in the DCFR on contract law, and the Commission's interest in ADR solutions for B2B contracts.

an established European approach to collective actions in which public enforcement sits alongside private enforcement 'often separating them for public norms and private rights respectively' and identifies that 'many Member States use ADR for disputes between the public sector and its contractors and citizens'.[83] The significance of this new European approach to designing the legal architecture from the objective to be achieved is reflected in the terminology that Hodges identifies had changed twice, from 'class action' to 'collective action' and then to 'collective redress'.

In the Commission's Recommendation on common principles for injunctive and compensatory collective redress, ADR procedures are positioned as an 'efficient way of obtaining redress in mass harm situations' that should 'always be available alongside, or as a voluntary element of, judicial collective redress'.[84] The Recommendation links the encouragement of parties to a mass harm situation to consensual or out-of-court settlement, at both the pre-trial and during the trial stages, to the requirements of the Mediation Directive.[85] At the EU level, the Directive applies only to mediation in cross-border disputes but encourages Member States to apply similar provisions to internal processes. The objectives of the Mediation Directive are set out in Article 1 and reflect the synthesis of options suggested above with the provision explicitly requiring 'a balanced relationship between mediation and judicial proceedings'. The combination of judicial and non-judicial processes is reinforced with provision for the courts to invite parties to a dispute already subject to litigation to use mediation to settle and to attend an information session on mediation if available.[86] This approach is reinforced in the Commission's Recommendation which suggests that collective redress mechanisms in the Member States are accompanied by collective ADR that is available both before and throughout any litigation.[87]

The collective interests of consumers have also been addressed in the Injunctions Directive of 2009 that sought to codify a number of amendments that had been made to its predecessor.[88] This new Injunctions Directive provides for collective actions to be brought on behalf of consumers by independent public bodies or organisations representing the collective interests of consumers or responsible for protecting the collective interests of consumers. Such actions are provided for in respect of infringements

[83] Hodges, 'Current Discussions on Consumer Redress' (n 81) 12.

[84] Commission Recommendation C(2013) 3539/3, preamble, para 16.

[85] Directive 2008/52/EC of 21 May 2008 on certain aspects of mediation in civil and commercial matters [2008] OJ L136/3.

[86] ibid, Art 5.

[87] Commission Recommendation C(2013) 3539/3, para 26.

[88] Directive 2009/22/EC of 23 April 2009 on injunctions for the protection of consumers' interests [2009] OJ L110/30, replacing Directive 98/27/EC of 19 May 1998 on injunctions for the protection of consumers' interests [1998] OJ L166/51.

applicable to a broad swath of the EU consumer *acquis*[89] with the joint objective of protecting the collective interests of consumers and ensuring the smooth functioning of the Internal Market.

4.3 Procedural Law in Civil Matters and the Broader Stockholm Programme

As part of its 2010–14 Stockholm Programme[90] the European Council called for the prioritisation of mechanisms that would facilitate access to justice 'so that people can enforce their rights throughout the Union'.[91] Aspects of the Stockholm Programme concern procedural law in civil matters, and include the abolition of *exequatur* that was accomplished with the recast of the Brussels I Regulation.[92] The main policy objective in the area of civil procedural law, beyond adjustments to European private international law, was to ensure that national borders between Member States 'should not constitute an obstacle either to the settlement of civil matters or to initiating court proceedings, or to the enforcement of decisions'.[93] The provision of easier access to justice, particularly in cross-border proceedings, is identified as a parallel objective to improving alternative methods of settling disputes, 'particularly in consumer law'.[94] The objectives in the Stockholm

[89] Directive 85/577/EEC of 20 December 1985 to protect the consumer in respect of contracts negotiated away from business premises [1985] OJ L372/31; Directive 2008/48/EC of 23 April 2008 on credit agreements for consumers [2008] OJ L133/66; Directive 89/552/EEC of 3 October 1989 on the coordination of certain provisions laid down by law, regulation or administrative action in Member States concerning the pursuit of television broadcasting activities [1989] OJ L298/23, Arts 10–21; Directive 90/314/EEC of 13 June 1990 on package travel, package holidays and package tours [1990] OJ L158/59; Directive 93/13/EEC of 5 April 1993 on unfair terms in consumer contracts [1993] OJ L95/29; Directive 97/7/EC of 20 May 1997 on the protection of consumers in respect of distance contracts [1997] OJ L144/19; Directive 1999/44/EC of 25 May 1999 on certain aspects of the sale of consumer goods and associated guarantees [1999] OJ L171/12; Directive 2000/31/EC of 8 June 2000 on certain legal aspects on information society services, in particular electronic commerce, in the internal market (Directive on Electronic Commerce) [2000] OJ L178/1; Directive 2001/83/EC of 6 November 2001 on the Community code relating to medicinal products for human use [2001] OJ L311/67, Arts 86–100; Directive 2002/65/EC of 23 September 2002 concerning the distance marketing of consumer financial services [2002] OJ L271/16; Directive 2005/29/EC of 11 May 2005 concerning unfair business-to-consumer commercial practices in the internal market [2005] OJ L149/22; Directive 2006/123/EC of 12 December 2006 on services in the internal market [2006] OJ L376/36; Directive 2008/122/EC of 14 January 2009 on the protection of consumers in respect of certain aspects of timeshare, long-term holiday product, resale and exchange contracts [2009] OJ L33/10.

[90] The Stockholm Programme—An Open and Secure Europe Serving and Protecting Citizens [2010] OJ C115/01.

[91] ibid, paras 1.1, 4.

[92] Regulation (EU) No 1215/2012 of 12 December 2012 on jurisdiction and the recognition and enforcement of judgments in civil and commercial matters (recast) [2012] OJ L351/1.

[93] (n 90) paras 3.3.2, 15.

[94] ibid, para 3.4.1.

Programme also promote e-Justice as an enabler for easier access to justice and recognised the potential for the cross-border procedural aspects of the European Payment Order and the European Small Claims Procedure to be dealt with online.[95]

The European Payment Order and the European Small Claims Procedure represent other strands in this ongoing reassessment of procedural law. Both are concerned with the functioning of the Internal Market and improving access to efficient justice, particularly in cross-border cases. The European Payment Order was established with the purpose of simplifying, speeding up and reducing costs in cross-border litigation and the setting of minimum standards for the free circulation of European orders for payment: an initiative that pre-empted the abolition of *exequatur* in the recast of the Brussels I Regulation by removing the need for any intermediate proceedings in the Member State of enforcement. The process is however an additional and optional means for the claimant, who remains free to resort to a procedure provided for by national law.

Whilst many Member States have pursued procedural simplification of civil procedures for small claims, in order to reduce the costs and delays of litigation, the reduction of obstacles in cross-border cases has been promoted at the EU level through the European Small Claims Procedure. Again, the objective is to facilitate simplified and accelerated access to justice in cross-border disputes for consumers and small businesses through the establishment of common procedural rules.[96]

5. CONCLUSIONS

If, as a direct consequence of consumer engagement with non-litigious redress the new ADR/ODR measures are expected to significantly boost access to justice and cross-border consumer trade, the premise appears flawed from a number of perspectives. The already established and extensive provision of ADR schemes provides only for a mixed and incomplete approach that, other than perhaps in some sectoral situations, appears to be sufficiently entrenched in diverse national traditions so as to limit the attraction of such schemes in cross-border consumer redress situations. Such national traditions link with individual aspects of consumer behaviour, motivation and awareness that suggest the new measures will only attract a limited increase of consumer engagement with ADR/ODR processes. The predicted positive social and economic impact of the new measures is unlikely therefore to

[95] Regulation (EC) No 1896/2006 of 12 December 2006 creating a European order for payment procedure[2006] OJ L399/1; and Regulation (EC) No 861/2007 of 11 July 2007 establishing a European Small Claims Procedure [2007] OJ L199/1 respectively.

[96] Regulation (EC) No 861/2007 (n 95) recitals 4 and 7.

be realised, at least within a short or medium time frame, and the empirical evidence shows little of the moral or ethical imperative for the win-win model of consumer and trader self-interest that leads to the common good in economic theory.

It is interesting, yet perhaps not surprising, to note from the empirical evidence that the most vulnerable of consumers are the oldest, the least well educated, and those who do not use computers or the Internet, and that it is these groups who are the most likely not to engage with any ADR scheme. This is however a reducing demographic, and in this context it is perhaps appropriate to view the new ADR/ODR provisions as being more compatible with the Digital Agenda and those other procedural and private law initiatives designed to promote the growth of cross-border trade in the Internal Market. Whilst it does not appear that the new measures will of themselves trigger an immediate increase in cross-border consumer trade, they are likely to become increasingly important as the collective effect of the broader framework of recent initiatives becomes recognised as providing a sufficiently safe and accessible platform for the development of cross-border trade and the digital market.

4

Top-Level Domains and ADR: What Protection of Consumer Interests Under ICANN's New gTLD Program?

CRISTINA M MARIOTTINI*

1. INTRODUCTION: ICANN'S NEW gTLD PROGRAM AND ADR PROCEDURE

THE INTERNET CORPORATION for Assigned Names and Numbers (ICANN)[1] was founded in 1998 as a not-for-profit, multi-stakeholder organization. ICANN operates the Internet Assigned Numbers Authority (IANA), and is in charge of maintaining the Domain Name System (DNS) root zone. One of ICANN's key mandates is to promote competition in the domain name market: the mission of ICANN, pursuant to its bylaws, is to coordinate at the overall level and to ensure the stable and secure operation of the Internet's unique identifier systems.[2] In addition to providing technical operations of vital DNS resources, ICANN also defines policies for how the 'names and numbers' of the Internet should run. ICANN's assignment specifically calls for the corporation to maintain and build on processes that will ensure competition and consumer interests without compromising the security and stability of the Internet.[3] Overall, while ICANN's task in not that of distributing domain names directly to users, the corporation nevertheless retains the ability to regulate the DNS and determine the available Top Level Domains (TLDs) that will ultimately

* Senior Research Fellow, Max Planck Institute Luxembourg for International, European and Regulatory Procedural Law.

[1] See www.icann.org.

[2] Art 1, Bylaws for Internet Corporation for Assigned Names and Numbers, as amended 7 February 2014, available at: www.icann.org/resources/pages/bylaws-2012-02-25-en.

[3] gTLD Applicant Guidebook, version 4 June 2012 (Applicant Guidebook), available at: newgtlds.icann.org/en/applicants/agb, Attachment to Module 2, at A-1. See also Core Value No 1, available at: www.icann.org/resources/pages/bylaws-2012-02-25-en.

be available for distribution: and while its decision-making process is based on an extended stakeholder community which encompasses private Internet users, businesses and governments,[4] the corporation plays an undisputed major role in shaping what the Internet ultimately looks like to end-users.[5]

Originally, the domain namespace was restricted and consisted of 22 generic Top Level Domains (gTLDs)—visible to Internet users as the suffix at the end of a domain name—and over 250 country code Top Level Domains (ccTLDs)[6] operating on various models.[7] Generally speaking, there are unsponsored and sponsored TLDs. An unsponsored TLD operates under policies established by the global Internet community directly through the ICANN process, while a sponsored TLD is a specialized TLD that has a sponsor representing the narrower community that is most affected by the TLD. The sponsor thus carries out delegated policy-formulation responsibilities over many matters concerning the TLD.

In the 1980s, the first seven gTLDs (.com, .edu, .gov, .int, .mil, .net, and .org) were created. In 2001 and 2002, four new unsponsored TLDs (.biz, .info, .name, and .pro) were introduced,[8] and another three new TLDs (.aero, .coop, and .museum) were sponsored.[9] After an evaluation period,

[4] Governments' contribution is provided essentially through ICANN's Governmental Advisory Committee (GAC). The GAC was formed to consider and provide advice on the activities of ICANN as they relate to concerns of governments. The GAC periodically issues communiqués to ICANN in relation to the gTLD process providing, inter alia, advice on sensitive issues, especially on any gTLD applications that the GAC considers problematic. GAC Advice may come into three forms: (i) the GAC advises ICANN that it is the consensus of the GAC that a particular application should not proceed. This will create a strong presumption for the ICANN Board that the application should not be approved; (ii) the GAC advises ICANN that there are concerns about a particular application. The ICANN Board is expected to enter into dialogue with the GAC to understand the scope of concerns. The ICANN Board is also expected to provide a rationale for its decision; (iii) the GAC advises ICANN that an application should not proceed unless remediated. This will raise a strong presumption for the ICANN Board that the application should not proceed unless there is a remediation method available in the Applicant Guidebook (such as securing the approval of one or more governments), that is implemented by the applicant. The GAC may also issue Early Warnings. An Early Warning is an indication that a formal GAC objection is possible (either through the GAC advice process or through the formal objection process). Applicants are notified of an Early Warning against their application and given the opportunity to address the concerns or to withdraw the application. See Applicant Guidebook, Module 3, 3–2. To track the history and progress of GAC Advice to the Board, *cf* https://gacweb.icann.org/display/gacweb/GAC+Recent+Meetings.

[5] On the long-standing debate on which institutions should be in charge of the Internet and how their legitimacy may be established see R Radu, JM Chenou and RH Weber (eds), *The Evolution of the Global Internet Governance. Principles and Policies in the Making* (Heidelberg, Springer, 2014).

[6] ccTLDs correspond to a country, territory, or other geographic location. The rules and policies for registering domain names in the ccTLDs vary significantly, and ccTLD registries limit use of the ccTLD to citizens of the corresponding country. For more information regarding registering names in ccTLDs, including a complete database of designated ccTLDs and managers, see www.iana.org/cctld/cctld.htm.

[7] *cf* Applicant Guidebook, preamble.

[8] At: www.icann.org/news/announcement-2004-08-31-en.

[9] ibid.

a further round of sponsored TLDs was introduced during 2003 and 2004 which included, among others, .mobi, for services relating to mobile phones, .jobs, for the human resources sector, and .travel for restricted use of travel industry operators.[10]

Each gTLD has a designated registry operator that enters into the Registry Agreement with ICANN[11] and is responsible for setting up and maintaining the operation of the registry: the registry operator is responsible for the technical operation of the gTLD, including all of the names registered in that gTLD. The gTLDs are served by over 900 registrars who interact with registrants to perform domain name registration and other related services.

Extending the gTLD market to new gTLDs has been at the forefront of ICANN's agenda since its outset. In 2011, ICANN's board eventually voted to end most restrictions on gTLD names. As a result of this decision and the subsequent adoption of ICANN's New gTLD Program, companies and organizations (but not individuals) are currently able to choose and apply for the exclusive registration of essentially arbitrary top-level Internet domains.[12]

Alongside the application procedure for new gTLDs, ICANN also laid out a New gTLD Dispute Resolution Procedure, a fully self-contained alternative dispute resolution mechanism that operates where claims are brought against an application.[13] The system laid out by ICANN includes a public comment period, where interested stakeholders may express their concerns about an applied-for registration: such concerns will be considered by the ICANN authorities during the so-called 'administrative evaluation period' of the application.[14] Pursuant to ICANN's New gTLD Dispute Resolution Procedure, four different types of claim may be brought against an

[10] ibid.

[11] The Registry Agreement is the agreement executed between ICANN and successful gTLD applicants, which appears as an attachment to Module 5 of the Applicant Guidebook.

[12] Information related to the New gTLD Program is available at: newgtlds.icann.org/en. On ICANN's expansion of gTLDs see: BW Borchert, 'Imminent Domain Name: The Technological Land-Grab and ICANN's Lifting of Domain Name Restrictions' (2010–11) 45 *Valparaiso University Law Review* 505; C Easton, 'ICANN's Core Principles and the Expansion of Generic Top-Level Domain Names' (2012) 20 *International Journal of Law and Information Technology* 273; LG Kruger, 'Internet Governance and the Domain Name System: Issues for Congress', Congressional Research Service (CRS Report for Congress) (2014) 7-5700, R42351; EM Weitzenboeck, 'Hybrid net: the regulatory framework of ICANN and the DNS' (2014) 1 *International Journal of Law and Information Technology* 22, 49; M McGillivray, 'Anticipating Conflict—An Evaluation of the New gTLD Dispute Resolution System' in D Wiese Schartum and AGB Bekken (red), *Yulex 2012* (Oslo, 2012); M Mahler, 'New Top-Level Domains and Legal Risks' in D Wiese Schartum and AGB Bekken (red), *Yulex 2012* (Oslo, 2012). Strong criticism against ICANN's New gTLD Program has been expressed in Annex C—NCUC Minority Statement, 25 July 2007, available at: http://gnso.icann.org/en/issues/new-gtlds/pdp-dec05-fr-parta-08aug07.htm. In NCUC's opinion the Program's objection and rejection processes are far too broad and unwieldy to be put into practice.

[13] At: http://newgtlds.icann.org/en/applicants/agb.

[14] Applicant Guidebook, Module 1, esp para 1.1.2.3.

application for a new gTLD registration, these claims being: String Confusion Objection; Legal Rights Objection; Limited Public Interest Objection; and Community Objection.[15]

During the first application window, opened in January 2012 and closed in April of the same year, ICANN received 1,930 new gTLD applications, of which 751 were contested during the public comment period from June to September 2012.[16] Examples of new gTLDS for which applications were filed are: .bank; .book; .energy; .health; .healthcare; .hospital; .insurance; .hotel; .lotto; .mail; .med; .medical; .food; .camera; .church. Eventually, 263 claims were brought: 23 claims based on Limited Public interest; 69 on Legal Rights; 67 on String Confusion; and 104 on Community Objection grounds.[17] Over 1,300 new names or 'strings' could become available in the next few years.[18]

In this chapter, I will consider the stance of ICANN's New gTLD Program towards consumer protection: I will try to establish whether and to what extent the interests of consumers have been considered in both the application procedure for the registration of New gTLDs (section 2) and ICANN's New gTLD Dispute Resolution Procedure (section 3).

2. THE APPLICATION PROCEDURE FOR A NEW gTLD: MEASURES PROTECTING THE INTERESTS OF CONSUMERS

Since ICANN was founded, one of its key mandates has been to promote competition in the domain name market: ICANN's mission specifically calls for the corporation to maintain and build on processes that will ensure competition and consumer interests without compromising Internet security and stability.[19] While introducing its New gTLD Program, ICANN repeatedly stressed that the Program aims at expanding and making accessible the top level of the Internet's namespace to foster diversity, encourage competition, enhance the utility of the DNS, create new options for consumers in the market, and generate significant benefit to Internet users across the globe.[20] Some stakeholders have welcomed the expansion of gTLDs as an excellent marketing and business opportunity which grants them the possibility to acquire their own gTLD and exercise greater control over their online presence. Nonetheless, strong concerns have been raised about the impact

[15] *cf* Applicant Guidebook, Module 3, para 3.2.1.

[16] See: http://newgtlds.icann.org/en/program-status/statistics.

[17] See: http://newgtlds.icann.org/en/program-status/odr/filings.

[18] The list of the currently delegated strings is available at: http://newgtlds.icann.org/en/program-status/delegated-strings.

[19] Art 1, Bylaws for Internet Corporation for Assigned Names and Numbers, as amended 7 February 2014, available at: www.icann.org/resources/pages/bylaws-2012-02-25-en.

[20] *cf* Applicant Guidebook, preamble.

of these new gTLDs not only on the market and on competition, but also on consumers: in the New gTLD Program consumer interests are only tangentially taken into account, and expansion opponents argue against such expansion as potentially creating consumer confusion, making the DNS more complicated, and increasing cybersquatting and commercial fraud.

In a letter of 16 December 2011,[21] the Federal Trade Commission (FTC) expressed the concern that a 'rapid, exponential expansion of gTLDs has the potential to magnify both the abuse of the domain name system and the corresponding challenges we encounter in tracking down Internet fraudsters'. The FTC urged ICANN to implement the New gTLD Program as a pilot program and substantially reduce the number of gTLDs that were introduced in the first application round, strengthen ICANN's contractual compliance program, develop a new ongoing program to monitor consumer issues that arose during the first round of implementing the new gTLD program, conduct an assessment of each new proposed gTLD's risk of consumer harm as part of the evaluation and approval process, and improve the accuracy of WHOIS data,[22] including by imposing a registrant verification requirement. The FTC further stated that 'ICANN should address these issues before it approves any new gTLD applications. If ICANN fails to address these issues responsibly, the introduction of new gTLDs could pose a significant threat to consumers and undermine consumer confidence in the Internet'. In a 27 December 2011 letter to ICANN,[23] the Senate and House Judiciary Committees strongly advised ICANN to 'strengthen protections for consumers and trademark holders who risk being harmed by the proliferation of domain names on the web'.[24] The letter also urged ICANN to work closely with the law enforcement community 'to ensure that the program's rollout does not adversely impact their efforts to fight fraud and abuse on the Internet'.[25]

[21] Letter from FTC to ICANN (16 December 2011), available at: www.ftc.gov/sites/default/files/documents/public_statements/icanns-plan-increase-available-generic-top-level-domains/111216letter-icann.pdf.

[22] The Whois Data Reminder Policy (WDRP) was adopted by ICANN as a consensus policy in 2003, and provides that all ICANN-accredited registrars must comply with the WDRP with respect to registrations they sponsor in all top-level domains for which they are accredited. Details of compliance requirements are available at: www.icann.org/resources/pages/wdrp-2012-02-25-en.

[23] Letter from the Chairmen and Ranking Members of the Senate and House Judiciary Committees to Rod Beckstrom, CEO, ICANN (27 December 2011), available at: www.icann.org/en/system/files/files/leahy-to-beckstrom-27dec11-en.pdf.

[24] ibid. See also 'Rockefeller Says Internet Domain Expansion Will Hurt Consumers, Businesses, and Non-Profits—Urges Delay', Press Release, Senate Committee on Commerce, Science and Transportation (28 December 2011), available at: http://commerce.senate.gov/public/index.cfm?p=PressReleases; and House Committee on Energy and Commerce, 'Committee Urges ICANN to Delay Expansion of Generic Top-Level Domain Program', Press Release, (21 December 2011), available at: http://energycommerce.house.gov/news/PRArticle.aspx?NewsID=9176.

[25] ibid.

Nonetheless, at the December 2011 US House and Senate hearings, ICANN indicated its intention to proceed with the gTLD expansion as scheduled.[26] ICANN defended its gTLD program arguing that the new gTLDs will offer more protections for consumers and trademark holders than current gTLDs; that new gTLDs will provide needed competition, choice and innovation to the domain name system; and that critics had already had ample opportunity to contribute input during a seven-year deliberative policy development process.[27] Ultimately, ICANN did not delay the initiation of the New gTLD Program, and the application window was opened on 12 January 2012, as planned.

2.1 Applicant's Eligibility: Measures for Pre-Emptive Screening

The Program's application round was implemented using a 'first come, first served' processing schedule. Each applicant had to show that it had a 'legitimate claim' to the name it applied for and had to also submit a detailed business plan, financial statements and technical documentation about how it intends to operate and manage its gTLD.[28] However, no definition or any other indication for the interpretation of 'legitimate claim' is provided in the Program. Such legitimacy may be scrutinized by means of the objections that are made available to third parties against the application. However, absent any objections, the legitimacy is only subject to the large-mesh filter provided by the pre-emptive screening measures that are laid out in the Program.

As concerns the eligibility of the entity applying for a New gTLD, a background screening is intended to protect the public interest in the allocation of critical Internet resources: based on any information identified during the background screening process, ICANN reserves the right to deny an otherwise qualified application.[29] Furthermore, in keeping with ICANN's Uniform Domain Name Dispute Resolution Policy (UDRP),[30] with the Anti-Cybersquatting Consumer Protection Act,[31] and with other

[26] Kruger (n 12) 15.

[27] ibid.

[28] Instructions for Completing the Registrar Accreditation Application, available at: www.icann.org/resources/pages/instructions-2014-02-05-en.

[29] Applicant Guidebook, Module 1, para 1.2.1.

[30] At: www.icann.org/resources/pages/udrp-2012-02-25-en.

[31] 15 USC § 1125(d). The Anti-Cybersquatting Consumer Protection Act (ACPA) was enacted by the US Congress in 1999 to establish a cause of action for registering, trafficking in, or using a domain name confusingly similar to, or dilutive of, a trademark or personal name. Instead of suing in a federal court under the ACPA, a trademark owner can choose to pursue an administrative proceeding under ICANN's Uniform Domain Name Dispute Resolution Policy (UDRP) which allows a trademark owner to challenge domain name registrations in expedited administrative proceedings. See www.icann.org/resources/pages/udrp-2012-02-25-en.

equivalent legislation, the Program states that applications from any entity that has been involved in a pattern of adverse, final decisions indicating that the applicant has been engaged in cybersquatting will be automatically disqualified from the Program.[32] These measures are meant to prevent access to the new gTLD system by those applicants who have a history of cybersquatting or equivalently undesirable cyber-behaviours, such as typosquatting or phishing. While anti-cybersquatting and similar legislation directly protects a trademark owner granting him standing to bring a claim against the alleged cybersquatter in order that the domain name be transferred to the trademark owner, the same legislation also indirectly provides a protection of consumer interests against the confusion and probable deception that would ensue from allowing a cybersquatter to maintain the domain name's registration in his name. Nonetheless, the boundaries established by such pre-emptive screening measures against applicants with an undesirable cyber-history are not necessarily insurmountable, as proven by the case—which, not detected at the application phase, reached the objection stage—where the applicant for the .bank gTLD was a member of a corporate family which, according to the Anti-Phishing Working Group (APWG) Report of October 2012, 'Global Phishing Survey: Trends and Domain Name Use in 1H2012',[33] accounted for the largest percentage of malicious domain name registrations of any named registrar.[34]

As concerns undesirable cyber-behaviours enacted after the registration of a new gTLD, cybersquatting 'to the right of the dot' in new gTLDs is less likely since the application process is burdensome and expensive.[35] Cybersquatting 'to the left of the dot' is also unlikely since most of the new gTLDs will be purchased by brand owners who wish to have complete control of the domain names within their gTLD.[36] Nonetheless, abuse may occur, in particular—but not only—where a 'non-brand' organization acquires a new gTLD and then sells malicious domain names under it: this should be reason for particular concern as harm to consumers, as well as to institutions, usually happens within hours of malicious domain names being purchased. This point was expressly addressed in letters submitted to the chairman of ICANN's Board by the governments of France, Italy and Portugal in June 2014 expressing concerns that the already heightened existing safeguards over the delegation of .vin and .wine adopted by

[32] Applicant Guidebook, Module 1, paras 1.2.1(m), 1-23–1-24.

[33] The Report is available at: http://docs.apwg.org/reports/APWG_GlobalPhishingSurvey_1H2012.pdf.

[34] ICC, Case No EXP/389/ICANN/6 *International Banking Federation (UK) v Dotsecure Inc (UAE)*, available at: http://newgtlds.icann.org/sites/default/files/drsp/06dec13/determination-1-1-1053-59307-en.pdf.

[35] *cf* http://meitar.com/180626.

[36] ibid.

the Governmental Advisory Committee (GAC) in Beijing[37] and endorsed by the ICANN Board may not prove sufficient as they would still allow non-legitimate rights holders to register second-level domain names under the .vin and .wine strings, and open the door for the potential violation of rights provided for under EU legislation to protect such geographical indications.[38] In this case, as the above-mentioned pre-emptive screening measures are meant to function beforehand, they would be clearly unable to provide relief, meaning that recourse to the traditional ex-post measures provided by ICANN's UDRP, as well as by the Anti-Cybersquatting Consumer Protection Act and other equivalent legislation, would be necessary. However, this recourse may not necessarily be sufficient or timely enough to prevent the harm of misdirection of consumers, hence undermining consumer confidence in a particular commercial sector and having an impact on its financial productivity.

To afford further protection of the interests of consumers and to strengthen the efficacy of the pre-emptive screening of applications for registration of a new gTLD, the Applicant Guidebook also provides that a final and legally binding decision by a national law enforcement authority or consumer protection authority that an applicant was engaged in fraudulent and deceptive commercial practices as defined in the Organisation for Economic Co-operation and Development (OECD) Guidelines for Protecting Consumers from Fraudulent and Deceptive Commercial Practices Across Borders[39] may cause an application to be rejected.[40]

2.2 Public Comment Period

A crucial element in ICANN's processes is the opportunity for public comment on each substantial piece of work before it is considered for approval: this opportunity also encompasses applications for new gTLDs. Comment mechanisms are part of ICANN's policy development, implementation, and operational processes: throughout ICANN's activity, bottom-up, consensus-based processes are in place to achieve wide representation of global Internet communities, and to develop policies appropriate to ICANN's mission.[41] To ensure the participation of stakeholder groups in a public discussion and to provide a means for the public to bring forward any other

[37] Governmental Advisory Committee, GAC Communiqué—Beijing (11 April 2013), available at: www.icann.org/en/system/files/correspondence/gac-to-board-18apr13-en.pdf, at para 1(c)(i).

[38] The letters may be retrieved at http://newgtlds.icann.org/en/program-status/correspondence.

[39] At: www.oecd.org/sti/consumer/oecdguidelinesforprotectingconsumersfromfraudulentanddeceptivecommercialpracticesacrossbordershtml.htm.

[40] Applicant Guidebook, Module 1, paras 1.2.1, 1-24.

[41] Kruger (n 12) 2.

relevant information or issues, the New gTLD Program provides that anyone (including consumers and consumer organizations) may comment in a public comment forum during the comment period through all stages of the evaluation process.[42] While public comments do not constitute formal objections—the latter having been created to allow a full and fair consideration of objections based on certain limited grounds[43]—and will not per se prevent an application from being evaluated, they will nevertheless be available to and may be subsequently considered by an expert panel during a dispute resolution proceeding. However, ICANN itself warned expert panels that 'the public comment forum should not be used as a mathematical polling mechanism ... [and that] the quantity of the comments is not in itself a deciding factor'.[44]

2.3 Interim Conclusions

Overall, as concerns the protection of consumer interests, the measures in ICANN's New gTLD Program and particularly in its application procedure appear to consider the impact that new gTLDs may have on consumers and provide some safeguards. In fact, at the very initial stage of the application, on the one hand, pre-emptive screening measures may be effective in blocking applicants with a history of undesirable cyber-behaviours and of fraudulent and deceptive commercial practices. On the other hand, the public comment period provides a valuable means of direct expression and communication of possible consumer and consumer organization concerns regarding applications for new gTLDs. Although the effectiveness of the public comment period is limited because (i) it may not directly affect an application, and (ii) its effects on the possible subsequent objection phase are not predictable given that the relevance afforded to public comments in the objection procedure is left to the expert panel's discretion, as explained below in section 3, the public comment period remains one of the few stages in the New gTLD Program where consumer concerns may be directly expressed.

[42] Applicant Guidebook, Module 1, para 1-6.

[43] See: http://newgtlds.icann.org/en/program-status/odr for more information on objections.

[44] New gTLDs Proposed Final Applicant Guidebook, Public Comment Summary (21 February 2011) 37, available at: http://archive.icann.org/en/topics/new-gtlds/summary-analysis-proposed-final-guidebook-21feb11-en.pdf. However, see ICC, Case No EXP/500/ICANN/117 *Universal Postal Union (Switzerland) v Charleston Road Registry Inc (USA)* (consolidated with Cases EXP/494/ICANN/111 *Universal Postal Union (Switzerland) v Victor Dale, LLC (USA)*; EXP/496/ICANN/113 *Universal Postal Union (Switzerland) v Whitepages TLD, LLC (USA)*; and EXP/497/ICANN/114 *Universal Postal Union (Switzerland) v GMO Registry, INC (Japan)*), available at: http://newgtlds.icann.org/sites/default/files/drsp/10feb14/determination-1-1-1141-82929-en.pdf, 139 expressly 'considering the small number of Posts which have filed public comments' as a factor to establish the expression of a substantial opposition (or lack thereof) to the application for a new gTLD.

3. A SELF-CONTAINED ADR SYSTEM FOR DISPUTES OVER A NEW gTLD APPLICATION

While consumer interests are to some degree recognized as relevant at the application stage, in none of the objections made available by ICANN's independent dispute resolution process against an application for a New gTLD are consumers or consumer organizations expressly granted standing,[45] nor are their interests explicitly included in the substantial grounds of the objection.

The New gTLD Program provides for four possible objections that may be brought within its framework.[46] Pursuant to Article 20 of the Procedure,[47] for each category of objection, the expert panel deciding on the objection shall apply the standards that have been defined by ICANN. In addition, the panel may refer to and base its findings on the statements and documents submitted and any rules or principles that it determines to be applicable.[48] The burden of proving that its objection should be sustained in accordance with the applicable standards lies with the objector.[49] The four objections made available by ICANN's New gTLD Program are: (1) String Confusion Objection; (2) Legal Rights Objection; (3) Limited Public Interest Objection; and (4) Community Objection.

3.1 String Confusion Objection

String confusion refers to the scenario in which the string is confusingly similar to an existing TLD or to another applied-for gTLD string—delegating two or more similar TLDs could cause user confusion.[50] Pursuant to

[45] Consumer organizations may be granted standing, especially in Community Objection claims, but they do not benefit from any particular provisions and are required, to the contrary, to comply with the general standards on standing and substance of the claim provided for any other objector. See, eg, ICC, Case No EXP/385/ICANN/2 *Hotel Consumer Protection Coalition (USA) v Booking.Com BV (The Netherlands)* (consolidated with Case No EXP/447/ICANN/64 *Hotrec, Hotels, Restaurants & Cafes in Europe (Belgium) v Booking.Com BV (The Netherlands)*), available at: http://newgtlds.icann.org/sites/default/files/drsp/25nov13/determination-1-1-1016-75482-en.pdf.

[46] *cf* Applicant Guidebook, Module 3. The various categories of dispute are administered by different Dispute Resolution Service Providers (DRSP) based upon the rights that are protected with each claim. Namely, the International Centre for Dispute Resolution (ICDR) administers disputes arising on the ground of string confusion; The Arbitration and Mediation Centre of the World Intellectual Property Organization (WIPO) administers disputes arising on the ground of Legal Rights; finally, the International Chamber of Commerce (ICC) administers disputes arising on the ground of Limited Public Interest as well as on grounds of Community Objection. See Module 3, para 3.2.3.

[47] Applicant Guidebook, Attachment to Module 3.

[48] ibid.

[49] ibid.

[50] Applicant Guidebook, Module 1, esp para 1.1.2.10.

ICANN's Applicant Guidebook, 'similar' means strings so similar that they create a probability of user confusion if more than one of the strings is delegated into the root zone. For a likelihood of confusion to exist, it must be probable, and not merely possible, that confusion will arise in the mind of the average, reasonable Internet user. While this requirement would appear to suggest a means of protection—or, at least, of consideration—of consumer interests, the standing to this objection is limited to operators who have an immediate interest in the string. Hence, consumers or consumer organizations do not fall within the categories of the entities that have standing for this objection. Therefore, although an indirect protection is afforded by this objection to deceiving or confusing strings, no direct protection is granted to consumers or their organizations.

3.2 Legal Rights Objection

In a Legal Rights Objection the objector alleges that the applied-for gTLD string infringes existing legal rights of the objector.[51] Examples of these legal rights that are internationally recognized include, but are not limited to, rights defined in the Paris Convention for the Protection of Industry Property[52] (in particular, trademark rights), as well as intellectual property treaties administered by the World Intellectual Property Organization (WIPO) and the WTO Agreement on Trade-Related Aspects of Intellectual Property (TRIPS).[53] Once again, only the holder of registered or unregistered trademarks or a service mark is acknowledged as having standing in this claim. In addressing the substance of the claim, the expert panel will determine whether the potential use of the applied-for gTLD by the applicant takes unfair advantage of or unjustifiably impairs the distinctive character or the reputation of the objector's trademark or service mark. Accordingly, consumer interests are not furthered by this objection.

3.3 Limited Public Interest Objection

In a Limited Public Interest Objection, the objector alleges that the applied-for gTLD string is contrary to generally accepted legal norms of morality and public order recognized under international principles of law. These

[51] *cf* Applicant Guidebook, Module 3, esp para 3.5.2. On legal rights and new gTLDs see J Lipton and M Wong, 'Trademarks and Freedom of Expression in ICANN's New gTLD Process' (2012) 38 *Monash University Law Review* 188.

[52] Paris Convention for the Protection of Industrial Property of 20 March 1883 and subsequent amendments, consolidated text, available at: www.wipo.int/treaties/en/text.jsp?file_id=288514.

[53] Text available at: www.wto.org/english/tratop_e/trips_e/t_agm0_e.htm.

grounds are, to name a few: incitement to or promotion of violent lawless action; incitement to or promotion of discrimination based upon race, colour, gender, ethnicity, religion or national origin, or other similar types of discrimination that violate generally accepted legal norms recognized under principles of international law; incitement to or promotion of child pornography or other sexual abuse of children; or a determination that an applied-for new gTLD string would be contrary to specific principles of international law as reflected in relevant international instruments of law. Examples of such principles of law include, but are not limited to,[54] the Universal Declaration of Human Rights (UDHR),[55] the International Covenant on Civil and Political Rights (ICCPR),[56] the Convention on the Elimination of All Forms of Discrimination against Women (CEDAW)[57] and the International Convention on the Elimination of All Forms of Racial Discrimination.[58]

Anyone may file a Limited Public Interest Objection, including a consumer or a consumer organization. However, the grounds upon which this objection may be raised address general principles of international law rather than consumer interests. Because the Limited Public Interest Objection aims at protecting a broad spectrum of general principles of international law addressing questions of morality and public order, consumer interests are unlikely to fall within the scope of this objection. While consumer interests may have been encompassed, at a regional level, in the scope of fundamental rights (*cf*, eg, Article 38 of the Charter of Fundamental Rights of the European Union, where it is stated that 'Union policies shall ensure a high level of consumer protection'),[59] apparently such characterization has not been implemented by expert panels when it comes to the DNS. In fact, in the expert determinations rendered on Limited Public Interest grounds as to 26 June 2014, consumers are seldom mentioned, and when they are mentioned it is usually simply to be cited as part of the objector's arguments. Moreover, in one case the expert panel expressly rejected the objector's arguments that allowing the .broker string to be operated by the applicant would harm the public by having a negative effect on consumers and on competition: while the expert panel acknowledged that the objector's arguments on this issue may be relevant in the broader context of the application procedures for gTLD strings, it also reiterated that its task is limited to assessing 'whether the gTLD string .broker is contrary to general or specific principles of international law for morality and public order',[60]

[54] Applicant Guidebook, Module 3, esp para 3.5.3.

[55] Text available at: www.un.org/en/documents/udhr.

[56] Text available at: www.ohchr.org/en/professionalinterest/pages/ccpr.aspx.

[57] Text available at: www.un.org/womenwatch/daw/cedaw/cedaw.htm.

[58] Text available at: www.ohchr.org/EN/ProfessionalInterest/Pages/CERD.aspx.

[59] Charter of Fundamental Rights of the European Union [2010] OJ C83/389, 399.

[60] ICC, Case No EXP/458/ICANN/75 *TD Ameritrade (USA) v IG Group Holdings Plc (UK)*, available at: http://newgtlds.icann.org/sites/default/files/drsp/16dec13/determination-1-1-1332-82635-en.pdf, esp para 93.

and accordingly the expert panel provided a clear indication that in its opinion consumer protection does not fall within the scope of the Limited Public Interest Objection.

3.4 Community Objection

In a Community Objection, the objector alleges that there is substantial opposition to the new gTLD application from a significant portion of the community which the new gTLD string may explicitly or implicitly target.[61] To qualify for standing for a community objection, the objector must prove it is an established institution and it has an ongoing relationship with a clearly delineated community. To evaluate whether the community is clearly delineated, the panel may consider, among others, the following factors: the level of public recognition of the group as a community at a local and/or global level; the level of formal boundaries around the community and what persons or entities are considered to form the community; the length of time the community has been in existence; the global distribution of the community; and the number of people or entities that make up the community.[62] For the substance of a claim for a Community Objection to be successful, the objector must prove that: (i) the community invoked by the objector is a clearly delineated community; (ii) community opposition to the application is substantial; (iii) there is a strong association between the community invoked and the applied-for new gTLD string;[63] and (iv) the application creates a likelihood of material detriment to the rights or legitimate interests of a significant portion of the community which the string may explicitly or implicitly target,[64] such (not better identified) rights or legitimate interests

[61] *cf* Applicant Guidebook, Module 3, esp para 3.5.4.

[62] In considering whether the 'clearly delineated community' test is met, the Procedure provides that the panel may consider, among others, the following factors: the number of expressions of opposition relative to the composition of the community; the representative nature of entities expressing opposition; the level of recognized stature or weight among sources of opposition; the distribution or diversity among sources of expressions of opposition, including (i) regional; (ii) subsectors of community; (iii) leadership of community; (iv) membership of community; the historical defence of the community in other contexts; and the costs incurred by the objector in expressing opposition, including other channels the objector may have used to convey opposition.

[63] To evaluate the existence of a strong association between the string and the community, the panel may consider, among others, the following factors: statements contained in the application; other public statements by the applicant; and associations by the public.

[64] To assess the existence of material detriment to the members of the community, the Procedure advises the panel to use, among others, the following factors: nature and extent of damage to the reputation of the community represented by the objector that would result from the applicant's operation of the applied-for gTLD string; evidence that the applicant is not acting or does not intend to act in accordance with the interests of the community or of users more widely, including evidence that the applicant has not proposed or does not intend to institute effective security protection for user interests; interference with the core activities of

being the ultimate object of protection that ICANN's ADR procedure aims at furthering by means of the Community Objection.

While these standards do not grant any explicit favourable treatment to consumers as concerns standing nor afford a direct, substantial protection to consumer interests, such interests have been, nonetheless, taken into account in some expert determinations. In a decision addressing the applied-for new gTLD string .architect, the expert panel pointed out that one of the aims of the introduction of new gTLDs is clearly the promotion of consumer choice and competition, and that promoting competition is not an absolute and unlimited goal.[65] To the contrary, among ICANN's Core Values is introducing and promoting competition in the registration of domain names where practical and beneficial in the public interest[66] which, in the expert panel's opinion, includes limitations imposed for reasons of consumer protection. Accordingly, the expert panel drew the conclusion that consumers should be entitled to assume that anybody using a gTLD such as .architect is in fact a licensed architect, as this is the only way the use of the gTLD .architect can promote consumer choice and competition.

In an objection raised against the registration of the .insurance string, the expert panel observed that consumers are entitled to assume that entities presenting themselves under the .insurance domain in whatever form, including gTLD, are regulated entities, and are subject to the same online registration requirements and applicable regulations as their offline counterparts. As the expert panel observed, because

> the Application does not provide any eligibility/validation restrictions on the registration of generic names or any subsequent control, it may result in entities which are not members of the insurance community registering generic names in the .insurance domain. If at present there already are a substantial number of malicious domain registrations on the basis of second level registrations, it is likely that the reliance placed by the consumers on the gTLD domain .insurance will increase the level of malicious use. If generic domain names are not subject to any registration or subsequent control, and consumers have placed their trust on the wrongful assumption that registration barriers and subsequent control exist, the likelihood of creating confusion in the mind of the end user will result in harm not only to the consumer, but ultimately, to the reputation of the internet activity of the insurance community.[67]

the community that would result from the applicant's operation of the applied-for gTLD string; dependence of the community represented by the objector on the DNS for its core activities; nature and extent of concrete or economic damage to the community represented by the objector that would result from the applicant's operation of the applied-for gTLD string; and level of certainty that alleged detrimental outcomes would occur.

[65] ICC, Case No EXP/384/ICANN/1 *The International Union of Architects (France) v Spring Frostbite, LLC (USA)*, available at: http://newgtlds.icann.org/sites/default/files/drsp/25sep13/determination-1-1-1342-7920-en.pdf, para 128.

[66] *cf* ICANN's Core Value No 6, available at: www.icann.org/resources/pages/bylaws-2012-02-25-en.

[67] ICC, Case No EXP/433/ICANN/50 *The Financial Services Roundtable (USA) v Dotfresh Inc (UAE)* (consolidated with Case No EXP/510/ICANN/127 *American Insurance*

Establishing a significant connection between consumer protection and the interests of the relevant community, the expert panel ruled that the application, if granted, would facilitate an increase in abusive behaviour and would result in loss of consumer trust, especially as the applicant 'had not committed to institute effective security protection for user interests, and was not acting in the interests of the insurance community'.[68]

Both in the .architect and in the .insurance objection, the expert panels found for the objector. Regardless of ICANN's dispute resolution process failing to provide direct means to ensure consumer protection, in both cases the ruling was based, inter alia, on reasons directly related to the protection of consumer interests. In fact, in their determinations the expert panels portrayed some of the deficiencies of ICANN's New gTLD Program and effectively acknowledged the potential negative impact of some new gTLDs on the interests of consumers.

This has not, however, always been the case. In the expert determination over the .lotto string, the applicant prevailed as the expert panel deemed that the objector had failed to prove the likelihood of the material detriment. In support of his claim for the likelihood of material damage, the objector argued that while European lotteries adhere to strict standards of responsible gaming, thereby minimizing potential harm on society and in particular vulnerable groups, the general availability of .lotto domain names may confer upon illegal operators the advantage of associating their website with state licensed lotteries which would damage the interests of unsuspecting consumers. The objector referred, inter alia, to the decisions of the CJEU in *Liga Portuguesa*[69] and *Sporting Exchange*[70] which express the view that online gambling produces an increased risk of overspending, fraud and addiction by consumers. The objector further cited a 2011 report of the European Parliament where it is acknowledged that '[o]nline gambling, if not properly regulated may involve a greater risk of addiction than traditional physical, location-based gambling, owing inter alia to increased ease of access and the absence of social control'[71] and that 'consumers must

Association (USA) v Dotfresh Inc (UAE)), available at: https://newgtlds.icann.org/sites/default/files/drsp/17feb14/determination-2-1-1063-32835-en.pdf, esp paras 187–89.

[68] ibid, 192.

[69] CJEU, Case C-42/07 *Liga Portuguesa de Futebol Profissional and Bwin International Ltd v Departamento de Jogos da Santa Casa da Misericórdia de Lisboa* [2009] ECR I-07633; EU:C:2009:519, esp para 70 where the Court observed that 'because of the lack of direct contact between consumer and operator, games of chance accessible via the internet involve different and more substantial risks of fraud by operators against consumers compared with the traditional markets for such games'.

[70] CJEU, Case C-203/08 *Sporting Exchange Ltd v Minister van Justitie* [2010] ECR I-04695; EU:C:2010:307, esp para 34, citing to *Liga Portuguesa*.

[71] European Parliament, Committee on the Internal Market and Consumer Protection, Report of 14 October 2011 on online gambling in the internal market, 2011/2084/INI (Rapporteur: Jürgen Creutzmann), available at: www.europarl.europa.eu/sides/getDoc.do?pubRef=-//EP//TEXT+REPORT+A7-2011-0342+0+DOC+XML+V0//EN, para 7.

be educated about the potential harm of online gambling and protected against dangers in this area, especially addiction, fraud, scams and underage gambling'.[72] The expert panel, however, was satisfied by the applicant's submission that, in view of its long-standing experience in the operation of large gTLDs such as .info and .org, the applicant could guarantee a high standard of protection for domain users and consumers and would act in the best interests of the community which the string targeted. One may argue that, in the Beijing Communiqué of 11 April 2013,[73] ICANN's Governmental Advisory Committee advised ICANN that strings that are linked to regulated or professional sectors should operate in a way that is consistent with applicable laws. As the GAC noted, these strings are likely to engender implied trust from consumers, and carry higher risk associated with consumer harm. Among such strings, the GAC identified .lotto. Indeed, the necessary connection to the applicable laws suggested by the GAC may assist in decreasing the chance of consumer deception and fraud, and may buttress the expert panel's statement that it was satisfied by the applicant's long-standing experience in the field of domain names to exclude the likelihood of material damage to the gambling community, which includes consumers. However, on the one hand, the expert determination failed to mention the Beijing GAC Advice at all to possibly ground its ruling, leading one to infer that the expert panel dismissed, per se, the objector's allegations as to the relevance of consumer interests and referred their protection to the applicant's alleged good reputation. On the other hand, the question remains open as to how and to what extent ICANN will ensure the operation of the .lotto string complies with the 'applicable laws', also in light of the notorious complexities that the effort of detecting infringements of the law governing online gambling entails.[74]

In a similar fashion, in the expert determination addressing the community objection against the application for the .mail gTLD,[75] the expert panel addressed the objector's concern that potential consumer confusion between the terms 'mail' and 'post' may mislead them from the websites of the posts or from .post websites to websites on the .mail TLD, thereby 'disrupting the activities of the Postal Community and harming the public'[76] by failing to

[72] ibid, preamble, lit I.

[73] Governmental Advisory Committee, GAC Communiqué—Beijing (11 April 2013), available at: www.icann.org/en/system/files/correspondence/gac-to-board-18apr13-en.pdf.

[74] J Hörnle and B Zammit, *Cross-border Online Gambling Law and Policy* (Cheltenham, Edward Elgar Publishing 2010).

[75] ICC, Case No EXP/500/ICANN/117 *Universal Postal Union (Switzerland) v Charleston Road Registry Inc (USA)* (consolidated with Cases EXP/494/ICANN/111 *Universal Postal Union (Switzerland) v Victor Dale, LLC (USA)*; EXP/496/ICANN/113 *Universal Postal Union (Switzerland) v Whitepages TLD, LLC (USA)*; and EXP/497/ICANN/114 *Universal Postal Union (Switzerland) v GMO Registry, INC. (Japan)*), available at http://newgtlds.icann.org/sites/default/files/drsp/10feb14/determination-1-1-1141-82929-en.pdf.

[76] ibid, para 52.

meet public expectations regarding the reliability, privacy and security of 'mail'.[77] After having acknowledged the potential misdirection of consumers, the expert panel nevertheless appears to place on consumers the burden of verifying the trustworthiness of the website to which the .mail gTLD is directing them. In fact, the expert panel considered that

> the degree of consumer care is becoming more heightened as the novelty of the Internet evaporates and online commerce becomes commonplace. The criterion to be applied here should take into consideration a reasonable consumer, not a sophisticated one, but one who actually acts prudently.[78]

One may reasonably wonder whether this suggested reversal of burden is in keeping with ICANN's Core Values which call for the corporation to maintain and build on processes that will ensure the preservation and enhancement of the stability, reliability, and security of the Internet,[79] and that promote limitations to competition in the registration of domain names for reasons of public interest.[80] This perplexity is all the more justified by the fact that the expansion of gTLDs is indeed a novelty, and is currently far from being considered as a commonplace feature of the Internet with which consumers may be familiar.

The expert panel further pointed out that the GAC in its Beijing Communiqué did not include the .mail gTLD in those strings that are linked to regulated or professional sectors and that should operate in a way that is consistent with applicable laws, as they are likely to engender implied trust from consumers, and carry higher risks associated with consumer harm. In spite of having acknowledged that the list provided by the GAC is expressly non-exhaustive, the expert panel found it meaningful in itself—for reasons that remain obscure—that, as of 11 April 2013, the GAC did not think that the .mail string was related to a regulated sector.[81] The expert panel stated that even if subsequently the GAC realizes that the mail string is linked with a regulated sector, its advice would not constitute a sufficient reason to block altogether the attribution of the string, and its effect would be to recommend that registry operators do not bypass applicable rules and regulations.[82] Startlingly, the expert panel concluded its determination on the likelihood on material detriment by stating that in the application for the registration of the .mail gTLD '[T]he harm is probable. However, most of the concerns expressed by the objector can be met and corrected by a sound policy taken by ICANN and solid rules to implement that policy and control its

[77] ibid.
[78] ibid, para 157.
[79] Applicant Guidebook, Attachment to Module 2, A-1. See also Core Value No 1 at www.icann.org/resources/pages/bylaws-2012-02-25-en.
[80] *cf* ICANN's Core Value No 6 at www.icann.org/resources/pages/bylaws-2012-02-25-en.
[81] See above, n 75, para 165.
[82] ibid, para 167.

application'.[83] This statement calls into question the clarity (or lack thereof) of ICANN's regulations regarding new gTLDs, and it raises questions on the expert panel's finding for the applicant by simply referring to and relying on ICANN's (to date) blurred policies and potential—and yet uncertain—future clarifications. In this case, it would have been perhaps more sensible to find for the objector, concurrently inviting ICANN to provide the necessary clarifications—both generally, and specifically as concerns the .mail string—on the rules and regulations that registry operators may not bypass where the applied-for string involves significant implied trust from consumers, and where its registration carries higher risks associated with consumer harm.

4. THE INDEPENDENT OBJECTOR

ICANN's New gTLD Dispute Resolution Procedure also provides for the potential involvement of an Independent Objector (IO).[84] The IO is entitled to lodge objections only on the Limited Public Interest and Community Objection grounds: for both grounds, the IO acts in complete independence, and exclusively in the best interests of the public who use the global Internet. In line with his public interest mission, the IO cannot object to an application (ie, he does not have standing) unless there is at least one comment in opposition to the application made in the public sphere. Moreover, he can only lodge an objection if no one else has previously filed an objection on the same ground which implies that, within ICANN's Dispute Resolution Procedure, the IO acts as a 'safety net'. On the one hand, the IO may provide a protection to those entities, such as individual consumers or consumer organizations, who raise a well-founded concern over an applied-for new gTLD string during the public comment period, but do not or may not follow up with a claim because, under the standards, they would not have (or would hardly have) standing to bring the objections. On the other hand, the fact that the IO is granted power to bring only objections on Limited Public Interest and Community grounds and that, in any event, the substance of those objections does not provide direct and immediate relief or protection to consumer interests is of little help in furthering those interests.

5. CONCLUDING REMARKS

While an, albeit limited, relevance is assigned to consumer interests at the application stage of ICANN's New gTLD Program as a result of the

[83] ibid, para 178.

[84] Applicant Guidebook, Module 3, para 3.2.5. The objections filed by the Independent Objector may be accessed at www.independent-objector-newgtlds.org/home/the-independent-objector-s-objections.

preliminary screening process and of the possible direct intervention by consumers in the public comment period, in ICANN's New gTLD Dispute Resolution Procedure consumer interests are not protected by any specific provisions. Under two of the available objections (String Confusion and Legal Rights), consumers and consumer organizations are denied standing and may only benefit from a secondary protection where their interests overlap with those claimed by the objector. And while under the Limited Public Interest Objection they may be able to establish standing, it is nevertheless unlikely that they will see their interests furthered or protected by complaints based on this objection.

The Community Objection appears to be best suited to try and establish a safeguard for consumer interests. Nonetheless, the argument may generally be made that—while the Community Objection clearly relies on the assumption that, if an application touches upon the core interests of a given community, that community will react by means of one of its major representatives ('an established institution' which has 'an ongoing relationship with a clearly delineated community')—this may not always be the case: reactions are not always necessarily timely, especially in such an innovative area as new gTLDs, because such a mechanism implies a constant and careful surveillance of the applications by unidentified 'established institutions' and then their immediate reaction.

Moreover, while in some Community Objection expert determinations the New gTLD Program's goal of promoting competition in gTLDs has been construed as predicated on the stability and reliability of the Internet and as complementary to the promotion of consumer protection, in other expert determinations claims of relevance of consumer interests have been radically dismissed in light of the applicant's alleged good reputation or deferred to ICANN's future regulations: such lack of consistency clearly leads to a scenario of uncertainty and instability.

Finally, the New gTLD Program does not provide for an 'ad hoc' appeal process. To the contrary, it relies on the Request for Reconsideration (RfR) mechanism,[85] that provides the possibility for any person or entity to submit a request for reconsideration or review of an ICANN action or inaction[86] and assigns to the Board Governance Committee the power to make a final determination or a recommendation to the ICANN Board New gTLD Program Committee (NGPC) with respect to a reconsideration request.[87] Further to a RfR from an applicant for the .med gTLD, on 21 June 2014

[85] On Request for Reconsideration *cf* Art IV, Bylaws for Internet Corporation for Assigned Names and Numbers, as amended 7 February 2014, available at: www.icann.org/resources/pages/bylaws-2012-02-25-en. The status update of the RfRs submitted is available at: www.icann.org/resources/pages/reconsideration-2012-02-25-en.

[86] Art IV, s 2.2, Bylaws for Internet Corporation for Assigned Names and Numbers, as amended 7 February 2014, available at: www.icann.org/resources/pages/bylaws-2012-02-25-en.

[87] ibid, Art IV, s 2.17.

ICANN overturned a Community Objection decision and allowed an applicant for the .med new gTLD back in the game on the grounds that the Independent Objector, who filed the Community Objection, lacked standing pursuant to section 3.2.5 of the Applicant Guidebook which prohibits the IO from filing an objection unless there is at least one public comment opposing the relevant application.[88] In the case at issue, ICANN based its decision on the fact that one of the two alleged comments on which the IO's standing was grounded actually purposefully did not oppose the requester's application for .med while the other was 'advisory' in nature and was not intended as an objection.

One first step has been recently taken to address the lack of an 'ad hoc' appeal process. On 5 February 2014, the ICANN Board New gTLD Program Committee (NGPC) directed the ICANN President and CEO to initiate a public comment period on the framework principles of a potential review mechanism to address perceived inconsistent String Confusion Objection expert determinations.[89] The framework principles address cases where objections were raised by the same objector against different applications for the same string and where the outcomes of the objections differ. The decision to initiate a public comment period was reached following the inconsistencies that resulted from several expert determinations on the .car/.cars and .cam/.com new gTLDs. Upon receiving feedback from the public comment forum, the NGPC will consider whether or not to adopt the proposed review mechanism. This recent chapter of the New gTLD Program, which touches upon a very sensitive issue such as that of a review mechanism of possible inconsistencies in the final outcomes of different expert determinations, is a clear indication that the New gTLD Program is a work-in-process. Perhaps, a sound review of the standards that ground the different objections could avoid such inconsistencies, and specific review mechanisms should be also adopted to provide a means to challenge expert determinations rendered under objection grounds other than String Confusion.

The inconsistent results in expert panel determinations leads to agreement with those commentators, such as the FTC, which suggested that ICANN should restrict the number of gTLDs introduced in the first application round and in the meantime conduct, inter alia, an assessment of the concrete risks of consumer harm posed by the new gTLDs. In addition to such a much needed preliminary assessment, one may also draw the conclusion

[88] Determination of the Board Governance Committee (BGC) Reconsideration Request 14-1 (21 June 2014) at www.icann.org/en/system/files/files/determination-medistry-21jun14-en.pdf.

[89] Proposed Review Mechanism to Address Perceived Inconsistent Expert Determinations on String Confusion Objections at www.icann.org/news/announcement-2014-02-11-en. The comment period started on 11 February 2014 and ended on 12 Mar 2014; the reply period opened on 13 March 2014 and ended on 3 April 2014. At the time this article was submitted for publication, the NGPC had not made public its decision.

that, to enhance the stability and reliability of the DNS, a rethinking of ICANN's New gTLD Dispute Resolution Procedure should be welcomed especially, but not only, as concerns the extent consumer interests are taken into account in the dispute resolution system. This would operate in the interests of all stakeholders, including ICANN, which is currently facing the risk that the deficiencies of the New gTLD Program undermine consumer (and institutional) confidence not only with respect to a given commercial sector, but the domain name system overall.

Part III

Simplified Procedures and Debt Collection: Much Ado About Nothing?

5

'Trusted with a Muzzle and Enfranchised with a Clog': The British Approach to European Civil Procedure

CARLA CRIFÒ*

1. INTRODUCTION

I am trusted with
a muzzle and enfranchised with a clog; therefore I
have decreed not to sing in my cage. If I had my
mouth, I would bite; if I had my liberty, I would do
my liking: in the meantime let me be that I am and
seek not to alter me.

Much Ado About Nothing, act 1 scene 3

IN SHAKESPEARE'S PLAY, Don John calls himself a 'plain-speaking villain', though in truth he is one of the tamest villains in the Shakespearean canon. Although it would not be entirely appropriate to equate the British Government or the British public with a 'villain' in the context of the development and implementation of a European law of civil procedure, this particular quote from Don John does reflect a certain conscious self-ghettoising, self-defeating attitude to be found in the British approach. This approach, in turn, has a negative effect on that field as well, as the United Kingdom could, with a different outlook towards Europe in general, and EU 'activism' in particular, exercise a profound influence on the development of many core legal concepts, by bringing its common law experience into the debate. Instead, the government line (regardless of political colour) so far has been to deliberately take a *de minimis* approach to implementation, and quite clearly also with regard to negotiations concerning new instruments, from the first principles to the exercising of the power not to opt in once a draft has been finalised.

* Senior Lecturer in law, University of Leicester.

The history and development of 'European civil procedure' is now quite well known.[1] A growing judicial and institutional awareness of the capacity of court procedures to limit, if not thwart, the full enjoyment of EC rights led to the creation of the Third Pillar (including 'Justice and Home Affairs') under the Treaty of Maastricht, whose Article K.1 brought 'judicial cooperation in civil matters' under the aegis of the matters of 'common interest'. This was subsequently followed by the Treaty of Amsterdam, which placed the policy area of judicial cooperation in civil matters in the First Pillar, and introduced the legislative competence to adopt measures under Articles 61 and 65 of the EC Treaty. The embryonic beginnings of a European law of civil procedure were thus laid out, through the piecemeal accretion of subject-specific, scope-limited instruments, loosely based on Article 65 and its definition of 'measures in the field of judicial cooperation in civil matters having cross-border implications', with the two explicit limitations to 'matters having cross-border implications' and 'insofar as necessary for the proper functioning of the internal market':

> Measures in the field of judicial cooperation in civil matters having cross-border implications, to be taken in accordance with Article 67, and insofar as necessary for the proper functioning of the internal market, shall include:
>
> (a) improving and simplifying:
> — the system for cross-border service of judicial and extrajudicial documents,
> — cooperation in the taking of evidence,
> — the recognition and enforcement of decisions in civil and commercial cases, including decisions in extrajudicial cases;
>
> (b) promoting the compatibility of the rules applicable in the Member States concerning the conflict of laws and of jurisdiction;
>
> (c) eliminating obstacles to the good functioning of civil proceedings, if necessary by promoting compatibility of the rules on civil procedure applicable in the Member States.

The Commission lost no time in testing the limits of its new competence (and that under the subsequent Treaty of Lisbon (Article 81 TFEU)) and began converting existing conventions into regulations. It converted the original measure in this field, the Brussels Convention on jurisdiction and the enforcement of judgments,[2] which codifies traditional rules of conflict of law in relation to recognition and enforcement of foreign judgments, into a regulation,[3] and followed it with a number of other regulations, including the

[1] See generally E Storskrubb, *Civil Procedure and EU Law—A Policy Area Uncovered* (Oxford, Oxford University Press, 2008) and W Kennett, *The Enforcement of Judgments in Europe* (Oxford, Oxford University Press, 2000) for the history of the Commission's legislative projects in civil procedures.

[2] Brussels Convention on jurisdiction and the enforcement of judgments in civil and commercial matters (consolidated version) [1998] OJ C27/1.

[3] Regulation (EC) No 44/2001 of 22 December 2000 on jurisdiction and the recognition and enforcement of judgments in civil and commercial matters [2001] OJ L12/1.

European Enforcement Order (EEO).[4] This was followed by the European Order for Payment (EOP) and finally the European Small Claims Procedure (ESCP).[5] Substantively, these three Regulations have the following effects. The EEO Regulation establishes a procedure for a speedier enforcement of a judgment of one Member State in another Member State if it complies with certain minimum standards. This procedure is of great value to an English judgment creditor, as it enables him or her to obtain the equivalent of a *formule exécutoire*, required to enforce a judgment in most civil law jurisdictions, which is unknown in common law as a legal concept. The EEO Regulation allows the litigant from one jurisdiction to bypass the foreign court processes where there is such a requirement for enforcement. The EOP Regulation goes one step further, as it creates a simple procedure to obtain, from the start, a special kind of court order for the payment of uncontested debts, which is immediately enforceable throughout the EU. There is no equivalent to this procedure in the English Civil Procedure Rules. The English litigant in a cross-border situation is faced with a choice between seeking a normal judgment which could subsequently be made enforceable through the EEO, or the different, unknown procedure which, however, is advantageous in that it is given in his or her own court and language, and it avoids the second step of obtaining the EEO. Finally, the ESCP Regulation attempts to create a uniform adversarial small claims procedure for cross-border claims. Unlike the two previous procedures, a small claims procedure exists in England and Wales, and is indeed one of the most successful procedures to have emanated from the 1998 civil procedure reforms.[6] With regard to the ESCP, therefore, a question arises as to the extent of the integration, competition and 'fit' of the European cross-border approach and the existing domestic procedure.

[4] Regulation (EC) No 805/2004 of 21 April 2004 creating a European Enforcement Order for uncontested claims [2004] OJ L143/15: see C Crifò, *Cross-Border Enforcement of Debts in the European Union* (Alphen aan den Rijn, Kluwer Law International, 2008) ch 2, and C Crifò, 'First Steps Towards the Harmonisation of Civil Procedure' (2005) 24 *Civil Justice Quarterly* 200. In the first draft of an amended regulation to substitute the Brussels I Regulation (COM(2010) 748 final), at its Art 92, Regulation (EC) 805/2004 would have been repealed in favour of a generalised abolition of *exequatur* proceedings in all cases except defamation and collective redress cases, complemented by 'three main remedies ... by which [the defendant] could prevent in exceptional circumstances that a judgment given in one Member State takes effect in another Member State': para 3.1.1. That proposal, however, did not survive the consultation and discussion process.

[5] Regulation (EC) No 1896/2006 of 12 December 2006 creating a European order for payment procedure [2006] OJ L399/1 and Regulation (EC) No 861/2007 of 11 July 2007 establishing a European Small Claims Procedure [2007] OJ L199/1, both of which were preceded by a Green Paper: EU Commission, 'Green Paper on a European order for payment procedure and on measures to simplify and speed up small claims litigation' COM(2002) 749 final. See A Fiorini, 'Facilitating Cross-Border Debt Recovery: The European Payment Order and Small Claims Regulations' (2008) 57 *International & Comparative Law Quarterly* 449.

[6] See, eg, R Turner, '"Actively": The Word that Changed the Civil Courts' and T Parkes, 'The Civil Procedure Rules Ten Years On: The Practitioners' Perspective' in D Dwyer (ed), *The Civil Procedure Rules Ten Years On* (Oxford, Oxford University Press, 2009).

Other important procedural fields in which the Commission has produced legislation include the cross-border service of judicial documents,[7] the taking of evidence abroad,[8] mediation,[9] legal aid,[10] and various procedural aspects of family proceedings[11] and insolvency proceedings.[12] Further developments are expected: the Commission has recently published a Proposal to amend the ESCP Regulation,[13] which will be discussed further below. The most recent development is the recently enacted European Account Preservation Order (EAPO).[14]

The United Kingdom has not been an enthusiastic participant in the negotiation and adoption of many of these measures, but rather has displayed at all times a strong reluctance to engage beyond the minimum it has perceived as necessary to maintain some real or perceived advantage for its own stakeholders, identified (or self-identified) through ad hoc calls for evidence. This was the case, for example, of the mention, amongst the permitted methods of service under the EEO, of 'postal service', which is the usual method in England and Wales.[15] Indeed, a privileged position had already been negotiated, reaffirmed in the Lisbon Treaty, with regard to measures taken under Title V of that Treaty (Area of Freedom, Security and Justice, Articles 67–89), which allows the UK to choose whether or not to take part and

[7] Regulation (EC) No 1393/2007 of 13 November 2007 on the service in the Member States of judicial and extrajudicial documents in civil or commercial matters and repealing Regulation (EC) No 1348/2000 of 29 May 2000 [2007] OJ L324/79.

[8] Regulation (EC) No 1206/2001 of 28 May 2001 on cooperation between the courts of the Member States in the taking of evidence in civil and commercial matters [2001] OJ L174/1.

[9] Directive 2008/52/EC of 21 May 2008 on certain aspects of mediation in civil and commercial matters [2008] OJ L136/3.

[10] Directive 2002/8/EC of 27 January 2003 to improve access to justice in cross-border disputes by establishing minimum common rules relating to legal aid for such disputes [2003] OJ L26/41.

[11] Regulation (EC) No 2201/2003 of 27 November 2003 concerning jurisdiction and the recognition and enforcement of judgments in matrimonial matters and the matters of parental responsibility, repealing Regulation (EC) No 1347/2000 [2003] OJ L338/1; Regulation (EC) No 4/2009 of 18 December 2008 on jurisdiction, applicable law, recognition and enforcement of decisions and cooperation in matters relating to maintenance obligations [2009] OJ L7/1.

[12] Regulation (EC) No 1346/2000 of 29 May 2000 on insolvency proceedings [2000] OJ L160/1, also subject to a recent proposal of amendment, COM(2012) 744 final.

[13] Proposal for a Regulation of the European Parliament and of the Council amending Regulation (EC) No 861/2007 of the European Parliament and the Council of 11 July 2007 establishing a European Small Claims Procedure and Regulation (EC) No 1896/2006 of the European Parliament and of the Council of 12 December 2006 creating a European order for payment procedure, COM(2013)794. The first official reactions from the UK can be found in the European Scrutiny Committee, *33rd Report of the session 2013–14* (HC 2013–14, 83-xxx) 44–48, available at: www.publications..uk/pa/cm201314/cmselect/cmeuleg/83-xxx/83xxx.pdf.

[14] Regulation (EU) No 655/2014 of 15 May 2014 creating a European Account Preservation Order procedure to facilitate cross-border debt recovery in civil and commercial matters [2014] OJ L189/59.

[15] Information obtained by the author during a telephone conversation with a member of the European legislation negotiating team of the Ministry of Justice.

opt in to the measures, or conversely refuse to participate at all or only at the negotiation or at the implementation stage. The most recent exercise of the opt-out process is with regard to the EAPO, for example, where the UK indicated that it would not opt in to the measure, but continued to take part in the negotiations.[16] Moreover, the UK Government recently conducted a review of the 'Balance of Competences'[17] with the express intention of gathering evidence to support a further withdrawal from the legal sphere of influence of the EU, which makes for sobering reading. Interestingly, however, few of the responses to the call for evidence provided the unqualified support that the Government was apparently seeking.

2. THE CASE OF THE SMALL CLAIMS PROCEDURE: AWARENESS, IMPLEMENTATION AND USE IN ENGLAND AND WALES

2.1 Practice and Empirical Data

Where they are applicable in England, the regulations which collectively form the embryonic European law of civil procedure present the domestic lawyer with a number of difficulties. The traditional process of common law court litigation, for example, would require very technical and almost exquisite refinements and the identification of boundaries for each and every aspect of litigation: you need only look at the bulk of the commentaries on the Civil Procedure Rules (CPR) (the so-called 'White Book',[18] for example) to realise that, even after the simplifying and revolutionary Woolf Reforms,[19] and despite a lack of academic interest comparable to that in other European jurisdictions, civil procedure remains one of the fields of English law that most justifies the use and cost of highly trained experts. However, when it comes to commentaries, both judicial and professional, on the European regulations the ground is bare, uncultivated and almost 'un-legal'. Thus, the

[16] On 31 October 2011 a Written Ministerial Statement was made to Parliament confirming that 'the UK would not be opting in to these proposals. Although the Government has decided that the UK should not opt in to the proposal now, it intends to participate fully in the negotiations with the hope that sufficient changes will be made to enable a post-adoption opt in'.

[17] The report on competence stemming from Art 81 TFEU is available online at: https://consult.justice.gov.uk/digital-communications/balance-of-competences, as are the submissions to the Call for Evidence.

[18] Constantly updated and widely available through the subscription-only online database Westlaw UK, it is published by Sweet & Maxwell with commentary on 'more than 10,000 cases': www.sweetandmaxwell.co.uk/whitebook/contents.aspx.

[19] On which see J Sorabji, *English Civil Justice after the Woolf and Jackson Reforms: A Critical Analysis* (Cambridge, Cambridge University Press, 2014).

ESCP and EOP Regulations are reproduced in full, appended to Part 78 of the CPR, with very few implementing additional rules[20]—a consequence of a very literal understanding of their nature as 'regulations', perhaps. Her Majesty's Courts & Tribunals Service (HMCTS), which provides a number of leaflets generally aimed at the litigant in person, provides a guidance leaflet,[21] written in cooperation with the unit within the Ministry of Justice in charge of negotiation and implementation of the European regulations,[22] which is notable in that it simply repeats much of the explanatory material of the regulations themselves, or refers directly to the guidance in the forms,[23] rather than attempting to provide any additional information as to how the European procedure—or any of its steps—fits in with existing English procedures or the technical English legal terminology. The leaflet tells the litigant to complete the form (to be found on the Judicial Atlas website) and pay the fee; the form must then be taken or sent to the court, which will check that it has been correctly completed and will then serve it on the defendant. Eventually a successful claimant will be required to send[24] the final order to the enforcement authorities in the destination country, to be identified through the online European e-Justice Portal. The leaflet provides the URL of the Judicial Atlas and the European e-Justice Portal and expects the litigant to navigate them independently.

It cannot be stressed enough that there is a clear advantage to simple, non-technical procedures; this has become increasingly apparent and acted upon even in the crustiest English legal circles. 'Technicalities', or procedural legal qualifications, may be required but ought always to be used sparingly and only where they serve to enhance and increase the quality of justice, avoiding as far as possible the unnecessary accretion of obstacles to access to the court and to a timely resolution of the claim.[25] Small claims and other

[20] A problem because there are several points in the life of one of these applications where there is a passage to 'national' law—and this is not detailed, except insofar as to say 'Part 7' will apply.

[21] Form 725, 'Making a Cross-Border Claim in the EU', available at: https://hmctsformfinder.justice.gov.uk/courtfinder/forms/ex725-eng.pdf.

[22] Information acquired by the author during a telephone conversation with a member of the unit.

[23] eg, at 10, 'All forms for the ESCP are available on the European Commission's Judicial Atlas website at: http://ec.europa.eu/justice_home/judicialatlascivil/html/index_en.htm. In England and Wales a claim must be commenced in the county court. The procedure introduces standard forms and Form A must be used to start proceedings. The form itself contains detailed guidance notes to assist you in completing it. It is important that you read them carefully. You will be asked to provide enough information about the evidence you have available to prove your claim, and to enable the defendant to be able to choose whether to defend the claim. This may include any relevant supporting documents where appropriate'.

[24] A non-technical use of the word.

[25] This is the gist of the Benthamian 'philosophy of justice' that is now prevalent within English civil procedure: see AAS Zuckerman, 'The Second Great English Reform of Civil Justice: A Triumph of Hope over Experience' (2000) 1(2) *Hibernian Law Journal* 178.

procedures traditionally left to the county court have always had, ever since the creation of that court in the middle of the nineteenth century, at the very least the expectation that they would be user-friendly.[26] To be 'user-friendly' in common law means also to be addressed to and understandable by the layperson, as one of the main procedural characteristics of common law is the 'right to self-represent'.[27] The UK Government's official website[28] shows a commendable commitment to explaining to self-represented litigants (LIPs) most of the basic steps of a claim and their procedural requirements. Additionally, it has been a goal of the Woolf Reforms[29] and a foreseen consequence of the Jackson Reforms,[30] or rather, of the concurrent legal funding reforms implemented by successive governments that, in order to reduce the costs of litigation, more ought to be done to encourage and enable self-representation, including to provide as much information as to how to proceed in what is clearly a layperson's terms.

Therefore, the simple non-technical approach to the on-the-ground implementation of the European regulations may appear to fall squarely within the norm, both because of their subject matter, especially the ESCP Regulation, and because of the general modern tendency to reduce the impact of 'proceduralese'. If such were the case, you would expect to see quite a robust take-up of these procedures, adjusting for their newness. However, this has not been the case, as figures collected for the years 2009–12 show, especially in comparison to the slightly more established procedure of the EEO. The number of applications regarding both obtaining and enforcing EOPs and ESCPs in England and Wales[31] appear to be relatively 'healthy',

[26] N Madge, 'Small Claims in the County Court' (2004) 23 *Civil Justice Quarterly* 201. But see for a 'reality check' as to their actual workings, P Lewis, 'The Consumer's Court? Revisiting the Theory of the Small Claims Procedure' (2006) 25 *Civil Justice Quarterly* 52 and P Lewis, 'Litigants in Person and their Difficulties in Adducing Evidence: A Study of Small Claims in an English County Court' (2007) 11 *International Journal of Evidence and Proof* 24.

[27] See R Assy, 'Revisiting the Right to Self-Representation in Civil Proceedings' (2011) 30 *Civil Justice Quarterly* 267, and A Zuckerman, *Zuckerman on Civil Procedure*, 3rd edn (London, Sweet & Maxwell, 2013) 143.

[28] At: www.gov.uk/make-court-claim-for-money; and see the leaflets available in relation to Form N1 (Claim form), such as 'I'm in a Dispute—What Can I Do?—For People Who Are in a Dispute' (Leaflet ex301); 'How Do I Make a Court Claim?—For People Who Want to Take a Dispute to Court' (Leaflet ex302); 'I've Started a Claim in Court—What Happens Next?' (Leaflet ex304) all, available at: http://hmctsformfinder.justice.gov.uk/HMCTS/FormFinder.do.

[29] Zuckerman, 'The Second Great English Reform of Civil Justice' (n 25).

[30] H Genn, 'Do-it-Yourself Law: Access to Justice and the Challenge of Self-Representation' (2013) 32 *Civil Justice Quarterly* 411; C McIvor, 'The Impact of the Jackson Reforms on Access to Justice in Personal Injury Litigation' (2011) 30 *Civil Justice Quarterly* 411.

[31] These figures were obtained from the Ministry of Justice, in March 2013, for the period up to the end of 2012, with the proviso that they had been collated manually and therefore could not be vouched for officially as free from error.

with a crescendo since 2009 regarding the number of applications for EOPs and a dip across all categories in the year of the global financial crisis:

Table 1: Applications to issue or enforce EOPs and ESCPs in England and Wales

	2009	2010	2011	2012	Total
Applications to issue a European Order for Payment	85	62	242	250	639
Applications to enforce a European Order for Payment	38	196	47	37	318
Applications to issue European Small Claims Procedure	200	105	176	45	526
Applications to enforce European Small Claims Procedure	138	202	183	164	687

What is notable, however, is that these numbers are still low in comparison with EEO requests from abroad and from England and Wales:

Table 2: Applications to issue or enforce EEOs in England and Wales

	2009	2010	2011	2012	Total
Applications to issue a European Enforcement Order	26	125	86	33	307
Applications to enforce a European Enforcement Order	696	2547	2134	406	5783

Additionally, the total numbers appear relatively small in comparison to the volume of claims typically issued in the county court: in 2011 there were domestic applications for roughly one million specified money claims, for example, of which 200,000 claims were for an unspecified amount of money. In general, the majority of claims issued at the county court are dealt with under 'small claims' rules[32] (for general claims of less than £5,000, until 1 April 2013, and subsequently claims of less than £10,000).[33]

[32] For the period from 2004 to 2008, a useful report is that prepared for Consumer Focus by IFF Research, *Consumer Experience of the Small Claims Court* (2010), available at: www.consumerfocus.org.uk/files/2010/10/Research-Report.pdf.

[33] CPR 26.6. The rules underwent a substantial amendment on 1 April 2013 to coincide with the enactment of most of Sir Rupert Jackson's reform proposals for tackling the spiralling costs of justice: the increase in the financial scope of the small claims track enables the automatic extension of the fixed costs rule, ie, that party costs beyond a fixed amount are not recoverable from the losing party.

2.2 Causes for Lack of Take-Up

What reasons can be given for the lack of take-up of these cross-border instruments that are supposed to be easy to access and use, and non-technical, that do not necessarily require the assistance of expensive lawyers, and that seem to fall within the recognised desire to simplify court procedures for the 'consumer'? The most common answer is the 'lack of knowledge' by potential litigants,[34] a lack of awareness of these procedures amongst the general public: for example, the Balance of Competences report refers to a Eurobarometer survey[35] on awareness, use and experience of the ESCP, with very low figures both throughout the EU and in the United Kingdom. This data suggests that the 'problem', if it is such, is not limited to the United Kingdom but is generalised and therefore can be resolved with a centralised drive to inform EU citizens of the available procedures. The additional disincentive to use the procedure, that it was only available for claims for a very low financial amount, was also mentioned in the UK Government's report.[36] If this is the case, then a greater use of and more advertising for these instruments, besides increasing the monetary scope of the procedure, would no doubt lead to an increase in the take-up of applications both with regard to the issue and enforcement of EOPs and ESCPs. (The Proposal to amend the ESCP Regulation[37] very clearly addresses the low financial limit and recommends that it be raised to EUR 10,000.) This is on the assumption that intra-Member State commerce in particular is of such a volume that there is a pocket of unmet legal needs which would specifically require and benefit from these instruments *if only the economic actors concerned knew about them*. It is possible to gain an insight into the value of the market—and its corresponding unmet legal needs—again from the Call for Evidence of the Balance of Competences exercise:[38]

> 3.56 Our Call for Evidence showed that UK goods and services' exports to the EU stood at around £234bn (around 47% of the UK's total exports) with

[34] See, eg, *Evaluation of the European Enforcement Order* (RAND Europe, 2012), the report written pursuant to the duty to evaluate the application of Regulation 805/2004. The report does not appear to be publicly available at the time of writing.

[35] At para 3.47. European Commission, Special Eurobarometer 351: EU Civil Justice (2010), available at: http://ec.europa.eu/public_opinion/archives/ebs/ebs_351_sum_en.pdf; European Commission, Special Eurobarometer 395: European Small Claims Procedure (2013), available at: http://ec.europa.eu/public_opinion/archives/ebs/ebs_395_en.pdf: 'A survey of 26,691 EU citizens on experiences with cross border civil and commercial disputes found … [that for the European Small Claims Procedure] [o]nly 1% had heard of the procedure and used it and only 7% had heard of it but not used it. Among UK citizens, only 5% had heard of it'.

[36] Para 3.44, reporting on the evidence gathered by the Brussels Workshop.

[37] COM(2013) 794 final.

[38] Citing Ministry of Justice, *Call for Evidence: Civil Judicial Cooperation* (2013), and HM Revenue and Customs, Department for Business, Innovation & Skills, *Call for Evidence: Review of the Single Market: Free Movement of Goods* (2013).

Germany, the Netherlands and France being the largest markets for UK exports. The UK has recorded a trade surplus with the EU since 2004, growing to record a net surplus of £15.9bn in 2011.

3.57 According to the Free Movement of Goods' Call for Evidence, around 132,000 UK companies imported goods from the EU and around 112,000 companies exported goods to EU destinations.

3.58 In relation to consumer activity, our Call for Evidence also reported on a Eurobarometer Survey on the European Small Claims Procedure which showed that around one in ten people living in the EU ordered or bought goods or services from sellers based in other EU countries; around one in five people made recent purchases while in another EU Member State on a holiday or business trip; and three in ten citizens purchased offline and online goods from businesses based in other Member States.

However, it is quite striking—though perhaps unsurprising in the current political climate—that the main, if not the only reason given for the lacklustre performance of these regulations consists very much in laying the blame for it on the consumers themselves, even if only through the prism of their ignorance. This is both patronising and disingenuous. There could be other, concurrent or alternative, causes for their poor performance, at an 'earlier' stage of their life, so to speak. First, the regulations themselves—objectively as pieces of legislation required to apply throughout the Union—might be poorly written, or their scope ill-defined. Uncertainty as to the actual procedure or the actual effect of an order so obtained can be a strong disincentive, especially if there is a concurrent commercial need for a timely resolution (in particular applicable to EOP procedures) that would be thwarted by the need to repeat the whole process once it has become apparent that the effects are different or insufficiently robust. Uncertainty as to a legal process and its effects is even more dampening on the one-time-user, do-it-yourself litigant, whose appetite for legal resolution is already rather thin. Second, there might be a bottleneck at an earlier stage in their application: there might be a lack of appetite not amongst litigants, but at the level of the state negotiators and legislators when participating in the creation of instruments within a 'European civil procedure' under Article 81 TFEU.

2.3 The 'Legal Quality' of the ESCP Regulation

To take the first point, the problem might simply be that the Regulation itself is badly written, in a way that is either too general for the professional, or conversely too 'legal' for the layman; in addition, its scope (be it the limitation to 'cross-border' cases in Article 3, or the various substantive limitations in Article 2) is perhaps poorly defined or too narrow. When creating an accelerated, simplified procedure for claims of a small value, the simplification must necessarily take the form of a reduction in procedural formalism. However, procedural formalism (usually in the shape of the protection of the defendant) tends to increase in relation to the consideration of such 'fair trial' rights as the right to be heard and the right to an adversarial trial (including the right to be informed of and to be able to meaningfully challenge any evidence), and therefore any 'accelerated' procedure must always toe a difficult line between a claimant's right of access to justice and a defendant's right of resistance.[39] The compromises to the latter may be justified where an increase in procedural complexity would increase the cost of professional advice to the point that it would dwarf the substantive value of the claim. This point is particularly sore in England and Wales, where legal advice costs are notoriously high.

With all account taken of the difficulty of the balancing exercise necessary in the creation of a procedure that might have the advantage of acceleration and 'informalism', without losing too many procedural guarantees of fair trial, the ESCP Regulation is still not a particularly well written one from a technical point of view. This author has written elsewhere about some of the more technical shortcomings.[40] From an English legal perspective the Regulation is not immediately applicable. It fails to pinpoint in precise legal terms the steps that the litigant must undertake to engage the procedure. Specific problems arise with the generic definition of the methods of service allowed, for example.[41] This is a consequence of the need for its provisions to apply in several different jurisdictions, court systems and litigation cultures, which is inherent in a Europe-wide piece of primary legislation and it is the inevitable challenge of a law of civil procedure that is truly European.

All that this means is that more ought to be done at the domestic level to explain, if not technically implement, the Regulation and its place within the domestic legal framework. The fact of the matter is, that in the wishful thinking of the Commission, the lack of specificity and technicality in the Regulation would have been more than compensated for by a robust, activist and almost paternalistic intervention by the court, whose duty it is to check the content and form of the claim, for example. If this reliance on the court taking the litigant by the hand raises any concern, it is in relation to the consequent lack of foreseeability of effects, as individual jurisdictions or even individual courts within a jurisdiction may interpret their roles very differently.

[39] The necessary balancing exercise is referred to, briefly, in the ESCP Regulation, preamble, recital 9.

[40] As to more specific and technical points, see C Crifò, 'Europeanisation, Harmonisation and Unspoken Premises: The Case of Service Rules in the Regulation on a European Small Claims Procedure (Reg No 861/2007)' (2011) 30 *Civil Justice Quarterly* 283.

[41] ibid.

Still, there is a great deal of leeway and informalism already inherent in the domestic small claims procedure in the Civil Procedure Rules,[42] and it could be argued that the ESCP Regulation does no more than provide more of the same informalism, if on a broader scale. Just as a claim in the small claims track is subject to a certain amount of judicial discretion (as to the exact extent of the procedure),[43] it could be argued that there is no need to fetter judicial action in an ESCP case, for it will simply be more of the same. However, there are two problems with this approach: the first is that the traditional reliance on a judicial 'common sense' approach in cases of low value may begin to seem misplaced as the financial scope of the small claims track creeps up to encompass claims of a higher value. The proposal for the reform of the ESCP Regulation includes an increase of the financial value of the claim to EUR 10,000. Increasing the limit to include, as the Commission itself acknowledges,[44] a separate category of users (small and medium-sized enterprises—SMEs) risks magnifying the flaws of informalism in the procedure, as the new category of users may be presumed to be a little more sophisticated than an individual consumer. The increased value of claims that could be brought under the ESCP Regulation is one of the aspects of the proposal that the UK Government does not oppose. It must be noted, however, that it does so against the background of its own increase of the small claims ceiling from £5,000 to £10,000 as a consequence of the Jackson Review of Costs. This increase must be viewed in the context of the peculiarities of the very expensive litigation in this jurisdiction, which are beyond the scope of this chapter.[45] The addition, in the proposal, of an oral hearing when the value of the claim exceeds EUR 2,000 does not necessarily resolve the tension between 'fair trial' rights, where procedural guarantees are curtailed in favour of informalism for low-value claims and attempting to extend the reach of the procedure to a larger number of claims including some where procedural guarantees may become necessary.

Indeed, the second and main problem with the reliance on a robust—and discretionary—activism/paternalism on the part of the court is the variance in legal cultures throughout the Union. The scope of the court's powers and activities varies in European jurisdictions, and the discretion to act (informally) in one may take quite a different colour in another. The role of the court is not always spelled out in the various domestic constitutions or

[42] CPR 26 PD, para 8.1(a): 'The small claims track is intended to provide a proportionate procedure by which most straightforward claims with a financial value of not more than £10,000 can be decided, without the need for substantial pre-hearing preparation and the formalities of a traditional trial, and without incurring large legal costs. (Rule 26.6 provides for a lower financial value in certain types of case)'.

[43] CPR Part 27.

[44] COM(2013) 794 final, para 3.1.1.

[45] See C Hodges, S Vogenauer and M Tulibacka (eds), *The Costs and Funding of Civil Litigation. A Comparative Perspective* (Oxford, Hart Publishing, 2010).

procedural codes, but rather typically emerges from the delicate balance of the rules therein: the simplest example, of course, is that of the rule which allows or regulates the intervention of the judge in the taking of evidence.[46] From that rule and its corollaries much can be gleaned—even if it is not made explicit elsewhere—about the role of the individual judge and the court, up to the limits of the judicial power and whether or not informal procedures are to be considered exceptional and 'extra-ordinary'. Words matter, even in a deliberately non-technical regulation of general applicability. The Commission chose a type of 'informalism' not only when it came to the specifics of the procedure (where words such as 'service' and 'hearing' are not defined), but also when it came to the actual framework within which that procedure would take place (so what is not defined is the Member State's 'ordinary' or 'domestic' law, for example). The crux is that informalism works when there is a shared understanding, if unspoken, as to what is an acceptable level of action by the court, what is required and what is positively not allowed. It may work within a jurisdiction, but within the EU it is dangerous to assume, as the Commission did, that 'mutual trust' would translate into 'broadly similar action', in particular in relation to the implementation of a regulation, which by definition ought not to require any meaningful level of legal implementation or adaptation.

The consistency of the ESCP Regulation with the rest of a Member State's domestic law is the aspect that creates the most uncertainty for the consumer, and a particular problem with regard to how the Regulation is implemented in the UK: the amount of adaptation in CPR Part 78 or even in the Practice Direction or the leaflet for litigants, is the very minimum possible, and both refer back to the (technically inadequate) text of the Regulation. The leaflet in question instructs the litigants to seek the aid of the court, itself not something that encourages—or is to be encouraged in the context of—a mass utilisation of the instrument.

2.4 Vagueness by Design: The Role of Negotiators and the Scope of Implementation

The implementation of the ESCP Regulation has taken a defensive or *de minimis* approach in the UK. This was possible because of the legal nature of the Regulation, but also because of the very terminology of the measure, and essentially its own limitation concerning cross-border matters. This, however, is not without cause: after all the Regulation was written after a relatively lengthy negotiation stage, so some of the causes of the inherent uncertainty of legal process and effects that a potential litigant may fear must rest not with that

[46] JH Langbein, 'The German Advantage in Civil Procedure' (1985) 52 *University of Chicago Law Review* 823.

consumer's ignorance, or at best lack of faith in her own legal system ('what will the court *do*?'), but with the negotiating and drafting agents, and those in charge of implementing the final legislative result.

At the UK Ministry of Justice, for example, it is felt that the rather timid, hands-off approach to implementation of the Regulation is entirely justified in that the instruments in question were always meant to be exceptional (and not harmonising),[47] which meant that it was almost obligatory to refrain from integrating them within the existing legal framework. Indeed, this lack of acceptance of a harmonising agenda applies both to implementation (withholding as much 'integration' as possible) and to negotiation, in that the UK and the other partially common law systems do not intend to impose the common law, but just wish to be left alone, and certainly do not want to be changed. In that regard, they are like Don John. The much vaunted 'mutual trust' is not used proactively to inform, persuade, work together for the best possible instrument that would benefit from the input of comparative civil procedure at a more abstract level; instead it is used to prevent accusations of protectionism (in other words only that which is necessary to remove the necessity of separate enforcement proceedings for a foreign judgment, or *exequatur*) but no more. The UK's participation in these endeavours is instead framed by the 'cross-border' limitation: this provides the justification for maintaining a wall of 'exceptionalism' around these procedures and therefore it is most vigorously defended at all stages of the process, first of all when the decision is made to opt in or opt out. Indeed, the Government's submission to the relevant House of Commons Committee indicates that, far from being convinced by the Commission's arguments for removing the cross-border limitation in the proposed reformed ESCP, it considers that a simple removal of the limitation is inconsistent with the Treaty on the Functioning on the EU itself.[48] Additionally, the United Kingdom, due to the Protocol to Title V of the Lisbon Treaty, can

[47] In Case C-292/10 *G v de Visser*, EU:C:2012:142, the CJEU confirmed, with regard to the EEO Regulation that certification under the EEO is an exception to domestic rules of procedure that requires a higher standard of notification of service.

[48] See the Report of the House of Commons European Scrutiny Committee (n 13) paras 11.15 and 11.16:

'Art 81(1) TFEU requires that measures adopted under that provision must have cross-border implications. The Government believes that this restriction must be reflected properly in this proposed regulation. While it will give further consideration to the Commission's changes to Art 2, it currently remains concerned that those changes will not properly respect the Treaty's cross-border restriction and would unduly extend the instrument's scope of application to cover cases which should remain subject to national law only.

11.16 As this proposal has been brought under Art 81 TFEU, the UK's Title V opt-in applies. The text was presented to the Council in English on 25 November. Therefore the eight-week period before which the Government will not make a decision on the opt in expires on 20 January. When deciding whether to opt in, the Government will consider the effect on UK citizens and businesses if the UK no longer participates in the Regulation; how effective the Commission's suggested changes will be in improving the quality and use of the procedure; and the negotiability of resisting the proposed changes to the cross-border restriction'.

opt out at all stages up to implementation. It has exercised the prerogative a few times, most recently in relation to the EAPO.[49] It therefore has no incentive to negotiate heavily at the creation stage, since it can always give up on the instruments.

This also explains why, whereas there are some parts of the European civil procedure regulations that clearly demonstrate the imprint of the common law approach (most notably, the rules relating to service in Article 14 EEO Regulation, transposed in the EOP Regulation and referred to in the ESCP Regulation),[50] for the vast majority there is a dearth of technicality, or at the very least common law intelligible technicality, which makes it difficult to understand, at times, exactly how 'domestic law' or 'national law' should intervene. It has taken the Court of Justice until 2013 to resolve the issue of the effect of an opposition to an EOP[51] and the UK did not even submit observations, even though the outcome is very similar to the solution found by the Rules Committee in enacting Part 78 CPR.[52] The UK's hands-off approach, post-adoption, in this case by not intervening in a Court of Justice case, quite clearly affects the very quality of the European legal discourse, as was pointed out during the Balance of Competences exercise:

> 3.54 The Law Society of England and Wales, the Bar Council, Dr Mills and participants at the London workshops stated that another way in which the ECJs decision-making could be improved was for the UK to intervene more frequently in cases before the ECJ. Of those respondents, the Law Society of England and Wales, including those practitioners who responded to its own consultation, said that the UK should intervene to ensure the 'commercial context was understood'. The other respondents said that intervening would allow the 'common law perspective to be represented'. At the Edinburgh and Brussels workshops, participants stated that some of the criticism over the rulings had arisen because the judgments have been misunderstood or people had failed to understand the context in which they had been made.

[49] '[The UK government] announced by way of a written Ministerial Statement to the House of Commons its decision not to opt in to the proposed Regulation because the Government's recent consultation revealed significant problems, including a concern that there was a lack of adequate safeguards for defendants. However, it stated that it will participate in the forthcoming negotiations with a view to opting in in the future (HC Db 31 October 2011, col 28WS (UK)). In February 2013 the European Scrutiny Committee of the UK Parliament examined a letter by the Ministry of Justice regarding the EAPO and stated that "several developments have gone the UK's way", but there are still "significant concerns" about various issues of the proposal': N Kyriakides, 'A European-wide preservation order: how the common law practice can contribute' (2014) 33 *Civil Justice Quarterly* 93, fn 36.

[50] See Crifò, 'Europeanisation, Harmonisation and Unspoken Premises' (n 40).

[51] Case C-144/12 *Goldbet Sportwetten*, EU:C:2013:393.

[52] According to the CJEU, opposition to EOP just finishes the EOP process, it is not 'entering an appearance' for the purposes of 24 BR, and therefore does not need to include challenges to jurisdiction. This point was clear to the Rules Committee when it enacted CPR 78.6, which clearly indicates how and when a challenge to the jurisdiction ought to be made, and that in such cases (a) rule 10.1(3) [reasons for filing an acknowledgement of service]; (b) rule 10.3 [time limits for filing an aos]; and (c) rule 15.4(1) [period for filing a defence] do not apply.

3. CONCLUSION: STRIKE UP, PIPERS?

Messenger
My lord, your brother John is ta'en in flight,
And brought with armed men back to Messina.
Benedick
Think not on him till to-morrow:
I'll devise thee brave punishments for him.
Strike up, pipers.

Much Ado About Nothing, act 5 scene 4

The recent decision on the EAPO laid bare the inner workings of the Government's approach to European developments: it relied on the criticisms of a few influential trade bodies instead of taking a principled approach to the problems of continent-wide enforcement of judgments. The recent submissions with regard to the proposal to reform the ESCP[53] are as revealing on the cross-border point. From a UK perspective, these regulations are merely extraordinary procedures that will not further coalesce into a coherent body of (harmonised) European civil procedure. Any analysis of their usefulness would require therefore a substantial amount of empirical research as to their impact on the individual problems they seek to resolve, within the limiting constraints of the improvement of the Internal Market.

Ultimately, Don John stirs up a little trouble but it peters out and the play culminates in a happy ending. In the final scene the villain, defeated and recaptured after an abortive escape attempt, is all but forgotten, save for a passing reference to his impending punishment. If the UK persists in its isolationist course, as the political landscape at the time of writing indicates is likely, it will definitely not be forced to any compromise with regard to the Commission's legislative competences but it may well be that, like the other players in *Much Ado*, the other Member States and the Commission will see the UK's attitude as nothing more than a minor distraction and continue on their legislative agenda unabated. Yet this would not be quite the happy ending. It is not just UK citizens, as opposed to the stakeholders—generally trade associations—with very specific agendas and who can be stirred into action by a call for evidence who will lose out. So too will the citizens of the other Member States, the UK's isolationist approach denying them the considerable weight of experience and tradition that the common law could bring to the nascent European law of civil procedure.

[53] Report of the House of Commons European Scrutiny Committee (n 13).

6

European Procedures on Debt Collection: Nothing or Noting? Experiences and Future Prospects[1]

XANDRA E KRAMER*

1. INTRODUCTION

IT HAS BEEN over seven years since the two first uniform European civil procedures were introduced, with the aim of facilitating the collection of debts in cross-border cases. The European Order for Payment Procedure (EOP) is a one-sided procedure for the collection of uncontested monetary claims,[2] whereas the European Small Claims Procedure (ESCP) applies to both contested and uncontested claims, and is as yet limited to claims with a maximum value of EUR 2,000.[3] These European procedures were

* Professor, Erasmus School of Law, Erasmus University Rotterdam.

[1] This publication has been made possible with the financial support of the Dutch Organisation for Scientific Research within its innovative research scheme (Vidi). This chapter results from a presentation at the conference 'Civil Justice in the EU—Growing and Teething?' co-organised by the Swedish Network for European Legal Studies in collaboration with the Faculty of Law at Uppsala University and the Max Planck Institute Luxembourg, Uppsala, October 2013. Part of the research and data on the Netherlands presented in section 3 relies heavily on earlier work, in particular XE Kramer, ML Tuil and I Tillema et al, 'Verkrijging van een executoriale titel in incassozaken', report for Research and Documentation Centre of the Ministry of Security and Justice, 2012, in particular 112–18, available at: www.wodc.nl/onderzoeksdatabase/executoriale-titel.aspx, English summary, available at: papers.ssrn.com/sol3/papers.cfm?abstract_id=2259557; and XE Kramer and EA Ontanu, 'The Functioning of the European Small Claims Procedure in the Netherlands: Normative and Empirical Reflections' (2013) 3 *Nederlands Internationaal Privaatrecht* 319. The empirical research has been solely (European order for payment) or primarily (European small claims) conducted by the present author; the co-authors have granted permission to reproduce some of the data. See also for a consolidating paper in Dutch, XE Kramer, 'Ervaringen met Europese civiele procedures in Nederland: een terugblik en wenkend toekomstperspectief' (2014) 2 *Nederlands Tijdschrift voor Europees Recht* 99–108.

[2] Regulation (EC) No 1896/2006 of 12 December 2006 creating a European order for payment procedure [2006] OJ L399/1, Arts 1 and 2 (EOP Regulation).

[3] Regulation (EC) No 861/2007 of 11 July 2007 establishing a European Small Claims Procedure [2007] OJ L199/1, Art 2 (ESCP Regulation).

introduced with a view to overcoming the hurdles that companies and consumers face when having to initiate legal proceedings to recover debts and to enforce rights across borders. The procedures generally aim to simplify, speed up, and reduce the costs of litigation in relation to uncontested claims and small claims.[4]

An important limitation to both procedures is that they are available only in cross-border cases. Article 3 of the respective Regulations defines these as cases in which at least one of the parties is domiciled or habitually resident in a Member State other than that of the court or tribunal seised. It should be noted further that both European procedures are optional; the claimant may still choose to initiate those domestic procedures available in the Member State of the court seised.[5] This means that the European procedures 'compete' with domestic procedures, particularly where these are effective or simply more familiar to the (domestic) claimant. To date, the European procedures seem to be underused, and this holds true particularly for the ESCP.

The conference lecture that gave rise to the current chapter was framed in a thematic session on European procedures and debt collection, and the organisers added the question as to whether these uniform procedures were 'much ado about nothing'. In Shakespeare's oft-quoted romantic comedy of the same title, apart from the 'nothing', the term 'noting'—as in 'to be noted'—plays an important role. The question is whether indeed these still relatively new European procedures are truly of little value to civil justice adjudication, or whether it is a matter of these procedures having received insufficient notice in practice and, to some extent, in academia. The conclusion that the ESCP is 'not used to its full potential' led the European Commission to put forward a proposal to amend the Regulation in November 2013.[6] The question is whether this proposal will enhance the use of European procedures and the ESCP in particular, and surpass the 'nothing' or 'noting'. To illustrate the discussion, this chapter will draw on practical experience of these two procedures in the Netherlands in particular, where the author has collected data and conducted interviews with, inter alia, courts.[7]

In this chapter the general impressions regarding the application of these two procedures in the Member States will be discussed first, as well as the extent of their potential (section 2). Subsequently the implementation of

[4] See Art 1 EOP Regulation and ESCP Regulation.

[5] ibid.

[6] Commission, 'Proposal for a Regulation amending Regulation (EC) 861/2007 of 11 July 2007 establishing a European Small Claims Procedure and Regulation (EC) 1896/2006 of 12 December 2006 creating a European order for payment procedure' COM(2013) 794 final.

[7] The chapter also benefits from lectures and a series of interactive training sessions that the author has provided for judges and other practitioners from all over the EU as well as discussions with Member States' representatives, inter alia, in the context of judicial training supported by the European Commission, a meeting of the European Judicial Network and a conference organised by the Lithuanian Council Presidency.

and practical experience of these two procedures in the Netherlands will be reviewed (section 3). Thereafter, the Commission proposal to amend the ESCP Regulation and the potential impact on the use and functioning of this procedure will be discussed (section 4). The chapter will conclude with some thoughts on the status and future of these two European civil procedures (section 5).

2. PROSPECTIVE AND GENERAL IMPRESSIONS OF EUROPEAN DEBT COLLECTION PROCEDURES

2.1 Rationale and Potential

Starting with the Green Paper of 2002 on the order for payment and small claims, it has been argued by the Commission that there is a genuine need for EU-wide procedures concerning these categories of claims.[8] The costs, delays, and complexity of domestic procedures are considered to be disproportionate for claims that are not disputed on their merits and for claims having a small value.[9] As recital 6 of the EOP Regulation contends, the EOP is of 'paramount importance for economic operators in the EU, as late payments constitute a major reason for insolvency threatening the survival of businesses, especially small and medium-sized enterprises, and resulting in numerous job losses'. Recital 8 adds that the differences in existing domestic procedures are impediments to access to efficient justice, and result in the distortion of competition in the EU. Likewise, for the ESCP the requirements of efficient access to justice and the economic desire to increase cross-border business have been used to underpin the need for this procedure,[10] as is also expressed in its recitals.[11]

The EOP has considerable potential. The Explanatory Memorandum to the legislative proposal of the Commission in 2004 observed that in fact between 50 and more than 80 per cent of claims in courts of first instance in the Member States are uncontested.[12] By way of illustration, in the Netherlands, data from 2012 demonstrate that 84 per cent of cases in the sub-district department of the District Court (*sector kanton*)[13] are

[8] Commission, 'Green Paper on a European order for payment procedure and on measures to simplify and speed up small claims litigation' COM(2002) 746 final.

[9] Green Paper (n 8) 10–11 and 59–60. See also EOP Regulation, recitals 6–9 and ESCP Regulation, recitals 7–8.

[10] Commission, 'Proposal for a Regulation establishing a European Small Claims Procedure' COM(2005) 87 final, Explanatory Memorandum, 3–4.

[11] ESCP Regulation, recitals 7 and 8.

[12] Commission, 'Proposal for a Regulation creating a European order for payment procedure' COM(2004) 173 final 3, Explanatory Memorandum, 5.

[13] This department of the district court has general competence for cases with a value up to EUR 25,000.

undefended.[14] It is for this reason that most Member States already had an order for payment mechanism under domestic law prior to the introduction of the European procedure.[15] The Impact Assessment of 2005 undertaken in relation to the proposed European small claims proposal indicated that the procedure might involve seven million citizens per year, and have a 'turnover' of at least EUR 8 billion.[16] However, because the Commission's proposal extended to domestic cases, these numbers were not limited to cross-border cases. The Impact Assessment of 2013, prepared for the Commission's proposal to amend this Regulation, however, points to an even greater potential impact. In view of the substantial increase in cross-border sales, it is estimated that the Regulation could cover up to 15 million potential claims, taking into account the current threshold of EUR 2,000.[17] A Eurobarometer survey conducted in 2012 shows that 71 per cent of consumer cases are below this threshold, which is also an indicator of its high potential.[18]

As noted above, an important limitation to the potential use is that both European procedures apply only in cross-border cases. However, reliable statistics on the number and the percentage of cross-border cases are lacking. The Heidelberg Report evaluating the Brussels I Regulation[19] indicated that only between 1 and 3 per cent of the cases are in fact international.[20] A Dutch empirical study on debt collection and default procedures revealed that in the sample of cases only 0.75 per cent were international in the sense that one of the parties was from a country other than the Netherlands.[21] However, as indicated by the aforementioned Eurobarometer survey and the Impact Assessment to the proposal amending the ESCP Regulation, the number of cross-border sales is growing steadily, and consequently, so is the potential of European debt collection procedures. It should be noted that the limitation imposed by the current definition of cross-border cases has led

[14] See NE de Heer-de Lange, BJ Diephuis and RJJ Eshuis (eds), *Rechtspleging Civiel en Bestuur 2012*, 86, available at: www.rechtspraak.nl/organisatie/publicaties-en-brochures/rapporten-en-artikelen/Documents/Rechtspleging-Civiel-en-Bestuur-2012.pdf.

[15] See also EOP Regulation, recital 7.

[16] Commission Staff Working Document, SEC(2005) 351, 18.

[17] Deloitte report, 'Assessment of the socio-economic impacts of the policy options for the future of the European Small Claims Regulation', July 2013, Executive summary, V. This number is based on data from Eurobarometer 395 (2013) that showed that 14.7 million cross-border sales are regarded as problematic, and would thus potentially result in litigation.

[18] Special Eurobarometer 395 on European Small Claims Procedure, 10, available at: ec.europa.eu/public_opinion/archives/ebs/ebs_395_sum_en.pdf.

[19] Regulation (EC) No 44/2001 of 22 December 2000 on jurisdiction and the recognition and enforcement of judgments in civil and commercial matters [2001] OJ L12/1 (Brussels I Regulation).

[20] B Hess, T Pfeiffer and P Schlosser, *Report on the Application of Regulation Brussels I in the Member States* (Heidelberg, Ruprecht-Karls-Universität, 2007) paras 40–49. See also B Hess, 'Procedural Harmonisation in a European Context' in XE Kramer and CH van Rhee (eds), *Civil Litigation in a Globalising World* (The Hague, TMC Asser Press, 2012) 162.

[21] Kramer, Tuil and Tillema (n 1) 82.

the European Commission to propose a significant extension of the definition in its amendment proposal.[22]

2.2 Use in Practice and Possible Explanations

Despite the reasonable assumptions and calculated estimations as to the need for and potential of these European procedures, only limited use is made of them in practice, particularly the ESCP. Little reliable data are available, but the data that are available, along with reports from the literature, show that these procedures are seldom used.[23] The Commission Report and the Impact Assessment on the EOP, which were due in December 2013, have not yet been published.[24] These should reveal in detail how many cases have been processed in the Member States, as well as how the Regulation operates. The above-mentioned Impact Assessment that was conducted in light of the Commission proposal to amend the ESCP Regulation also does not contain extensive numbers. It is estimated that in 2012 a total of 3,500 cases were dealt with in the Member States.[25] This estimation is made on the basis of the average number of applications per million citizens in seven Member States for which data or estimates were available, and transposing this number to all EU citizens. This of course is only a rough estimate, but it supports the general conception and—at least to some—the concern that the ESCP is underused. These data show that only in Austria did this procedure find its way to court practice in greater numbers.[26]

[22] Commission Proposal (n 6). See further section 4.2 below.

[23] See, inter alia, R Mánko, European Parliamentary Research Service, 'Briefing: Orders for payment in the EU. National procedures and the European order for payment', December 2013, 5, which contains some numbers on Poland and several other countries, available at: www.europarl.europa.eu/eplibrary/Orders-for-payment-in-the-EU.pdf. In the Briefing note, reference is made to P Rylski in (2012) 12 *Prawo w Działaniu—Sprawy Cywilne* 145, 147 and S Amrani-Mekki in *Droit processuel civil de l'Union européenne* (Paris, LexisNexis, 2011) 249, 253. See for some data on the European Small Claims Procedure, European Parliament, Directorate General for Internal Policies, 'Cross-Border Alternative Dispute Resolution in the European Union', IMCO 2011, 54–63, available at: www.europarl.europa.eu/meetdocs/2009_2014/documents/imco/dv/adr_study_/adr_study_en.pdf. For some data on both procedures in the Baltic States, reference can be made to I Kacevska and others, *Practical application of European Union regulations relating to European Union level procedure in civil cases: The experience in Baltic states* (Riga, Vilnus, Talinn, 2012), available at: www.just.ee. See also for data from the consumer perspective on the use of the European Small Claims Procedure, *ECC-Net Small Claims Procedure Report* (2012), available at: ec.europa.eu/consumers/ecc/docs/small_claims_210992012_en.pdf, 25, 27. See further section 3 below on data for the Netherlands, and on Germany and the United Kingdom.

[24] See Art 32 EOP Regulation.

[25] Deloitte report (n 17) 63.

[26] ibid, 63. According to these statistics (some based on estimates), in Austria in 2012 there were 26.4 applications per one million citizens, followed a considerable distance behind by Finland, where 8.5 applications per one million citizens were made among the countries listed, France has the lowest number of applications—only 0.8 cases per one million citizens.

As regards the ESCP, the European Commission concluded based on the Impact Assessment and several consultations that under-usage of the procedure is a result of the limited scope of application as well as of the fact that the procedure is still 'too cumbersome, costly and lengthy', and 'does not reflect the technological progress achieved in the Member States' justice systems'.[27] The Commission further mentions a lack of awareness.[28] Careful reference is made to poor implementation of the current rules in the Member States, and to the lack of transparency.[29] It is submitted that actually poor implementation is very likely to have had a significant impact so far on the limited attractiveness of the ESCP. A review of the information provided by the Member States demonstrates that many of them do not offer adequate guidance to potential users.[30] Information is limited and incomplete, and reference is often made to provisions of domestic procedural law and rules on court fees.[31] This requires a potential litigant to pore over domestic procedural rules that are not likely to be even linguistically accessible for foreign parties. This is likely to scare off any party that does not want to engage a lawyer—as the Regulations allow[32]—or is financially not able to do so. Only a few Member States allow low threshold electronic communication. Transparency relating to the procedure or to the costs incurred is lacking.

Though no extensive data are yet available, the EOP is more successful in most Member States. The following explanations seem plausible to explain the greater attraction of the EOP compared with the ESCP. First, the value of the claim is not limited under the EOP Regulation. Second, users of this procedure will often be businesses, while the ESCP is aimed primarily, though not exclusively, at consumers. Third, potential litigants and their lawyers may have been more familiar with the concept of the EOP, since similar procedures for the collection of uncontested debts (payment orders) already existed in the domestic laws of many Member States. Fourth, the ESCP may be regarded as a more 'risky' procedure since—unlike the EOP—it also and primarily applies to adversarial cases. Fifth, the one-sided character of the

[27] Commission Proposal (n 6) Explanatory Memorandum, 3.

[28] ibid.

[29] ibid.

[30] This information is available on the European Judicial Atlas in Civil Matters, section on Cross-Border Procedures, Documents (consolidation of information on the Member States) and Communications of the Member States (per Member State by clicking on the map).

[31] For implementation in general and in several Member States, see XE Kramer, 'Enhancing Enforcement in the European Union: The European Order for Payment Procedure and its Implementation in the Member States, Particularly in Germany, the Netherlands, and England' in CH van Rhee and A Uzelac (eds), *Enforcement and Enforceability: Tradition and Reform* (Antwerp, Intersentia, 2010) 27–36 and XE Kramer, 'Small Claim, Simple Recovery? The European Small Claims Procedure and Its Implementation in the Member States' (2011) 1 *ERA Forum: Journal of European Law* 119, 128–31.

[32] See Art 24 EOP Regulation and Art 10 ESCP Regulation according to which legal representation shall not be mandatory.

EOP more easily enables/facilitates electronic procedures, thereby lowering the costs of and thresholds for using this procedure. For example, a successful pilot project between Germany and Austria in 2009 resulted in the implementation of the electronic handling of this procedure.[33] A final explanation may be that in several Member States alternative dispute resolution mechanisms, such as consumer complaint boards, are widely available for consumer cases, or are even compulsory in the first instance.

3. EXPERIENCES IN A MEMBER STATE: THE NETHERLANDS

3.1 Implementation into Dutch Law

This section will focus on the implementation and application of the two European procedures in the Netherlands. It will discuss the main findings as derived from the published case law and experiences in the Netherlands as evidenced by empirical research to illustrate the functioning of the European procedures in this Member State.[34] In short, the empirical research consisted of interviews based on questionnaires together with the collection of data from participating courts and the Dutch Council for the Judiciary.[35]

In the Netherlands, the two European civil procedures dealt with in this chapter are applied by means of two separate Implementation Acts,[36] instead of being implemented in the Code of Civil Procedure. These separate Implementation Acts are concise and incorporate most of the information items that have to be communicated pursuant to Article 29 EOP Regulation and Article 25 ESCP Regulation. Both procedures are regarded as so-called petition procedures under Dutch law, and the rules on petition procedures apply, unless provided otherwise.[37] This has several important consequences, notably that the procedure is not initiated—as are ordinary procedures—by summoning the defendant using a bailiff, but by a petition to the court. The petition procedure, which is otherwise used mostly in family law matters and a few other specific matters, is generally less formal,

[33] See, inter alia, Project for electronic processing of the European order for payment procedure on the website of the Austrian *Bundeskanslerambt* at www.epsa-projects.eu/index.php?title=Project_for_electronic_processing_of_the_European_order_for_payment_procedure. See also www.epractice.eu/en/cases/euopa.

[34] Parts 3.2.2 and 3.3.2 of this section rely heavily on data obtained and reported in earlier research; see (n 1).

[35] For the methodology and further references see sections 3.2 and 3.3.

[36] Implementation Act European Order for Payment Procedure (*Uitvoeringswet verordening Europese betalingsbevelprocedure*), Act of 29 May 2009, Staatsblad 2009, 232 (hereafter Implementation Act EOP); Implementation Act European Small Claims Procedure (*Uitvoeringswet verordening Europese procedure voor geringe vorderingen*), Act of 29 May 2009, Staatsblad 2009, 234 (hereafter Implementation Act ESCP).

[37] See Art 12 Implementation Act EOP and Art 9 Implementation Act ESCP.

as well as cheaper and faster. This explains the choice of this type of process for the two European procedures (EOP and ESCP).

The handling of matters falling under the EOP is concentrated at the District Court of The Hague.[38] Competence for matters falling under the ESCP lies with the sub-district department of District Courts, of which there are currently 11.[39] A particularity of the two Dutch Implementation Acts is that they limit the period of review, which must be done 'promptly' on the basis of Article 20 EOP Regulation and Article 18 ESCP Regulation, to four weeks.[40] In the ESCP, appeal is excluded.[41] The development of electronic communication is at an advanced stage in the Dutch judicial system; however, applications under these procedures must, to date, still be submitted to the relevant court by hand or by way of postal delivery.

Another important point is that ordinary court fees apply in these procedures.[42] These fees are relatively high in the Netherlands. Particularly for low- and medium-value claims, the fees are substantial. In 2014, the fee for natural persons for claims up to EUR 500 is EUR 77; for claims with a value up to EUR 12,500 it is EUR 219; and for claims up to EUR 25,000 it is EUR 462. For legal persons, the proportional fee for these categories is EUR 115, EUR 462, and EUR 923 respectively. A fixed fee of EUR 77 applies to only a limited category of financially disadvantaged natural persons. In the EOP, the defendant lodging an opposition within the meaning of Article 17 EOP Regulation does not have to pay court fees, but fees must be paid if the defendant subsequently continues to defend the case and the matter is transferred to be dealt with in ordinary civil proceedings.[43]

3.2 Experience of the European Order for Payment Procedure

3.2.1 Introduction

To date, 13 cases have been published in the Dutch national open access database.[44] These concern primarily the review procedure on the basis of Article 20 EOP Regulation as well as the continuation of the procedure under the ordinary rules of civil procedure after an opposition has been

[38] This does not follow from the Implementation Act EOP, but from a temporary resolution. A proposal to amend the Act is pending.

[39] See Art 2 Implementation Act ESCP. Until 1 January 2013 there were 19 district courts.

[40] See Art 9(2) Implementation Act EOP and Art 6(2) Implementation Act ESCP.

[41] See Art 2(2) Implementation Act ESCP. However, cassation at the Supreme Court is possible on limited grounds. This is different from domestic cases, since—on the basis of Art 332 of the Dutch Code of Civil Procedure—appeal is possible for cases with a value of EUR 1,750 and higher, including costs and interest.

[42] See Art 11 Implementation Act EOP and Art 3 Implementation Act ESCP referring to the *Wet griffierechten in burgerlijke zaken* (law court fees in civil cases).

[43] See Arts 11(2) and 11(3) Implementation Act EOP.

[44] See www.rechtspraak.nl.

lodged pursuant to Article 17 EOP Regulation. In contrast to many other Member States, the Netherlands does not have a national order for payment procedure. The national procedure was actually abandoned in 1991 because it was seldom used in practice.[45] To obtain a better appreciation of how the European procedure is conducted and functions in Dutch legal practice, empirical research was undertaken. Data were collected from the Council for the Judiciary and the competent court in The Hague. Two interviews based on extensive questionnaires were held with professionals who are closely involved in the handling of such matters.[46] One was with a judge and two staff members of The Hague Court, and the other was with a senior employee in a bailiff's office located in The Hague. At the request of and in consultation with The Hague Court, this bailiff's office serves the orders for payment that need to be served abroad, or that for other reasons cannot be served by the Court itself by means of the postal service.[47] The interviews and the primary data collection took place in 2012,[48] with additional data collected in 2013 and at the beginning of 2014.

In contrast to the Dutch procedure for judgment in default,[49] under the EOP the defendant in principle has only one opportunity to defend the case. The order is issued in a one-sided procedure upon assessment of formalities.[50] The order becomes enforceable if the defendant does not oppose the claim within 30 days.[51] However, pursuant to Article 20 EOP Regulation a 'review in exceptional cases' is possible. These exceptional cases concern, in the first instance, a situation in which the order was served without an acknowledgement of receipt, and service was not effected in sufficient time to enable the defendant to arrange for his defence, without any fault on his part, or in which the defendant was not able to defend himself for reasons of force majeure or extraordinary circumstances.[52] The defendant must request a review promptly in the Member State where the order was issued. A second case in which the defendant is entitled to a review is where the order was 'clearly wrongly issued, having regard to the requirements laid down in this Regulation, or due to other exceptional circumstances'.[53] As mentioned

[45] See Kramer, Tuil and Tillema (n 1) 62–63.

[46] These interviews were conducted during a study carried out for the Dutch Ministry of Security and Justice; see Kramer, Tuil and Tillema (n 1).

[47] The postal delivery of orders with acknowledgement of receipt, as prescribed by Art 13(c) EOP Regulation, proved to be problematic. As discussed above in section 3.1, in the Netherlands, courts in ordinary claim cases (introduced by summons) are not involved in the service of notification.

[48] Some findings may therefore not be up to date, and certain shortcomings may have been remedied in the meantime.

[49] This is an ordinary summons procedure that ends in a default judgment in the event that the defendant does not enter an appearance or fails to pay the court fee; see Art 139 Dutch Code of Civil Procedure.

[50] Art 12 EOP Regulation.

[51] See Arts 16 and 18 EOP Regulation.

[52] Art 20(1) EOP Regulation.

[53] Art 20(2) EOP Regulation.

above, the Dutch Implementation Act for the EOP provides that 'promptly' means within four weeks.[54] This four-week period is also prescribed in the second situation in which a review is allowed, even though strictly speaking the Regulation does not require the defendant to act promptly.

3.2.2 Lessons from Case Law: Going Once, Going Twice?

The Hague Court has interpreted the above-mentioned four-week deadline in a strict manner.[55] The Court has held that, if a defendant was not aware that the order for payment was issued for reasons other than those mentioned in Article 20 EOP Regulation, it cannot invoke a limitation period in relation to the claim.[56] In one case, the defendant declared that he did not recognise the document as being an order for payment, and that it was lost in other mail. In another case, the Court decided that the defendant was required to secure adequate representation to receive postal documents during his absence.[57] The fact that the concierge of a building where many companies and persons have offices had accepted the document and did not pass it on to the defendant in time to meet the four-week deadline was the responsibility of the defendant; the risk was entirely his own. In three other cases, the review was dismissed simply because the four-week deadline had not been met; in one case, the review was requested after one month and a few days.[58] The Hague Court reasoned that the four-week deadline was reasonable, since the opposition period prescribed by Article 16 EOP Regulation is 30 days.

It is submitted that the general interpretation of Article 20 by The Hague Court is in line with the exceptional character of the review procedure as well as with the ruling of the Court of Justice of the European Union in *Novontech-Zala*.[59] The Court ruled in this case that—due to negligence on the part of the defendant's representative—the failure to observe the deadline for lodging a statement of opposition within the meaning of Article 16 EOP did not justify a review. However, it may be doubted whether the strict

[54] See section 3.1 above and (n 40). Art 9(2) Implementation Act EOP reads as follows (my translation, XEK): 'The request must be fulfilled: (a) in the case of Art 20, first paragraph, under "a" of the Regulation, within four weeks after the enforceable payment order becomes known to the defendant; (b) in the case of Art 20, second paragraph, under "b" of the Regulation, within four weeks after the grounds mentioned have ceased to exist; (c) in the case of Art 20, second paragraph, of the Regulation, within four weeks after the grounds mentioned for review have become known to the defendant'.

[55] See also Kramer, 'Ervaringen met Europese civiele procedures in Nederland' (n 1).

[56] District Court The Hague, 25 September 2010, NL:RBSGR:2010:BN9631.

[57] District Court The Hague, 24 January 2012, NL:RBSGR:2012:BV2920.

[58] District Court The Hague, 30 September 2010, NL:RBSGR:2010:BN9635 (two months); District Court The Hague, 3 November 2010, NL:RBSGR:2010:BO3259 (one month and 4 days); District Court The Hague, 10 August 2012, NL:RBSGR:2012:BX6433 (one month and 5 days).

[59] Case C-321/12 *Novontech-Zala*, EU:C:2013:205.

observance of the four-week deadline laid down in the Dutch Implementation Act and not at the European level is reasonable. This pivotal deadline might come as a surprise especially to foreign defendants. An interesting development is that the Commission's proposal to amend the ESCP includes a uniform review period, which is set at 30 days.[60] Setting such a uniform deadline for the EOP would also be a step forward.

3.2.3 Significant Findings

The most important data obtained from the Council for the Judiciary and The Hague District Court concern the number of applications for a EOP, the period within which the order is issued, and the number of cases in which a statement of opposition was filed.[61] The most extensive data available are for the research period from 2009 to 2011. However, additional data as to the number of applications were provided on request for 2012 and 2013.

As is clear from Table 1, the number of applications for a EOP in the Netherlands is low. In the first three years, the number of applications was on the rise; however, the growth did not continue in 2012 and 2013. It is also apparent that the number is low compared with the potential number of cases. In 2012, the number of default judgments in the sub-district department of the District Court (*sector kanton*)—which has general jurisdiction for claims with a value of up to EUR 25,000—was 370 241.[62] In the District Court (claims over EUR 25,000), 2,467 default judgments were rendered.[63] Even if one were to consider, as discussed earlier,[64] that probably less than 1 per cent of these cases are cross-border, the number of EOPs is still far below the procedure's potential reach.[65]

Table 1: Total number of applications per year under the EOP Regulation (District Court, The Hague)[66]

2009	2010	2011	2012	2013[67]
295 cases	343 cases	372 cases	334 cases	284 cases

[60] Commission Proposal (n 6), Art 2(11) amending Art 18(2).
[61] See for additional data and analyses Kramer, Tuil and Tillema (n 1) 112–13.
[62] De Heer-de Lange, Diephuis and Eshuis (n 14) 228–29; Tables 4.2 and 4.3.
[63] ibid.
[64] Section 2.1 above.
[65] In the research of Kramer, Tuil and Tillema (n 1) 80, the sample of cases in the sub-district department of the District Court shows that 97% of them concern monetary claims arising from the contract; these are typically cases that would be suitable for the EOP.
[66] Data obtained from the Council for the Judiciary demonstrated clearly that in the first two years seven additional cases were registered in other District Courts for unknown reasons.
[67] The number of cases had not been finally determined at the time these data were obtained (in January 2014), but are mostly accurate.

The data available for 2009–11 showed that the duration of the proceedings was on average 152 days, calculated from the moment of submitting the request to issuing the payment order (Table 2). This is remarkable, since it is a simple, one-sided procedure, yet the time it took is clearly much longer than the 30 days that the EOP Regulation prescribes as the period within which the order should ordinarily be issued.[68] The data also show that in the vast majority of cases (71–83 per cent) the duration was more than three months.[69] Data made available by The Hague Court during 2011 show that if one were to disregard the cases in which no payment order was issued (because the case has been withdrawn), actually 95 per cent of the cases took more than three months to be concluded. It should be noted that these figures exclude the period needed to serve the order and the 30-day period to oppose it. No data are available on how many days this adds to the duration of the proceedings. Unfortunately, no data have been made available for 2012 and 2013. The long duration of the proceedings was a point of attention of The Hague Court itself, and it might be that in the meantime the period has been shortened.

Table 2: Average duration of the procedure to issue the order (year of issuing)

2009	2010	2011
144 days	162 days	151 days

The data available for 2009–11 show that the order for payment was opposed in on average 24 per cent of the cases (Table 3).[70] This appears to be a relatively high number, though there is little comparative material available. A briefing from the European Parliamentary Research Service, referring to empirical research in Poland, indicates that in Poland only 7 per cent of the EOPs were contested.[71]

Table 3: Concluded cases divided into opposition/no opposition (year of issuing)

	2009	2010	2011
Opposition	31	93	80
No opposition	89	285	269

The most important findings from the interviews with The Hague Court and the bailiff's office concerning the service of payment orders may be

[68] See Art 12 EOP Regulation.
[69] See Kramer, Tuil and Tillema (n 1) 113.
[70] See also Kramer, Tuil and Tillema (n 1) 113–14.
[71] Mánko, 'Briefing: Orders for payment in the EU' (n 23) 5.

summarised as follows.[72] Initially there were a number of questions on how service should be effected, but the Court soon developed a practice in consultation with the Ministry of Security and Justice and the Council for the Judiciary. Users initially had many questions as well, but these seem to have been settled in the meantime. The procedure is regarded as a so-called stamp procedure, and in the vast majority of cases it is handled entirely by the Court's administrative staff.

There is a large variation in the types of cases and claims for which a EOP is used. The amounts for which the order is requested vary from a few dozen euros to, in one case, EUR 7 million. Both companies and consumers make use of the procedure, and it is estimated that parties are represented in more than half of the cases, usually by a lawyer, a bailiff's office, or a debt collection agency. This is remarkable, since according to the EOP Regulation legal representation is not compulsory.[73] The Court indicated that the delay in the handling of the procedure is in part caused by the fact that in many cases information in the request form is missing or needs to be corrected, for example, essential data regarding the debtor or the requested interest.[74] This requires the Court to call for additional information. Missing data are usually requested informally by phone or by e-mail, as this is quicker than using the designated forms. Another difficulty that the Court identified is the question regarding international jurisdiction; consumers in particular seem to have difficulties filling in this item.[75]

Most delays, however, occur only after the order is issued and needs to be served. Both the Court and the bailiff's office consider the service of payment orders abroad to be difficult and time-consuming. The bailiff's office handles the service when the postal service with acknowledgement of receipt turns out to be impossible, or where the order has to be served abroad. The interviewee at the bailiff's office indicated that on average the case is concluded six weeks after an order has been issued. However, the service abroad causes excessive delays in some cases, even up to one year.

To the concluding question as to how the EOP is generally assessed, interviewees answered that the procedure is simpler than the Dutch procedure for judgment in default, particularly because the procedure is to a great extent handled through electronic forms. They regard the generally high court fees in the Netherlands as a threshold. Interviewees at the Court saw the fact that the claim is not reviewed in any way as a disadvantage of this procedure, whereas in the Dutch default procedure there is a marginal

[72] See more in detail Kramer, Tuil and Tillema (n 1) 114–18.

[73] See Art 24 EOP Regulation.

[74] eg, the address or exact name of the debtor is missing. Another frequent occurrence is that a party ticks more than one box concerning the requested interest (item 7 in the Application Form, Annex I EOP Regulation): eg, both statutory and contractual interest.

[75] See item 3 in the Application Form, Annex I EOP Regulation.

check.[76] The extrajudicial debt collection costs, as part of the claim, are also not reviewed, whereas this is the case in the Dutch default procedure. In fact, research has shown for the Dutch default procedure that the claim is partially rejected in 25 per cent of the cases, mainly because the court reduces the requested interests and costs.[77] Legal protection in the EOP is therefore very limited. From the 2012 case *Banco Español de Crédito* of the Court of Justice of the European Union, it may be concluded that some review within the order for payment procedure is nevertheless required.[78] The Court required an *ex officio* review of moratory interest in a Spanish order for payment procedure on the basis of Council Directive 93/13/EEC on unfair terms in consumer contracts. However, the same would hold true for the EOP. The interviewees also pointed to the fact that the debtor runs a big risk under this procedure; if he does not respond to the order within 30 days, there is no second chance to oppose the claim. For this reason, proper service of the payment order is considered essential.

3.3 Experiences with the European Small Claims Procedure

3.3.1 Introduction

To date, 21 cases regarding the application of the ESCP have been published in the Netherlands.[79] These are usually short judgments that provide little insight into the conduct and functioning of the procedure. For this reason, further research was conducted in 2012, consisting of data collection and interviews on the basis of questionnaires.[80] At my request, several courts have provided additional information in 2013 and 2014. A problem is that there is no uniform registration system for this procedure, as the courts register it under different categories. An overview of cases per court obtained from the Council for the Judiciary was far from complete. This lack of registration is remarkable in view of Article 27(2) ESCP Regulation that requires the Member States to inform the Commission on the functioning of the procedure, including its duration, effectiveness and user-friendliness. For the purpose of our research, a first interview was held with the ECC-NL. Questionnaires were distributed to eight other courts (sub-district departments of the district courts) out of the then 19 courts having jurisdiction.[81]

[76] Art 139 of the Dutch Code of Civil Procedure states that the claim will be awarded unless it appears to be unjustifiable or unfounded. Art 11(1)(b) EOP Regulation also prescribes that the application shall be dismissed if it is clearly unfounded. However, sending supporting documents is not required, and apparently the court interprets these provisions differently.

[77] Kramer, Tuil and Tillema (n 1) 91 and Table 4.7.

[78] Case C-618/10 *Banco Español de Crédito*, EU:C:2012:349.

[79] See www.rechtspraak.nl.

[80] See further on the methodology, Kramer and Ontanu (n 1) 319–20.

[81] Meanwhile, the number of District Courts has been reduced to 11. See also section 3.1 above and (n 39).

These were selected on the basis of their size and location in a border region, which means that the data might not be representative for all courts, since only the largest courts and courts in border regions were approached. Face to face interviews were held with seven of these; the eighth court had only a few cases, and it was sufficient for it to simply fill in the questionnaire.

3.3.2 Case Law: Characteristics and Trends[82]

All cases but one concerned consumer cases; that one case was a consumer-to-consumer case involving the online sale of second-hand goods. In more than 75 per cent of the cases the consumer was the claimant; in all cases it concerned a Dutch consumer against a company located in another Member State. Most of the cases, 75 per cent, concerned claims against airlines on the basis of Regulation 261/2004 for compensation due to a delayed or an annulled flight.[83] The amount claimed varied from EUR 99 to 1,607. In all but three of the cases, the claim was granted, including legal expenses and the costs for extrajudicial debt collection. As far as could be derived from the data the average duration of the cases was four to five months.

Published case law does not reveal specific problems, though in one instance the application of the language rules laid down in Article 6 ESCP Regulation and Article 8 Service Regulation seemed problematic.[84] In one remarkable case, the judge decided that Regulation 261/2004 does not give a right to compensation in the case of flight delays, and that the *Sturgeon* ruling[85] of the Court of Justice of the European Union cannot change this, since the Court is not the legislature and cannot change the law.[86] However, in later cases in the same Court this obviously wrong judgment from an apparently determined judge was not repeated. One case concerned the possibility of appeal. As was discussed earlier, the Dutch legislature excluded the possibility of appeal.[87] This choice to exclude appeal—whereas in national cases appeal is possible in instances involving claims above EUR 1,750 including costs and interest[88]—was made deliberately to enable a simple

[82] See for a more detailed analysis, Kramer and Ontanu (n 1) 322–23.

[83] Regulation (EC) No 261/2004 of 11 February 2004 establishing common rules on compensation and assistance to passengers in the event of boarding being denied and of cancellation or long delays involving flights, and repealing Regulation (EEC) No 295/91 [2004] OJ L46/1. See also joined cases C-402/07 and C-432/07 *Sturgeon and others* [2009] ECR I-10291; EU:C:2009:716; joined cases C-581/10 and C-629/10 *Tui Travel and others* EU:C:2012:657.

[84] See District Court Amsterdam, 30 August 2010, NL:RBAMS:2010:BO2995. The Latvian defendant raised an objection against the Dutch claim form. The judge decided that this was in conformity with Art 6(1) ESCP Regulation. However, this concerns submission of the claim form to the court, and not service of the document to the defendant.

[85] See (n 83).

[86] District Courts-Hertogenbosch, 19 January 2012, NL:RBSHE:2012:BV1931.

[87] See section 3.1 above.

[88] Whereas the EUR 2,000 threshold of the ESCP excludes costs and interest (see Art 1 ESCP Regulation).

and fast procedure.[89] For these reasons, the Court of Appeal did not want to make an exception to the prohibition to appeal. In this case, the ground for appeal was the apparent lack of international jurisdiction. The Court of Appeal judged that matters of international jurisdiction could nevertheless be brought to the Supreme Court.[90]

3.3.3 Significant Findings

In view of the lack of a national registration system for this procedure, the eight courts that participated in the research were asked to provide data, though not all courts were able to provide precise data or records per year. Based upon the data provided, a total of 178 applications were made in these eight courts between January 2009 and mid-2012 (Table 4). If one were to transpose this to all the Dutch courts according to available data on the share of the selected courts in the total number of civil cases handled, it would come to a rough estimate of about 330 cases in total in the Netherlands.[91] However, since the eight courts selected may very well not be representative because they have not been randomly selected, this figure may not be accurate.[92]

Table 4: Total applications in the ESCP in the eight participating courts (2009 to mid-2012)[93]

Amsterdam	Den Haag	Rotterdam	Utrecht	's-Hertogenbosch	Arnhem	Maastricht	Zutphen
28	16	32	26	50	10	11	5

Data from courts that were able to provide it per year did not show a substantial increase in the number of cases. However, the courts of 's-Hertogenbosch and to a lesser extent Amsterdam did witness a substantial increase. This was due to an increase in claims for delayed flights following the case law of the Court of Justice of the European Union concerning Regulation 261/2004.[94] In other courts this was not the case. For example, in the District Court of Rotterdam, 10 cases were completed in 2010, and 18 cases in 2011; in 2012

[89] See *Kamerstukken II* (Parliamentary Documents) 31 596, fn 3.

[90] Cassation at the Supreme Court is possible; see Art 2(3) Implementation Act ESCP.

[91] Available figures from 2005 show that these eight courts account for 54.3% of the cases handled. See BCJ van Velthoven, 'Civiele rechtspraak in eerste aanleg 2005: Een eerste stap op weg naar kwantificering van de maatschappelijke betekenis van de rechtspraak', Report for the Council for the Judiciary, 2005, available at: media.leidenuniv.nl/legacy/BvV-2007-02.pdf, 17.

[92] The courts were selected by size and by location, see section 3.3.

[93] Not all data are complete; hence there may be a small difference between the actual number of applications and estimates provided by some courts.

[94] See (n 83).

the number of cases dropped to 13, and in November 2013 (when these data were provided) only 7 cases were completed.[95]

In line with what was concluded on the basis of published case law, in the courts that participated in our research, the procedure is on average concluded within three to five months (Table 5). This is certainly reasonable, and in conformity with the general scheme of the ESCP Regulation.[96]

Table 5: Average duration of cases concluded in the eight participating courts, in months (rounded)

Amsterdam	Den Haag	Rotterdam	Utrecht	's-Hertogenbosch	Arnhem	Maastricht	Zutphen
5	4.75	4	4.5	4	3	4.5	3

Other important data that were collected concern primarily the number of oral hearings that were requested and held, as well as the number of requests for review within the meaning of Article 18 ESCP Regulation.[97] In five cases the court ordered an oral hearing. In only three cases one of the parties had requested an oral hearing, which was granted in two instances.[98] This practice is in conformity with the spirit of the Regulation, which limits oral hearings in order to save costs and time.[99] A request for a review was only registered in one case. Under the ESCP there seems to be little need for this review mechanism, though there may be other reasons for its limited use, for example, that parties are not familiar with the possibility of review.[100]

Some of the most important observations during interviews with the ECC-NL and the courts include the following.[101] As regards how the procedure is managed internally, some of the courts remarked that they had been somewhat taken aback by the introduction of the ESCP, but all of them had established a fixed practice. Specific judges and staff members are charged with the handling of the procedure. A few courts considered that it was

[95] Data provided by email at the author's request. The author is deputy judge in this District Court.

[96] The Regulation does not provide a deadline for the entire procedure, but only for steps within the procedure (see Arts 4, 5, 7 and 14 ESCP Regulation). The Commission Proposal (n 10) did include an overall deadline of six months.

[97] See for a more complete overview of data, Kramer and Ontanu (n 1) 324. Other items regarded the number of cases in which cassation at the Supreme Court is lodged, and the requests for a refusal, stay, or limitation of enforcement in relation to an ESCP judgment rendered in another Member State. No cases were registered.

[98] In the third case, an additional written round of arguments was held.

[99] See Art 5(1) ESCP Regulation.

[100] On the contrary, published case law on the EOP reveals that the review mechanism is regularly invoked. See section 3.2.1 above.

[101] See for a more extensive report and analysis, Kramer and Ontanu (n 1) 323–27.

difficult to develop a good practice in view of the small number of cases. In the event that parties have questions on the procedure, they are referred to the website of the European Judicial Atlas, to the Dutch judiciary website, or to the *Juridisch Loket*, a subsidised agency that provides independent free legal advice to citizens.[102] Not all courts were familiar with the role of the ECC-NL (which is headed under the *Juridisch Loket*) in European matters. The ECC-NL stated that they regularly advise consumers on the ESCP and, in collaboration with ECCs in other Member States, mediate between consumers and companies located in other Member States. If mediation is not successful, the ECC-NL provides help to fill in the forms and, where necessary, to translate them.

In line with what appears from the reported case law, almost all cases concerned consumer cases, with the consumer being the claimant. In most cases it concerned online sales or service contracts and—in designated courts—airline cases regarding flight delays. In many cases the parties were represented. For example, in airline cases EUclaim is one of the big players representing consumers.[103]

The courts indicated that there were no serious problems with the use of the standard forms, though information is often lacking or incorrect. Completion or correction is requested using the designated Form B or more informally by e-mail or phone. The most problematic item, particularly for consumers, is the question regarding international jurisdiction, since the simple tick box format on the claim form and the information used to determine jurisdiction is misleading.[104] Several courts indicated that they found the forms too rigid, and that a case cannot be completed only with a claim form and an answer form if there is a serious defence. Sometimes an extra round of written submissions is ordered in such a case.[105] Some courts regard it as a clear disadvantage that the possibilities of holding an oral hearing are limited, since a case can often be resolved more easily in an oral hearing.

Another difficulty encountered by the courts has to do with language issues and the requirements of Article 6 ESCP Regulation in this regard. Forms are regularly submitted in a foreign language. In order to save time and cost, some courts do not require a translation if they are able to

[102] Some basic information on both the ESCP and the EOP is available on the official website of the courts and the Council for the Judiciary, at: www.rechtspraak.nl.

[103] This is a no cure no play agency that offers its services to handle claims relating to flight delays and annulations.

[104] Question 4 of the Claim Form (Annex I, Form A of the ESCP Regulation) suggests that the Dutch court has jurisdiction if the consumer is domiciled in the Netherlands; however, Art 17 of the Brussels I-bis Regulation has further requirements and, for example, does not apply to contracts of transport other than travel packages (eg, flight only). See also for this problem, Kramer and Ontanu (n 1) 325.

[105] According to the present author this is in line with the possibility to request further information in accordance with Art 7 ESCP Regulation.

understand the form. In conformity with Article 6(2) ESCP Regulation, they only require a translation of the supporting documents if this is necessary to give judgment. One of the interviewees suggested introducing English as *lingua franca* for this procedure. However, other interviewees did not—understandably, in my view—regard this as a plausible alternative, since not all courts and certainly not all parties are fully equipped and capable of conducting the whole procedure in English. Questions have also arisen as to who should bear the costs of translating the forms to be served to the defendant or the claimant. Some courts carry the costs themselves, but this would create budgetary difficulties if the number of cases were to rise substantially. It is submitted that translation costs are costs of the procedure that, as far as these are not unnecessarily incurred and are not disproportional to the claim, should in the end be borne by the losing party in accordance with Article 16 ESCP Regulation.

Most problematic is the service of documents. As the primary method of service, Article 13 ESCP Regulation prescribes postal delivery attested by an acknowledgement of receipt. However, particularly since Dutch courts are ordinarily not involved in the service or notification process, they are not well equipped to perform this task. Practice differs between courts. Most courts do not translate forms or documents to be served to the foreign defendant, and neither do they enclose the standard form regarding the right to refuse documents if the addressee does not understand these (Annex II of the Service Regulation). In the event that no acknowledgement of receipt is received, some courts extend the period of time to answer, or they make another attempt to send the documents. One court indicated that after a certain lapse of time it gives a default judgment, assuming that the defendant has received the document. One court indicated that it simply sends the documents by post, without requiring an acknowledgement of receipt. It is submitted that such practices may seriously undermine a fair trial, and in particular the right to be heard.

In addition to language obstacles and jurisdiction problems, the EEC-NL regarded the way interest had to be calculated as being particularly problematic. It further pointed to practical problems that parties encounter in the enforcement of judgments in other Member States.[106] Another point raised was that court fees are high in the Netherlands, also in comparison to neighbouring Member States.

Most courts were reserved in their appreciation of the added value of the ESCP. One interviewee qualified the procedure as merely a 'political gesture'. Some interviewees mentioned that the low number of cases might be an indication that there is little need for this procedure. For courts, an

[106] See to this end also *ECC-Net European Small Claims Procedure Report: the Study*, September 2012, available at: ec.europa.eu/consumers/ecc/docs/small_claims_210992012_en.pdf.

additional procedure that is seldom used is burdensome. One interviewee said that this procedure has to date only been useful for airline cases, since this is a typical European and cross-border matter. Another court officer said that it is a procedure accessible to consumers, but doubted whether procedural rights could always be fully guaranteed.

3.4 Concluding Remarks

Both the EOP and the ESCP are not used very frequently in the Netherlands. As regards the ESCP, this appears to support the general trend in the Member States. The EOP, however, should have more potential, but it is not yet popular in the Netherlands. One reason might be that a similar procedure is not available in domestic law. However, this would only explain why Dutch creditors do not request a EOP, as it is clear that foreign creditors do not address the Dutch courts in great numbers either.[107] The research carried out by the present author in collaboration with others on debt collection practices and procedures in the Netherlands[108] has led the Dutch legislature to conclude that the EOP or a similar procedure will not be introduced for domestic cases.[109] The conclusion is that the domestic procedure for judgment in default works well; it is fast, and gives more legal protection than does the EOP.

General deficits in the Dutch application of these procedures are that the service of documents is generally problematic, language obstacles still persist, procedural rights are not always fully guaranteed, and—as regards the EOP—the procedure takes too long. However, this latter shortcoming may be relatively easily remedied by restructuring the working process. A general obstacle to access to justice, not only in European procedures, is that court fees are high. A recent report by the Council of the Judiciary showed that in 2013 there were 26 per cent fewer civil law suits brought in court than in 2010.[110] This is attributed to the substantial rise in court fees in 2010 and 2011, particularly for cases with a value between EUR 500 and EUR 12,500.

[107] There are no exact numbers as to how many applicants are Dutch or foreign, but a list provided by the bailiff's office involved in the service indicated that this is approximately 50/50.

[108] Kramer, Tuil and Tillema (n 1).

[109] See the proposal and explanatory memorandum in the context of *Programma Kwaliteit en Innovatie rechtspraak (KEI)* (Program Quality and Innovation judiciary), available at: www.rijksoverheid.nl/onderwerpen/rechtspraak-en-geschiloplossing/vernieuwing-in-de-rechtspraak/programma-kwaliteit-en-innovatie-rechtspraak-kei. The goal of the programme is to simplify and digitalise court procedures. See also XE Kramer, I Tillema and ML Tuil, 'De verstekprocedure getoetst: een empirisch onderzoek naar de verstekprocedure in het licht van het KEI-programma' (2014) *Tijdschrift voor civiele rechtspleging* 1.

[110] F van Tulder, 'In de schaduw van de rechter, Individuele en maatschappelijke kosten en baten van de juridische infrastructuur' (Raad voor de rechtspraak 2014) report available at: www.rechtspraak.nl.

4. IMPLICATIONS OF THE COMMISSION'S AMENDMENT PROPOSAL ON SMALL CLAIMS

4.1 Most Significant Changes

In this section, the Commission's proposal to amend the ESCP Regulation adopted in November 2013 will be discussed briefly.[111] In its Explanatory Memorandum, the Commission emphasises the importance of promoting efficiency of justice in a time of economic crisis.[112] The revision of the Regulation is summarised in eight points.[113] These regard the extension of its scope; the use of electronic communication; videoconferencing and other means of distance communication; a maximum court fee; distance means to pay fees; the translation of Form D (Certificate of Enforcement); information regarding court fees and payment methods; and assistance in filling in the forms.

As discussed above, the Commission concludes that the procedure is still little known and remains underused, and that the rules have several deficiencies.[114] Although the Commission, according to the Explanatory Memorandum, seems primarily to put the blame on deficiencies in the rules rather than on the implementation in Member States for the procedure's lack of success,[115] most of the proposed amendments actually involve implementation. Several of the proposed revisions aim at converting the current rules on the possible use of ICT for the purpose of oral hearings and the taking of evidence to become a genuine obligation on the Member States to have these means available. These obligations have been subject to debate in the negotiations, since Member States are required to invest in ICT infrastructure. For example, the position of the Dutch Government is that the proposed obligations are disproportionate.[116] The government also fears that the obligations interfere with the current national programme to digitalise court procedures and processes. The more stringent obligations regarding information on court fees, payment methods and the available assistance in fact also concern the implementation or the transparency regarding implementation.

It is submitted that there is indeed much to be gained from improving the implementation and imposing obligations combined with providing more detailed rules to this effect. Research in the Netherlands and in several other Member States, discussions with Member States' representatives,

[111] Commission Proposal (n 6).
[112] ibid, Explanatory memorandum, 2.
[113] ibid, Explanatory memorandum, 5.
[114] See section 2.2 above.
[115] See section 2.2 above and Commission Proposal (n 6), Explanatory memorandum, 3.
[116] See *Tweede Kamer* (Parliamentary documents) 2013–2014, 22 112, no 1758 (under point 2).

and experiences shared with judges and practitioners during judicial training sessions and seminars have made clear that a lack of proper implementation and the interaction with domestic civil procedures are particularly problematic.

The Commission's proposal additionally seeks to make an amendment to the EOP Regulation. It is proposed to amend Article 17 EOP Regulation as regards the effect of lodging a statement of opposition. The current provision provides that if the debtor opposes the order for payment, the procedure continues under the national rules of civil procedure. As a first option, the amendment includes the possibility to continue the procedure in accordance with the rules of any applicable simplified procedure, in particular the ESCP procedure. This rule is to be welcomed, since it links the two European procedures in small claims cases.

4.2 Scope of the Regulation

The most prominent part of the Commission's amendment proposal concerns raising the current threshold of application of the Regulation to EUR 10,000.[117] Though most consumer transactions are below the current threshold of EUR 2,000, raising the limit will make the procedure available to SMEs as well.[118] This may in the end also benefit consumers and the overall conduct of the procedure, since the procedure will be used more often, and courts and practitioners will be more familiar with it.[119] It is submitted that raising the threshold is generally to be welcomed. However, at the same time it is important that the conduct of the procedure is improved and that procedural rights are fully guaranteed. With the aim that an oral hearing may not be refused if the value of the claim exceeds EUR 2,000, the proposed amendment of Article 5 is one of the elements that may facilitate important procedural guarantees.[120] As is now clear from the Agreement between the Council and the European Parliament on this proposal, reached on 29 June 2015, by way of compromise the threshold will be raised to EUR 5,000.

The second proposed amendment that would have substantially broadened the scope of the Regulation involves extending the definition of 'cross-border cases' as defined in Article 3 ESCP Regulation.[121] The proposal contains a negative definition. The Regulation shall not apply when all the following elements are present in one Member State alone: (a) the domicile or habitual residence of the parties; (b) the place of performance of the

[117] See Art 1 Commission Proposal (n 6), amending Art 2 ESCP Regulation.

[118] Commission Proposal (n 6), Explanatory memorandum, 5. See also Kramer and Ontanu (n 1) 328.

[119] See Kramer and Ontanu (n 1) 328.

[120] Art 1(4) Commission Proposal (n 6), amending Art 5.

[121] See section 1 above.

contract; (c) the place where the facts on which the claim is based arose; (d) the place of enforcement of the judgment; or (e) the court or tribunal with jurisdiction.[122] Some of the proposed elements are drawn from the criteria applied to establish jurisdiction under the Brussels I Regulation, particularly (a), (b) and (c).[123] However, point (c) is not confined to the place where the harmful event occurred within the meaning of Article 7(2) Brussels I-bis Regulation, but seems to take into account every single fact connected to the claim and that occurred in another Member State. These criteria, as well as the place of enforcement of the judgment (d), may be ambiguous and lead to far-fetched assumptions. In some cases the proposed criteria may require the court to undertake extensive fact-finding in order to establish whether the ESCP is applicable, and lead to discussions as to where facts occurred or where assets are located. In any case, the proposed new definition will blur the distinction between cross-border and domestic cases, and may bring up the old discussion of the legislative competence of the EU under Article 81 of the Treaty of the Functioning of the European Union. However, a case undeniably has some kind of 'cross-border implication' if it fulfils the proposed new criteria. An evident shortcoming of the current definition is that it may force a party to bring its case in a Member State other than the one where both parties are domiciled or habitually resident although the case may have a clear cross-border aspect.[124] As is meanwhile clear, this proposal is not part of the abovementioned Agreement between the Council and the European Parliament and will therefore not be introduced in the new Regulation.

4.3 Maximum Court Fees

Another far-reaching proposal of the Commission is to introduce a limit to court fees. According to the proposal, the court fees may not exceed 10 per cent of the value of the claim, excluding interest, expenses and disbursements.[125] In the event that a Member State charges a minimum fee, this may not be more than EUR 35. This proposal has been debated extensively and met with resistance, since it would affect the financing in the Member States of their judicial systems, many of which are already under pressure.

For example, the Netherlands had responded negatively to this proposal, and has contested EU competence to legislate on court fees.[126] As discussed

[122] Art 1(1) Commission Proposal (n 6), amending Art 2.

[123] See Arts 2, 5(1) and 5(3) Brussels I Regulation (n 19).

[124] eg, that the contract underlying the claims was or needed to be performed in another Member State, or that the tort occurred in another Member State.

[125] Art 2 Commission Proposal (n 6), inserting a new Art 15a.

[126] See *Tweede Kamer* (Parliamentary documents) 2013–2014, 22 112, no 1758 (under point 2).

earlier, court fees are high in the Netherlands, and have been raised substantially in the past few years to make the court system more cost-effective.[127] The minimum fee by far exceeds the current minimum of EUR 77 for natural persons and EUR 115 for legal persons. For low-value claims, the stepwise Dutch court fee system is also clearly not in conformity with the proportional 10 per cent fee. An extreme example is a claim of EUR 500, for which the consumer-claimant would pay EUR 219 and a defendant legal person EUR 462 in fees under the current Dutch rules, whereas EUR 50 would be the maximum fee in this case under the rules proposed by the Commission. Only for claims starting from EUR 2,000 (consumers) and EUR 4,500 (legal persons) is the Dutch fee system closer to or more favourable than the limit proposed to be imposed by the amended regulation. Other Member States, including the United Kingdom, also opposed the proposal on this point, and it is not surprising that this rule is not part of the abovementioned Agreement between the Council and the Parliament. In the text of this Agreement, Recital 10 modestly reads that the fee should not be disproportionate to the claim and that it should not be higher than the court fees charged for national simplified court procedures.

5. CONCLUSION AND OUTLOOK

Though over a dozen European instruments covering a wide range of procedural issues have been established in the meantime, it may be said that European civil procedure is still in its infancy. National civil procedure has developed over the course of centuries and is deeply rooted in the various legal traditions. The European instruments are only of recent date and have to a certain extent been established ad hoc; they arise from policy priorities and are inevitably the result of political compromises. The instruments take various legislative forms, have different legislative techniques and scopes, and establish different degrees of coordination, harmonisation and unification.

The specific European procedures that have been dealt with in this chapter occupy a special position in this spectrum of instruments on various procedural and private international law matters. The EOP and ESCP Regulations were the first to establish genuine European civil proceedings—a novelty that 15 or 20 years ago many proceduralists would have thought impossible. In 2014, the third procedure, the European Account Preservation Order, has been adopted with the aim of contributing to improving cross-border debt collection.[128] Another breakthrough is the establishment

[127] See section 3.1 above.

[128] Regulation (EU) No 655/2014 of 15 May 2014 establishing a European Account Preservation Order procedure to facilitate cross-border debt recovery in civil and commercial matters [2014] OJ L189/59.

of the Council Agreement on a Unified Patent Court that together with the (draft) Rules of Civil Procedure provides an all-encompassing procedural framework for European patent cases.[129]

Although experiences of the past five years of application of the EOP and ESCP have not all been positive, one should realise that any change and innovation in procedural law takes a long time to calibrate. Scepticism in relation to the European procedures, and particularly the ESCP, is understandable. However, it is a fact that the number of cross-border transactions is increasing and so are the disputes resulting from these. Most of the amendments that the Commission has proposed in relation to the ESCP—and that might be followed in the EOP revision—are realistic as to what the bottlenecks are. Nevertheless, one may argue as to how they may and can best be tackled, particularly in times of financial distress.

As regards the European debt collection procedures, there is still a great deal to do to raise awareness. For the European policymaker and legislature, along with the individual Member States, the time has come to invest in the further consolidation, implementation and evaluation of the instruments. Empirical evidence concerning what works and what does not is of the utmost importance, especially where European idealism and economic rhetoric no longer suffice as driving forces. Member States' judges have to adopt a reactive approach in the application of the European civil procedures to fill in the gaps between European and domestic procedure in daily practice. Finally, academics have an important role to play in this, and the recently initiated ELI/UNIDROIT project to establish European rules of civil procedure, is most welcome in this regard.[130] They should contribute to shaping the new architecture and to connecting the dots of European civil procedure.

[129] Council Agreement on a Unified Patent Court [2013] OJ C175/1 and Preliminary Set of Provisions for the Rules of Procedure ('Rules') of the Unified Patent Court (15th draft of 31 May 2014), available at: www.unified-patent-court.org/images/documents/draft-rules-of-procedure.pdf.

[130] See also XE Kramer, 'The Structure of Civil Proceedings and Why it Matters: Exploratory Observations on Future ELI-UNIDROIT European Rules of Civil Procedure' 1 (2014) *Uniform Law Review* 218, 237–38.

7

The Small Claims Regulation: On the Way to an Improved European Procedure?

CRISTIAN ORO MARTINEZ*

1. INTRODUCTION

THE EUROPEAN SMALL Claims Procedure (ESCP), established by Regulation 861/2007[1] (ESCP Regulation), is facing an important challenge: it needs to overcome its staleness and underuse. The ESCP was designed as one of a number of simplified mechanisms offered by EU law for the collection of debt along with the European Enforcement Order (EEO)[2] and the European Order for Payment Procedure (EOP).[3] The ESCP Regulation is the second instrument creating a European procedure, after the adoption of the EOP,[4] but it is the first fully adversarial European procedure. Therefore, the implications of the ESCP for the future development of a European system of civil procedure, going well beyond the mere promotion of 'the compatibility of the rules on civil procedure applicable in the Member States' provided for by Article 81(2)(f) TFEU[5] should not be

* Senior Research Fellow, Max Planck Institute Luxembourg for International, European and Regulatory Procedural Law.

[1] Regulation (EC) No 861/2007 of 11 July 2007 establishing a European Small Claims Procedure [2007] OJ L199/1 (ESCP Regulation). For a general overview of the Regulation see XE Kramer, 'The European Small Claims Procedure: Striking the Balance between Simplicity and Fairness in European Litigation' (2008) 2 *Zeitschrift für europäisches Privatrecht* 355.

[2] Regulation (EC) No 805/2004 of 21 April 2004 creating a European Enforcement Order for uncontested claims [2004] OJ L143/15 (EEO Regulation).

[3] Regulation (EC) No 1896/2006 of 12 December 2006 creating a European order for payment procedure [2006] OJ L399/1 (EOP Regulation).

[4] The EEO Regulation does not establish a fully-fledged procedure but merely a mechanism to certify judgments and other judicial decisions arising out of national procedures. The EOP is aimed at exempting such decisions from *exequatur*, hence making their enforcement in other Member States swifter, but in any event always relying on a previous procedure based on national procedural law.

[5] Treaty on the Functioning of the European Union (consolidated version) [2012] OJ C326/47.

underestimated.[6] The step by step approach followed by the EU legislator for the development of some areas of procedural law (eg, the abolition of *exequatur*) points in this direction: a first, sectorial instrument is likely to end up functioning as a testing ground for the expansion of its principles to other more broad instruments. It is hence necessary to come up with a working, well-founded and balanced procedure from which sound general principles of procedural law, or even a general EU civil procedure, may legitimately stem.[7]

The ESCP, however, is for now far from being an example of a working procedure. Indeed, it has almost become commonplace to highlight the scarce use of the Regulation. Several studies on the impact of the ESCP Regulation, carried out from different perspectives by different institutions and with different methodologies, have reached essentially similar conclusions: this procedure is far from well known, not only by the general public, but also by judges, lawyers and other stakeholders like consumer associations who should be actively involved in its use and promotion.[8] This low degree of awareness has an obvious consequence: the ESCP is rarely used. This trend was confirmed by a study conducted by the Max Planck Institute Luxembourg on the occasion of the consultation launched by the Commission in the spring of 2013. The study gathered published case law from nine Member States[9] to evaluate the impact of the Regulation mainly from a quantitative perspective (the number of cases in which the Regulation was used, or even simply mentioned), but also from a qualitative point of view (assessing how national courts had applied the ESCP and trying to identify some aspects which may have proved to be particularly problematic and lead national courts to misapply the provisions of the Regulation). From a quantitative perspective, the results were rather discouraging. In four of the nine jurisdictions no published case applying the ESCP Regulation could be found.[10] In four other Member States the number of published cases was

[6] The ESCP has been described as an important step towards integration insofar as the adversarial proceeding leading to an EU-wide enforceable title created by the EU legislator is the first entirely European procedure: see B Hess, *Europäisches Zivilprozessrecht* (Heidelberg, CF Müller, 2010) 576.

[7] The sectoral approach has of course its risks: among others, fragmentation, lack of transparency and lack of coherence, as pointed out by XE Kramer, 'Small Claim, Simple Recovery? The European Small Claims Procedure and its Implementation in the Member States' (2011) 12 *ERA Forum* 119, 132.

[8] See eg, ECC-Net, *European Small Claims Procedure Report* (2012), available at: ec.europa.eu/consumers/ecc/docs/small_claims_210992012_en.pdf, 3, pointing to the 'overall lack of awareness among judges and also consumers' as the main problem faced by the Regulation. See also the Special Eurobarometer 395 on the ESCP, published in April 2013, available at: ec.europa.eu/public_opinion/archives/ebs/ebs_395_sum_en.pdf.

[9] Namely Austria, Belgium, Bulgaria, France, Germany, Greece, Italy, the Netherlands and Spain.

[10] This was the case in Belgium, Bulgaria, Italy and Greece. However, in Italy there were a few cases in which the Regulation was cited, but only to confirm the parallelism between its provisions on costs (Art 16 and recital 29 ESCP Regulation) and the equivalent provisions of

very limited, ranging from one to four.[11] The most successful country quantitatively was the Netherlands where the study found around 20 cases.[12] The fact that judgments delivered by lower courts are not always published does of course partially account for these results. But at the same time, the limited number of cases reaching the appellate level[13] indirectly demonstrates that few cases are lodged with lower courts. On the other hand, from a qualitative perspective, the available judgments showed that, in general terms, the use of the Regulation did not pose major practical problems.[14] One could conclude, therefore, that the basic condition for increased use of the Regulation would be to raise awareness among its potential users (consumers, consumer associations, and small and medium-sized enterprises (SMEs)) and among practitioners and authorities entrusted with its application. That, together with the widely repeated increase of the threshold value of a claim,[15] could improve the success of the ESCP Regulation.

However, it is hard to ignore other causes which, besides the lack of awareness of the existence and availability of the Regulation, have had an influence on the current staleness of the ESCP. Some of these questions have been addressed by the Commission in its Proposal for a Regulation amending

national law: see, eg, the judgments of the *Tribunale Foggia Sez II* of 13 March 2012, or of the *Tribunale Roma Sez XII* of 27 April 2012 (DeJure no 529) 17 May 2012, 12 September 2012 and 13 March 2013 (DeJure nos 35028 and 35039–042). Moreover, evidence as to some instances of application of the Regulation could be found in Bulgaria (by means of interviews with judges) and Belgium.

[11] One in France (judgment of the *Juridiction de proximité Angers* of 6 December 2010, no 91.10-438, Juris Data no 2010-025575); two in Germany (judgment of the *Amtsgericht Gießen* of 23 April 2013, BeckRS 2013, 08741 and judgment of the *Amtsgericht Geldern* of 9 February 2011, BeckRS 2011, 03927); three in Spain (order of the *Audiencia Provincial de Alicante* of 27 October 2010, Roj AAP A 159/2010, judgment of the *Audiencia Provincial de Barcelona* of 26 September 2012, Roj SAP B 15507/2012, and order of the *Audiencia Provincial de Madrid* of 19 October 2012, Roj AAP M 16975/2012, in which the Regulation is referred to and allegedly applied, although the Court seems to be actually dealing with an EOP; additionally, the search produced two cases in which the ESCP Regulation was merely cited in *obiter dicta* to support a restrictive interpretation of the domestic concept of 'counterclaim' in line with the EU concept, which requires both claims to be based on the same contract or facts: judgments of the *Audiencia Provincial de Madrid* of 29 October 2008, Roj SAP M 15568/2008, and of 21 February 2011, Roj SAP M 1842/2011) and four in Austria (judgments of the *Bezirksgericht Schwechat* of 12 October 2011, 4 C 580/11v-10, of the *Landgericht Korneuburg* of 28 June 2012, RRa 2013, 53, of the *Landesgericht St. Pölten* of 7 January 2010, 21 R 373/09z, and of the *Landesgericht Feldkirch* of 14 June 2012, 2 R 131/12y).

[12] For an empirical study in the Netherlands based on field research carried out by interviews with judges and legal staff charged with the handling of the ESCP, see XE Kramer and EA Ontanu, 'The Functioning of the European Small Claims Procedure in the Netherlands: Normative and Empirical Reflections' (2013) 3 *Nederlands Internationaal Privaatrecht* 319.

[13] In those Member States where an appeal is available: see below, section 3.

[14] Similarly Kramer and Ontanu (n 12) 322.

[15] Following the path taken by some Member States in their domestic equivalent procedures, the Commission enquired in its consultation of 2013 (question 5) whether the EUR 2,000 threshold currently provided for by Art 2(1) ESCP Regulation for the value of the claim, excluding all interests, expenses and disbursements, should be raised to EUR 10,000.

the ESCP Regulation, presented on 19 November 2013[16] (the Commission Proposal). This Proposal is a consequence of the Commission's obligation, set forth in Article 28 ESCP Regulation, to draft a report reviewing the operation of the ESCP by 1 January 2014 and, if appropriate, suggest proposals for adaptation. The Report on the application of the Regulation,[17] also presented on 19 November 2013 (the Commission Report), assesses rather positively the overall functioning of the ESCP,[18] but acknowledges the need to address some of its shortcomings. Accordingly, the Commission Proposal envisages a number of modifications to the procedure.[19]

In this chapter, I will analyse some of the causes which, as stated before, have arguably influenced underuse of the ESCP. As we will see, the Commission Proposal addresses some of these problematic issues, while others remain unchanged. Where applicable, I will also assess to what extent the amendments suggested by the Commission are likely to solve the problems detected. My contribution will basically revolve around two broad categories of issues: those linked to the scope of application of the ESCP Regulation (section 2), and those relating to the interaction of the Regulation with other EU procedural instruments and with the internal law of the Member States (section 3).

2. PROBLEMS ARISING FROM THE SCOPE OF APPLICATION OF THE ESCP REGULATION

2.1 Territorial Scope of Application

The scope of application of the ESCP Regulation is arguably narrower than it should be. From a material point of view, Article 2(1) of the Regulation

[16] Commission, 'Proposal for a Regulation amending Regulation (EC) 861/2007 of 11 July 2007 establishing a European Small Claims Procedure and Regulation (EC) 1896/2006 of 12 December 2006 creating a European order for payment procedure' COM(2013) 794 final.

[17] Report from the Commission on the application of Regulation (EC) 861/2007 establishing a European Small Claims Procedure COM(2013) 795 final.

[18] The Report addresses the issue of the scarce use of the procedure, although presenting it rather as a problem of imbalance between the number of applications filed in different Member States, and stating that 'this difference in the uptake of the European Procedure seems to be linked in particular with the awareness of its existence and operation. This conclusion is supported by the fact that the number of applications under the Regulation has constantly increased since its entry into application in 2009': see Commission Report (n 17) s 2, 2–3.

[19] The Committee of Legal Affairs of the European Parliament adopted on 26 February 2014 a Working Document on the Proposal, reference no PE529.833v01-00 (EP Working Document) which welcomes and agrees with most of the Commission's suggestions; however, this is only a first general reaction, since the formal deliberations of the European Parliament on the Commission Proposal will only take place under the new formation of the Parliament issued from the May 2014 elections. The European Economic and Social Committee adopted on 25 March 2014 its Opinion on the Proposal, reference no INT/724 (EESC Opinion). This Opinion is in general terms positive, but raises a number of issues for further examination during the legislative procedure.

uses the same wording as most of the procedural instruments adopted by the EU legislator in the field of judicial cooperation in civil matters: it defines the substantive scope of the Regulation by reference to 'civil and commercial matters', with the usual clarification that such notion does not cover revenue, customs or administrative matters, or actions for the liability of the state for acts and omissions in the exercise of state authority (*acta jure imperii*).[20] Also similarly to most of the other procedural instruments, the ESCP Regulation contains in Article 2(2) a list of matters expressly excluded from its scope of application. Some of these exclusions, however, can only be found in this instrument: employment law (Article 2(2)(f)), tenancies of immovable property, with the exception of actions on monetary claims (Article 2(2)(g)), and violations of privacy and of rights relating to personality, including defamation (Article 2(2)(h)).[21] Even without discussing their justification,[22] these express exclusions clearly narrow the material scope of the Regulation. The Commission Proposal does not suggest removing any of them.[23]

Nonetheless, the main reason to describe the scope of the Regulation as being too narrow is not the material, but the territorial perspective.[24] Article 2(1) states that the Regulation only applies to cross-border cases, whereas Article 3 determines which cases should be deemed to be cross-border. According to this provision, the ESCP is limited to a rather narrow category of cross-border cases: those where at least one of the parties is domiciled or habitually resident, on the date in which the claim form is

[20] *cf* Art 1(1) of Regulation (EC) No 44/2001 of 22 December 2000 on jurisdiction and the recognition and enforcement of judgments in civil and commercial matters [2001] OJ L12/1 (Brussels I Regulation), soon to be replaced by Art 1(1) of Regulation (EU) No 1215/2012 of 12 December 2012 on jurisdiction and the recognition and enforcement of judgments in civil and commercial matters (recast) [2012] OJ L351/1 (Brussels I recast Regulation). Only the latter provision contains the *acta jure imperii* clarification which was however already read into the Brussels I Regulation by the Court of Justice of the European Union (CJEU) in Case C-292/05 *Lechouritou* [2007] ECR I-01519; EU:C:2007:102, para 45.

[21] The latter exception can be found in Art 1(2)(g) of Regulation (EC) No 864/2007 of 11 July 2007 on the law applicable to non-contractual obligations (Rome II) [2007] OJ L199/40, which is nevertheless not a procedural but a conflict-of-law instrument.

[22] Employment law was arguably excluded because the simplified, mostly written procedure established by the Regulation, which only allows oral hearings as an exception (see Art 5(1)), could undermine the protection of employees and the thorough assessment of the sensitive issues discussed in employment law disputes: see M Vargas Gómez-Urrutia, 'Artículo 2. Ámbito de aplicación' in F López Simó and FF Garau Sobrino (eds), *El Proceso Europeo de Escasa Cuantía. Comentarios al Reglamento (CE) no 861/2007, del Parlamento Europeo y del Consejo, de 11 de julio de 2007* (Madrid, Dykinson, 2010) 76–77. The other two exclusions were introduced by the European Parliament without giving a justification: see the Report of the Committee on Legal Affairs of the European Parliament, adopted on 7 November 2006, A6-0387/2006 final.

[23] See the proposed new Art 2(3).

[24] In the sense of its applicability to international situations, and not of the purely geographical applicability of the ESCP Regulation which is determined by Art 2(3) together with recital 38. Under these provisions, the Regulation applies in all Member States except Denmark.

received by the court or tribunal with jurisdiction, in a Member State other than the Member State where the court is located. This narrow definition echoes the one we find in Article 3 of the EOP Regulation—a definition which was contested by the Commission upon its adoption.[25] It does not comport, however, with the broader approach retained by most of the procedural instruments adopted by the EU legislator, and in particular by the general instrument on European procedural law: the Brussels I Regulation.[26] It seems therefore advisable to broaden this definition to allow the inclusion of cases where both parties are domiciled or habitually resident in the same Member State where the court is located but which have a cross-border connection (such as the place where a harmful event occurs, the place where a contract is performed or where the object of the contract is located, etc), or even cases where one of the parties is resident or domiciled in a non-EU state and the other party brings the claim before the courts of its own Member State: Article 18(1) of the Brussels I recast Regulation will[27] indeed allow EU domiciled consumers to bring proceedings in the courts of their own domicile against third state defendants. Since the ESCP Regulation does not establish rules on jurisdiction, but implicitly relies on the rules of the Brussels I/Brussels I recast Regulations,[28] a greater coherence between both Regulations would ensue from broadening the scope of the ESCP Regulation. This would also bring about an increase in the application of the Regulation in cases where it would be sensible to have a procedure designed for cross-border litigation.

Some courts have already started to move in this direction: for example, the above-mentioned Max Planck Institute study identified an Austrian judgment of 2012 in which the court, disregarding Article 3, applied the ESCP Regulation to a case where both parties were domiciled in a Member State but the place of arrival of an international flight was in another

[25] Indeed, in its Communication to the European Parliament pursuant to the second subparagraph of Art 251(2) of the EC Treaty concerning the common position of the Council on the adoption of a Regulation creating a European order for payment procedure, COM(2006) 374 final, the Commission regretted 'the limitation [of the European Order for Payment Procedure Regulation] to cases where both parties are domiciled in a Member State' and therefore made the following declaration: 'The Commission declares that the definition of the term "cross-border case" in the context of this Regulation is not an interpretation of the obligation provided for in Article 65 of the Treaty [currently Art 81 TFEU] to limit the action of the Community to matters having cross-border implications, but only one among other possibilities to limit the scope of application of this Regulation in the context of Article 65. It is not necessary to limit the scope of application by reference to a general definition of "cross-border" in the instruments relating to private international law'.

[26] *cf* Case C-281/02 *Andrew Owusu v N B Jackson, trading as 'Villa Holidays Bal-Inn Villas' and Others* [2005] ECR I-1383, EU:C:2005:120, para 26 (applicable mutatis mutandis to the Brussels I Regulation).

[27] From 10 January 2015 onwards (see Art 81 Brussels I recast Regulation).

[28] See below, section 3.2.

Member State.[29] Admittedly this is not very orthodox, and should be plainly qualified as a misapplication of the ESCP Regulation. Nevertheless, it shows that some courts have felt the need to amend the narrow concept of 'cross-border cases' established by Article 3(1) of the Regulation.

Consequently, the amendment suggested by the Commission Proposal to broaden the scope must be positively assessed. According to the proposed new drafting, Article 2(1) of the amended ESCP Regulation would no longer make reference to cross-border cases, and the current Article 3 would be deleted. This is surely a bold suggestion, since the notion of cross-border cases would formally disappear from the Regulation as a positive condition of applicability. Instead, there would be a new Article 2(2) which would determine the non-applicability of the Regulation to purely domestic cases. Hence, the ESCP would no longer be available only if a case is cross-border (using a narrow definition thereof), but would as a matter of principle be available unless a case is not cross-border (using a broad definition of 'cross-border'). According to the amended Article 2(2), the Regulation would not apply

> where, at the time when the claim form is received by the court or tribunal with jurisdiction, all of the following elements, where relevant, are in a single Member State: (a) the domicile or habitual residence of the parties; (b) the place of performance of the contract; (c) the place where the facts on which the claim is based arose; (d) the place of enforcement of the judgment; (e) the court or tribunal with jurisdiction.

The enlargement of the scope of the Regulation would be significant, and the negative method used by the proposed provision, in contrast with the positive method of the current version of Article 3, would definitely be more in line with the broad approach of the Brussels I/Brussels I recast Regulations.[30]

However, some of the criteria suggested in the Commission Proposal may trigger difficulties for their application in concrete cases. For example, the ambiguous reference to 'domicile or habitual residence' in paragraph (a), currently also present in Article 3(1) ESCP Regulation, may give rise to legal uncertainty. The concept of 'domicile' is deferred to the definitions of

[29] Judgment of the *Bezirksgericht Schwechat* of 12 October 2011, 4 C 580/11v-10. The place of arrival was considered relevant as it is one of the relevant places under Art 5(1)(b) Brussels I Regulation (see Case C-204/08 *Peter Rehder v Air Baltic Corporation* [2009] ECR I-6073, EU:C:2009:439, para 43).

[30] For which the existence of an international element is undisputedly required: see Case C-281/02 *Owusu* (n 26) para 25. However, if the amendment is accepted, it would create an arguably unjustified imbalance with the parallel provision of the EOP Regulation which would then remain as the only example of a narrow approach to the definition of a cross-border case. The Regulation creating a European Account Preservation Order to facilitate cross-border debt recovery in civil and commercial matters (Regulation (EU) No 655/2014 [2014] OJ L189/59) will only apply to cross-border cases (Art 2(1)), but its definition thereof (Art 3) is relatively broad.

the Brussels I (Articles 50 and 60) or Brussels I recast (Articles 62 and 63) Regulations. In contrast, the concept of 'habitual residence', placed on an equal footing with the concept of 'domicile', is still an equivocal notion in EU law in spite of its widespread use in private international law instruments. The reference in paragraph (d) to the place of enforcement of the judgment may equally give rise to difficulties especially as regards defendants with assets located in several Member States. Indeed, it may be problematic to determine, at the earliest stage of the procedure ('at the time when the claim form is received by the court or tribunal with jurisdiction') where the judgment will have to be enforced. To benefit from the application of the ESCP, the plaintiff may argue that the judgment might have to be enforced in a Member State other than the Member State where the court is located, where the parties are domiciled or resident and where the contract has to be performed, for example if the defendant tries to prevent enforcement by removing its assets from that Member State. The defendant could then contest the applicability of the Regulation by stating that the assets situated in that Member State at that very moment should be sufficient to face an eventual judgment in favour of the plaintiff. Moreover, the fact that the amount of this eventual judgment is obviously not determined at the moment when the court receives the claim form makes it even more difficult to determine whether assets located in a different Member State will have to be used for the future enforcement.[31]

In any event, these potential difficulties do not prevent a positive assessment of the proposed approach to the cross-border requirement so as to trigger the applicability of the ESCP Regulation. A requirement which should nevertheless disappear sooner rather than later: as long as European procedures remain an optional tool for the claimant, along with the equivalent national procedures, there is no reason why their scope should be limited to cross-border cases.[32] The 'cross-border test' is almost inevitably arbitrary to a greater or lesser extent. Freezing it at the stage of the filing of the claim form by no means ensures that the case will not become a cross-border one. And moreover, as I have just pointed out, some factors used as indicators that a case has a cross-border character (such as the place of enforcement) may give rise to complex discussions.

[31] It should be noted that the likely increase of the value of the claim, currently set at EUR 2,000, will equally increase the difficulties deriving from the potential need to establish the place of enforcement *in limine litis*.

[32] See in this respect the arguments advanced by the Commission, in its initial proposal for a ESCP Regulation, in favour of not limiting it to cross-border cases: 'Proposal for a Regulation establishing a European Small Claims Procedure' COM(2005) 87 final, s 2.2.1, 5–6. Against, see A Fiorini, 'Facilitating Cross-Border Debt Recovery: The European Payment Order and Small Claims Regulations' (2008) 57 *International & Comparative Law Quarterly* 449, 461–63.

2.2 Material Scope of Application

From a broad perspective of the material scope of application, the ESCP is to some extent ill-designed: the Regulation does not seem to be fully aware of its own purpose. In some aspects the procedure is designed as a weak party protection tool, while at the same time it features aspects which do not respond to this protective scope. It is beyond any doubt that the ESCP Regulation applies both to consumer claims and to commercial claims.[33] However, the overall design of the procedure rather seems to have in mind consumers or, more generally, weak parties.[34] Indeed, it is foreseen as a mainly written procedure based on standard forms,[35] in which the court should have a proactive role in supporting the parties;[36] the parties are exempted from legal representation,[37] and will not be required to make any legal assessment of the claim.[38] Against this background, and considering that the purpose of the Regulation is to create a simplified and swift procedure, with reduced costs both in terms of money and time, the EU legislator's decision to limit the availability of oral hearings[39] may be justified. It is clear that the right to a public hearing guaranteed by Article 6(1) of the European Convention on Human Rights and by Article 47 of the Charter of Fundamental Rights of the EU[40] can be subject to some

[33] Recital 4 states that both types of claims lay at the basis of the creation of 'common procedural rules for simplified and accelerated cross-border litigation', foreseen by the Tampere Conclusions of the European Council in 1999.

[34] F Gascón Inchausti, 'Un nuevo instrumento para la tutela de los consumidores y de los créditos transfronterizos: el proceso europeo de escasa cuantía' (2008) 1 *Ius et Praxis* 167, 174. In the Netherlands, the reported case law confirms this impression from an empirical perspective: see Kramer and Ontanu (n 12) 325, stating that B2B cases do exist but they are exceptional.

[35] See Arts 4 and 5 ESCP Regulation, as well as the standard forms contained in Annexes I to III.

[36] eg, Art 4(4) establishes that if the information provided by the claimant is inadequate or insufficiently clear, or if the claim form is not filled in properly, the court must *sua sponte* give the claimant an opportunity to complete or rectify the claim, or to supply further information or documents. The Regulation contains a standard form (form B, set out in Annex II) which is specifically intended for this purpose. Another example of the proactive role that the Regulation expects from national courts is Art 12(2), which establishes an obligation to inform the parties about procedural questions.

[37] Art 10 ESCP Regulation; Art 11 tries to facilitate this exemption by placing on the Member States an obligation to ensure that the parties can receive practical assistance in filling in the forms, an obligation which unfortunately has not been fully complied with by many Member States: *cf* Commission Report (n 17) s 6, 7.

[38] Art 12(1) ESCP Regulation.

[39] Art 5(1) ESCP Regulation determines that an oral hearing shall be held only if the court considers it to be necessary; parties may request an oral hearing, but courts may refuse such a request if they consider that it is 'obviously not necessary for the fair conduct of proceedings'. The refusal must be reasoned and given in writing but it is clear from the wording of this provision that the judge has substantial leeway when it comes to refusing the oral hearing.

[40] Charter of Fundamental Rights of the European Union [2010] OJ C83/389. Recital 9 of the ESCP Regulation expressly declares to take into account the principles recognised by the Charter and encourages national courts to respect the right to a fair trial and the principle of an adversarial process when deciding, among others, on the necessity of an oral hearing.

restrictions.[41] As the Court of Justice of the European Union (CJEU) recently held in relation to the right to a fair trial,

> fundamental rights do not constitute unfettered prerogatives and may be subject to restrictions, provided that the restrictions in fact correspond to objectives of general interest ... and that they do not constitute, with regard to the objectives pursued, a manifest and disproportionate breach of the rights.[42]

The protection of weak parties seems to be a sensible objective to potentially hinder the full right to an oral hearing, along the lines of Article 5(1) ESCP Regulation. However, this does not seem to be so self-evident in purely commercial disputes, which usually present more complex issues and therefore require an oral hearing. It is in this respect that the ESCP Regulation seems not to be fully aware of its own purpose, insofar as it features weak-party protection devices but at the same time intends to be used by commercial parties. Moreover, the Regulation seems to identify the smallness of the claim with its simplicity, both from a legal and from a factual point of view. This assumption justifies the whole procedural configuration of the ESCP. But it is an assumption which in many cases has proved to be wrong. This incongruity would become even more evident if the threshold regarding the value of the claim were to be substantially raised, even up to EUR 10,000, as suggested by the Commission Proposal.[43]

Therefore, since the ESCP Regulation is not only not restricted to weak-party litigation but likely to become more used in commercial litigation, the limitations to oral hearings should be seriously reconsidered. The absence of an oral hearing reduces the possibilities to ascertain the real problem at stake in the litigation, especially if it has some complexity, and also makes it difficult to settle, something which runs against the principle underlying Article 12(3) ESCP Regulation.[44] Finally, the principle of not holding an oral hearing is also questionable in light of the absence of a right to appeal. Article 17 does not guarantee that parties have a right to appeal, but defers

[41] The European Court of Human Rights has determined that a hearing may not be required where there are no issues of credibility or contested facts which necessitate a hearing and the Court may fairly and reasonably decide the case on the basis of the parties' submissions and other written materials: see, eg *Saccoccia v Austria* App no 69917/01 (ECtHR, 18 December 2008) para 73.

[42] Case C-619/10 *Trade Agency Ltd v Seramico Investments Ltd*, EU:C:2012:531, para 55.

[43] See the proposed new wording of Art 2(2). The justification of this amendment is mostly related to allowing an increased use of the ESCP by SMEs: see Commission Proposal, s 3.1.1, 5–6. eg, the EP Working Document, at 3, not only welcomes this proposal, but even suggests raising the threshold slightly higher in order to further enlarge its availability for businesses and consumers. The EESC Opinion, s 4.2.2, has a more nuanced approach and qualifies the proposed threshold as 'rather high'.

[44] According to which 'Whenever appropriate, the court or tribunal shall seek to reach a settlement between the parties'.

this question to domestic law.[45] As far as the Regulation is concerned, a ESCP can simply be a single-instance procedure. In such case, depriving the parties of the right to an oral hearing may pose a serious threat to their right to a fair trial. Under Article 6(1) of the European Convention on Human Rights, in proceedings before a court of first and only instance, the right to a public hearing entails an entitlement to an oral hearing, unless there are exceptional circumstances that justify dispensing with such a hearing.[46] It would therefore be advisable to reconsider whether the system created by the Regulation takes sufficiently into consideration the rights guaranteed by the Convention.

From this perspective, the amendments to Article 5(1) ESCP Regulation suggested in the Commission Proposal seem to go in the right direction. On the one hand, the Proposal emphasises more strongly the exceptional character of the court's ability to hold oral hearings of its own motion. In the current version of Article 5(1) the court can hold an oral hearing only 'if it considers this to be necessary', while under the amended version the court would only be allowed to hold a hearing 'if it considers that it is not possible to render the judgment on the basis of the written evidence submitted by the parties'. This rewording is arguably intended more as a clarification of the status quo than as a reduction of the margin of appreciation of the courts. On the other hand, concerning the possibility for parties to request an oral hearing, the new wording of Article 5(1) would introduce some changes. Unlike in the current situation, courts would not be allowed to refuse such a request in two situations: for claims with a value exceeding EUR 2,000, or where the parties intend to conclude a court settlement and request a court hearing for that purpose. The first condition proposed by the Commission acknowledges the need to improve the procedural treatment of higher-value claims, which are potentially more complex. However, it regrettably leaves untouched the current situation as regards claims not exceeding the EUR 2,000 threshold. Hence, these will continue to be potentially dealt with in a single-instance procedure and without the right to an oral hearing, because the Commission Proposal would not introduce any change in relation to the availability of an appeal. As regards the second condition, the Proposal takes into consideration the pro-settlement rationale of Article 12(3) ESCP Regulation although in a slightly reformulated manner, insofar as it shifts the settlement initiative from the court[47] to the will of the parties.

[45] See below, section 3.1.

[46] *Göç v Turkey* App no 36590/97 (ECtHR, 11 July 2002) para 47.

[47] Art 12(3) ESCP Regulation determines that the court shall seek to reach a settlement.

3. THE INTERPLAY OF THE REGULATION WITH NATIONAL LAWS AND WITH OTHER EU INSTRUMENTS

3.1 Interplay with National Laws

The ESCP Regulation does not establish a fully-fledged procedure, but rather a partial procedure which has to be inserted into the domestic procedural systems, including the judicial structure and organisation, of the Member States. The EU legislator expressly deferred to internal procedural law the definition or regulation of some specific questions which are by no means minor aspects. Thus, Article 21(1) of the Regulation subjects the enforcement procedure to the law of the Member State of enforcement, subject to the respect of Articles 21 to 23; recital 13 defers to national law for the definition of the concepts[48] of 'clearly unfounded' in the context of the dismissal of a claim and 'inadmissible' as regards the dismissal of an application; recital 29 establishes that the costs of the proceedings should be determined in accordance with national law; and finally, Article 17(1) and recital 26 make the availability and time limits of an appeal dependent upon domestic law. The EU legislator also established the existence of some rights which derive directly from the ESCP Regulation but which are not directly regulated by it: for example, Article 18 determines the cases in which the defendant 'shall be entitled to apply for a review of the judgment' given in the ESCP, but does not deal with the review procedure itself. Therefore, this procedure necessarily has to be regulated by the national legislator.[49] More generally, Article 19 sets out a general reference to the law of the Member State where the ESCP is conducted for all the issues which are not directly addressed by the ESCP Regulation. Arguably the EU legislator did not have any other practicable option but to rely on the existing domestic judicial structures and procedures as well as on the general 'coordinating effect' of the principles of equivalence and effectiveness which characterise EU law. However, this complex framework comes at a price.

An example of a problem caused by the reliance of the ESCP Regulation on national law is inconsistencies that can arise as the fallback domestic procedure may not be adapted to the requirements of the ESCP. For instance, in Spain the so-called 'verbal procedure' (*juicio verbal*) has been designated to supplement the ESCP,[50] since it is the judicial track designed for claims of up to EUR 6,000. However, as its name indicates, it is an essentially oral

[48] Used by Art 4(4) ESCP Regulation.

[49] The Commission Proposal suggests introducing an element of harmonisation in the review procedure: according to the wording suggested for a new version of Art 18(2), the time limit to apply for a review would be determined by the ESCP Regulation and no longer by the Member States.

[50] See the 'final provision' (*disposición final*) no 24(2) of the Spanish Law of Civil Procedure (*Ley de Enjuiciamiento Civil*).

procedure which comports rather badly with the written character of the ESCP.[51] On another note, the restrictive approach regarding oral hearings has a negative impact on the taking of 'personal' evidence—ie, statements of witnesses, parties and experts.[52] This poses problems for the integration of the ESCP in some national procedural systems and discourages courts from making use of the Regulation,[53] so that they may end up not advising parties to use the ESCP Regulation or even advising them not to use it.

A striking consequence of the ESCP Regulation's interplay with domestic law can be found in the widely differing systems of review of decisions between Member States. As already pointed out, the ESCP Regulation does not guarantee the existence of a right to appeal: Article 17(1) leaves for the Member States the right to decide whether an appeal is available under their procedural law against a judgment given in the ESCP and, where applicable, what is the time limit to lodge the appeal. This entails an uneven level of protection of rights across the EU, since the decision whether to allow an appeal or not is undoubtedly a core feature of any procedural device. Every legislator clearly has some leeway to decide whether or not to grant an appeal within each procedure; and when it does grant the right, it also has a margin of appreciation to establish the conditions of admissibility of the appeal.[54] However, the decision as to whether or not to grant a right of appeal within one specific procedure—as the ESCP is, or at least claims to be—should not have different outcomes depending on the Member State where it is conducted.[55] The availability of an appeal in the framework of

[51] AJ Valencia Mirón, 'El proceso europeo de escasa cuantía' in A de la Oliva Santos (ed), *Derecho Procesal Civil Europeo. Volumen III: Tutela judicial del crédito en Europa* (Cizur Menor, Aranzadi/Thomson Reuters, 2011) 259, 294. Should the threshold of the value of the claim be raised to EUR 10,000, following the Commission Proposal, the Spanish fallback procedure could end up being split between the 'verbal procedure' (*juicio verbal*) for claims of up to EUR 6,000 and the 'ordinary procedure' (*juicio ordinario*) for claims above EUR 6,000: see arts 249 and 250 of the Spanish Law of Civil Procedure (*Ley de Enjuiciamiento Civil*).

[52] This is clear in Art 9(2) ESCP Regulation, which has a very restrictive stance as regards the taking of expert evidence and oral testimony, making the court's decision dependent upon costs.

[53] Gascón Inchausti (n 34) 196.

[54] According to the European Court of Human Rights in *Luordo v Italy* App no 32190/96 (ECtHR, 17 July 2003) 547, para 85.

[55] eg, an appeal is permitted in Spain (A Bernardo San José, 'Artículo 17. Recurso' in F López Simó and FF Garau Sobrino (eds), *El Proceso Europeo de Escasa Cuantía. Comentarios al Reglamento (CE) no 861/2007, del Parlamento Europeo y del Consejo, de 11 de julio de 2007* (Madrid, Dykinson, 2010) 265, 266–72) or in Italy (E D'Alessandro, *Il procedimento uniforme per le controversie di modesta entità* (Turin, G Giappichelli, 2008) 93), while in Germany it is in principle reserved to claims exceeding a value of EUR 600 (Hess (n 6) 580). On the contrary, appeal is not allowed in France (F Ferrand, 'Procédure européenne de règlement des petits litiges' in S Guinchard (ed), *Droit et pratique de la procédure civile. Droits interne et de l'Union européenne*, 7th edn (Paris, Dalloz, 2012) 888, 891), whereas it is excluded as a matter of principle in the Netherlands, although there is a very limited possibility to lodge an appeal based on jurisdictional issues before the Dutch Supreme Court (Kramer and Ontanu (n 12) 321). For a comparative overview of the situation in most Member States, see HP Mayer et al, *Small Claims*

a European instrument should lie with the EU legislator.[56] The situation is even more paradoxical if we bear in mind that the ESCP Regulation seems to take for granted that an appeal will be available when it establishes that some decisions of the court 'may not be contested separately':[57] this is the case of the refusal of a party's request to hold an oral hearing (Article 5(1)) and of the decision whether a non-monetary claim comes within the scope of the Regulation or else exceeds the claim value threshold (Article 5(5)). If such decisions may not be contested separately, this implies that they can only be contested when the judgment itself is contested—that is to say, by means of an appeal. The right of review granted by Article 18 ESCP Regulation cannot be used in this respect: first, because it is only available for the defendant, whereas the decisions addressed in Articles 5(1) and 5(5) can potentially be contested by either party; and second, because it only applies to a very limited number of grounds, which do not include the reasons according to which these decisions could be contested. Unfortunately, the Commission Proposal does not address this issue, as it does not foresee any change in Article 17(1) ESCP Regulation.[58] It is submitted that the amended regulation should introduce uniform rules on the availability of appeals following the Brussels I model.[59] It could even be conceivable to establish a minimum threshold, stating that appeals would only be possible for claims exceeding a certain (ideally low) amount. After all, the key issue is not so much introducing an unrestricted right of appeal in the ESCP, but rather harmonising its availability across the EU.

3.2 Interplay with EU Instruments

The ESCP Regulation is bound to find its place within the different instruments which comprise the European law of civil procedure.[60] This is only a

Verordnung. Klage, Verfahren, Urteil und Vollstreckung geringfügiger Forderungen in Europa (Munich, CH Beck, 2009) 157–62. This lack of consistency is obviously an open door for *forum shopping*, as pointed out by R Miquel Sala, *El proceso europeo de escasa cuantía* (Cizur Menor, Aranzadi/Thomson Reuters, 2009) 48.

[56] *cf* in this respect Art 43(1) Brussels I and Art 49(1) Brussels I recast Regulation, which determine that decisions which put an end to the first instance of the procedure they regulate 'may be appealed against by either party'. If a mere procedure for a declaration of enforceability (Brussels I) or for a refusal of enforcement (Brussels I recast Regulation) can be appealed as a matter of EU law, then a fortiori a fully European procedure should be subject to the same principle.

[57] Valencia Mirón (n 51), 274.

[58] It only suggests amending Art 17(2) so that the new Art 15a, which caps court fees and enables payment by means of distance payment methods, would apply also to the appellate level.

[59] And of course keeping the principle according to which appeals do not necessarily entail the stay of enforcement: see Arts 15(1), 23 and recital 25 ESCP Regulation.

[60] An example of this is the suggestion to amend Art 17 of the EOP Regulation (see Art 2 of the Commission Proposal) in order to create a procedural bridge between this Regulation and

natural consequence of the ever-growing competence of the EU in the field of judicial cooperation in civil matters. In some cases the relationships between the Regulation and other procedural instruments is expressly stated. This is the case with the EEO Regulation,[61] as regards the methods of service to be used if postal service attested by an acknowledgement of receipt is not possible.[62] In turn, recital 24 defers the calculation of the time limits established by the ESCP Regulation to Regulation 1182/71.[63] In other cases the relationship between the ESCP Regulation and other EU instruments is only implied: for example, Article 6(3) ESCP Regulation implicitly refers to the grounds for refusing the service of a document for linguistic reasons provided for by Article 8(1) of the Service Regulation.[64] But unfortunately, this interplay with other EU instruments can sometimes also hinder the swift application of the ESCP Regulation.

In this respect, the relationship between the ESCP Regulation and the Brussels I Regulation is far from well designed. This is unfortunate, as filing a claim with the competent court is of the utmost importance: indeed, it is the only way to effectively commence the procedure (Article 4(1)) or to fix the moment relevant for establishing the cross-border character of a case (Article 3(3)). The Regulation does not create an obligation for the court to advise the parties in this respect, whereas it does provide for such an obligation for other possible mistakes in the complaint (Articles 4(3) and 4(4)). This is all the more regrettable if we bear in mind that establishing jurisdiction is far from easy even for some sophisticated lawyers; it can thus be close to impossible for plaintiffs who appear before a court without legal assistance. The first problem is that the ESCP Regulation does not expressly mention that jurisdiction should be established by having recourse to the Brussels I Regulation.[65] Fortunately, however, the Brussels I Regulation is mentioned in Section 4 of the standard claim form contained in Annex I of the ESCP Regulation.[66] This Section provides an open list of possible

the ESCP Regulation. This would imply that when a defendant files a statement of opposition in a EOP procedure the case could be transferred not only to a national adversarial proceeding, but also to an ESCP, of course provided that the dispute falls within its scope of application.

[61] EEO Regulation.

[62] See Art 13 ESCP Regulation, esp para (2).

[63] Regulation (EEC, Euratom) No 182/71 of 3 June 1971 determining the rules applicable to periods, dates and time limits [1971] OJ L124/1.

[64] Regulation (EC) No 1393/2007 of 13 November 2007 on the service in the Member States of judicial and extrajudicial documents in civil or commercial matters (service of documents) and repealing Regulation (EC) No 1348/2000 of 29 May 2000 [2007] OJ L324/79. See in this respect Hess (n 6) 581. Unfortunately, courts often do not inform the defendant of his or her right to refuse the service on linguistic grounds although the Service Regulation requires it: see Kramer and Ontanu (n 12) 326.

[65] The Brussels I Regulation is only incidentally referred to as regards the determination of the concepts of 'domicile' (Art 3(2)) and of 'counterclaim' (recital 16).

[66] See Form A, which additionally refers the plaintiff to the website of the European Judicial Atlas and to a glossary of legal terms on the website of the DG Justice.

heads of jurisdiction, which it expressly characterises as non-exhaustive, and simply expects plaintiffs to be able to choose between complex legal concepts such as 'place of performance of the obligation in question',[67] 'place of the harmful event' or even 'domicile of the consumer', without any reference, for example, to the need to establish whether he or she was an active or passive consumer, thus giving the impression that a consumer may sue in his or her own domicile regardless of any other condition. Additionally, since many cases of application of the ESCP Regulation derive from online consumer transactions,[68] the elaborated interpretation of the CJEU as regards the concept of 'activity directed' in the sense of Article 15(1)(c) of the Brussels I Regulation[69] must also be taken into consideration, in spite of the silence of Annex I regarding these matters. To sum up, the extremely misleading drafting of Section 4 may entail serious consequences for the consumer's right of access to justice.[70]

Additionally, it is worth pointing out that that neither the ESCP Regulation nor its Annex C (which contains the standard answer form) invite the defendant to contest the jurisdiction of the court. Since parties may appear without legal representation, this may easily give rise to unnoticed tacit submissions under Article 24 of the Brussels I Regulation.[71] Hence, clear guidelines are needed explaining to the defendant the consequences of entering an appearance without contesting the jurisdiction of the court. Admittedly, the forthcoming applicability of Article 26(2) of the Brussels I recast Regulation will partially remedy this problem, insofar as it places an obligation on the court, before assuming jurisdiction, to inform weak-party defendants of their right to contest the jurisdiction and of the consequences of entering or not entering an appearance. However, as pointed out, this remedy will only be partial, because the rule of Article 26(2) of the Brussels I recast Regulation will not apply in commercial disputes. SMEs not represented by a lawyer may still incur the risk of inadvertently entering an appearance.

Therefore, the establishment of international jurisdiction should be carefully rethought to enhance its working in the interest of potential claimants

[67] Which is not even accurate, since there is no mention of the criteria of Art 5(1)(b) Brussels I (place of delivery of goods/place of provision of services) that take precedence over the rule of letter (a).

[68] As advanced by Miquel Sala (n 55) 83. This has been confirmed by empirical data, eg, regarding the Netherlands, see Kramer and Ontanu (n 12) 325.

[69] See Joined Cases C-585/08 and C-144/09 *Pammer* and *Hotel Alpenhof* [2010] ECR I-12527, EU:C:2010:740; Case C-190/11 *Daniela Mühlleitner v Ahmad Yusufi and Wadat Yusufi* EU:C:2012:542; and Case C-218/12 *Lokman Emrek v Vlado Sabranovic*, EU:C:2013:666.

[70] The EESC Opinion stresses that the forms should be improved in order to make them clearer and easily understandable by all kinds of potential parties: see ss 1.13, 4.1 and 5.3.

[71] The *Goldbet* doctrine of the CJEU would not apply in this case, as there is only one proceeding and—contrary to the European Order for Payment Procedure—contesting the claim does not put an end to the ESCP: see Case C–144/12 *Goldbet*, EU:C:2013:393, not yet published, para 31.

and defendants and especially also weak parties.[72] The information on jurisdictional rules provided in the forms should be substantially improved so as to facilitate its use by parties not represented by a lawyer. The need to prevent unnoticed tacit submissions should also be considered, in addition to the weak-party protection mechanism which the full applicability of the Brussels I recast Regulation will bring about. It would thus be advisable to insert in Annex C a clear indication of the defendant's right to contest the jurisdiction of the court. Unfortunately, the Commission Proposal deals with these issues in an insufficient and unsatisfactory manner: it simply suggests redrafting Article 11 ESCP Regulation so as to establish explicitly that the obligation of the Member States to provide practical assistance to the parties in filling in the forms should cover, among others, the determination of the court with jurisdiction.[73] Member States have so far not been very diligent in complying with this obligation,[74] so the usefulness of this possible new provision remains to be seen. In any event, the problems arise from the drafting of the standard forms (particularly Forms A and C). Consequently, the wording of the forms should be substantially improved.

4. CONCLUSIONS

The Commission Proposal is a good first step towards an enhanced functioning of the ESCP as it addresses some of the issues which have so far curtailed the full working of the Regulation. However, it would be necessary to amend other aspects for which the Commission has either not suggested any change or suggested insufficient adjustments. For example, as regards the narrow territorial scope of the ESCP Regulation, the proposal to enlarge the definition of cross-border cases is positive and would enhance the coherence of the system of EU procedural instruments, in particular given the central role played by the Brussels I/Brussels I recast Regulations. However, some of the criteria advanced by the Commission for the delineation of cross-border cases should be refined. More generally, the possibility of opening the ESCP to purely domestic disputes should seriously be considered.

The ESCP Regulation features weak-party protection devices although its scope includes commercial cases. In addition, in the future it could be extended to disputes of a sensibly high value, up to (or even above) EUR 10,000. This brings about some inconsistencies of which the Commission seems to

[72] See Kramer (n 1) 363, suggesting creating within the ESCP Regulation specific jurisdictional rules for the protection of consumers, similar to Art 6 of the EOP Regulation.

[73] The proposed drafting for a new Art 11(1) would also oblige Member States to assist the parties as regards the question whether the ESCP may be used to resolve the dispute concerned, the calculation of interests and the identification of the documents which need to be attached to the claim.

[74] See Commission Report (n 17), s 6, 7.

be aware, especially when it suggests removing the court's ability to refuse oral hearings requested by a party in cases exceeding EUR 2,000. In any case, the consequences deriving from the principle of not holding oral hearings, especially in combination with the non-mandatory existence of a right to appeal, should be carefully rethought. The Regulation's approach to appeals is moreover a prime example of the severe consequences of deferring many aspects of the ESCP to the internal law of the forum. In order to have a real unitary procedure, as the ESCP should be, it would be necessary to harmonise the availability of appeals and the basic conditions for their admissibility following the example of the Brussels I/Brussels I recast Regulations. This is an issue which the Commission Proposal unfortunately does not even consider.

Enhancing the interplay of the ESCP Regulation with other EU instruments is also important to increase the coherence of the whole system of European civil procedural law. From this point of view, the relation between the ESCP Regulation and the Brussels I/Brussels I recast Regulations can and should be significantly improved. The proposal to provide practical assistance by the Members States in this respect is a first step in the right direction, but the Annexes of the Regulation should be adjusted so as to guarantee the effective protection of the rights of both claimants and defendants.

On the whole, the success of the Regulation depends on a little more than mere publicity and increased awareness. The amendments suggested by the Commission acknowledge this, although there is arguably still room for further adjustments in the ESCP. The legislative process triggered by the Proposal provides the European Parliament and the Council with an opportunity to tackle the issues I have underlined, among others. After all, improving the working of the ESCP could have an important role in the further development of the European system of civil procedural law. This is why it is fundamental to improve its usability and make it well regarded among its potential users and the authorities entrusted with its application. Otherwise, the ESCP may end up being perceived not as a high-quality alternative to the equivalent domestic procedures, but as a mere second best for those cases where the national systems do not provide access to justice at all.

Part IV

Family Law

8

The Nordic Input on the EU's Cooperation in Family and Succession Law: Exporting Union Law Through 'Nordic Exceptions'

MAARIT JÄNTERÄ-JAREBORG*

1. SWEDEN AND FINLAND AS 'BACK-SEAT DRIVERS'

1.1 How a State Can Gain the Reputation of Being a Troublemaker

Sweden applied for EU membership in 1991 and Finland in 1992 in the aftermath of the radically changed geopolitical situation in Europe following the collapse of the Soviet Union and the Iron Curtain. Both states joined the EU on 1 January 1995 (together with Austria). The applications by Sweden and Finland were motivated predominantly by political and economic concerns, whereas the legal implications of membership raised mixed feelings and, in general, much less enthusiasm.

I feel tempted to refer to the two states as 'back-seat drivers', who have not been entrusted with the driving of the vehicle called 'the EU's cooperation in family and succession law' but who feel a need to intervene, often irritating the driver. I aim to analyse whether the interventions by Sweden and Finland have prevented the EU from finding and taking the optimal course or whether, on the contrary, their contributions have enabled the vehicle to stay on the road/on course and to reach the destination in a more stable manner. The reason for this focus is the reputation of the two states as troublemakers in the context of cooperation in family and succession law.

* Professor of Private International Law and International Civil Procedure, Uppsala University; Legal consultant at the Swedish Ministry of Justice; Member of the Curatorium of The Hague Academy of International Law.

This label[1] dates back to the negotiations on the Brussels II Convention,[2] which was subsequently replaced by the Brussels II Regulation[3] and later by the Brussels II *bis* Regulation.[4] Sweden and Finland's decision not to take part in the Rome III Regulation[5] reinforced the reputation of the two states as 'states difficult to negotiate with' and 'half-hearted' Member States.

The requests by Sweden and Finland for the right to apply in their mutual relations a given inter-Nordic convention instead of the regulation in question can be expected to have contributed to this reputation. Such a request has been made each time a family or succession law regulation has been under negotiation. Such requests may, at first sight, appear to be 'legal irritants', reducing the impact of each regulation and raising concerns about 'split loyalties', ie, to the EU on the one hand and the Nordic Region on the other. The exceptions granted to Sweden and Finland as a result of these requests (the Nordic Exceptions) will be dealt with in further detail below.

1.2 Negotiating the Brussels II Instruments

When joining the then pending negotiations on the Brussels II Convention in 1995, the EU's first purely family law instrument, both Sweden and Finland had serious reservations regarding the project's added value. Both states would have preferred measures encouraging all the Member States of the EU to ratify the 1970 Hague Convention on the recognition of foreign divorces and legal separations,[6] and to concentrate on the ongoing

[1] In the Explanatory Report to the Brussels II Convention, Alegría Borrás mentions that the negotiations between the Member States had been very difficult and that they had not been facilitated by new Member States which joined the Union in 1995. While the Austrian position on important issues rarely differed from the mainstream, Sweden and Finland emerged as the troublemakers. This semi-official report by Borrás is published in [1998] OJ C221/27. According to the German delegate to the negotiations, Dr Jörg Pirrung, the Nordic states should be blamed for the adoption of an almost unlimited jurisdiction favouring the plaintiff and forum shopping. J Pirrung, 'Europäische justitielle Zusammenarbeit in Zivilsachen—insbesondere das neue Scheidungsübereinkommen' (1999) *Zeitschrift für Europäisches Privatrecht* 844. As the Brussels II Convention was adopted within the framework of multilateral civil law cooperation within the EU, Denmark participated in its adoption and shared the concerns of Finland and Sweden.

[2] Convention on jurisdiction and the recognition and enforcement of judgments in matrimonial matters, adopted on 28 May 1998.

[3] Regulation (EC) No 1347/2000 of 29 May 2000 on jurisdiction and the recognition and enforcement of judgments in matrimonial matters and in matters of parental responsibility for children of both spouses [2000] OJ L160/19.

[4] Regulation (EC) No 2201/2003 of 27 November 2003 concerning jurisdiction and the recognition and enforcement of judgments in matrimonial matters and the matters of parental responsibility, repealing Regulation (EC) No 1347/2000 [2001] OJ L338/1.

[5] Regulation (EU) No 1259/2010 of 20 December 2010 implementing enhanced cooperation in the area of the law applicable to divorce and legal separation [2010] OJ L343/10.

[6] Convention on the Recognition of Divorces and Legal Separations, concluded at The Hague Conference on Private International Law on 1 June 1970.

negotiations within the Hague Conference on Private International Law on a global child protection convention.[7]

Both states feared that a special Union instrument on marriage dissolution would subject their citizens and inhabitants to more conservative and even oppressive rules, and make divorce proceedings much more complicated and expensive. In their opinion, this spoke for a multitude of jurisdictional grounds. Bearing in mind the differences in divorce law among the Member States of the EU, they feared, in addition, that their own divorce decrees would not be recognised in all the other Member States if granted upon the request of one spouse only. Both states had abolished all divorce grounds (other than a spouse's wish to terminate the marriage) in their domestic law (as well as, in effect, in their private international law through the application of the *lex fori* to divorce claims), in addition to abolishing the institutions of legal separation and marriage annulment.[8]

The concerns of Sweden and Finland were taken into account to a considerable degree in the final drafting of the Brussels II Convention. First, the Brussels II Convention came to include several alternative grounds for divorce jurisdiction, with no hierarchy among them. Second, an explicit provision was included, prohibiting any Member State from refusing the recognition of another Member State's divorce decree, on the ground that the divorce could not have been obtained in that state based on the same facts.[9] Both solutions were inspired, indirectly or directly, by the 1970 Hague Convention,[10] to which both Sweden and Finland are parties. These solutions were later transferred, unaltered in substance, to the Brussels II Regulation of 2000 and the Brussels II *bis* Regulation of 2003.[11]

[7] Convention on Jurisdiction, Applicable Law, Recognition, Enforcement and Co-operation in Respect of Parental Responsibility and Measures for the Protection of Children was concluded at The Hague Conference on Private International Law on 19 October 1996. This Convention, which preceded the Brussels II Convention, came to include a so-called disconnection clause, Art 52(2), aimed in favour of the Brussels II Convention (and the subsequent EU regulations).

[8] The Swedish law reform to this effect took place in 1973. See answer to Q2 (by M Jänterä-Jareborg) in K Boele-Woelki, B Braat and I Sumner (eds), *European Family Law in Action, Volume I: Grounds for Divorce* (Antwerp, Intersentia, 2003) 52–53. The Finnish law reform was carried out in 1988. See answer to Q2 (by M Savolainen) in Boele-Woelki, Braat and Sumner, ibid, 29–30.

[9] This provision is currently found in Art 25 'Differences in applicable law' of the Brussels II *bis* Regulation. Mutual recognition is, explicitly, not made dependent on any kind of harmonisation regarding the applicable choice-of-law rules or substantive law.

[10] The jurisdictional grounds of Brussels II, ie, Arts 3–5, can be compared with the 'indirect jurisdictional grounds' for recognition in Arts 2–5 of the 1970 Hague Convention. Regarding the irrelevance of the grounds for divorce, see in particular Art 6(2) of the 1970 Hague Convention, to be compared with Art 25 in the Brussels II *bis* Regulation.

[11] As we know, this Convention never entered into force but was replaced by the first Brussels II Regulation in 2000, but basically unaltered in substance. It was only in the Brussels II *bis* Regulation, adopted in 2003, that considerable changes took place, since the new Regulation aimed to cover all issues concerning parental responsibilities. The provisions on marriage dissolution remained intact.

1.3 The Enactment of the Rome III Regulation

The apparent resentment in several other Member States against these two solutions encouraging, according to critics, forum shopping and a race to court turned into a driving force behind the adoption of the Rome III Regulation. This Regulation containing 'universally applicable' Union rules regarding the law applicable to divorce and legal separation was adopted in 2010, as the European Union's first 'test case' of enhanced cooperation in the field of civil justice and specifically family law with, originally, 14 Member States on board.

It cannot have been a source of surprise for any initiated body that the Rome III initiative on the unified conflict rules for marriage dissolution was 'a mission impossible' from the very beginning from the Swedish and Finnish points of view.[12] As Sweden's Minister of Justice Beatrice Ask expressed it during the course of the negotiations, 'Our position is solid. As representatives for a modern and equal state in the north of Europe we cannot compromise fundamental rights'.[13] In her statement, 'fundamental rights' refer to the basic right of each spouse to request a divorce without the state imposing any restrictions on this right, ie, the Swedish outlook on divorce law. Even if Sweden was the only Member State to raise a veto against the adoption of the Regulation, Finland shared Sweden's concerns. In a note to the Council (Coreper), Finland raised concerns regarding the EU's choice of enhanced cooperation in a field closely linked to fundamental values and traditions in each Member State.[14] Finland found this unfortunate, because the chosen procedure disregarded the differences between the Member States' outlooks on divorce. Even if Sweden for some reason abstained from a similar statement, it shared Finland's view.[15]

Seen from the point of view of Sweden and Finland, and their reasons for abstaining from the cooperation, the rhetoric of a 'two-speed Europe' indicating the existence of two camps of Member States—a progressive one and a conservative one—makes little sense when related to the Rome III Regulation. It appears to me that those who resented the fact that not all Member States were willing to participate, chose to disregard the underlying complexity of the issues at stake.

1.4 Later Contributions

The EU's later initiatives in the field of cooperation in family and succession law have been less problematic, at least from the Swedish and Finnish

[12] These states could be expected to endorse only a pure *lex fori* approach.

[13] Reported, eg, in *Upsala Nya Tidning* (27 January 2008).

[14] JUSTCIV 128, JAI 583, 11429/10 (Brussels 5 July 2010).

[15] See M Jänterä-Jareborg, 'EU:s internationella familje- och successionsrätt—mot harmonisering eller fragmentering?' (2010) *Europarättslig Tidskrift* 678.

perspective. Irrespective of how well new initiatives have corresponded to their national laws (private international law included), Sweden and Finland have chosen to emphasise the expected practical benefits, the added value from the citizens' point of view, and the compliance of the measures with the principles of subsidiarity and proportionality. Both states accepted from the beginning that the Maintenance Regulation (with Protocol) would require them to accept foreign rules and decisions which went beyond their own outlook, according to which any duty to provide maintenance was restricted to parents in respect of their under-aged children and to interspousal relations.[16] Both states were also ready to accept common rules which are less progressive than those in their national private international law. More choices were, for example, available according to Finland's conflict rules on a deceased person's right to choose the law applicable to succession than according to the EU's Succession Regulation.[17] The forthcoming Regulation on Matrimonial Property Relations is expected to endorse a more limited party choice of law than the one provided by the current universally applicable Swedish and Finnish conflict rules.[18]

In part, of course, this willingness to cooperate might be explained as a necessity considering the prevailing narrow understanding within the EU regarding what qualifies as 'family law'. Neither the adoption of the Maintenance Regulation[19] nor the adoption of the Succession Regulation[20] qualified as family law measures, giving each Member State the right to a veto.[21]

A new test case can, nevertheless, be envisaged. The Commission's proposal for a special regulation concerning registered partners' property relations[22] has been received with mixed feelings by the Member States. In Sweden and Finland, registered partners enjoy the same rights as married couples and

[16] Furthermore, under the domestic laws of Sweden and Finland, a court can only exceptionally grant post-divorce maintenance between the former spouses.

[17] See Code of Succession (40/1965), Ch 26 § 6 (as amended in 2001). These rules continue to apply when the death occurred before 17 August 2015, when the Succession Regulation entered into force.

[18] For Sweden, see Act (1990:272) on international issues concerning the property relations of spouses and informally cohabiting couples, § 3. For Finland, see Marriage Act (234/1929), § 130 (as amended in 2001).

[19] Regulation (EC) No 4/2009 of 18 December 2008 on jurisdiction, applicable law, recognition and enforcement of decisions and cooperation in matters relating to maintenance obligations [2009] OJ L7/1.

[20] Regulation (EU) No 650/2012 of 4 July 2012 on jurisdiction, applicable law, recognition and enforcement of decisions and acceptance and enforcement of authentic instruments in matters of succession and on the creation of a European Certificate of Succession [2012] OJ L201/107.

[21] Art 81(3) of the Treaty on the Functioning of the European Union. See M Jänterä-Jareborg, 'Family Law in the European Judicial Space—Concerns Regarding Nation-State's Autonomy and Legal Coherence' in EJ Hollo (ed), *National Law and Europeanisation* (Helsinki, Suomalainen Lakimiesyhdistys, 2009) 57–58.

[22] Commission, 'Proposal for a Regulation on jurisdiction, applicable law and the recognition and enforcement of decisions regarding the property consequences of registered partnerships' COM(2011) 127 final.

are subject to the same rules (private international law included).[23] Sweden has gone as far as to abolish the institution of registered partnership in connection with a law reform in 2009, which introduced a gender-neutral marriage concept into Swedish legislation. It is an explicit legislative policy that the same rules should always apply to both same-sex and opposite-sex couples, leaving no scope for any kind of *lex specialis* on same-sex relationships. In Finland, as of 1 March 2017, same-sex couples will be able to marry and can no longer register a partnership.[24] It cannot be ruled out that both Sweden and Finland will be opposed to the forthcoming regulation, *if* the adopted final solutions differ significantly from those applicable to spouses. In the pending negotiations, the policy of both states has been to act for the same or essentially similar rules for both spouses and registered partners. More conservative EU states, on the other hand, might be opposed towards the proposal if it endorses solutions very similar to those applicable to the property relations of spouses. If enhanced cooperation is chosen as the model with which to proceed, the rhetoric of a 'two-speed Europe' will once again not adequately reflect the reasons given by the Member States for not participating. Whatever decision a Member State makes, it will require a complex balance between national conceptions of justice and European goals. Considering that registered partnerships are an institution which was originally (in Denmark in 1989) created for *same-sex couples*, and that such couples are not recognised in all Member States, the adoption of the Regulation can, indirectly, be expected to put pressure on those Member States which are opposed to formalising same-sex unions. This kind of an impact would as such be politically welcomed in the Nordic states.

All in all, the input of Sweden and Finland concerning the more recent regulations would appear to have been at an average level or even above average. Both were among the group of Member States which pleaded in favour of an increased certainty regarding the concept of habitual residence in the EU's Succession Regulation, for example, by linking it to a fixed minimum period of residence (such as a duration of five years or, at least, two years). As we know, this proposal was not adopted, but the states' concerns are to some extent met in the preamble of the Regulation.[25] Nor were Sweden

[23] See K Boele-Woelki and A Fuchs (eds), *Legal Recognition of Same-Sex Relationships in Europe. National, Cross-Border and European Perspectives*, 2nd edn (Antwerp, Intersentia, 2012) in particular contributions by I Lund-Andersen and M Jänterä-Jareborg. In the Nordic countries' domestic laws, the institute of registered partnership is reserved for same-sex couples.

[24] A bill to this effect was adopted by the Finnish Parliament in December 2014. Finland was the last of the five Nordic states to extend its legal marriage concept to same-sex couples. Same-sex couples' access to marriage has made the (same-sex) institution of registered partnership superfluous in the Nordic states' domestic laws. The domestic enactments on registered partnerships continue, however, to apply to previously concluded registered partnerships (which have not been converted into a marriage).

[25] Preamble to the Regulation, recitals 23–25.

and Finland convinced that the law applicable to succession should cover the procedural aspects of estate administration, in addition to matters of substantive law, due to their domestic law systems of estate management.[26] They needed to retrace their steps also in this respect.[27]

1.5 Requests for Nordic Exceptions

In one specific respect, Sweden and Finland have set their joint footprint on each of the family and succession law regulations they have participated in. Each of these regulations includes, namely, an explicit provision mandating Sweden and Finland to apply, in their mutual relations, certain provisions in a given inter-Nordic convention, instead of the relevant regulation. These concessions, often called 'Nordic exceptions', originate from requests by Sweden and Finland, made during the negotiations.

I indicated above (section 1.1) that these requests have contributed to the reputation of the two countries as half-hearted partners in EU cooperation on family and inheritance law. What lies behind the requests from the two states, and how have these requests been met by the EU? What is the effect of the concessions granted on the EU's vision of a common European area of justice?

In the following section, my focus will be on the Nordic exceptions. I wish to show that the exceptions granted have not been detrimental to the visions of the EU. On the contrary, the EU has in this manner in part exported its rules to three non-participating states, namely Denmark, Iceland and Norway, to be given effect within the application of inter-Nordic conventions (in their mutual relations and in relation to Sweden and Finland).

2. INTER-NORDIC CONVENTIONS ON CROSS-BORDER FAMILY OR INHERITANCE LAW

2.1 Background

Since the early 1930s, the five Nordic countries, ie, Denmark, Finland, Iceland, Norway and Sweden, have adopted conventions for their mutual relations containing rules on the various aspects of private international law, in some cases following the adoption of harmonised Nordic

[26] When a person dies, his or her assets are not immediately transferred to the heirs (etc). Instead, the estate is regarded as a legal subject of its own, governed by special rules on administration until the estate is divided between the heirs.

[27] Art 29 of the Succession Regulation tries to meet the concerns of Sweden and Finland to some extent. The provision has, however, been drafted in an extremely complicated manner. Opinions can be expected to become divided on how it should be interpreted and applied.

substantive law legislation.[28] The inter-Nordic conventions have from the beginning aimed to facilitate the mobility of Nordic citizens within the Nordic region, and the administration of justice in such cases. The criteria for the applicability of each convention vary to a certain extent, depending on the subject matter. Normally, however, relevant connecting factors must exist, with at least two of the (Nordic) countries, usually in the form of both citizenship in one of the states and habitual residence in another.[29] According to the main common principle of the conventions, jurisdiction is vested in the Nordic state of habitual residence. Correspondingly, the rules on choice of law refer to the law of the Nordic state of habitual residence. The applicable law changes either automatically, when a Nordic citizen assumes habitual residence in another Nordic country, or after a certain period of residence in the new state. Decisions by a competent authority in any one of the (Nordic) countries (if covered by an inter-Nordic convention) are automatically recognised in the other (Nordic) states and are directly enforceable there.

2.2 Topicality: Civil Justice Cooperation in the EU

The Nordic countries have had a common labour market since 1955, but the mobility of the citizens in the region dates much further back. Once the EU initiated measures in the fields covered by the inter-Nordic conventions in family and succession law, the Nordic countries appointed a working party to compare and evaluate the inter-Nordic rules with the proposed EU measures.[30] The structure and basic principles of the conventions (see above section 2.1) were found to be solid and, in certain respects, essentially superior to those under consideration in the EU. This relates in particular to the system of mutual or automatic recognition and the enforcement of judgments. The following quotation from a 2011 joint proposal by Finland and Sweden to the EU working party in charge of the drafting of the Succession Regulation captures the concerns of the two countries about changes for the

[28] In family law this cooperation reached its peak in the 1920s, with the result that in some fields, in particular with regard to marriage, the legislation in the Nordic countries became almost uniform.

[29] When the Conventions were drafted, the eastern Nordic countries (Sweden and Finland) followed the principle of nationality in cross-border family and inheritance matters, whereas the western Nordic countries (Denmark, Iceland and Norway) adhered to the principle of domicile. These two approaches were accommodated by focusing on Nordic citizens with their habitual residence in another Nordic country, prioritising the principle of habitual residence.

[30] This task was given to the inter-Nordic working group in matters of family law which has existed since the early 1990s. Maarit Jänterä-Jareborg has been a member of this working party since 1995.

worse if Sweden and Finland in their mutual relations were to be covered by Union rules:

> Having to introduce less flexible rules and, not least, rules on *exequatur* after more than 70 years without such provisions would send the wrong message to our citizens on the benefits of further EU integration, and we are strongly opposed to this.[31]

In other words, how would it affect the legitimacy of EU cooperation on civil law if restrictions to mutual trust had to be introduced just because EU regulations, due to greater diversities between EU Member States, are not able to enhance a corresponding trust? It is also possible to identify a concern regarding a threat towards continued inter-Nordic unity, hampering mobility between the Nordic countries.[32] The request for the Nordic exceptions, by Sweden and Finland, in each of the EU regulations adopted, must be seen against this background (section 3). A corresponding request is pending regarding the forthcoming regulation on the property relations of spouses.[33]

3. THE NORDIC EXCEPTIONS IN THE REGULATIONS ON FAMILY AND SUCCESSION LAW

3.1 The Relationship Between the EU Regulations and Existing International Conventions

All of the EU regulations adopted include provisions on the relationship between each regulation in question and existing international conventions,

[31] Brussels, 4 November 2011, 16386/11, LIMITE, JUSTCIV 290, CODEC 1893.

[32] Over the years, I have attended several hearings in the Swedish Parliament on whether special Nordic rules can be regarded as entailing an added value. Each time I have been able to observe the politicians' (irrespective of political party) unreserved support for such rules in cross-border matters of family and inheritance law. Facilitating citizens' mobility between the states is an important political concern. See also K Kjaerheim Fredwall, 'Nordisk konvensjon om arv och dødsboskifte—till nordisk nytte?' (2013) 517 *Utviklingen i nordisk arverett—tegn i tiden, TemaNord* 52.

[33] No corresponding request has been made regarding the proposed regulation on the property relations of registered partners. The explanation is that registered partnerships are not covered specifically by any of the inter-Nordic conventions. This, in turn, finds its explanation in the fact that the institution of registered partnership did not evolve in Nordic legal cooperation. Instead, each Nordic state acted on its own. The enactments (adopted between 1989 to 2001) follow the original Danish model. See I Lund-Andersen, 'The Danish Registered Partnership Act', 13–23; M Savolainen, 'The Finnish and Swedish Partnership Acts—Similarities and Divergencies', 24–40 and M Jänterä-Jareborg, 'Registered Partnerships in Private International Law: The Scandinavian Approach', 137–58, all in K Boele-Woelki and A Fuchs (eds), *Legal Recognition of Same-Sex Couples in Europe*, European Family Law Series Vol 1, (Antwerp/Oxford/New York, Intersentia, 2003). For more recent Scandinavian developments, see the book's second edition, K Boele-Woelki & A Fuchs (eds), *Legal Recognition of Same-Sex Relationships in Europe, National, Cross-Border and European Perspectives*, European Family Law Series Vol 32 (Cambridge/Antwerp/Portland, Intersentia, 2012).

even if the solutions chosen differ. The position of the Brussels II *bis* Regulation is to replace the conventions applicable in the Member States.[34] The Maintenance Regulation, on the contrary, gives priority to existing conventions, unless the mutual relations between Member States are at stake.[35] The same applies under the Succession Regulation.[36] The stipulations regarding the Nordic exceptions are found in this context. Each of the three regulations has an explicit provision concerning how it relates to a given inter-Nordic convention, in the mutual relations between Sweden and Finland. In the next sections, I will comment on each of the Nordic exceptions that have been granted and their impact on the common area of justice within the EU.

3.2 The Outcome of the Requests for Nordic Exceptions

3.2.1 The Brussels II bis *Regulation*

The precedent for granting inter-Nordic exceptions was created in the Brussels II Convention of 1998 and transferred unchanged to the first Brussels II Regulation and, later the Brussels II *bis* Regulation.[37] According to this provision, Finland and Sweden have the option of declaring that the (so-called) 1931 Nordic Marriage Convention[38] will apply, in whole or in part, in their mutual relations, instead of the rules of the Regulation.

The exception granted is tricky in several respects. It has enabled Sweden and Finland, once they made the required declaration, to continue applying the more simple rules of recognition in the 1931 Convention compared with those in the Brussels II instruments. The relevant content of the Convention is an automatic recognition which cannot be refused on any grounds.[39] This continues to apply between Sweden and Finland. The exception granted does not cover *exequatur* proceedings. Enforcement between the Nordic countries of, for example, judgments on custody and contact with children is regulated in another inter-Nordic convention from 1977, which was not included in the exception, contrary to the request made by the

[34] See Art 59.

[35] See Arts 75(1)–75(2).

[36] See Arts 69(1)–69(2).

[37] Art 38 of the Brussels II Convention, Art 36(2) of the Brussels II Regulation and Art 59(2) of Brussels II *bis* Regulation.

[38] The Convention between Denmark, Finland, Iceland, Norway and Sweden containing private international law provisions on marriage, adoption and guardianship, concluded in Stockholm on 6 February 1931. Because of the dominance of the provisions on marriage, this Convention is commonly referred to as 'The Nordic Marriage Convention'. Occasionally, the title 'Nordic Family Law Convention' is also used.

[39] See Art 22 of the 1931 Convention. In case law see, eg, the decision by the Swedish Supreme Court *NJA 1978 C 480*, making it clear that recognition cannot be refused on the grounds of public policy *(ordre public)*.

two countries.[40] As a result, *exequatur* proceedings in accordance with the Brussels II *bis* Regulation became applicable between Finland and Sweden. A further limitation to any priority of inter-Nordic rules is subject to the interpretation of the concept of 'civil law matters', as established by the Court of Justice of the European Union (CJEU) in respect of issues concerning parental responsibilities to be covered by the Regulation.

Two preliminary rulings of the CJEU in cases concerning child protection with a Swedish–Finnish connection, namely case C-435/06 and case C-523/07, both delivered upon a referral from the Finnish Supreme Administrative Court, make it clear that unless otherwise provided, the Brussels II *bis* Regulation is exclusively applicable between the two states. According to these rulings, placement orders taking children into care (outside the parental home) without the consent of the children's parents, qualify as 'civil law matters' under the Brussels II *bis* Regulation. This prevents the application of harmonised inter-Nordic rules on the enforcement of (public law) care orders, in accordance with an agreement between the Nordic countries from 1970.[41] This interpretation was contrary to the expectations in Finland and Sweden regarding the scope of application of the Regulation, and one which they had not taken into account.[42] Due to this 'miscalculation', no request for a corresponding exception was made during the negotiations. The outcome from a Swedish–Finnish perspective entails that informal and simple rules, which do not require *exequatur*, have been replaced by more complicated EU rules.

The right for a continued application of the 1931 Convention was, furthermore, made conditional on that:

(i) the principle of non-discrimination on the grounds of nationality between citizens of the Union is respected; and
(ii) the rules on jurisdiction in any future agreement between Finland and Sweden and related to matters governed by the Regulation are in line with those laid down in this Regulation.[43]

[40] The Convention of 11 October 1977 between Denmark, Finland, Iceland, Norway and Sweden on the recognition and enforcement of judgments on civil and commercial matters. As a framework convention the 1977 Convention has enabled each contracting state to implement it in accordance with its own preferences. Iceland has not ratified this Convention. In relation to Iceland, the Convention's predecessor from 1932 continues to be applicable.

[41] These rules aim primarily to facilitate the return to care in an institution in another Nordic country for people on the run, but also apply to (public law) care orders made in any of the Nordic countries.

[42] See K Boele-Woelki and M Jänterä-Jareborg, 'Protecting Children Against Detrimental Family Environments Under the 1996 Hague Convention and the Brussels II *bis* Regulation' in K Boele-Woelki et al (eds), *Convergence and Divergence in Private International Law, Liber Amicorum Kurt Siehr* (The Hague, Eleven International Publishing, 2010) 143–45.

[43] Furthermore, contrary to the generally applicable prohibition to review the jurisdiction of the Member State of origin, such a review appears to be obligatory in every EU Member State whenever the judgment originates from Sweden or Finland, see Art 59(2)d.

Even if the concession due to its narrowness was a disappointment from a Nordic perspective, the countries concluded that the advantages outweighed the disadvantages. As the quotation above shows, the exception granted was made conditional on two grounds. According to the second condition above, the future inter-Nordic rules (on jurisdiction) must be in line with the Union rules. The Nordic countries saw the advantages of this. It obliged them to modernise the existing inter-Nordic rules. Consequently, in 2001, the rules of the 1931 Convention on jurisdiction and *lis pendens* were remodelled on the Brussels II Regulation. The revised rules apply in situations where both spouses are both citizens of and habitually resident in the contracting states.[44] The Nordic countries considered this combination of connecting factors sufficient to exclude any alleged discrimination on the basis of nationality and, thus, in conformity with the first condition.

3.2.2 The Maintenance Regulation

According to Article 69(3), the Maintenance Regulation does not preclude the application of the 1962 Nordic Convention on the recovery of maintenance, due to the said Convention's 'simplified and more expeditious procedures' and its system on 'legal aid which is more favourable' than that provided in the Regulation. The application of the Convention may not, however, deprive the defendant of certain protection, specifically guaranteed by the Regulation.[45]

The exception granted is the most generous of the Nordic exceptions.[46] From the point of view of Sweden and Finland, it is of great practical relevance. The Nordic countries recover more maintenance payments from the other Nordic countries than from any other foreign state, which illustrates both how common it is for families to be split among the Nordic countries and the effectiveness of the 1962 Convention.

Until the adoption of the Maintenance Regulation, jurisdiction in issues of maintenance was covered by the Brussels I Regulation (earlier Brussels I Convention). Since the Brussels I and Lugano instruments corresponded to each other, the Nordic countries agreed already in 2000 to repeal the rules on jurisdiction in the 1962 Nordic Convention in favour of these common EEA rules. This is an additional example of the impact of European civil law cooperation.

[44] The revised rules on jurisdiction in matrimonial matters and matters of parental responsibility of the Nordic Marriage Convention still reflect those of the first Brussels II Regulation.

[45] Art 69(3) refers in this respect to Art 19 (right to apply for a review) and to Art 21 (refusal or suspension of enforcement).

[46] Art 69(1) starts by giving priority to existing conventions. Para 2 declares, however, that the Regulation shall take precedence in relations between Member States, whereas para 3 grants a special, favourable status to the inter-Nordic Maintenance Convention.

3.2.3 The Succession Regulation

Articles 75(1)–(2) of the Succession Regulation provide that international conventions to which one or more Member States were party at the time of the adoption of the Regulation remain unaffected, unless they were concluded exclusively between two or more Member States. The generally drafted provision is followed by a specific stipulation in Article 75(3), according to which Sweden and Finland are not precluded from applying, in their mutual relations, provisions in the inter-Nordic Convention on Inheritance of 2012, as regards procedural aspects of estate administration, and simplified and more expeditious procedures for the recognition and enforcement of judgments. The drafting of this provision raises several concerns.

The exception granted refers to a convention from 2012 on the amendment of the 1934 Convention, an amendment which had not yet entered into force in the states in question. The amended convention was adopted and signed just before the Succession Regulation, on 1 June 2012. It is modelled on the conflict rules of the Succession Regulation,[47] but with the exception of estate administration which continues to be governed by the *lex fori* (as in the 1934 Convention). From the Nordic perspective, estate administration is largely about proceedings whereby the application of the *lex fori* has practical advantages. The original plan of having the revised rules enter into force simultaneously with the Succession Regulation, ie, on 17 August 2015 was not feasible, due to certain unexpected events delaying the ratification procedures.[48] Instead, the 2012 Convention entered into force on 1 September 2015, following ratification by the five states.

I have previously mentioned (section 1.4 above) that Sweden and Finland would have preferred the procedural aspects of estate administration to be governed by the law of the state where the administration of the deceased person's estate takes place. The Succession Regulation, on the other hand, entails that 'succession as a whole' under the law applicable to succession is to be determined on the basis of the deceased person's last habitual residence (Article 21) or his or her choice of the law of nationality (Article 22). In their mutual relations, thanks to the exception granted, Sweden and Finland will be able to distinguish between the law applicable to 'substantive issues' and

[47] Negotiations for a revision of the 1934 Convention were initiated in 2006, and a draft Convention was presented in 2009, approximately at the same time as the proposal by the Commission on a Succession Regulation. Once the Member States had reached an agreement on the final content of the Regulation, the Nordic draft Convention was adjusted to the Regulation. Concerning the content of the contemplated but abandoned draft of inter-Nordic rules on inheritance, see M Jänterä-Jareborg, 'Inter-Nordic Exceptions in EU Regulations on Matters of Family and Inheritance Law' in AL Verbeke et al (eds), *Confronting the Frontiers of Family and Succession Law, Liber Amicorum Walter Pintens* (Antwerp, Intersentia, 2012) 743–45.

[48] These include the unexpected Danish parliamentary election in June 2015, delaying the ratification.

the law applicable to 'procedural aspects'. They may also continue to follow the inter-Nordic rules on recognition and enforcement, when asked to enforce each other's judgments.

An explanation for the Nordic countries' interest in a revision of the inter-Nordic Inheritance Convention, in accordance with the conflict rules in the EU's Succession Regulation, can be found in their wish to maintain where possible a continued inter-Nordic unity of assessment of succession.[49] In the amended convention, Finland and Sweden explicitly undertake to give precedence to the Succession Regulation in all respects, unless otherwise provided. In essence, this means that they will apply the rules on jurisdiction and choice of law in the Regulation also in relation to the three other Nordic countries (with the exclusion of procedural aspects of estate administration). This demonstrates a highly pragmatic approach on behalf of Sweden and Finland and a loyalty towards the EU's visions, accepted as necessary by the other Nordic countries.

3.2.4 The Marital Property Regulation

In a Note dated September 2013 to the working party in charge of the planned regulations on the property relations of spouses and registered partners, the Finnish and Swedish delegations pleaded for a Nordic exception in favour of the continued application, in the relations between Finland and Sweden, of the rules in the previously mentioned 1931 and 1977 Conventions.[50] The request was drafted following the wording and the terms of the exception granted in the Brussels II instruments.

This request exceeds the scope of the exceptions previously granted to the two states. For the first time, modernised inter-Nordic conflict rules are at stake, adopted as late as in 2006 in the form of an amendment to the 1931 Convention. These rules differ in several relevant respects from the planned EU rules, in the light of the Commission's proposal from 2011.[51] The most striking difference between the inter-Nordic conflict rules and those of the forthcoming regulation is probably the Nordic solution of full mutability of the law which is applicable, once the new habitual residence has lasted for two years in the new Nordic country of habitual residence, unless the

[49] See the report by the working party in charge of the 2012 reform, Den nordiska konventionen om arv, testamente och boutredning (antagen i Köpenhamn 19.11.1934), En översyn av konventionsregleringen föreslagen av den nordiska expertgruppen för familjerättsfrågor (2013) 528 TemaNord 31. See also M Jänterä-Jareborg, 'Överenskommelsen av den 1 juni 2012 om ändring av den nordiska arvskonventionen', Utviklingen i nordisk arverett—tegn i tiden (2013) 517 TemaNord 78 and Kjaerheim Fredwall (n 32) 62.

[50] JUSTCIV 191, 13543/13 (Brussels, 30 September 2013).

[51] Commission, 'Proposal for a Regulation on jurisdiction, applicable law and the recognition and enforcement of decisions in matters of matrimonial property regimes' COM(2011) 126 final.

spouses agree otherwise.[52] On the other hand, according to the EU proposal, the principle of immutability applies unless the spouses agree otherwise.[53] The options in the proposed regulation regarding a party choice of law are more limited than those of the Convention.[54] The inter-Nordic conflict rules are, however, not universal but drafted in such a manner that they can only lead to the application of the law of the referred Nordic country.

The revised inter-Nordic conflict rules entered into force in the five countries in 2008. Bearing in mind both their novelty and the fact that they have been carefully adjusted to the (reasonably harmonised) domestic laws of the Nordic countries, the interest of the Nordic countries in revisiting these rules in order to bring them in line with the forthcoming EU rules cannot be taken for granted. Equally, in the light of previous negotiations, it is unlikely that the EU will be willing to accept that Finland and Sweden in their mutual relations are able to apply these rules.[55] The other parts of the request, which focus on aspects of recognition and enforcement in accordance with the Nordic Conventions, should be less controversial from the EU perspective since corresponding exceptions have been granted in the other regulations.

3.3 Impact Analysis

The requests by Sweden and Finland to be permitted to apply inter-Nordic rules in their mutual relations instead of an EU regulation have been met only in part, indicating an irritation on behalf of the EU and its other Member States. Swedish and Finnish delegates to the negotiations have reported that considerable difficulties have prevailed regarding gaining any understanding for the requests for exceptions.[56] This applies even in cases where the Nordic countries have mutually achieved what the EU is aspiring to achieve, namely the direct recognition and enforcement of the other states' judgments due to the long since prevailing mutual trust.

[52] On the content of the inter-Nordic rules on marital property, see Jänterä-Jareborg, 'Inter-Nordic Exceptions' (n 47) 746–49. See also E Meurling, 'Less surprise for spouses moving within the Nordic countries? Amendments to the 1931 Convention on Marriage' (2009) 11 *Yearbook of Private International Law* 385–94.

[53] Art 17 of the Proposal (n 51).

[54] Arts 16 and 18 of the Proposal (n 51). On the other hand, according to the proposed Regulation, the spouses may choose whether their choice-of-law agreement, concluded during the marriage, shall cover the whole of their property relations or only have effect for the future.

[55] Both states remain bound by the 2006 Amendment Convention (to the 1931 Convention), in relation to Denmark, Iceland and Norway, which will delimit the scope of application of the EU conflict rules. Art 351 TFEU remains, nevertheless, problematic in this context.

[56] See M Helin, *Suomen kansainvälinen perhe- ja perintöoikeus* (Helsinki, Talentum, 2013) 687 on the Finnish perspective.

Two of the three concessions granted so far were made conditional on a future law reform in a relevant inter-Nordic convention, to be modelled on the EU rules. This, if anything, demonstrates how seriously the Union takes its mission to develop a common European area of justice. From the Union's point of view, the Nordic cooperation must respect the principles of the Community legal order. As a result, three additional states, namely Denmark, Iceland and Norway, are now in part covered by rules modelled on the EU regulations insofar as inter-Nordic relations are at stake. This adjustment of the existing inter-Nordic conventions has taken place either after the adoption of a regulation within the EU, which was the case with the rules on jurisdiction regarding marriage dissolution in the 1931 Convention, or in anticipation of measures to be taken by the EU, as in the case of the 2012 amendment Convention on Inter-Nordic Inheritance. In essence, this means that the EU has succeeded in exporting its own rules to three non-participating states, through the Nordic exceptions granted to Sweden and Finland. The Nordic countries have gained a safeguarded unity of approach regarding inter-Nordic situations, in accordance with modernised rules corresponding to what applies within large parts of Europe. These outcomes are well in line with the spirit of Article 351 TFEU, which obliges Member States to take all appropriate measures to eliminate any incompatibilities between Union law and international agreements with third countries. It appears not to be far-fetched to expect that preliminary rulings by the CJEU will have a spin-off effect on the application of the corresponding inter-Nordic rules.[57]

4. CONCLUDING REMARKS

The aim of this chapter has been to critically evaluate the contributions of Sweden and Finland within EU cooperation on family and succession law. The two states wielded considerable influence in the final drafting of the (first) Brussels II instrument. They objected to the adoption of the Rome III Regulation, which would have undermined their previous achievements. This opposition was legitimate, considering each Member State's right of veto in EU cooperation on family law and that fundamental rights were at stake from their own point of view. The actions of Sweden and Finland have contributed to the creation of a more 'divorce-friendly' Europe, which I believe best meets the expectations of European citizens. Both states have welcomed the later initiatives by the EU and have played an active role in the negotiations.

[57] An example could be rulings by the CJEU on a deceased person's habitual residence.

The Nordic exceptions in the regulations adopted granting Finland and Sweden the right to apply a given inter-Nordic convention instead of the corresponding EU regulation may, initially, appear to be 'legal irritants', reducing the impact of each regulation. Upon a closer analysis, the concessions have turned out to be very limited in scope. Besides, under general EU law the level of rights guaranteed by EU law cannot be downgraded. The requests for exceptions have provided an opportunity for the EU to take an explicit position, on the aimed impact of each regulation on existing inter-Nordic conventions. From this perspective, the Nordic exceptions can be regarded as clarifications or even restrictions to what would otherwise follow from the general rules of treaty law bearing in mind that the inter-Nordic conventions according to usual treaty law qualify as multilateral conventions. All in all, Sweden and Finland and the other Nordic countries have accepted the outcomes and used them to their mutual advantage. Inter-Nordic situations are, as a result, largely governed by rules essentially similar to those of the EU. The added value, in general European terms, is an increased predictability and legal certainty, due to the achieved unity of approach.

It is important to emphasise that the exceptions granted have not been detrimental to the EU's visions. On the contrary, the common area of justice has reached beyond the participating EU Member States, without any special efforts by the EU to export its own rules. It remains to be seen what scope, if any, there can be left for mutual actions between the Nordic states considering the European Union's continuously increasing competence within cross-border family and succession law (and related areas).

9

The European Certificate of Succession: Portrait of a New Instrument in European Private International Law

BJÖRN LAUKEMANN*

1. INTRODUCTION

INCREASINGLY, EU CITIZENS leave their country on a temporary or permanent basis. This fundamental right of free movement is currently enjoyed by some 12 million people. Put differently, 450,000 successions (10 per cent of the annual total), with an estimated value of EUR 120 billion, contain a cross-border element[1]—the actual number is likely to be significantly higher. There are multiple reasons for this phenomenon. Denouncing it as 'death tourism' would be unfounded. One has to keep in mind that a cross-border change of habitual residence in the context of succession—quite different from the case of (looming) bankruptcy—is rarely aimed towards death. On the contrary: it is not unusual that relationships are established and property is acquired in the State of destination. However, unlike the bourgeois death of winding up one's business ventures through bankruptcy, which these days enjoys the miracle of resurrection (considering the discharge of residual debts),[2] physical death is (or at least seems to be) permanent.

* Senior Research Fellow, Max Planck Institute Luxembourg for International, European and Regulatory Procedural Law, *Habilitand* with Professor Dr Burkhard Hess, and *Maître en droit*, Aix-en-Provence.

[1] H Dörner, 'EuErbVO: Die Verordnung zum Internationalen Erb- und Erbverfahrensrecht ist in Kraft!' (2012) *Zeitschrift für Erbrecht und Vermögensnachfolge* 505; J Kleinschmidt, 'Optionales Erbrecht: Das Europäische Nachlasszeugnis als Herausforderung an das Kollisionsrecht' (2013) 77 *Rabels Zeitschrift für ausländisches und internationales Privatrecht* 723, 725ff, with reference to A Röthel, 'Ist unser Erbrecht noch zeitgemäß?: Gutachten A zum 68. Deutschen Juristentag' (2010) *Verhandlungen des 68. Deutschen Juristentags* A17.

[2] *cf Local Court of Göttingen*, 10 December 2012—74 IN 28/12 (2013) *Neue Zeitschrift für das Recht der Insolvenz und Sanierung* 206 with note B Laukemann, 'Die ordre public-Kontrolle bei Erschleichung von Zuständigkeit und Restschuldbefreiung im Europäischen Insolvenzverfahren: eine Gläubigerperspektive (AG Göttingen, S. 285)' (2014) *Praxis des Internationalen Privat- und Verfahrensrechts* 258.

In the light of heterogeneous and inconsistent national rules, a purely national regulatory approach is broadly considered incapable of overcoming the diverse and complex legal issues arising in succession matters with cross-border implications.[3] To simplify succession planning and administration, the EU Succession Regulation primarily aims at reducing the length of proceedings and enable successions to be settled more efficiently and rapidly.[4] The Regulation which entered into force in August 2012[5] and which is principally applicable as of August 2015[6] in all Member States except the United Kingdom, Ireland and Denmark,[7] took around 10 years to prepare.[8] The legislative act not only deals with all aspects emblematic of private international law (such as international jurisdiction, applicable law and recognition or enforceability of decisions), but also breaks new ground regarding the acceptance of authentic instruments and the creation of a European Certificate of Succession (ECS).[9] So what are the basic architecture and general principles of this ambitious and universally applicable EU instrument?[10]

First, reflecting the objectives of simplicity and predictability, the Regulation's key principle is the synchronization of the competent court and the applicable law. Second, the habitual residence of the deceased at the time of death (in lieu of nationality) is adopted as the general criterion for determining both jurisdiction and the applicable law which enhances flexibility (at the risk of weakening legal certainty and predictability).[11] At the same time, party autonomy can, to a limited extent, come into play:[12]

[3] The drafting of last wills; the determination of heirs or persons entitled to a reserved share in the light of a foreign testator; the interplay between succession and matrimonial regimes, and the competence of courts or the way to prove entitlement to succession, to name but a few, *cf* PW Vollmer, 'Die neue europäische Erbrechtsverordnung' (2012) *Zeitschrift für die Steuer- und Erbrechtspraxis* 227ff.

[4] *cf* Regulation (EU) No 650/2012 of 4 July 2012 on jurisdiction, applicable law, recognition and enforcement of decisions and acceptance and enforcement of authentic instruments in matters of succession and on the creation of a European Certificate of Succession [2012] OJ L201/107, recitals 7, 67 (Succession Regulation).

[5] 16 August 2012.

[6] 17 August 2015, see Art 84 Succession Regulation.

[7] Recitals 82, 83.

[8] Regarding the adaptation of German law to the EIR see the ministerial draft from 5 March 2014 (Referentenentwurf zum Internationalen Erbrecht und zur Änderung von Vorschriften zum Erbschein); its lacking provisions concerning the interplay of the EIR with bilateral agreements is criticized by D Lehmann, 'Der Referentenentwurf für ein Begleitgesetz zur EuErbVO' (2014) *Zeitschrift für Erbrecht und Vermögensnachfolge* 232ff.

[9] *cf* recital 8. Dutta compared this new regulatory act to a quantum leap in the Europeanization of private international law, A Dutta, 'Das neue internationale Erbrecht der Europäischen Union—Eine erste Lektüre der Erbrechtsverordnung' (2013) *Zeitschrift für das gesamte Familienrecht* 4, 14.

[10] Following the principle of *universal application*, Art 20 provides that any law specified by the Regulation shall be applied whether or not it is the law of a Member State.

[11] The connecting factor is established through an overall assessment of the relevant factual elements, *cf* Arts 4, 21; recital 23.

[12] The aim is to mitigate the side effects of the potential abstractness and inadequacy of habitual residence as a general connecting factor and to facilitate the organization of a succession in advance.

Article 22 empowers the testator to designate (only) the law of the state of his nationality as the law governing his or her succession as a whole.[13] Third, the Regulation sets forth the principle of the unity of the succession (the monistic approach) for reasons of legal certainty and to avoid the fragmentation of succession.[14] Accordingly, the applicable law will govern the succession as a whole regardless of the nature of the assets (movables or immovables) and irrespective of whether the assets are located in another Member State or in a third country.[15] Fourth, the Regulation addresses the legal status and effects of authentic instruments, which shall have, as a matter of principle, the same evidentiary effects in another Member State as they have in the Member State of origin.[16] Finally, the Regulation provides for the creation of a uniform certificate, the ECS, demonstrating the status and/or rights of beneficiaries or the powers to execute the will or to administer the estate.[17] This instrument, producing equal effects throughout the EU, is doubtlessly one of the most innovative instruments of the Regulation.[18]

This chapter focuses on the ESC. From the abundant field of questions related to this supranational instrument, the chapter will focus on the interplay between the European and national certificates of inheritance (section 4) and consider the residual relevance of the *lex rei sitae* (section 5). First, a brief overview of the national systems of certification will however be provided (section 2) and basic characteristics and legal effects of the EU instrument dealt with (section 3).

2. DIVERGING NATIONAL SYSTEMS OF CERTIFICATION

The way succession is certified varies considerably amongst the Member States' legal orders—first, concerning the issuing authority. Judicial certificates can, for instance, be found in Germany, Austria and Greece. Especially

[13] *cf* also recital 38ff; B Hess et al, 'Note for the European Parliament on the Regulation (EC) No 650/2012 of July 2012 on jurisdiction, applicable law, recognition and enforcement of authentic instruments in matters of succession and on the creation of a European Certificate of Succession' (2012) 4.

[14] *cf* D Martiny, 'Lex rei sitae as a connecting factor in EU Private International Law' (2012) *Praxis des Internationalen Privat- und Verfahrensrechts* 119, 126, concerning justifications for a unitary approach.

[15] Arts 21(1), 22(1), 23(1); recital 37, s 4.

[16] Agreements as to succession (*cf* the definition under Art 3(1)(b)) vary significantly amongst the Member States. Therefore, the Regulation determines the law to govern the admissibility of such arrangements, their substantive validity as well as their binding effects between the parties, *cf* recital 49 and Arts 25, 27.

[17] Arts 63, 69; recital 67.

[18] *cf* R Wagner, 'Aktuelle Entwicklungen in der justiziellen Zusammenarbeit in Zivilsachen' (2012) *Neue Juristische Wochenschrift* 1333, 1334 ('The Succession Regulation is regarded as one of the most difficult projects of judicial cooperation in civil matters'). According to recitals 16, 34, 46, the Succession Regulation also aims at improving judicial coordination as well as access to relevant information for (potential) creditors.

in Latin (European) countries, notarial certificates of inheritance prevail such as the French *acte de notariété*, whereas countries like Sweden and Finland provide for private (court-confirmed) inventories of the estate.[19] Further differences exist with regard to the intensity of examination (*ex officio* or not) and, most importantly, the function and effects of the national instrument.[20] Not all certificates are designed to establish a presumption[21] or have the effect of protecting persons acquiring succession property or making payments to the alleged heir in good faith.[22] In addition, we face practical and legal difficulties pertaining to the cross-border use of national certificates of succession: different terminology and legal effects are one aspect; refusing the substitution or adaptation of foreign certificates, as not only German courts are inclined to do,[23] may urge heirs to apply for an additional certificate in the state in which the succession property is located in order to attain legitimating effect vis-a-vis register offices.[24] These time- and cost-consuming drawbacks are exacerbated by a lack of common rules of recognition and uniform recognition practice within the EU Member States.

Generally speaking, settling inheritances in a less complex way, as well as more quickly and more efficiently can be achieved through either a supranational certificate (such as the ECS) or an optimized circulation of national certificates of inheritance. One instrument for realizing the latter objective is the acceptance of authentic instruments laid down in Articles 59–61 of the Regulation. I will, however, begin with the alternative mechanism, the ECS, by first addressing its basic characteristics and legal effects.

[19] *cf* Max Planck Institute for Comparative and International Private Law, 'Comments on the European Commission's Proposal for a Regulation in matters of succession and the creation of a European Certificate of Succession' (2010) 74 *Rabels Zeitschrift für ausländisches und internationales Privatrecht* 522, paras 266ff.

[20] Kleinschmidt (n 1) 723, 729ff denies any connection between the system of transfer by succession and the concrete form of certification. He also doubts that the certification of succession on the one hand, and the range of effects incumbent upon recordings in land registers on the other, correlate with each other.

[21] The lack of presumption is true, for instance, for the Italian *atto di notorietà*, *cf* Deutsches Notarinstitut (DNotI), *Rechtsvergleichende Studie der erbrechtlichen Regelungen des Internationalen Verfahrensrechtes und Internationalen Privatrechts der Mitgliedstaaten der Europäischen Union* (2002) 285ff.

[22] *cf* §§ 2366ff BGB (German Civil Code).

[23] *cf* with regard to § 35(1) GBO (German Land Registry Act): Kammergericht Berlin, 25 September 2012, (2013) *Neue juristische Wochenschrift-Rechtsprechungs-Report Zivilrecht* 79; OLG Bremen, 19 May 2011, (2011) *Neue juristische Wochenschrift-Rechtsprechungs-Report Zivilrecht* 1099 (concerning a certificate issued by the District Probate Registry at Brighton); Kammergericht Berlin, 25 March 1997, (1997) *Neue juristische Wochenschrift-Rechtsprechungs-Report Zivilrecht* 1094.

[24] *cf* for instance, the certificate of inheritance limited to the objects located within the country according to § 2369 BGB (German Civil Code).

3. BASIC CHARACTERISTICS AND LEGAL EFFECTS OF THE ECS

3.1 Purpose and Procedure

The ECS is an instrument[25] designed to enable heirs, legatees, executors of wills and administrators of an estate[26] to easily demonstrate their status and/or their rights and powers in another Member State (Article 63), for instance when succession property is located there.[27] Upon the application of those persons,[28] the courts or notaries exercising judicial functions[29] of the Member State are competent to issue the certificate according to the general rules in Articles 4–6.[30] The issuing authority verifies the information, declarations and documents provided by the applicant[31] and issues a certified copy[32] following the procedure laid down in the Regulation,[33] thereby resorting to a standard form;[34] the certified copies are principally valid for a limited but extendable period of six months.[35] Article 68 determines the far-reaching content of the Certificate including, inter alia, the factual elements of the authority's competence; information concerning the matrimonial property regime; the law applicable to the succession; the share of each heir; the rights for any given legatee; or the restrictions on their rights. Under Article 71, the issuing authority can rectify, modify or withdraw the

[25] *cf* recital 69.

[26] Creditors are not mentioned as applicants. Those provisions under German law conferring creditors a right to request a certificate of inheritance in the context of enforcement (§§ 792, 896 ZPO) could be amended by a forthcoming implementation Act allowing them to apply for an ECS, see M Buschbaum and U Simon, 'EuErbVO: Das Europäische Nachlasszeugnis' (2012) *Zeitschrift für Erbrecht und Vermögensnachfolge* 525.

[27] According to M Buschbaum, 'Europäisches Nachlasszeugnis und Annahme öffentlicher Urkunden—neue Mechanismen zur grenzüberschreitenden Nachlassabwicklung und ihr Verhältnis zum materiellen Sachenrecht' in J Hager (ed), *Die neue europäische Erbrechtsverordnung* (Baden-Baden, Nomos, 2013) 61, the legal nature of the ECS is determined by the *lex fori* of the issuing authority.

[28] Arts 65, 63(1). Regarding applications, Art 65(2) provides for the use of standard forms.

[29] This is the case, for instance, with notaries in Baden-Württemberg pursuant to § 38 LFGG BW (Landesgesetz über die freiwillige Gerichtsbarkeit).

[30] The issuing authorities are obviously not allowed to confine the Certificate to assets located in a third country pursuant to Art 12 to which Art 64(1) does not refer, see also Dutta, 'Das neue internationale Erbrecht der Europäischen Union' (n 9) 4 and 14; Buschbaum and Simon (n 26) 525f.

[31] See Arts 65(3), 66(1).

[32] Art 70(1). Pursuant to Art 70(2), the issuing authority keeps a list of persons to whom certified copies have been issued. Under German law, however, issuing certified copies is not admissible, J Mayer in FJ Säcker and R Rixecker (eds), *Münchener Kommentar zum BGB*, 6th edn (Munich, CH Beck, 2013) § 2353, para 122.

[33] Arts 66ff. Differences may arise with regard to the application procedure (Art 66(3)): Pursuant to § 2356(2) BGB (German Civil Code), a statutory declaration in lieu of an oath is mandatory.

[34] Art 67(1), s 2. The standard form is still to be established in accordance with the advisory proceedings (*Beratungsverfahren*) referred to in Art 81(2).

[35] Art 70(3).

Certificate where national law permits.[36] Finally, persons entitled to apply for a Certificate may challenge its issue or, by demonstrating a legitimate interest, request its rectification, modification or withdrawal without a time limit.[37]

3.2 Legal Effects

Apart from those procedural aspects, the Regulation also provides for specific legal effects attached to the Certification. To begin with, the ECS is not an enforceable title in its own right, particularly not a European Enforcement Order related to a national certificate, as suggested by some legal scholars.[38] Pursuant to Article 69(2), the certified copy of the Certificate[39] is instead presumed to accurately demonstrate elements (*Tatsachen*) established under the applicable law. Additionally, the person mentioned in the Certificate as heir, legatee, executor of wills or administrator of the estate is considered to have the status or to hold the rights or powers stated in the Certificate with no conditions or restrictions other than those stated in the Certificate. This evidentiary effect (*Beweiswirkung*) referring both to the correctness and the completeness of the Certificate's content might prove to be a problem for information falling outside the ambit of the Regulation such as the matrimonial regime.[40] Both categories of refutable[41] presumptions apply to register proceedings. The ECS constitutes a valid document for the recording of succession property in public registers[42] (*Legitimationswirkung*), however, without prejudice to national register law.[43] Finally, any person

[36] *cf* § 2361 BGB (German Civil Code): revocation or declaration of invalidity of an inaccurate certificate of inheritance. The Regulation does not prevent the risk of irreconcilable certified copies since only the incorrect certificate itself may be withdrawn. In that situation, Buschbaum and Simon (n 26) 525f plead for the application of § 2362 BGB conferring on the true heir a claim for the return of the incorrect certificate of inheritance to the probate court.

[37] To avoid acquisitions in good faith during redress procedures, the effects of the ECS may be suspended either by the issuing authority or by the judicial authority, Art 73.

[38] M Buschbaum and M Kohler, 'Vereinheitlichung des Erbkollisionsrechts in Europa' (2010) *Zeitschrift für das Privatrecht der Europäischen Union* 162, 166; *cf* W Rechberger, 'Das Europäische Nachlasszeugnis und seine Wirkungen' (2012) *Österreichische Juristen-Zeitung* 14, 19. Explicitly recital 71, s 2.

[39] In this sense: Buschbaum and Simon (n 26) 525, 527.

[40] For this aspect see: B Hess in B Hess, E Jayme and T Pfeiffer (eds), *Stellungnahme für den Rechtsausschuss des Europäischen Parlaments zum Vorschlag für eine Europäische Erbrechtsverordnung* Version 2009/147 (COD) from 16 January 2012 (hereafter the Heidelberg Report) 52.

[41] The Regulation is silent on this issue. See also Dutta, 'Das neue internationale Erbrecht der Europäischen Union' (n 9) 4, 15; U Janzen, 'Die EU-Erbrechtsverordnung' (2012) *Deutsche Notar-Zeitschrift* 484, 493. *cf* in German Law § 292 ZPO (Code of Civil Procedure): for the benefit as well as at the expense of the person mentioned in the Certificate.

[42] With regard to § 35(1) GBO (German Registry Act): H Wilsch, *Beck'scher Online-Kommentar GBO*, § 35 GBO, para 34; Kammergericht Berlin, 25 September 2012, (2013) *Neue juristische Wochenschrift-Rechtsprechungs-Report Zivilrecht* 79, 80 (obiter dictum).

[43] For this aspect see below section 5.

making payments or passing on property to the person authorized in the ECS on the basis of the certified information is deemed to have transacted in good faith with an authorized person unless he knows that the content of the Certificate is not accurate or is unaware of such inaccuracy due to gross negligence.[44] According to Article 69(4), the same principle applies to persons mentioned in the Certificate as authorized to dispose of the succession property in question.

This protection, however, is conditional on the presentation of a certified copy, the accuracy of which the person acting in good faith is relying on—the mere existence of the certified copy is, unlike in domestic German law,[45] insufficient to give presumption.[46] In cross-border succession cases this condition may require considerable effort, since beneficiaries will commonly be obliged to apply for an extension of the six-month validity period of the certified copy.[47]

These rules constitute substantive succession law directly applicable in the Member States[48] and specific to corresponding national rules on good faith which insofar do not apply.[49] As a consequence, Article 69(4) allows for the good faith acquisition of succession property where national rules do not or only do so to a limited extent.[50] Conversely, the protection of good faith conferred by the ECS may also fall behind the standard guaranteed by the laws of individual Member States. Taking, for instance, the need to act on the basis of the certified copy presented or the autonomous subjective conditions laid down in Article 69(4): the gross negligence criterion might differ from the prerequisites of respective national provisions in the sense that they require positive knowledge to rebut the presumption of good faith.[51]

This demonstrates that the ECS directly impacts on aspects of national substantive law, even exerting a direct influence over the allocation of

[44] Art 69(3).

[45] Under German law, the third person acting in good faith does not need to be aware of the existence of the Certificate, BGH, 23 November 1960, BGHZ 33, 314, 317; (1961) *Neue juristische Wochenschrift* 605, 606; H Brox and WD Walker, *Erbrecht*, 24th edn (Munich, Vahlen, 2010) para 618; R Frank and T Helms, *Erbrecht*, 6th edn (Munich, CH Beck, 2013) § 16, para 13.

[46] Arts 69(3) and (4); recital 71 ss 4, 6; against Buschbaum and Simon (n 26) 525, 528.

[47] *cf* Art 70(3). In this sense also Vollmer (n 3) 227, 233; *cf* also H Wilsch, 'EuErbVO: Die Verordnung in der deutschen Grundbuchpraxis' (2012) *Zeitschrift für Erbrecht und Vermögensnachfolge* 530, 532.

[48] Therefore, the Certificate is not subject to a substitution when applying national law (§§ 2366ff of the German Civil Code), also the Heidelberg Report (n 40) 52.

[49] See recital 71. National rules on good faith, however, remain applicable to the question whether the deceased was the owner of individual assets forming part of the estate.

[50] As in case of English or Portuguese law, see Kleinschmidt (n 1) 723, 776ff with further references.

[51] Under German law, § 2366 BGB (German Civil Code) requires so-called positive knowledge of the information documented in the national certificate of succession to rebut the legal presumption in § 2365 BGB.

assets.[52] A need for a further vertical coordination arises with regard to the coexistence of national and supranational certificates of succession. This raises the issue of whether an optimized circulation of national certificates could prove a credible alternative to the supranational counterpart. The acceptance of authentic instruments is the implementing instrument provided for by the Regulation (Article 59).

4. THE INTERPLAY BETWEEN THE ECS AND NATIONAL CERTIFICATES OF INHERITANCE

4.1 The Acceptance of Authentic Instruments: A Credible Alternative to the ECS?

The term 'authentic instrument', unknown to Scandinavian and Anglo-American legal orders, is legally defined as 'a document in the matter of succession ... the authenticity of which relates to the signature and the content of the authentic instrument'.[53] Prima facie, every national certificate of succession drawn up by a court or notary[54] meets that definition. In particular, the Regulation did not take up the recommendation to exempt national certificates from the scope of Article 59.[55] Under Article 59(1), an authentic instrument produces the same evidentiary effects in another Member State as it does in the Member State of origin, at least the most comparable effects.[56] Avoiding the term 'recognition', which is reserved for court decisions,[57] the Regulation introduces the as yet unknown term 'acceptance'.[58] This means an extension of evidentiary effects provided for in the State of origin (*Wirkungserstreckung*)[59] without further need for legalization, other similar formalities (such as an apostille)[60] or any examination of a functional

[52] This raises the question of EU competence, and whether national rules governing the system of property are respected in accordance with Art 345 of the Treaty on the Functioning of the European Union (TFEU), *cf* B Akkermans and E Ramaekers, 'Article 345 TFEU (ex Article 295 EC), Its Meanings and Interpretations' (2010) 16 *European Law Journal* 292ff.

[53] Art 3(1)(i).

[54] Within the meaning of recital 20, s 4.

[55] *cf* the Heidelberg Report (n 40) 45.

[56] This is subject to the condition that producing those evidentiary effects is not manifestly contrary to the public policy of the Member State concerned, Art 59(1).

[57] As laid down in Art 59, authentic instruments are not technically recognized but rather accepted. Nonetheless, by equating national certificates with decisions in the meaning of Art 39, some legal scholars advocate an automatic recognition of those certificates according to this provision, see T Rauscher (ed), *Europäisches Zivilprozess- und Kollisionsrecht EuZPR/EuIPR* (Munich, Sellier, 2010) Art 29 proposal, para 38.

[58] See J Fitchen, '"Recognition", Acceptance and Enforcement of Authentic Instruments in the Succession Regulation' (2012) *Journal of Private International Law* 323, 334ff.

[59] This concept is contrary to the concept of equation with the probative value of a domestic authentic instrument.

[60] Art 74.

equivalence in procedure, issuing authority or scope of evidentiary effects.[61] Depending on the law of the State of origin, those effects may encompass not only the authenticity of the document and the factual elements recorded in the instrument,[62] but also its content as to the substance, ie, the legal acts or legal relationships such as the determination of the heirs, their respective shares or the existence of a reserved share.[63]

The term 'content' in the wording of Article 3(1)(i) proves imprecise and open to ambivalent interpretation. Likewise for Article 59(1) referring to the abstract term 'evidentiary effects', yet in the German version to '*formal* evidentiary effects' (*formelle Beweiskraft*), thereby suggesting the explicit exclusion of effects regarding the substantive correctness of the recorded information from a German law perspective. It gives justified cause for criticism that recital 63 indicates an answer to that central question by stating that the evidentiary effects produced by an authentic instrument extend to its recorded contents as to substance (*materieller Inhalt*).[64] Article 59(3) refers to this issue only indirectly, in the context of a jurisdictional provision, by providing that challenges against the substantive validity of legal acts or relationships recorded in an authentic instrument shall be made before the courts having jurisdiction under the Regulation.[65]

Obviously, the acceptance of the legal consequences stated in the decision of the issuing authority from the perspective of the applicable law,[66] this so-called acceptance of substantive legal positions, essentially depends on the harmonization of conflict of laws rules in succession matters. Under the premise of harmonization, the extension of evidentiary effects provided for in the State of origin is not capable of undermining the fundamental rationale attributed to the conflict of laws rules by the state in which the foreign certificate will be used.[67] In my view, as the new Regulation guarantees that condition, leaving aside the impacts of preliminary questions[68] and non-harmonized matrimonial property law, Article 59 does not describe a paradigm shift from a conflict of laws system towards a system of recognition or acceptance pertaining to the substantive content of authentic instruments.[69] Article 59(3) mirrors this conclusion as challenges relating to the

[61] Upon request the issuing authority describes the evidentiary effects which the instrument produces in the State of origin, using a standard form, Art 59(1) subpara 2, referring to Art 81(2).

[62] *cf* recital 62.

[63] Also Kleinschmidt (n 1) 723, 739; Dutta, 'Das neue internationale Erbrecht der Europäischen Union' (n 9) 4, 13; Buschbaum (n 27) 43, 59.

[64] This aspect is not taken into consideration by Buschbaum (n 27) 43.

[65] Also Kleinschmidt (n 1) 723, 738ff. However, Art 59(4) accepts a binding effect in the context of incidental questions relating to the certified legal acts or legal relationships.

[66] The Heidelberg Report (n 40) 53.

[67] In that sense the Heidelberg Report (n 40) 47ff.

[68] For instance, as to the status or legal capacity of natural persons.

[69] Also the Heidelberg Report (n 40) 53; Kleinschmidt (n 1) 723, 740.

substantive content of an authentic instrument (legal act or relationships) are governed by the law applicable under the harmonized conflict of laws rules of the Succession Regulation. This situation, however, is obviously different from the recognition of a legal situation irrespective of the applicable law in the State of origin.

4.2 The ECS as a Special Instrument?

4.2.1 Optional Instrument

Against this backdrop, demands have been expressed for the ECS to be regarded as a special instrument taking precedence over Article 59: to extend the effects of national certificates to other Member States would unnecessarily increase complexity and be dispensable next to the implementation of a new supranational instrument.[70] However, the legal interaction between the European instrument and national certificates of inheritance is not yet satisfactorily clarified. As a starting point, the ECS is designed as an optional instrument[71] for use in another Member State and, thus, requires a cross-border element. However, once issued for that purpose, the Certificate also produces effects in the Member State of origin according to the clear wording of Article 62(3), section 2. Optionality means that its use is—as a quasi-28th regime[72]—neither mandatory nor replaces domestic instruments used for similar purposes in the Member States.[73] Furthermore, a national certificate of inheritance may not prevent the competent authority from issuing an ECS for a transnational use. As a matter of principle, once the European instrument has been established, a national certificate of inheritance need not be withdrawn or may even still be issued, at least as long as that national instrument (like under German law) confers a broader protection of good faith to that of the ECS.[74] In cases where this condition is not met, it is questionable whether a legitimate interest remains to uphold or to issue a national certificate which might potentially cause confusion. This is especially true if the information recorded in the ECS cannot be certified in the national certificate, such as the rights of legatees with a direct proprietary effect.[75] Given that the *situs*-reservation does not comprise non-registered

[70] MPI Hamburg (n 19) 522, 670, para 257 (with regard to court decisions); Buschbaum (n 27), 57.

[71] Under a general perspective see H Fleischer, 'Optionales europäisches Privatrecht ("28. Modell")' (2012) 76 *Rabels Zeitschrift für ausländisches und internationales Privatrecht* 235ff.

[72] Generally see M Fornasier, '"28." versus "2. Regime."—Kollisionsrechtliche Aspekte eines optionaleneuropäischen Vertragsrechts' (2012) *Rabels Zeitschrift für ausländisches und internationales Privatrecht* 401ff.

[73] Arts 62(2) and 62(3).

[74] Buschbaum and Simon (n 26) 525, 528, however, advocate a complete dispensability.

[75] *cf* Buschbaum (n 27) 62ff.

movable property (Article 69(5))[76] the ownership of those assets, governed by a *legatum per vindicationem*,[77] directly passes to the beneficiary. A national certificate, not certifying that foreign and unknown right,[78] would be inaccurate and therefore incapable of producing a good faith presumption. This outcome, however, is very far from being satisfactory.

Another example: an ECS issued by an Austrian authority according to the provisions of the Regulation constitutes a valid document for the recording of immovable succession property located in Germany.[79] Hence, an Austrian heir has no further need to apply in Germany for an additional national certificate of inheritance limited to the objects located in that country (*Fremdrechtserbschein*). Nonetheless, the Austrian heir may, in my view, still request this limited German certificate, given its more far-reaching effects of good faith. This costly and time-consuming alternative, however, is unlikely to happen.

4.2.2 Limited Circulation of National Certificates

In that light, should the ECS be considered as a special instrument? This proposal overlooks, on the one hand, the intention of the EU legislator to design the ECS as an optional instrument.[80] In view of the broad wording of 'authentic instrument' and the lacking provisions on the hierarchy and coordination of both mechanisms, it is difficult, *de lege lata*, to justify a primacy of the ECS over well-established national instruments which now can also be accompanied by standard forms.[81] On the other hand, the circulation of national certificates of succession remains limited. This is because they may only produce those evidentiary effects conferred on them by the Member State of origin—Article 59 does not secure substitution, ie, equation with the probative value of a domestic authentic instrument. This aspect sheds further light on the concern, especially articulated by Austrian scholars familiar with a very formalized procedure (*Einantwortung*), that land registers will be obliged to accept authentic instruments established by notaries without

[76] For that aspect see below section 5.

[77] The *legatum per vindicationem* applies in countries such as France, Belgium, Italy, Poland, Portugal, Spain, Hungary, Rumania and numerous Latin American countries, *cf* R Süß, 'Das Vindikationslegat im Internationalen Privatrecht' (2001) 65 *Rabels Zeitschrift für ausländisches und internationales Privatrecht* 244, 255ff, addressing the correlation between the acquisition system of property law and the implementation of legacies. *cf* also JP Schmidt, 'Die kollisionsrechtliche Behandlung dinglich wirkender Vermächtnisse' (2013) 77 *Rabels Zeitschrift für ausländisches und internationales Privatrecht* 1ff; D Martiny (n 14) 119, 128 (fn 158ff).

[78] *cf* OLG Köln, 14 July 1982, (1983) *Neue Juristische Wochenschrift* 525; BayObLG, 28 November 1974, BayObLGZ 1974, 460, 466.

[79] *cf* Art 69(5) and recital 18, s 5. Mayer (n 32) § 2353, para 193; Dörner (n 1) 505, 512.

[80] Only where a person opts for an ECS, the choice of instrument has to be respected by authorities or persons in another Member State, Arts 62(2) and 62(3); recital 69.

[81] See Art 59(1) subpara 2. With the same result: Kleinschmidt (n 1) 723, 741ff.

a detailed assessment.[82] Under the Succession Regulation, an Italian *atto di notorietà* will still lack any legitimating effects if, for example, an Italian heir seeks to re-register immovable property located in Germany.[83] Apart from that, it remains an outstanding issue whether good faith protection forms part of the cross-border evidentiary effects subject to Article 59(1), thus also binding foreign authorities. And finally, in court proceedings with incidental questions relating to legal acts or legal relationships recorded in an authentic instrument, the evidentiary effects of the instrument are *de lege lata* determined by national rules on evidence.[84] All these aspects will rather strengthen the attractiveness of the European Certificate.

4.3 Interim Conclusions

It needs to be noted first that, while it is a legal policy concern, the ECS is not a special instrument excluding the provisions on the acceptance of authentic instruments. It rather constitutes an optional instrument principally coexisting with and partially differing from national types of certification. However, to reduce confusion, national legislators should take the opportunity to inform the legal traffic about diverging effects.[85]

Second, the ECS considered as a whole, may be revealed as an important instrument in cross-border successions avoiding the multiplication of documents. Together with the introduction of a genuine European standard form, the new instrument will help beneficiaries to prove their rights or status vis-a-vis register offices, banks and insurance companies, especially in countries such as Italy with no or very weak instruments of certification. If preliminary questions are to be determined according to the conflict of laws rules of the *lex causae*, frictions can be avoided. Finally, the Certificate's effects across the EU call for a harmonized investigation procedure.[86]

Yet, every legislative innovation comes at a price, which is, with regard to the ECS, a lack of regulatory coherence: the coexistence of two mechanisms related to the extension of evidentiary effects, one through the new legal concept of 'acceptance' according to Article 59, the other through the implementation of a supranational instrument of certification, requires either a hierarchy or the coordination and adjustment of those mechanisms. Both are lacking. What solution, for instance, is to be adopted if the contents of a European and a national certificate of inheritance contradict each other? Should the conflict be resolved by the principle of temporal priority?[87] Does

82 Rechberger (n 38) 14f.
83 *cf* Kleinschmidt (n 1) 723, 728.
84 Art 59(4).
85 In that respect, the Heidelberg Report (n 40) 53.
86 ibid, 51.
87 The certificate issued first prevails; the second has to be withdrawn or adjusted.

the ECS prevail a priori over the national instrument or does the certificate with the more far-reaching effects take precedence over the other?[88] In my opinion, there is merit in a territorial delimitation related to the basic function of the respective certificate. Whereas the national instrument should prevail in a domestic context, the ECS should, in cases of contradiction, be given priority for uses abroad unless the national instrument exceptionally produces wider effects.

5. THE ECS AND THE RESIDUAL RELEVANCE OF THE *LEX REI SITAE*

5.1 Legal Policy Background

The EU legislator aims to reduce objections in the context of cross-border successions. Given this objective, should regulatory differences arising from diverging concepts of transfer by succession still be taken into account? This becomes particularly prominent when national succession regimes abstain from protecting publicity under property law when determining the transfer by universal succession (*ipso jure*-acquisition of all assets),[89] but coevally do so with regard to individual assets when executing the will of the deceased through dispositions *inter vivos*.[90] In this matter, the protection of publicity as well as the principle of speciality can usually not be considered to be a mandatory principle, ie, a priori not suitable to be balanced against other principles in the context of succession, such as the direct acquisition by reason of death or the universal succession. This latter principle, aiming at legal clarity (as for the identity of right holders) and preserving the unity of liable assets in the interest of the creditors of the estate, (co-)heirs and the general public,[91] allows, for instance under German law, a transfer of property without entry into the land register, thereby outweighing concerns of publicity otherwise safeguarded by property law.

Moreover, if a beneficiary were required to involve a notary twice, this could come into conflict with the proper functioning of the Internal Market. To take the example of a co-heir beneficiary under French succession law of an immovable located in Germany: *L'acte de partage*, ie, the division of the

[88] Moreover, it seems to me that the characteristics, mechanisms and effects of an optional procedural instrument at European level still need further clarification and research investigation.

[89] Under German law: § 1922 BGB (German Civil Code).

[90] According to German law: § 2174 BGB (German Civil Code). Directions given by the deceased for partitioning of the estate (*Teilungsanordnung* according to § 2048 BGB) shall serve as another example.

[91] *cf* D Leipold in FJ Säcker and R Rixecker (eds), *Münchener Kommentar zum BGB*, 6th edn (Munich, CH Beck, 2013) § 1922, paras 123ff; for a detailed commentary, K Muscheler, *Universalsukzession und Vonselbsterwerb* (Tübingen, Mohr Siebeck, 2002) 96ff.

estate, must first be certified by a French notary.[92] If German law applied cumulatively with regard to that immovable, an additional declaration of conveyance (*Auflassung*) would have to be made in the presence of both parties before a German notary,[93] thereby realizing the right of succession.[94]

5.2 Delineation Between Property and Succession Law Regarding the Transfer of Ownership

5.2.1 General Considerations

This triggers the general question of how to delineate succession rules from the *lex rei sitae* and, in particular, how to proceed with legal orders which do not provide for a transfer of individual assets by succession, instead executing dispositions of property upon death through dispositions *inter vivos*. The claim-based construction of legacies under German law (*legatum per damnationem*),[95] excluded from the content of the Certificate,[96] may serve as a notable example.[97]

From a general point of view, regulatory concepts effecting the transfer of ownership (of all or merely individual assets) not upon death, but through a subsequent legal transaction or court decision (combined with an acceptance of inheritance), are in principle attributable either to property law structures and policies such as the protection of publicity, the principle of speciality or the *numerus clausus* principle,[98] or (rather) to considerations of succession law, which are mirrored by the respective system of liability for the debts under succession balancing conflicting interests of beneficiaries and creditors.[99] Due to a different weighting of legally protected third-party interests with regard to the acquisition of rights in succession and property law, the transfer of ownership by reason of death differs in many countries from the types of acquisition common to their property law regimes—from

[92] Art 835(2) Code Civil (French Civil Code) stipulates: 'Lorsque l'indivision porte sur des biens soumis à la publicité foncière, l'acte de partage est passé par acte notarié'.

[93] §§ 873(1), 925 BGB (German Civil Code); §§ 19ff, 29 GBO (German Land Registry Act).

[94] The reserve of the *lex rei sitae* is capable of encroaching on the regulatory system of the succession law applicable according to Arts 21–23. Art 883 of the French Civil Code, for instance, cannot be 'displayed' by German rules on the partitioning of the estate; for further details see the Heidelberg Report (n 40) 33 with further references.

[95] The *legatum per damnationem* is provided for in countries such as Germany, the Netherlands, Austria, Switzerland or China, *cf* also with regard to common law countries, Süß (n 77) 244, 247ff.

[96] The ECS is exclusively dedicated for use by legatees with direct rights in succession, Arts 63(1), 63(2)(b). These rights are to be documented according to Art 68(m).

[97] § 2147 BGB (German Civil Code); *cf* also § 2048 BGB regarding directions by the deceased for partitioning.

[98] Regarding the key principles of German property law, see F Baur, JF Baur and R Stürner, *Sachenrecht*, 18th edn (Munich, CH Beck, 2009) § 4, paras 35ff.

[99] See the Heidelberg Report (n 40) 34ff.

a functional and constructive viewpoint.[100] This aspect deserves particular attention when delimitating the *lex rei sitae* from the *lex successionis.*

5.2.2 Autonomous Interpretation

This raises the problem of classification. Both the scope of succession law and the criteria for its delineation with respect to other areas of law, especially the *lex rei sitae*, should be determined by an autonomous interpretation of the Succession Regulation. Otherwise, a uniform application and, as a consequence, the *effet utile* of the Succession Regulation would be considerably weakened if the Member States were competent to freely decide on this central question, thereby trying to assert their diverging policy concepts of succession law. By stipulating the scope of subject matters governed by the law of succession, subsumed under the term 'succession as a whole' according to Article 23(1) and exemplified by section 2 of that Article, the Succession Regulation addresses two aspects which are closely interrelated and characteristic of a rule on conflict of laws. First, the delineation between succession matters and other areas of law excluded from the ambit of the Regulation and, second, the binding scope of succession law from an autonomous perspective. The specific regulatory objective pursued is based on the assumption that any right or legal instrument, provided for by the law of succession, must be, as a matter of principle, classified uniformly, thus excluding (a part from Article 30)[101] any diverging classification by the law of the state in which the succession property is located.

Referring to a different view on the legal position of legatees amongst Member States, the Regulation refrains from autonomously defining central notions of substantive succession law, such as 'beneficiaries'.[102] Accordingly, national laws of succession are called upon to determine who the beneficiaries are in any given succession.[103] Thereby, the Regulation does not give up its competence to classify autonomously, since the definition of 'succession' in a technical sense is understood to cover all forms of transfer of assets, rights and obligations by reason of death.[104]

[100] To that aspect from the perspective of German law see B Laukemann, 'Die lex rei sitae in der Europäischen Erbrechtsverordnung—Inhalt, Schranken und Funktion' in R Geimer (ed), *Festschrift Rolf A Schütze* (Munich, CH Beck, 2014) 325, 327ff.

[101] *cf* A Dutta, 'Succession and Wills in the Conflict of Laws on the Eve of Europeanisation' (2009) 73 *Rabels Zeitschrift für ausländisches und internationales Privatrecht* 547, 558ff.

[102] To this issue see C Baldus, 'Erbe und Vermächtnisnehmer nach der Erbrechtsverordnung' (2012) *Zeitschrift für das Privatrecht der Europäischen Union* 312, 313.

[103] Recital 47.

[104] Art 3(1)(a). As a consequence of this definition, the ECS is reserved to legatees receiving a direct share in the estate, Arts 63(2)(a), (b), 68(m).

5.2.3 The Principle Laid Down in Article 23(2)(e)

On the one hand, the Regulation applies the term 'succession' to all forms of transfer of assets, rights and obligations by reason of death, be it by way of a voluntary transfer under a disposition of property upon death or by a transfer through intestate succession.[105] According to Article 23(2)(e), the transfer of any asset to heirs and, as the case may be, to legatees, is governed by the law applicable to successions. In other words, it is in principle within the scope of succession law to determine the allocation of property by means of either universal or singular succession.[106] This is mirrored by the extension of succession law to the partitioning of the estate[107] as well as to the liability for the debts under the succession.[108] Correspondingly, the ECS certifies the attribution of a specific asset forming part of the estate to heirs or legatees having direct rights in the succession, Article 63(2)(b).

5.2.4 Reservation of the Lex Registrationis

On the other hand, the Regulation does not apply to areas of civil law other than that of succession: Article 1(2)(g). Subject to recital 11, a number of questions, which could be seen as having a link with matters of succession, should be explicitly excluded from the scope of the Regulation for reasons of clarity. In that respect, special attention should be devoted to Article 69(5), stipulating that the ECS itself constitutes a 'valid document' (meaning a sufficient condition) for the recording of succession property only as long as the reservations of Articles 1(2)(k) and (l) do not apply. Accordingly, Article 1(2) excludes from the scope of the Regulation not only the nature of rights *in rem* (lit k), but also any recording in a register of rights in immovable or movable property, including the legal requirements for and the effects of both recordings or failing thereof (lit l).[109]

5.2.4.1 Ambiguous Scope of Article 1(2)(l)

Recital 18 specifies that it is the law of the Member State in which the register is kept (*lex registrationis*) which determines under what legal conditions

[105] Arts 1(1) and 3(1)(a).

[106] The wording of Art 23(1), referring to the succession *as a whole*, does not point in the opposite direction. As recital 37, s 4 demonstrates, the Regulation aims for a uniform application of the succession law (*cf* Art 21(1)), avoiding a territorial fragmentation of the estate, but does not foreclose a singular succession provided for by national law, in that direction also P Wautelet in A Bonomi, *Le droit européen des successions—Commentaire du Règlement no 650/2012 du 4 juillet 2012* (Bruxelles, Bruylant, 2013) 129, para 132.

[107] Art 23(2)(j). By contrast, the partitioning of the estate under German law is, regarding the transfer of ownership, governed by general (property) rules, I Lohmann, *Beck'scher Kommentar BGB* (Munich, CH Beck, 2014) § 2032, para 7; § 2042, para 12.

[108] Art 23(2)(g).

[109] French version: 'exigences légales applicables à une telle inscription'; German version: 'einschließlich der gesetzlichen Voraussetzungen für eine solche Eintragung'.

and how the recording must be carried out. And finally, as supplemented by recital 19, the effects of the recordings, ie, whether they are declaratory or constitutive in nature, are excluded from the scope of the Regulation and instead determined by the law of the Member State in which the register is kept. Article 1(2)(l) thus encompasses the registration effects on substantive (property) law including the moment of acquisition.[110]

In the light of this, recital 19 transcends formal register law typically regulating the range and formal conditions of registrations, forms of evidence or the technical implementation of and inspections in the register, rather than whether and under what substantive conditions property rights are to be registered and what effects on substantive (property) law can be attributed to such recordings. Recital 19 therefore, contradicts the principle laid down in Article 23(2)(e).[111] Given that the preamble to a EU act '*has no binding legal force and cannot be relied on either as a ground for derogating from the actual provisions of the act in question or for interpreting those provisions in a manner clearly contrary to their wording*',[112] this conflict could easily be resolved in favour of Article 23(2)(e). Nonetheless, the intricate question, similarly important from a dogmatic and practical viewpoint, whether the reservation of the *lex registrationis* comprises substantive legal conditions and effects of recordings, is highly contested and, regarding the delimitation between Articles 1(2)(l) and 23(2)(e), subject to ambiguous interpretation.[113]

It should be clear, however, that the exception in Article 1(2)(l) is limited to property rights recorded in registers; all non-registered rights *in rem* are, apart from Article 1(2)(k), governed by the law applicable to the

[110] See recital 19, s 3.

[111] However, there is no contradiction in that, according to Art 69(5) and recital 18, sentences 4 and 5, the ECS should constitute a *valid* document for the recording of succession property in a register of a Member State. In that regard, the Succession Regulation seeks to avoid the duplication of documents in a registration process, thus formulating a provision of *formal* register law.

[112] In that respect the case law of the CJEU, Case C-136/04 *Deutsches Milch-Kontor GmbH v Hauptzollamt Hamburg-Jonas* [2005] ECR I-10095; EU:C:2005:716, para 32, with further references.

[113] In favour of a broad interpretation of Art 1(2)(l) encompassing formal *and* substantive legal conditions: P Lagarde, 'Les principes de base du nouveau règlement européen sur les successions' (2012) 101 *Revue critique de droit international privé* 691, 716; K Lechner, 'Die ErbVO im Spannungsfeld zwischen Erbstatut und Sachenrecht' (2013) *Praxis des Internationalen Privat- und Verfahrensrechts* 497, 499ff; C Hertel, 'Anmerkung zu einer Entscheidung des OLG Bremen, Beschluss vom 19.05.2011 (3 W 6/11; DNotZ 2012, 687)—Zum Nachweis der Erbfolge im Grundbuchverfahren mittels im Ausland erstellten Erbscheinen' (2012) *Deutsche Notar-Zeitschrift* 688, 690ff; Buschbaum (n 27) 53; J Remde, 'Die Europäische Erbrechtsverordnung nach dem Vorschlag der Kommission vom 14. Oktober 2009' (2012) *Rheinische Notarzeitung* 65, 81; against Kleinschmidt (n 1) 723, 763, confining the wording of recital 18 to formal register law; Wautelet and Bonomi (n 106) 126 ff, paras 124ff; S van Erp, 'The New Succession Regulation: The lex rei sitae rule in need of reappraisal?' (2012) *European Property Law Journal* 187, 188ff.

succession.[114] Therefore, the *ipso jure* transfer of non-registered property rights, effected by a *legatum per vindicationem*, cannot be questioned by the authorities of another Member State which only provides for legacies with a compulsory effect. Consequently, the lacking relevance of Article 1(2)(l) is irrespective of whether or not the *lex rei sitae* accomplishes a specific protection of publicity common to property law when executing the legacy.[115]

5.2.4.2 Conclusions Based on a Broad Interpretation of the *Lex Registrationis*

Those who advocate a broad interpretation of Article 1(2)(l), meaning to execute the succession right according to the substantive legal conditions of local property law, allude to the legislative process of the Succession Regulation, taking into account the criticisms directed against the far-reaching proposal of the Commission[116] and its understanding of the law applicable to succession.[117] Accordingly, a *legatum per vindicationem* under Italian law,[118] for instance, granting the beneficiary a right to immovable property located in Germany, would have to be executed by a declaration of conveyance between the heir and the legatee before a German notary and a recording in the land register.[119] This adaptation of a *legatum per vindicationem* to a legacy with compulsory effect[120] would guarantee the conformity of the substantive legal situation with the information documented in the land register.[121] The same principle would apply with respect to the partitioning of the estate, as exemplified by a co-heir beneficiary under French succession law of immovable property located in Germany. However, an additional declaration of conveyance, made in the presence of both parties before a German notary, should be substituted by the division of the estate

[114] Buschbaum (n 27) 53 ('there is good reason to believe'); Hertel (n 113) 688, 691; Dörner (n 1) 505, 509.

[115] *cf* Laukemann, 'Die lex rei sitae in der Europäischen Erbrechtsverordnung—Inhalt, Schranken und Funktion' (n 100) 325, 333.

[116] Commission, 'Proposal for a Regulation on jurisdiction, applicable law, recognition and enforcement of decisions and authentic instruments in matters of successions and the creation of a European Certificate of Succession' COM(2009)154 final.

[117] See Lechner (n 113) 497, 499 referring on the Heidelberg Report (n 40) 32ff, para 5.2.

[118] Art 649(2) of the Italian Civil Code *('Acquisto del legato. Quando oggetto del legato è la proprietà di una cosa determinata o altro diritto appartenente al testatore, la proprietà o il diritto si trasmette dal testatore al legatario al momento della morte del testatore (2648)')*. *cf* also L Salomon, 'The Acquisition of Possession in Legacies *per vindicationem* in Classical Roman Law and its Influence in the Modern Civil Codes' (2006) 3 *Roman Legal Tradition* 65, 73ff.

[119] §§ 873, 925 BGB (German Civil Code); §§ 19, 20, 29 GBO (German Registry Act).

[120] *cf* BGH, 28 September 1994, (1995) *Neue Juristische Wochenschrift* 58, 59 (III.3.b); Kammergericht Berlin, 26 February 2008, (2008) *Neue juristische Wochenschrift-Rechtsprechungs-Report Zivilrecht* 1109, 1110; OLG Köln, 14 July 1982, (1983) *Neue juristische Wochenschrift* 525; BayObLG, 28 November 1974, BayObLGZ 1974, 460, 466.

[121] Buschbaum (n 27) 53; Buschbaum and Simon (n 26) 525, 529.

(*l'acte de partage*) already certified by a French notary. Yet, this approach leaves open whether Article 1(2)(l) should solely apply to registered property rights on individual assets inherited through singular succession or rather in the context of universal succession, too.[122]

5.2.4.3 Critical Assessment and Proposal for a Delimitation

Granting the *lex rei sitae* exception a wider scope of application amounts to a *titulus-and-modus* doctrine, generally differentiating between the title of acquisition determined by succession law and the process of acquisition, governed by the property law of the state in which the asset is located.[123] This, however, contradicts the Regulation's aim to avoid a differentiated treatment of assets with regard to their nature or location and to ease the settling of cross-border successions.[124] In that light and given the diverging accentuation of publicity interests of third parties protected by succession and property law with regard to acquisition, [125] there are good (and better) reasons for concluding that the *lex registrationis* has to be interpreted in a narrow sense, confining its scope to provisions protecting specific concerns of property law such as publicity, speciality or the integrity of registry systems[126] also in the context of (direct) acquisition by reason of death.[127] This is generally not expected to be the case if the application of property law is deemed to be indispensable for emplacing genuine policy interests of succession law. If legal instruments are, on the basis of a functional analysis, predominantly justified by succession interests, especially by liability considerations—as is the case, for instance, with the *titulus-and-modus* doctrine in the Austrian system of a dormant estate—the law of succession should, as a matter of principle, solely apply to the substantive conditions for the transfer of ownership, also with regard to property rights requiring

[122] The wording of Art 1(2)(l) ('any recording in a register') pleads in favour of the latter alternative.

[123] Generally in that sense: Martiny (n 14) 119, 127; R Wagner, 'Der Kommissionsvorschlag vom 14. 10. 2009 zum internationalen Erbrecht: Stand und Perspektiven des Gesetzgebungsverfahrens' (2010) *Deutsche Notar-Zeitschrift* 506, 512ff; Dutta, 'Succession and Wills' (n 101) 547, 556ff; different, however, Dutta, 'Das neue internationale Erbrecht der Europäischen Union' (n 9) 4, 12; critically also Wautelet and Bonomi (n 106) 122, para 111.

[124] Recital 37, ss 4, 5, Art 21(1).

[125] To this issue see above section 5.2.1 and Laukemann (n 100) 325, 327ff. In that context, the complexity of delineating property and succession law also stems from the problem of distinguishing between dissimilar aspects of publicity. The decision of the German Bundesgerichtshof, refusing the recognition of a foreign *legatum per vindicationem*, serves a prominent example. The Court, applying the *lex rei sitae*, primarily relied on the argument that legacies with obligatory effects under German law (§ 2174 BGB) aimed at protecting the creditors of the estate, BGH, 28 September 1994, (1995) *Neue juristische Wochenschrift* 58, 59 (III.3.b).

[126] *cf* Lechner (n 113) 497, 500.

[127] Regarding that delineation see the Heidelberg Report (n 40) 34ff. Regarding the *numerus clausus* principle ('nature of property rights') see below section 5.2.5.

registration in the state in which the asset is located. The law of the state in which the property is located only governs the *formal* aspects (conditions) of registration. If, for instance, German law applies under Articles 21 or 22, an ECS issued by a German authority legitimates a sole heir not only with respect to his or her right of succession, but also to his or her right to immovable property located in Austria, without a further need for a decision by an Austrian court (*Einantwortungsbeschluss*).[128]

It seems doubtful, for instance, whether those conditions of Article 1(2)(l) are fulfilled with regard to the *legatum per damnationem* under German law. This is because the decision of the German legislator in favour of a legacy with obligatory effects and, inversely, against its Latin counterpart, essentially aims at preserving the unity of liable assets, thereby facilitating a transparent, predictable and uniform allocation of assets and their right holders (mainly) in the interest of creditors of the estate.[129]

5.2.5 *Reservation of the* Lex Rei Sitae

5.2.5.1 Differentiation Between the Nature of Rights *In Rem* and the Transfer of Property by Reason of Death

The principle of *numerus clausus* aims at protecting interests of publicity, too. The Succession Regulation accommodates that key principle of property law. As indicated by its preamble, sustaining specific forms of *acquisition* of property rights seems less urgent than respecting the *numerus clausus* principle. Recital 15 differentiates between the transfer of rights by succession (governed by succession law)[130] and the nature of rights *in rem* (*numerus clausus*) excluded from the Regulation's scope according to Article 1(2)(k).[131] Against this backdrop, raising the *numerus clausus* principle may, in particular cases, impair the *effet utile* of the Succession Regulation. Therefore, the delineation between Article 1(2)(k) (the nature of rights *in rem*) and Article 23(2)(e) (transfer of ownership by reason of death) plays a major role, proving more intricate than it might appear at first glance.

[128] The Austrian law of succession abstains from protecting publicity interests with regard to the acquisition of immovable property by reason of death, *cf* the Heidelberg Report (n 40) 35ff with further references; *cf* also I Ludwig, 'Anmerkung zum Beschluss des Notariats Villingen vom 12.09.2012 (II NG 801; ZEV 2013, 150)—Zur Frage der internationalen Zuständigkeit deutscher Gerichte' (2013) *Zeitschrift für Erbrecht und Vermögensnachfolge* 151, 152, with regard to the reverse situation (Austrian succession law applies to property located in Germany).

[129] *cf* BGH, 28 September 1994, (1995) *Neue juristische Wochenschrift* 58, 59 (III.3.b); Muscheler (n 91) 19ff; GJ Venrooy, 'Inländische Wirkung ausländischer Vindikationslegate' (1986) 85 *Zeitschrift für Vergleichende Rechtswissenschaft* 205, 233; G Otte, *Staudinger, BGB* (Berlin, Sellier de Gruyter, 2013) § 2174, para 4; D Leipold, 'Wandlungen in den Grundlagen des Erbrechts?' (1980) 180 *Archiv der civilistischen Praxis* 160, 208.

[130] Art 23(2)(e).

[131] *cf* also Wautelet and Bonomi (n 106) 121, para 110.

This is particularly true since the scope and content of the *numerus clausus* principle diverge considerably between Member States.[132] In particular, there is no common understanding of whether or not the *transfer* of a property right determines its content or—regarded from the private international law perspective of Article 1(2)(l)—forms part of its *nature*.[133]

However, according to the differentiation of recital 15, there are justifiable grounds to assume that the *numerus clausus* principle could not be opposed to the foreign legal instrument as such and its direct effects of transferring ownership by reason of death, but only to the specific content and effects of the property right itself transferred by that foreign instrument. In other words, the *numerus clausus* principle should not be understood as an undifferentiated right of veto extending the public policy exception.[134] Going along with the basic objective of the Succession Regulation to put an end to the competition for the better law of succession, the *numerus clausus* of property rights (concerning their content and effects) and the *numerus clausus* deriving from succession law (concerning types of disposal by reason of death) are to be distinguished.[135]

5.2.5.2 The *Numerus Clausus* Principle and the Adaptation of Property Rights

Opening the floodgates to unknown rights *in rem*[136] and their inconsistencies with domestic register law and enforcement or insolvency law can (also) be avoided through a narrow interpretation of the principle of *numerus clausus* of property rights and the instrument of adaptation. According to Article 31, an adaptation of the foreign property right to the closest (functionally) equivalent right *in rem* under domestic law should prevail to the greatest possible extent.[137] Interpreted in the light of Article 1(2)(k) and recital 15 sections 2, 3,[138] Article 31 underlines a restricted understanding of the *numerus clausus* of rights *in rem*. As a consequence of that approach,

[132] *cf* B Akkermans, *The Principle of Numerus Clausus in European Property Law* (Antwerp, Intersentia, 2008) 6ff, 565ff.

[133] Including, but without justification: HH Seiler, *Staudinger, BGB*, Einleitung zum Sachenrecht (2012) para 40; Martiny (n 14) 119, 122; Schmidt (n 77) 1, 21; also BGH (1995) *Neue juristische Wochenschrift*, 58, 59 (under III.3.a) against (in principle) Wautelet and Bonomi (n 106) A 121, para 110.

[134] Art 35.

[135] For further details see Laukemann, 'Die lex rei sitae in der Europäischen Erbrechtsverordnung—Inhalt, Schranken und Funktion' (n 100) 325, 336ff.

[136] *cf* Martiny (n 14) 119, 122ff; *cf* also M Brinkmann, *Kreditsicherheiten an beweglichen Sachen und Forderungen* (Tübingen, Mohr Siebeck, 2011) 322ff.

[137] *cf* also recital 16, s 3 providing an exchange of information on the nature and the effects of foreign property rights.

[138] According to Wautelet (n 106) 123ff, para 116, Arts 1(2)(k) and 31 are in conflict with each other. This conclusion, however, goes back to a broad understanding of the *numerus clausus* principle comprising the acquisition of property rights.

an adaptation of an unknown *legatum per vindicationem* to an equivalent right confined to obligatory effects might prove unnecessary in the sense of Article 31,[139] as long as the property right, transferred by that legacy, is commonly known to the legal order of the Member State in which the right *in rem* is invoked. Whatever the case, the European Court of Justice will have the final say over that intricate question.

[139] 'that right shall, *if necessary* ... be adapted'.

Part V

Collective Redress

10

'Opt-In is Out and Opt-Out is In': Dimensions Based on Nordic Options and the Commission's Recommendation

LAURA ERVO*

1. THE PRELUDE

'OPT-IN IS OUT and opt-out is in' wrote Lindblom in 2008.[1] However, still in 2013, the EU recommends a system of collective redress based on opting in. In the Commission's Recommendation C(2013) 3539 (Chapter V), 'Common principles for injunctive and compensatory collective redress mechanisms in the Member States concerning violations of rights granted under Union Law'. Specific principles relating to compensatory collective redress, with the title 'Constitution of the claimant party by "opt-in" principle', reads:

21. The claimant party should be formed on the basis of express consent of the natural or legal persons claiming to have been harmed ('opt-in' principle). Any exception to this principle, by law or by court order, should be duly justified by reasons of sound administration of justice.
22. A member of the claimant party should be free to leave the claimant party at any time before the final judgement is given or the case is otherwise validly settled, subject to the same conditions that apply to withdrawal in individual actions, without being deprived of the possibility to pursue its claims in another form, if this does not undermine the sound administration of justice.
23. Natural or legal persons claiming to have been harmed in the same mass harm situation should be able to join the claimant party at any time before the judgement is given or the case is otherwise validly settled, if this does not undermine the sound administration of justice.

* Professor of Law, Örebro University.

[1] PH Lindblom, 'Utvärdering av lagen om grupprättegång' (2008) 10 *Svensk Juristtidning* 833, 843.

24. The defendant should be informed about the composition of the claimant party and about any changes therein.

As we can see, the main recommendation of the Commission is that Member States enact an opt-in rule, which can be deviated from only for reasons of the sound administration of justice ('any exception to this principle, by law or by court order, should be duly justified by reasons of sound administration of justice'). This proposed slim possibility to make exceptions in the name of the 'sound administration of justice' is a very open ended policy proposal and places a great deal of responsibility on a Member State which chooses to enact such an opt-out option. Several questions come to mind: how much is needed to 'justify' such a decision, and which composites make the administration of justice 'sound'; what elements do 'the administration of justice' de facto include, and how high must the threshold be to depart from the main rule? And last but not least: why should the system mainly (and solely) be based on opt in?

2. THE CURRENT NORDIC SITUATION

2.1 The Scope and Nature of Group Actions

In Sweden, the system of group actions[2] has been in force since 2003.[3] The possibility of group actions covers civil cases, which belong to the competence of the general courts, as well as cases concerning environmental damages in the environmental courts.[4] The possible group actions in Sweden are: (i) group actions by private parties, (ii) governmental (public) group actions as well as (iii) group actions brought by specific organisations.[5] The system is based on the opt-in method.[6] Any party, which is a member of the group concerned, can bring a lawsuit against a defendant in the case of private group action. Natural or legal persons have standing to bring

[2] In Sweden, Norway and Denmark the term 'group action' is used, whereas in Finland the term 'class action' is used. The interesting peculiarity is that in Finland the scope of 'class actions' is the most restricted compared with the other Scandinavian countries even if the name refers more directly to the American type of broad class actions.

[3] Lindblom has commented on the earlier Swedish proposals, see PH Lindblom, 'Group Actions and the Role of the Courts—A European Perspective' (1997) 23 *Forum internationale* 15–21.

[4] Class Action Act, s 2, and Code of Environmental Matters, ch 32, s 13.

[5] Class Action Act, ss 1, 4, 5 and 6.

[6] Class Action Act, s 14. The committee report was based on an opt-out system (SOU 1994:151 *Grupprättegång. Betänkande av Grupptalanutredningen*) but it was turned into an opt-in system in Government Bill 2001/02:107 (Sweden) *Regeringens proposition 2001/02:107 Lag om grupprättegång*. The topic was again discussed in the follow-up report, Ds 2008:74. *Utvärdering av lagen gruppgättegång*, but the proposal put forward was not to change the system.

a private group action.[7] In group actions brought by organisations, the plaintiff is a non-profit-making association representing the interests of, for example, consumers or of employees.[8] In environmental cases, non-profit associations can bring group actions if they work for the interests of nature or environmental conservation. Also associations for fishermen, farmers, reindeer management and forest communities can bring an organisational group action regarding environmental issues.[9] Public group action is possible in cases where an action has not been brought in the form of a private group action or by the one of the organisations mentioned above.[10] The authorities, which may initiate a public group action, are the Consumer Ombudsman and the natural conservation authorities in environmental cases.[11]

In Finland, class actions are possible in disputes between consumers and companies. The Act on Class Actions came into force on 1 October 2007. Even if the name of the Act seems to cover class actions in general, class actions are possible only in consumer disputes.[12] Participation in a class action requires registration as a member of the class.[13] The system is therefore based on the opt-in method. Only governmental (public) class action is possible and it is the Consumer Ombudsman who will bring the class action and act as the representative of the class, thereby ensuring that an action cannot be brought for malicious purposes.[14]

In Norway, the legislation on group actions came into force on 1 January 2008.[15] The field of group actions is open.[16] The possible group actions are private group actions, governmental (public) group actions as well as group actions brought by organisations or associations.[17] The system is normally based on the opt-in system. Even the opt-out system may be used in certain situations.[18] The court may decide in favour of the opt-out system if a case covers small values or interests that cannot be expected to be promoted through individual action, and is not expected to raise questions that require individual treatment.[19] The aim seems to be to guarantee access to justice and courts as well as well-functioning proceedings.

[7] Class Action Act, s 4.
[8] ibid, s 5.
[9] Code of Environmental matters, ch 32, ss 13 and 14.
[10] Government Bill 2001/02:107, 54.
[11] Class Action Act, s 6 and decisions 1995:868 and 2001:1096 of the Council of State.
[12] s 1 of the Act.
[13] ibid, s 2.
[14] ibid, s 4. See also Government Bill 154/2006 (Finland) Hallituksen esitys eduskunnalle ryhmäkannelaiksi ja laiksi Kuluttajavirastosta annetun lain muuttamisesta, 20.
[15] See: www.lovdata.no/all/nl-20050617–090.html.
[16] The Code of Judicial Procedure in Civil Cases, ch 35, s 2.
[17] ibid, s 3.
[18] See more about the opt-out system in Norway in HB Berg and A Nordby, *Gruppesøksmål* (Oslo, Gyldendal Juridisk, 2012) 119.
[19] The Code of Judicial Procedure in Civil Cases, ch 35, ss 6 and 7.

In Denmark, Chapter 23a of the Danish Civil Procedural Code on group actions came into force on 1 January 2008. The field of group actions is open.[20] Group actions can be private group actions, group actions brought by authorities or by organisations or associations.[21] Both the op-in and opt-out systems are possible. However, the opt-out system is only possible in group actions brought by an authority. The other requirement for the opt-out system is that the individual claims have a very low monetary value which would be otherwise too small for court proceedings.[22] The aim is to guarantee access to justice and the fair use of the system at the same time since the opt-out system is only authority-based.

In class actions, access to justice and access to courts should be maximised. At the same time, sufficient safeguards for well-functioning procedures and the fair use of the system should be guaranteed. Public class action based on opt-out safeguards all the aforementioned aims very effectively. There seems to be no risk of abuse and in addition access to justice is maximised if the authorities work effectively and have enough resources for bringing class actions whenever needed. Have we found a class action paradise in Denmark?

2.2 Case Law

In Sweden, by the beginning of 2014, 17 group actions had been brought before the courts. Some cases have been dismissed or cancelled, or they have ended with a settlement or been dealt with in arbitration. Almost all the group actions have been private group actions but one case is a public group action, brought by the Consumer Ombudsman in which the intermediate judgment ordered the respondent to pay damages to the consumers. However, the question of how much each consumer was entitled to receive was settled by an agreement between the Consumer Ombudsman and the company when the case was still pending. Although final judgment was never obtained, the Ombudsman was satisfied with the half amount claimed.[23] In addition, up until now there has been only one successful case, which has been decided by a judgment. See below details of the successful case and the above-mentioned consumer case:

Svea Court of Appeal, 21 December 2009, T 3552-09, Veterinärutbildningen

Private group action. Damages due to discrimination regarding university entrance. Affirmed by Svea Court of Appeal.

[20] The Civil Procedural Code, ch 23a, s 254b.
[21] ibid, s 254c.
[22] ibid, s 254e.
[23] See: www.konsumentverket.se/Nyheter/Pressmeddelanden/Pressmeddelanden-2014/Ersattning-till-tusentals-konsumenter-efter-tio-ars-rattsprocess.

The Court of Appeal for Northern Norrland, 4 November 2011, T 154-10, Kraftkommission

Public group action. Damages due to the defendants' failure to supply electric power. The intermediate judgment was delivered and subsequently affirmed by the Court of Appeal for Northern Norrland. Liability for damages was established in the intermediate judgment and the Supreme Court denied leave to appeal. This means that the intermediate judgment is final and binding. The next step would have been for the Court to establish quantum of the damages to be awarded to the group members, but as explained above the case was settled by an agreement between the Ombudsman and the company before that.

It must be underlined that there are more successful cases as settlements and arbitral awards may also be victorious. However, these are often not publicly available.

Until now there has been no case in Finland, which has caused some debate in the media.[24] The Ombudsman has been criticised because her threshold for initiating a group action seems to be very high. The other actors in the field are of the opinion that there have been several situations where a group action could have been a good tool to ensure access to the justice system and access to the courts especially with regard to consumer cases. However, according to the Ombudsman there has been no need to initiate a group action because the mere availability of the group action mechanism has worked as a deterrent or threat and it has been possible to resolve the cases by other means. She considers that up until now it has been sufficient to have the threat of group action and to use that threat when promoting the rights of consumers.[25] The Consumer Agency also maintains that another reason for the lack of initiated cases is that there is a fear that a group action would be difficult and entail lengthy legal proceedings, which could become expensive for the Agency. If a group action were to be dismissed, the government would have to pay the defendant's costs, while all the work and attorney's fees would have to be paid by the Agency itself. Therefore, the Consumer Ombudsman may decide in her discretion not to bring a group action on the grounds that the procedure is too complicated due to the complexity of the current case.[26]

In Norway, there were four class actions in 2010 and 13 in 2011.[27] In Denmark, there have been nine cases so far.[28] When the rules on group

[24] See eg, www.hs.fi/kotimaa/AL+Ryhm%C3%A4kanteet+eiv%C3%A4t+etene+kuluttaja-asiamiehelt%C3%A4+oikeuteen/a1305581561697.

[25] See: kuningaskuluttaja.yle.fi/node/2234.

[26] See eg, www.hs.fi/kotimaa/AL+Ryhm%C3%A4kanteet+eiv%C3%A4t+etene+kuluttaja-asiamiehelt%C3%A4+oikeuteen/a1305581561697.

[27] Domstolene i Norge. Årsmelding 2011, available at: http://aarsmelding.domstol.no/data/2011/aarsmelding.pdf. Statistic 2012 did not include any information on class actions: http://aarsmelding.domstol.no.

[28] U 2012.2938 H, U 2012.1561 V, U 2012.1228 H, U 2011.1596 V, U 2011.1168 Ø, and U 2010.2389 H, U 2013 2651 H, U 2014 100 V and U 2014 487 H.

actions were enacted, the government inserted a 'sunset clause' to make sure that the need to adjust the rules would be considered at a later date. This clause was first postponed because the practical experiences were too few to evaluate the rules. Now, the Danish Ministry of Justice has proposed deleting the clause because the rules seem to function well.[29] One very interesting case concerns the new digital land register system, which caused registration delays entailing extra costs for individuals who needed to register their property. The group action is being brought against the state.[30]

To sum up, Nordic experience is overall lacking and there is limited case law. However, group actions have been a working instrument in all Nordic countries bar Finland. The reason for that is obvious. In the other Nordic countries private and organisation brought group actions exist while in Finland only governmental group actions are possible. Therefore, to promote access to courts through a class action system requires that private parties or at least organisations or associations are also given standing. In addition, it would be more effective to allow opt-out actions as well as in Norway and Denmark.

3. THE NATURE OF COLLECTIVE REDRESS

The procedural instrument we are analysing has been defined broadly as 'collective and representative[31] actions'. The idea is for redress to be collective, which is different from a normal multiparty procedure that may be available in accordance with the general procedural rules relevant in the matter.[32] There is commonly nothing to prevent one action including several plaintiffs when a multiparty situation exists and all parties wish to cooperate. However, in such a case the action takes the shape of a 'normal' civil action under the general procedural rules and the plaintiffs will not reap the benefits of an easier procedure thanks to a specific collective redress mechanism. That is why there should be certain differences between collective redress and regular multiparty litigation. As long as collective redress is more or less identical to general multiparty proceedings, there is no reason to make a distinction between these two different tools. In which case,

[29] See: www.hoeringsportalen.dk/Hearing/Details/23623.

[30] See: http://gruppesoegsmaal.nu.

[31] Regarding collective standing, see A Gidi, 'Class Actions in Brazil—A Model for Civil Law Countries' (2003) LI *American Journal of Comparative Law* 311, 363–64.

[32] See also Gidi, 'Class Actions in Brazil' (n 31) 337, where he wrote that it is common to say that a class action is, by definition, brought without the consent of all the people represented. Taruffo has stressed that even if the nature of class actions is to be collective they do not only represent collective rights, but also individual rights collectively which is important to bear in mind. M Taruffo, 'Notes on Collective Protection of Rights' in *Procesos colectivos class actions* (International Conference and XXIII Iberoamerican Procedural Law Convention, Buenos Aires, June 2012) 23–30, 24.

cooperative multiparty plaintiffs are able to reach the same result through their own activity.

In addition, there is every reason to ask whether it is useful to have two separate systems if the differences are so small and if collective redress is in actual fact not very collective or representative at all. In such a situation there is no reason to make the procedural map more fragmented. In order to offer a real alternative, the differences and benefits must be substantial enough. To be collective and representative, the system should preferably be based on opt-out. The nature of collective redress requires it.

4. ACCESS TO THE COURTS AND THE PASSIVITY PROBLEM

The aim of a collective redress system is to guarantee access to justice and access to courts in situations where traditional procedures do not fulfil these aims well enough.[33] Access to justice and access to courts are essentially linked with the idea of collective redress. The whole system of collective and representative litigation is to promote this 'access' and to make it easier to litigate and more achievable to reach the courts of first instance and finally to get justice. Since access to courts and to justice is all about fundamental and human rights, everyone, not only active citizens, but equally passive and marginalised citizens should be included. It is not only about rights of 'winners'; the less fortunate should be included as well. Active, intelligent, healthy and wealthy adults who belong to the local population and who also represent the majority, seldom have problems realising their rights and gaining access to justice. They have the necessary knowledge and tools to do so. Mostly, collective redress is not there to help them but instead it aims to bring fairness and justice even when a vulnerable citizen does not have the capacity to struggle in a situation where the opponent is strong, like for instance a major company. It is a question of protection and the provision of legal services for those who need them most and who have the least power and capacity to demand them. Therefore the opt-out system realises the procedural human rights and even the rights of defendants better.[34]

[33] See, eg, R Mulheron, *The Class Action in Common Law Legal Systems. A Comparative Perspective* (Oxford, Hart Publishing, 2004) 52–57.

[34] See section 4. See also PH Lindblom, *Grupptalan Det anglo-amerikanska class actioninstutet ur svenskt perspektiv* (Stockholm, Norstedts Juridik, 1989) 210–11, where he describes the American amendments made in 1966. One reason behind the reform was to protect the right of defence. However, after the reform the number of class actions rose dramatically which was seen as a drawback from the defendant's perspective. Some were of the opinion that the reason for this increase was the 1966 reform. Still, a too weak or too complicated instrument is not the solution to prevent the risk of abuse. The class action system should be created in such a way that it can be used whenever it is needed. This is the only basis that is fair to all the actors. It is not fair to protect the right of defence with procedural tools that are impractical and which do not work. If the safeguards are needed, they should be created, just as in Denmark where only public class actions can be based on opt-out. See EL Andersen, *Gruppesøksmål* (Copenhagen, Thomson, 2007).

In many systems, collective redress only covers consumer and environmental matters. In those jurisdictions a collective tool for litigation is a natural continuation of substantive consumer and environmental protection rules and we should regard collective redress from this point of view and not isolate it from its context and design. Again, in such a context it seems to be natural to favour opt-out.

One of the objectives of collective redress is to solve the passivity problem among potential parties.[35] There is no need for collective action among active people as explained above. They can solve their problems through individual claims. However, the aim is to include inactive people and for that the opt-in system does not help much. According to empirical studies, only 8 per cent of group members opted out while 60 per cent 'opted out' by not opting in.[36] Inactive people seem to stay passive in all situations. Others have to be active in order to help them. If the aim is to serve passive and marginalised people, the right tool is not opt-in but opt-out.

5. ECONOMIC REASONS AND THE RATIONAL USE OF RESOURCES

Procedural economy is one indicator where rational litigation is concerned.[37] Quite often it is not rational to initiate an individual lawsuit where the claim is small and where the procedure would entail costs in the form of money, time, extra work and discomfort. In such a situation, the plaintiff party often does not want to go to court and decides not to pursue the case even if it would have substantive law on its side. The defendant party often knows this and thus takes a risk and will not pay damages voluntarily even if it understands that it would probably lose the case in court. This risk is worth taking especially if there are a substantial number of potential plaintiffs. By refusing to pay, the defendant can save a lot of time and money if the individual plaintiff parties do not have the capacity or energy to react. This is the very essence of collective redress: to avoid the latter situation and to make it easier for individuals in small claims situations. To save resources, a collective lawsuit should reach and cover all the parties who would not otherwise bring a lawsuit against the defendant. The answer is again the opt-out system. In the opt-in system, despite the collective action, there are still a number of inactive people who fall outside the case, the court and the justice system.

However, the situation can be seen even from the defendant's perspective. The defendant will also save resources of all kinds if the conflict is solved

[35] Mulheron has written a very informative chapter on this theme: 'Balancing Judicial Activism and Personal Autonomy' in Mulheron, *The Class Action in Common Law Legal Systems* (n 33) 60–63.

[36] PH Lindblom, *Grupptalan i Sverige* (Stockholm, Norstedts Juridik, 2008) 225.

[37] See also Mulheron (n 33) 57–60, on these economic reasons.

as a whole at once through one action with the *res judicata* and *ne bis in idem* effects.[38] Also, the judicial relief of the defendant is an additional argument for the opt-out system. By doing so, the defendant can be sure that the conflict will be solved as a whole at once and there is no uncertainty for the future either. This helps the defendant to consider the risks and the economic value of the action and therefore makes it easier to reach a settlement in the case. As long as the defendant can only guess the real value of the claim, he or she is probably not that willing to pay and settle the case.

6. THE FUNCTIONS OF CIVIL PROCEEDINGS

Currently, the most important function in adjudication is that contextual decisions, which the parties are satisfied with, are produced through fair proceedings. Therefore, civil proceedings and the justice system can be held to have two main goals, namely procedural fairness and satisfaction of its users. There has even been a change in the doctrinal and policy perspective on civil proceedings from solely providing formal justice towards also emphasising the perception of procedural justice. There is a change from focusing on the adjudicative power of the courts towards seeing the courts as providing a service, which means that it is not enough to follow normative fairness but the actors should additionally feel that the procedure was fair and what is doctrinally called an experimental sense of fairness is nowadays a significant factor in due process. Adjudication can now be called a service of the courts.[39]

The new court culture and the change in the procedural paradigm can easily be seen as a kind of counter-effect stemming from the population at large. Citizens prefer individual service, not only the traditional state control. They want to feel experimental procedural justice and perceive the ultimate effect of civil proceedings as conflict resolution for their personal purposes. In this new paradigm there is a need for a different attitude and a different type of state authorities.

[38] More detailed information on *res judicata* in class actions in Gidi, 'Class Actions in Brazil' (n 31) 384–99 and A Gidi, 'Issue Preclusion & Class Certification' (2012) 63 *Hastings Law Journal* 1023.

[39] K Ervasti, *Käräjäoikeuksien sovintomenettely—Empiirinen tutkimus sovinnon edistämisestä riitaprosessissa* (Helsinki, Oikeuspoliittinen Tutkimuslaitos, 2004) 168; V Haavisto, Court Work in Transition. An Activity–Theoretical Study of Changing Work Practices in a Finnish District Court (University of Helsinki, 2002) 20; S Laukkanen, *Tuomarin rooli* (Helsinki, Suomalainen Lakimiesyhdistys, 1995) 214; J-P Takala, *Moraalitunteet rikosten sovittelussa* (Helsinki, Oikeuspoliittinen Tutkimuslaitos, 1998) 3–5; J Tala, *Luottamus tuomioistuimiin—mitä se on ja tarvitaanko sitä lisää?* (Helsinki, Lakimies, 2002) 3, 21–23; TR Tyler, *Why People Obey the Law* (New Haven, CT, Yale University Press, 1990) 94; and J Virolainen and P Martikainen, *Pro et contra: tuomion perustelemisen keskeisiä kysymyksiä* (Helsinki, Talentum, 2003) 5.

Civil proceedings can also be seen as micro politics[40] and as a forum for moral discussions. Recently there have been many cases that have also had a societal impact outside the courts and where the discussions and deliberations during the proceedings are more interesting from the general public's point of view than the outcome of any individual case. Some examples can be mentioned: the cases against the tobacco industry, cases concerning the bank crisis at the beginning of the 1990s and, for instance, cases concerning bullying. In these situations, with the help of the media, the public procedure is a new place for moral discussions and sometimes they even include political elements that lead to societal choices.[41] At their best, moral discussions mean that the legal discourse in trials becomes more transparent and democratic. To realise this, the legal concepts must be developed in such a way that they better meet the grass roots level and by doing so provide a forum for moral discussions.[42]

The Swedish Ministry of Justice commissioned a broad research project on the trust of the citizens in courts in 2008. According to this report, there are several factors which are important as regards people's trust and confidence in the courts. The list is as follows: the accessibility of the courts and the court staff for parties and people giving evidence; the courts' reception of parties and people giving evidence; the processing times at the courts; the transparency of the courts' decision-making processes; the way in which judgments and decisions are formulated; the way in which the activities of the courts are portrayed by the media; the knowledge of the general public about what goes on in the courts; and finally the conduct of judges.[43] All elements refer to a new kind of role for the judges where the action is based more on social than legal skills. The public is looking for help and a service in their cases. They are no longer satisfied with distant and formal judges whose authority is based on the law and the institution as such. They are no longer looking for authoritative and final decisions made by someone in power. They are seeking cooperative skills to help solve a conflict and to be able to get on with their lives.

There has also been a very broad doctrinal discussion in Sweden on the purpose of civil proceedings, based on which the current understanding is that the purpose is mainly a matter of conflict resolution. Traditionally, to grant judicial relief has been held to be the main purpose of civil procedure.[44] In other words, the purpose of procedure has been to grant the

40 Sometimes judges also make political resolutions.

41 T Wilhelmsson, '(Media)julkinen oikeudenkäynti moraalikeskustelun tilana' (2002) 3 *Oikeus* 252, 252–53.

42 ibid, 262.

43 SOU 2008:106. *Ökat förtroende för domstolarna—strategier och förslag—Statens offentliga utredningar* (Committee Report, Sweden) 26.

44 The goal of civil procedure has traditionally been said to be the realisation of the interests and the rights of civil law. That is also why the procedural values have been regarded as being

interests of civil law. The proceedings are the instrument needed to ensure access to justice strictly according to substantive law. The traditional point of view is thus internal, focusing on the object or substantive case at hand with which the specific procedure is concerned. However, based on current doctrinal understanding the purposes are broader and aspects of society are taken into consideration. In the current discourse, the main purpose of the procedure has been held to be the resolution of disputes[45] or conflicts,[46] or even both.[47] Those who regard the purpose of procedure to be dispute resolution understand the process as a sanction mechanism. The idea is that the procedure strengthens the influence of substantive law and therefore judgments should be passed strictly according to substantive law. The point of view is external and procedure is seen as an instrument. The purpose of the proceedings as an instrument is to guide the behaviour of people so that they obey the norms of substantive law. At the same time, civil proceedings have the task of maintaining and advancing morals in society. This approach to the purpose of proceedings is quite close to the traditional doctrinal line of thought. The main difference is, however, that the point of view is not internal but external and that proceedings are held to have effects on the whole of society.[48]

The other current doctrinal line of thought is to see conflict resolution as a purpose of court proceedings, which seems to be the most popular and current trend among both academics and the legislator. According to that train of thought the most important aspect is for the proceedings to resolve the entire conflict between the parties not only the judicial problems. The correctness of the judgment and its contents are not the most important aspect; instead the task is to resolve the conflict in such a way that it will exist no more and the parties can get on with their lives and even get on with each other. The latter is especially important in a case where the parties are, for instance, neighbours, colleagues, former spouses or business partners who still have joint activities and will continue to do so even in the future. In order to achieve this aim, the parties should participate broadly in a procedure and have a wide set of possibilities to make dispositions as well.[49]

The most recent doctrinal trend is to see the purpose of civil proceedings as conflict resolution and to underline those kinds of characteristics.

identical with the values of substantive law. See for instance W Henckel, *Prozessrecht und Materielles Recht* (Göttingen, Otto Schwartz, 1970) 409.

[45] eg, Hägerström, Lundstedt, Olivekrona, Ekelöf, Andenæs, Boman, Werin, Scott and Fiss.

[46] eg, Aubert, Bolding, Eckhoff, Lindell and Palmgren. According to Lindell the procedure in non-mandatory civil cases should be conflict resolution and in mandatory cases dispute resolution. B Lindell, *Partsautonomins gränser* (Hallsberg, Iustus, 1988) 87.

[47] Eg, Lindblom and Strömholm see in the procedure the influences of both theories. PH Lindblom, 'Processens funktioner—en resa i gränslandet' in *Progressiv process. Spridda uppsatser om domstolsprocessen och samhällsutvecklingen* (Hallsberg, Iustus, 2000) 41, 52–58.

[48] Aggregated in Ervasti (n 39) 507.

[49] ibid.

In practice, the legislator, academics and actors seem to both seek and appreciate elements which realise this type of civil litigation. Mediation and class actions are examples of more communal conflict resolution methods that correspond to such an ethos. By introducing such methods in the procedural system the legislator tries to achieve the goal regarding access to justice and experimental fairness better and in a more effective way.[50]

The current elements in civil litigation, namely, court service, experimental justice, conflict resolution and dispute resolution as functions of civil procedure, court proceedings as micro politics and the scene for moral discussions provide more support for the opt-out system than the opt-in system.[51] There is arguably a mental readiness for opt-out and the general public expects a new type of kind, tactful and above all service-providing authority.

Traditionally, all of the above thinking has been included in the idea of the welfare state, which has, for instance, provided general education and health services. Why should it not also provide court services? The line of reasoning that everyone must have decision-making power to be able to opt in does not rhyme well with our current social order and people's expectations. Additionally, it is not a question of 'compulsory treatment'. There is always the possibility to opt out.

7. PROCEDURAL REASONS

There are also several procedural arguments which speak against opt-in and in defence of opt-out. Namely, it takes approximately two years to constitute the group, at least according to Nordic statistics.[52] In addition, that part of the proceedings requires a great deal of work. Even if the opt-out system also requires good information, it is still easier and cheaper to inform and update people in such cases.

In the case of collective redress, the joinder of actions is allowed and therefore the court may join other group actions or other pending cases into

[50] L Ervo, 'Party Autonomy and Access to Justice' in A Jokela, L Ervo and M Gräns (eds), *Europeanization of Procedural Law and the New Challenges to Fair Trial* (Groningen, Europa Law Publishing, 2009) 21; L Ervo, 'The Role of Judges and Party-Autonomy in Court-Facilitated Settlement' in R Stürner and M Kawano (eds), *International Contract Litigation, Arbitration and Judicial Responsibility in Transnational Disputes* (Tübingen, Mohr Siebeck, 2011) 336; and L Ervo, 'Substantive Law and the Newest Procedural Trends in Scandinavia' in R Stürner and M Kawano (eds), *International Contract Litigation, Arbitration and Judicial Responsibility in Transnational Disputes* (Tübingen, Mohr Siebeck, 2011) 147.

[51] Lindblom has stressed the same covering the micro politics and the scene for moral discussions aspects. Lindblom, *Grupptalan i Sverige* (n 36) 175.

[52] TemaNord 2006:583 'Consumers' Right of Action in Antitrust Cases—Current Problems and Future Solutions', available at: www.norden.org/fi/julkaisut/julkaisut/ 2006-583.

the group proceedings.[53] Also intervention is allowed according to the normal rules. In the case of intervention, the new subject in the lawsuit is given party status in group proceedings.[54] These procedural possibilities water down the nature and aims of opt-in. At the same time they bring the opt-in type of collective redress closer to the opt-out system because even if you have not opted in it is still possible to do so later via other procedural rules. Of course, the procedural consequences vary depending on which of these alternative procedural tools is attempted but they are still instruments to try to get more parties involved in the same action at a later stage. The aim is to achieve a synergy effect, to resolve all claims covering the same situation and the same defendant all at once; in other words to realise those aims and to reach those benefits which have already been presented above. Still, the same advantages and even more could be achieved through opt-out. In such cases, it is possible to minimise the need for joinder and intervention and all group members will obtain the benefits the group action gives them.

As regards *res judicata*, its effect and its limits may be more or less unclear as long as the system is based on opt-in. In those cases, the *res judicata* effect only covers the group members in most cases. However, there may be marginalised areas where the group action and the result thereof have an impact on later cases in the form of evidentiary effect or as a precedent. Even if the latter does not belong to *res judicata* it affects later proceedings. That is why it is clearer and fairer to admit that whenever the collective and representative tool is possible and is used, its effects will cover all people in the same situation regardless of whether they do not obviously opt out. 'The opt-in system also guarantees that the judgment will not bind other potentially qualified claimants who did not join' the Commission wrote in its Communication.[55] Therefore, the Commission does not seem to appreciate the benefits of *res judicata* but sees it as a risk. From the procedural law point of view, this argument is difficult to understand. As already explained, both practical and institutional procedural reasons are grounds for covering *res judicata* by one action and the tool to reach these 'savings' is naturally opt-out.

To summarise, the sound administration of justice seems to require opt-out even if the Commission sees the procedural situation the other way around. Last but not least, the very fundamental principles of law and order as well as public peace, are strong arguments for opt-out. It is only by opting out that the conflict will be resolved as a whole and without any uncertainties in the future. It is in that way and that way alone that public peace, and law and order can be achieved.

[53] Lindblom, *Grupptalan i Sverige* (n 36) 502–03.
[54] Code of Judicial Procedure, ch 14.
[55] See more about this Communication in section 8.

8. A CRITICAL DISCUSSION BASED ON THE COMMISSION'S COMMUNICATION

In the Communication from the Commission to the European Parliament, the Council, the European Economic and Social Committee and the Committee of the Regions COM(2013) 401 with the title 'Towards a European Horizontal Framework for Collective Redress', there are grounds for the opt-in system in section 3.4:

> A significant number of stakeholders, in particular businesses, strongly oppose the 'opt-out' model, arguing that it is more prone to abuse and that it may be unconstitutional in some Member States, or at least incompatible with their legal traditions. On the other hand, some consumer organisations argue that 'opt-in' systems may fail to deliver effective access to justice for all consumers who have been harmed. In their view, the availability of 'opt-out' is therefore desirable, at least as an option in appropriate cases and subject to approval by the court.

The possibility to abuse the system is the most traditional argument against class actions generally and especially against the opt-out system. However, this argument does not hold. Because, in such a case, substantive law—for instance tort law and the material basis for the right to obtain damages—does not change; and collective redress will not do so either. If punitive damages are not allowed according to substantive law or if the threshold for establishing negligence or liability has not been lowered, the fear of this type of negative Americanisation is amateurish. Collective redress is just a procedural tool to realise substantive law like all procedures. Therefore, it is surprising to me to read again and again these arguments where people try to explain that we need to avoid effective procedural tools; in other words we may not maximise access to justice but we have to torpedo it—to eliminate the risk of abuse. To put it in a different way, this means protecting wrongdoers. Where substantive law provides for liability, there should be effective tools to realise it and to ensure access to justice. When substantive law is not responsive, the problem lies in substantive law and not in the procedural tools. The aim of proceedings is to guarantee access to justice; in other words to realise substantive law. All of this means that there is always a link between procedural law and substantive law, and procedural law is just a method of execution. The method should be well functioning, otherwise it is useless.

The other often repeated argument is 'legal tradition'. The Commission notes that opt-out does not fit into the legal traditions of all Member States without giving any examples or descriptions of the kind of legal traditions those countries have. A great number of questions arise again. Is it not true that access to justice and access to the courts belong to various legal traditions, like consumer and environmental protection? Legal traditions should not prevent legal development. At least legal traditions should be defined and described first otherwise this argument is just empty words without any content:

> In the Commission's view, it should be ensured that the represented *group is clearly defined* so as to allow the court to conduct the proceedings in a manner consistent with the rights of all parties, and in particular with the rights of the defence.
>
> The 'opt-in' system *respects the right of a person to decide* whether to participate or not. It therefore better preserves the autonomy of parties to choose whether to take part in the litigation or not. In this system the value of the collective dispute is more easily determined, since it would consist of the sum of all individual claims. The court is in a better position to assess both *the merits* of the case and *the admissibility* of the collective action.

It is argued that the opt-in system is easier for the courts and for case management. However, the aim of the procedure should be to serve the parties and to provide them with access to justice. The court is not the object of proceedings. There should not be any process just due to the process itself. In addition, the opt-out model makes the procedure more orthodox as far as, for example, *res judicata* and public peace are concerned. They are ancient procedural values that are of significant importance in any legal system. Opting out realises both principles effectively whereas opting in leaves many questions open in this context:

> The 'opt-out' system gives rise to more fundamental questions as to the *freedom* of potential claimants to decide whether they want to litigate. The right to an effective remedy cannot be interpreted in a way that *prevents people from making (informed) decisions* on whether they wish to claim damages or not.

This is just a practical question regarding information. Regardless of whether the system is based on opt-in or opt-out, the information and notifications should work inclusively. Without that both systems are invalid. Opting in is even more defenceless when information is lacking because in the particular case in hand, the potential parties have missed the possibility of using this easier way to achieve their rights whereas opting out is not that risky from this point of view. Class members will not lose anything even if they did not know that they were involved. As you can see, I see collective redress as a positive possibility to obtain my rights more easily with the help of collective power. I also see the counter-arguments—where collective redress has been seen as a risk regarding access to justice for individuals meaning that their right to join in or stay out of the group should be maximised by the opt-in system—as artificial. Collective redress should be seen as an instrument when achieving material rights and not the other way around; an effective tool to realise substantive law correctly and when needed is not a risk:

> In addition, an 'opt-out' system *may not be consistent with the central aim of collective redress*, which is to obtain compensation for harm suffered, since such persons are not identified, and so the award will not be distributed to them.

This sounds like very empty rhetoric. Arguably, exactly the opposite is true. The very aim of collective redress is to be a collective instrument and to do it together and for all at the same time with the help of one action. By doing so, all people can gain access to justice regardless of their level of activity and their capability. It sounds sound, equal and fair. It sounds just. It sounds even better when enforcement also occurs collectively. Only the opt-out system can guarantee compensation for the harm suffered by people, and collective enforcement will guarantee that it is also distributed to them. It looks like the Commission lacks valid arguments when trying to defend the opt-in system. Almost all its arguments in favour of the opt-in system are in fact arguments in favour of the opt-out system.

9. THE FINALE

Without courage and a little bit of risk-taking there will be no progress. Too many adaptations will water down the original nature of collective redress. There is no need for such instruments as long as they only remain laws in books but not useful in practice. To ensure that collective redress is effective and works well, it must be based on the opt-out system.

11

The Crux of the Matter: Funding and Financing Collective Redress Mechanisms

STEFAAN VOET*

1. INTRODUCTION

TWO DECADES AGO, class actions were as good as a non-issue on the European continent. They only flourished in the US and related to common law jurisdictions.[1] But times have changed.[2] Mainly in order to manage high profile mass cases,[3] European countries have increasingly adopted procedures that share some characteristics of the US class action and that are often termed 'class actions',[4] although substantial differences

* Associate Professor of Law University of Leuven, Visiting Professor University of Hasselt, Programme Associate CMS/Swiss Re Research Programme on Civil Justice Systems (Centre for Socio-Legal Studies University of Oxford).

[1] R Mulheron, *The Class Action in Common Law Legal Systems: A Comparative Perspective* (Oxford, Hart Publishing, 2004).

[2] DR Hensler, 'The Future of Mass Litigation: Global Class Actions and Third-Party Litigation Funding' (2011) 79 *George Washington Law Review* 306 (listing 21 jurisdictions that currently have class actions). In the US, class actions seem to be on the decline (see RH Klonoff, 'The Decline of Class Actions' (2013) 90 *Washington University Law Review* 729 and LS Mullenix, 'Aggregate Litigation and the Death of Democratic Dispute Resolution' (2013) 107 *Northwestern University Law Review* 511).

[3] eg, the *Deutsche Telekom AG* case in Germany leading to the 2005 German Act on Model Case Proceedings in the Capital Markets or *KapMuG* (see M Stürner, 'Model Case Proceedings in the Capital Markets: Tentative Steps Towards Group Litigation in Germany' (2007) 26 *Civil Justice Quarterly* 250, 253) and the *DES* case in the Netherlands leading to the 2005 Collective Settlements Act or *WCAM* (see I Tzankova and D Lunsingh Scheurleer, 'The Netherlands' (2009) 622 *Annals of the American Academy of Political and Social Science* 149, 155).

[4] eg, Germany (see n 3; see also L Röckrath, 'Germany' in PG Karlsgodt (ed), *World Class Actions. A Guide to Group and Representative Actions around the Globe* (New York, Oxford University Press, 2012)), the Netherlands (see n 3; see also J Fleming and JJ Kuster, 'The Netherlands' in Karlsgodt, *World Class Actions*), Sweden (2002 Swedish Group Proceedings Act; see G Sparrman and L Göransson, 'Sweden' in Karlsgodt, *World Class Actions*), Norway (2005 Norwegian Dispute Act; see P Kiurunen and N Lindström, 'Norway' in Karlsgodt, *World Class Actions*), Finland (2007 Finnish Act on Class Actions; see P Kiurunen, 'Finland'

remain. Over time, European policymakers have also started to focus on the class action debate, especially in the fields of consumer redress[5] and competition law.[6] In 2013, this culminated in the European Commission launching a Recommendation on common principles for injunctive and compensatory collective redress mechanisms.[7] Although non-binding, these principles will shape the future debate. European policymakers have always used the term 'collective redress' rather than 'class action' to describe their procedural aims.[8] The goal is to establish 'a procedural mechanism that allows, for reasons of procedural economy and/or efficiency of enforcement, many similar legal claims to be bundled together into a single court action'. The purpose of such a mechanism is to

> facilitate[s] access to justice in particular in cases where the individual damage is so low that potential claimants would not think it worth pursuing an individual claim. It also strengthens the negotiating power of potential claimants and contributes to the efficient administration of justice, by avoiding numerous proceedings concerning claims resulting from the same infringement of law.[9]

Any jurisdiction wanting to introduce a collective redress mechanism will be confronted with the same design options: will its scope be trans-substantive

in Karlsgodt, *World Class Actions*), Denmark (1992 Danish Administration of Justice Act; see P Kiurunen, N Lindström and M Bylov Rath, 'Denmark' in Karlsgodt, *World Class Actions*), Portugal (see C Gonçalves Borges and M Serra Baptista, 'Portugal' in Karlsgodt, *World Class Actions*), Poland (see M Tulibacka, 'Poland' (2009) 622 *Annals of the American Academy of Political and Social Science* 190) and Spain (see F Malaga, 'Spain' in Karlsgodt, *World Class Actions*). In 2014, Belgium and France adopted a consumer class action system (see S Voet, 'European Collective Redress: A Status Quaestionis' (2014) 4 *International Journal of Procedural Law* 97; and S Voet, 'Consumer Collective Redress in Belgium: Class Actions to the Rescue?' (2015) 1 *European Business Organization Law Review* 121.

5 Commission, 'Green Paper on consumer collective redress' COM(2008) 794 final and European Parliament Resolution of 2 February 2012, 'Towards a Coherent European Approach to Collective Redress' 2011/2089 (INI).

6 Commission, 'Green Paper on damages actions for breach of the EC antitrust rules' COM(2005) 672 final and 'White Paper on damages actions for breach of the EC antitrust rules' COM(2008) 165 final.

7 Recommendation 2013/396/EU on common principles for injunctive and compensatory collective redress mechanisms in the Member States concerning violations of rights granted under Union Law [2013] OJ L206/60. For a first analysis see C Hodges, 'Collective Redress: A Breakthrough or a Damp Squib?' (2014) 37 *Journal of Consumer Policy* 67 and E Silvestri, 'Towards a Common Framework of Collective Redress in Europe? An Update on the Latest Initiatives of the European Commission' (2013) 1 *Russian Law Journal* 47. Together with the Recommendation, the Commission published a Communication, 'Towards a European Horizontal Framework for Collective Redress' COM(2013) 401, and a 'Proposal for a Directive on certain rules governing actions for damages under national law for infringements of the competition law provisions of the Member States and of the European Union' COM(2013) 404 final.

8 'Commission recommends Member States to have collective redress mechanisms in place to ensure effective access to justice' press release, 11 June 2013, available at: europa.eu/rapid/press-release_IP-13-524_en.htm.

9 Communication (n 7) 4.

or restricted?[10] Who will have standing?[11] How will the class be notified?[12] Will it be an opt-in or opt-out regime?[13] And what remedies will be available?[14] However, the question of how the mechanism will be funded and financed transcends all these issues, simply because without appropriate and clear funding rules, they will remain a dead letter. Funding rules are an essential precondition for the proper functioning of any civil justice system.[15] In that sense the funding and financing issue is the crux of the matter, because it goes to the heart of the class action system.

In this brief chapter, I will not assess how the optimal funding regime of a European class action should be organized. For that there are too many legal and cultural differences in both the existing (and future) European collective redress mechanisms and in the one-on-one litigation funding rules.[16] The goal of this chapter is simply to map the various funding options and assess their pros and cons in a collective litigation context.[17] The leitmotif will be the Recommendation of the European Commission. It should be noted that the latter does not explicitly state how collective redress mechanisms should be funded. The accompanying Communication reads: 'the European Parliament is not in favour of setting out conditions or guidelines for the private funding of damages claims at EU level'.[18] In order to strike a balance between access to justice and avoiding abusive litigation,[19]

[10] Trans-substantive rules apply broadly to all civil lawsuits regardless of the substantive law underlying the claims and regardless of the size of the litigation or the stakes involved (SN Subrin, 'The Limitations of Transsubstantive Procedure: An Essay on Adjusting the "One Size Fits All" Assumption' (2010) 87 *Denver University Law Review* 377, 378).

[11] An individual class member as in the US, or an association, foundation or governmental body. The latter are sometimes defined as ideological plaintiffs, Mulheron (n 1) 303. See on the standing issue, chapter 12 in this volume by R Money-Kyrle.

[12] Individual notice or non-individual notice (eg, notice through television, newspaper advertisements, the Internet, etc).

[13] Opt-in means that the class includes only those individuals or legal persons who actively opt in to become part of the class. Opt-out means that the class is composed of all individuals who belong to the defined class and claim to have been harmed by the same or similar infringement unless they actively opt out of the group, Communication (n 7) 11. For the opt-in versus opt-out issue, see chapter 10 in this volume by L Ervo.

[14] Injunctive, declaratory or damages relief. With respect to injunctive relief see Directive 2009/22/EC of 23 April 2009 on injunctions for the protection of consumers' interests [2009] OJ L110/30.

[15] M Cappelletti and B Garth (eds), *Access to Justice: A World Survey* (Leyden, Sijthoff/Giuffre, 1978) 1.

[16] For a comprehensive overview see C Hodges, S Vogenauer and M Tulibacka (eds), *The Costs and Funding of Civil Litigation. A Comparative Perspective* (Oxford, Hart Publishing, 2010).

[17] See also S Voet, 'Cultural Dimensions of Group Litigation: The Belgian Case' (2013) 41 *Georgia Journal of International and Comparative Law* 433, 464–69 and S Voet, *Een Belgische vertegenwoordigende collectieve rechtsvordering* (Oxford, Intersentia, 2012) 126–36.

[18] Communication (n 7) 9.

[19] ibid, 15.

the Commission only sets out key principles that form a framework based on its policy preferences.

2. COMPLEX ISSUE AND LOSER PAYS RULE

Funding and financing class actions is a complex issue.[20] It is challenging to embed this kind of procedure in the existing one-on-one litigation funding rules. In individual litigation the costs and lawyer fees are (pre)financed by the identifiable plaintiff pursuing his individual claim, or a third party (eg, a lawyer, a legal expenses insurer, a legal aid scheme or a third-party litigation fund) directly connected with that plaintiff. In class action litigation, and at least at the outset of the procedure, the plaintiff acts on behalf of a group of unquantifiable and unidentified class members. Rational apathy and free-rider problems minimize the incentive for those members to invest in the litigation, leaving the funding to be paid for or organized by their agent (ie, the class representative) who will in most cases be confronted with wealthy and sophisticated repeat players as counterparties in the litigation. This results in an investment asymmetry.[21]

The fees and costs in question are also substantial. Collective redress procedures not only entail court costs and lawyer fees, but also specific class action related costs connected to: an intensive preparation stage; a complicated certification phase; multiple individual or non-individual notifications to class members; reaching a settlement; court ordered investigations;

[20] The literature is abundant. A brief selection: JC Coffee, 'Understanding the Plaintiff's Attorney: The Implications of Economic Theory for Private Enforcement of Law through Class and Derivative Actions' (1986) 86 *Columbia Law Review* 669; D Collins, 'Public Funding of Class Actions and the Experience with English Group Proceedings' (2005) 31 *Manitoba Law Journal* 211; EH Cooper, 'Class Action Advice in the Form of Questions' (2001) 11 *Duke Journal of Comparative and International Law* 215, 245–46; D Grave and K Adams, *Class Actions in Australia* (Sydney, Lawbook Co, 2005) 435–84; DR Hensler, 'Financing Civil Litigation: The US Perspective' in M Tuil and L Visscher (eds), *New Trends in Financing Civil Litigation in Europe: A Legal Empirical and Economic Analysis* (Cheltenham, Edward Elgar, 2010) 155; C Hodges, *Multi-party Actions* (Oxford, Oxford University Press, 2001) 135–202; MJ Legg, 'Reconciling Litigation Funding and the Opt Out Group Definition in Federal Court of Australia Class Actions. The Need for a Legislative Common Fund Approach' (2011) 30 *Civil Justice Quarterly* 52; V Morabito, 'Federal Class Actions, Contingency Fees, and the Rules Governing Litigation Costs' (1995) 21 *Monash University Law Review* 231; V Morabito, 'Class Actions Instituted Only for the Benefit of the Clients of the Class Representative's Solicitors' (2007) 29 *Sydney Law Review* 5; Mulheron (n 1) 435–79; TD Rowe, 'Shift Happens: Pressure on Foreign Attorney-fee Paradigms from Class Actions' (2003) 13 *Duke Journal of Comparative and International Law* 125; I Tzankova and J Kortmann, 'Remedies for Consumers of Financial Services: Collective Redress and Improvement of Class Representation' (2010) *European Journal of Consumer Law* 117 and J Walker, S Khouri and W Attrill, 'Funding Criteria for Class Actions' (2009) 32 *University of New South Wales Law Journal* 1036.

[21] I Tzankova, 'Funding of Mass Disputes: Lessons from the Netherlands' (2012) 8 *Journal of Law, Economics & Policy* 549, 554.

a possible elaborate trial on the merits of the case; internal administration and communication processes; and potential distribution procedures etc. All these costs and fees need to be pre-financed, irrespective of the outcome of the case.

Due to the loser pays rule, which is well entrenched in the European legal tradition,[22] the final outcome of the case will ultimately determine who will have to bear some or all of these costs and fees. That the loser pays rule also should apply in collective redress procedures is suggested as the preferred policy option by the Commission in its Recommendation: 'the Member States should ensure that the party that loses a collective redress action reimburses necessary legal costs borne by the winning party ("loser pays principle"), subject to the conditions provided for in the relevant national law'.[23] The rule is viewed as a safeguard against abusive litigation.[24]

In a one-on-one setting, there are two principal actors: the plaintiff pursuing his individual claim and his (representing) counsel. Collective redress procedures are, from the plaintiff's side, characterized by a triangular structure.[25] In addition to the class representative and the class lawyer, there are a number of unquantifiable and unidentified class members. Although they are not formal parties to the procedure, it is their rights that are being adjudicated in a decisive manner, in the sense that they are directly bound by the *res judicata* effect of the decision, unless they have not opted in or have opted out. Therefore, the funding issue should first and foremost be approached from this triangular structure, and more specifically from the standpoint of the class representative and/or the class members (section 3) and the class counsel (section 4). Similarly as in one-on-one litigation, class action litigation can be funded and financed by third parties (section 5): legal expenses insurers, government funds, legal aid schemes and, most recently, third-party litigation funders.

3. FUNDING AND FINANCING BY THE CLASS REPRESENTATIVE

A first and significant provision of the Recommendation is that the plaintiff, regardless of his or her capacity, should declare to the court at the outset of the proceedings, the origin of the funds that he or she is going to use to support the legal action.[26] In other words, the representative plaintiff is subject to a full financial disclosure.

22 Communication (n 7) 16. However, the Communication clarifies that the rule is not present in every jurisdiction of the EU and that the way in which it is applied differs between jurisdictions.

23 Recommendation (n 7) Art 13.

24 Communication (n 7) 9.

25 LL Casey, 'Class Action Criminality' (2008) 34 *Journal of Corporation Law* 153, 225.

26 Recommendation (n 7) Art 14.

The most obvious option is that the collective redress action is financed in the same manner as an individual action, namely by the person or entity initiating the procedure: the class (or representative) plaintiff. This means that all the fees and costs regarding the preparation, initiation, settlement and adjudication of the action will have to be pre-financed by him or her. This plaintiff can be an individual class member (section 3.1), a governmental body (section 3.2) or an association or foundation (section 3.3). With regard to the standing issue—which falls outside the scope of this chapter[27]—the Recommendation stipulates that Member States should designate or certify,[28] in an ex ante manner,[29] representative or ad hoc entities, that satisfy certain minimum qualification criteria,[30] to bring representative actions.[31] Public authorities should also be empowered to bring such actions.[32]

3.1 An Individual Class Member as Class Representative

If the class representative were an individual class member, this would mean that there would be no funding at all. This would certainly be the case for small claims, but also for individually recoverable claims. In those cases, funding a class action would boil down to a personal and unprofitable investment, which no one would wish to make. If at the end of the procedure the class member ran the risk of also having to pay the costs of the defendant because of the loser pays rule,[33] there would be 'a disincentive to bringing

[27] See generally Voet, 'Cultural Dimensions of Group Litigation' (n 17) 457–64. See also chapter 12 in this volume by R Money-Kyrle.

[28] In its Communication, the Commission rejects an ad hoc certification (ie, allowing the court to check the adequacy of the representative entity on a case-by-case basis). The ex ante governmental designation or certification is motivated by the fact that mass harm situations could span across a border. Therefore representative entities originating from Member States other than the one where a representative action is being brought should have the possibility to continue performing their role, Communication (n 7) 11.

[29] Recommendation (n 7) Art 6.

[30] These criteria are: (a) the entity should have a non-profit-making character; (b) there should be a direct relationship between the main objectives of the entity and the rights granted under Union law that are claimed to have been violated in respect of which the action is brought; and (c) the entity should have sufficient capacity in terms of financial resources, human resources, and legal expertise, to represent multiple claimants acting in their best interest, Recommendation (n 7) Art 4.

[31] A representative action is defined as 'an action which is brought by a representative entity, an ad hoc certified entity or a public authority on behalf and in the name of two or more natural or legal persons who claim to be exposed to the risk of suffering harm or to have been harmed in a mass harm situation whereas those persons are not parties to the proceedings', Recommendation (n 7) Art 3(d). This needs to be distinguished from group actions where the action can be brought jointly by those who claim to have suffered harm, Recommendation (n 7) recital 17. Representative and group actions are two types of collective actions.

[32] Recommendation (n 7) Art 7.

[33] See (n 23). See also GD Watson, 'Class Actions: The Canadian Experience' (2001) 11 *Duke Journal of Comparative & International Law* 269, 274–77 ('the Ontario costs rule is

grouped proceedings, and [this] might in fact create yet another barrier to access to legal remedies of the kind which the recommended procedure itself aims to overcome'.[34]

Theoretical methods for creating greater incentives or pooling class member resources seem unlikely to succeed. It would be possible to reward the class member who stands as a class representative with a financial bonus, which would constitute an impetus to act. Mulheron pertinently points out, however, that this could lead to conflicts of interest:

> Where a representative plaintiff benefits from the class proceeding to a greater extent than the class members, and such benefit is as a result of the extraneous compensation paid to the representative plaintiff rather than the damages suffered by him or her, there is undoubtedly an appearance of a conflict of interest between the representative plaintiff and the class members. This view holds that a class action should not be viewed as a method by which persons can seek to receive personal gain over and above any damages or other remedy to which they would otherwise be entitled on the merits of their claims.[35]

This view can be shared. Allowing a class member with a greater interest than his fellow members (whose claims he alone is pursuing) to steer the litigation entails a real danger of conflict of interest. Moreover, this is at odds with the historical origin of an individual class member as class representative. In order to prevent abuses and conflicts, the class representative was required to have 'the same interest' as the other class members. Their interests needed to be aligned.[36] This is hardly the case if one of them is eligible for a bonus.

It would also be conceivable to allow the class representative to solicit other class members for financial contributions.[37] This is, for example,

problematic and causes difficulties because it raises the issue of who, properly advised, would agree to become a representative plaintiff': ibid, 275).

[34] Australian Law Reform Commission, 'Grouped Proceedings in the Federal Court. Report No 46' (1988) 107.

[35] Mulheron (n 1) 466. See also *In re* Gould Sec Litig, 727 F Supp 1201, 1209 (ND Ill 1989) ('if class representatives expect routinely to receive special awards in addition to their share of the recovery, the representative may be tempted to accept sub-optimal settlements at the expense of the class members whose interests they are appointed to guard'). Under the US Private Securities Litigation Reform Act, such awards are expressly prohibited (15 USC § 78u-4(a)(2)(A)(vi) (2012)).

[36] This is still a requirement in the US rule. See *Wal-Mart Stores, Inc v Dukes*, 131 S Ct 2541 (US 2011) (the class action is 'an exception to the usual rule that litigation is conducted by and on behalf of the individual named parties only. In order to justify a departure from that rule, a class representative must be part of the class and possess the same interest and suffer the same injury as the class members'). See also JC Coffee, 'Class Action Accountability: Reconciling Exit, Voice, and Loyalty in Representative Litigation' (2000) 100 *Columbia Law Review* 370 (stating that the Supreme Court has accepted an implicit theory of representation: a representative is entitled to bind only those persons whose interests and legal positions match those of the representative). This also explains why the representative plaintiff must fairly and adequately protect the interests of the class (Rule 23(a)(4) US Federal Rules of Civil Procedure).

[37] Morabito, 'Federal Class Actions' (n 20) 236.

possible in British Columbia: 'with leave of the court, notice under this section may include a solicitation of contributions from class members to assist in paying solicitors' fees and disbursements'.[38] This would create a challenge, however, because the class representative would act on behalf of an unknown group of class members, who would be difficult to reach, and sometimes even to identify. In small claims cases, it would be hard to persuade them to pay for the litigation. Therefore, Mulheron observes that this model

> is unlikely to be much utilised because of the disincentive to class member participation which up-front funding would entail. In any event, the practicalities are that any potential benefit is surely a bit remote at the time that this request for contributions is normally made, at such an early stage of the proceedings.[39]

3.2 Governmental Body as Class Representative

If the class representative were a governmental body,[40] funding the collective redress action would come down to taxpayer-funded litigation. Due to limited resources, they would only finance meritorious cases that are in line with their policy. According to the Commission 'public authorities could be potential gatekeepers when funding collective redress, refusing to allocate resources to unmeritorious claims'.[41] However, a possible danger is that they could be caught by political imperatives or the interests of particular stakeholder groups, which could raise concerns regarding access to justice.

3.3 An Association or Foundation as Class Representative

One may assume that funding would be easier, or at least less problematic, if the class plaintiff were an association or (ad hoc or special purpose) foundation, than if an individual member would act. It could be argued that at least the successful ones would have more financial resources, such as membership contributions, subsidies and other income.[42] More importantly, associations and foundations would not pursue a personal interest, but only

[38] s 19(7) Class Proceedings Act.

[39] Mulheron (n 1) 465.

[40] eg, in Denmark, the Consumer Ombudsman, who is a regulator, has exclusive standing to bring an opt-out class action (n 4). In Belgium, the Consumer Ombudsman Service also has standing, but only to conclude a collective settlement. See Voet, 'European Collective Redress' (n 4).

[41] 'Green Paper on consumer collective redress' (n 5) 13.

[42] S Issacharoff and GP Miller, 'Will Aggregate Litigation Come to Europe?' (2009) 62 *Vanderbilt Law Review* 179, 199.

the interests of the class. Because class interests overlap with their statutory aim,[43] a class action goes to the heart of their existence.[44] Just like governmental bodies, organizational plaintiffs will therefore act as gatekeepers, because it would be unlikely for them to invest in frivolous or meritless cases with the objective of profit.

That associations might be willing to finance this kind of litigation is illustrated by the Dutch *Dexia* case, one of the cases under the Dutch Collective Settlements Act.[45] The representing consumer association (*Consumentenbond*) was able to concentrate the representation and aggregate claims by setting up a special purpose vehicle for the (purpose of the) collective action, hiring one lawyer and law firm, and raising a substantial fund by requiring a modest contribution (EUR 45) from its members.[46] Another example is the Belgian *Lernout & Hauspie* case.[47] In 2001, Lernout & Hauspie Speech Products (L&H), a speech recognition technology company based in Ypres, went bankrupt due to overstated earnings, fictitious transactions and improper accounting methods. The major administrators of L&H and its financial and accounting partners (ie, Dexia and KPMG) were indicted before a criminal court. According to Belgian law, and contrary to common law jurisdictions, crime victims are formal parties to the criminal proceedings, just as the Public Prosecutor and the defendant are formal parties. They are able to bring their civil claims during the criminal proceedings. After the criminal judge has dealt with the criminal aspect of the case and has convicted the defendant, he or she is obliged to rule upon the civil claims. This is the so-called piggyback, or *partie civile*, technique.[48] During the L&H criminal trial in 2007, it took several days for the more than 15,000 piggybacking victims to bring their civil claims. Most of them were represented by consumer or minority shareholder associations. One consumer association, acting on behalf of its 4,000 members, did not charge anything. The members pay an annual EUR 150 contribution. They were not charged an extra fee for the L&H case. The legal support in the case was offered pro bono. The only condition the association imposed was that their members had to retain their membership until the end of the proceedings, which made it a perfect excuse to work on customer relations.

[43] Recommendation (n 7) Art 4(b).

[44] Issacharoff and Miller (n 42) 193–94.

[45] See (n 3) and (n 4).

[46] Tzankova (n 21) 579.

[47] S Voet, 'The L&H Case: Belgium's Internet Bubble Story' in DR Hensler, C Hodges and I Tzankova (eds), *Class Actions in Context: How Economics, Politics and Culture Shape Collective Litigation* (forthcoming).

[48] Voet, 'Cultural Dimensions of Group Litigation' (n 17) 446–47 and S Voet, 'Public Enforcement and A(O)DR as Mechanisms for Resolving Mass Problems: A Belgian Perspective' in C Hodges and A Stadler (eds), *Resolving Mass Disputes: ADR and Settlement of Mass Claims* (Cheltenham, Edward Elgar, 2013) 279–84.

Ideally, and to incentivize this, the direct funding and financing of collective redress actions by governmental bodies or associations could be coupled with one-way cost shifting:[49] when the class representative wins the procedure, the losing defendant has to pay the plaintiff's lawyer fees and costs. In case of a government fund,[50] these costs could be transferred back to this fund to finance future class action litigation. If the defendant wins the procedure, the governmental body or association is exempted from paying lawyer fees and costs. This dispensation could be justified by the public interest in class actions as a legal protection tool.

4. FUNDING AND FINANCING BY THE CLASS COUNSEL

A second option to address the issue of class action funding is allowing the class lawyer to fund and finance the litigation[51] on the basis of a contingency fee agreement, which is the default rule in the US.[52] If the case is successful, the lawyer receives a contingent fee. If the case is lost, he does not get anything. The contingent fee is usually calculated on a lodestar or percentage of recovery basis. The lodestar method is a technique where the court multiplies a reasonable hourly rate by a reasonable number of hours expended. The percentage of recovery method implies that the class counsel receives a fixed percentage (usually between 25 and 30 per cent)[53] of the awarded damages. Because contingent lawyer fees could be a major driving

[49] See on cost-shifting in a class action context: L Inglis, K McCabe, S Rassenti, D Simmons and E Tallroth, 'Experiments on the Effects of Cost-Shifting, Court Costs, and Discovery on the Efficient Settlement of Tort Claims' (2005) 33 *Florida State University Law Review* 89; Morabito, 'Federal Class Actions (n 20) 262 and TD Rowe (n 20) 125.

[50] See below section 5.1.

[51] Generally, class action lawyers use four funding mechanisms: (a) self-finance, which depends on the law firm's financial situation (ie, its cash flow) and the parameters of the case; (b) through a bank loan: most banks will only issue a loan based on the individual partners' collateral and personal credit; (c) a partnership with another law firm to share the cost burden; or (d) approaching a private financing company that specializes in funding contingency litigation through private financing. For an overview see NF Engstrom, 'Re-Re-Financing Civil Litigation: How Lawyer Lending Might Remake the American Litigation Landscape, Again' (2013) 61 *UCLA Law Review Discourse* 110.

[52] See JC Alexander, 'Contingent Fees and Class Actions' (1998) 47 *DePaul Law Review* 347; LA Baker, MA Perino and C Silver, 'Setting Attorneys' Fees in Securities Class Actions: An Empirical Assessment' (2013) 66 *Vanderbilt Law Review* 1677; T Eisenberg and GP Miller, 'Attorney Fees and Expenses in Class Action Settlements: 1993–2008' (2010) 7 *Journal of Empirical Legal Studies* 248; and RS Jeffrey, 'Facilitating Welfare Rights Class Action Litigation: Putting Damages and Attorney's Fees to Work' (2003) 69 *Brooklyn Law Review* 281. See generally on contingency fees: L Brickman, *Lawyer Barons: What Their Contingency Fees Really Cost America* (Cambridge, Cambridge University Press, 2011); and HM Kritzer, *Risks, Reputations, and Awards. Contingency Fee Legal Practice in the United States* (Stanford, CA, Stanford University Press, 2004).

[53] LL Casey, 'Reforming Securities Class Actions from the Bench: Judging Fiduciaries and Fiduciary Judging' (2003) 4 *Brigham Young University Law Review* 1239; and JL Tuxbury, 'A Case for Competitive Bidding for Lead Counsel in Securities Class Actions' (2003) 1 *Columbia Business Law Review* 285.

force behind a class counsel's motives to represent class members, and could lead to abuses or conflicts of interest, US courts assess and award reasonable lawyer fees and costs in certified class actions.[54]

In Europe, contingency fees are considered to violate public order and to be incompatible with the ethics of the legal profession.[55] The Code of Conduct for European Lawyers states:

> A lawyer shall not be entitled to make a *pactum de quota litis*. By '*pactum de quota litis*' is meant an agreement between a lawyer and the client entered into prior to final conclusion of a matter to which the client is a party, by virtue of which the client undertakes to pay the lawyer a share of the result regardless of whether this is represented by a sum of money or by any other benefit achieved by the client upon the conclusion of the matter. '*Pactum de quota litis*' does not include an agreement that fees be charged in proportion to the value of a matter handled by the lawyer if this is in accordance with an officially approved fee scale or under the control of the Competent Authority having jurisdiction over the lawyer.[56]

Only intermediate forms of contingency fee arrangements are possible. An agreement by which the lawyer fees partially depend on the outcome of the case is allowed.[57] This comes down to a permissible enhancement of the lawyer fees based on success in the litigation.[58]

Therefore, it is no surprise that the Recommendation rejects contingency fees.[59] As a general rule, the Member States should ensure that in collective redress procedures the lawyers' remuneration and the method by which it is calculated do not create any incentive to litigation that is unnecessary from the point of view of the interest of any of the parties.[60] Contingency fees create such an incentive. The rationale is clearly to avoid an abuse of the system or a conflict of interest.[61] Nevertheless, in its Recommendation the Commission has not entirely ruled out contingency fees as a policy option for collective redress cases. The Commission proposes that if Member States exceptionally allow them, they should provide appropriate national regulation, taking into account the right to full compensation of the members of the claimant party.[62]

[54] Rule 23(h) US Federal Rules of Civil Procedure.

[55] M Faure, F Fernhout and N Phillipsen, 'No Cure, No Pay, and Contingency Fees' in M Tuil and L Visscher (eds), *New Trends in Financing Civil Litigation in Europe: A Legal Empirical and Economic Analysis* (Cheltenham, Edward Elgar, 2010) 33–56. In Belgium, Art 446 of the Judicial Code explicitly forbids a fee arrangement linked to the outcome of the dispute.

[56] See: www.oa.pt/upl/%7B2f103317-16f3-4f86-9f8e-6d93d82312d9%7D.pdf.

[57] Faure, Fernhout and Phillipsen (n 55) 42.

[58] See, eg, the possibility of conditional fee agreements (CFA) in the UK which allow the client to transfer some risk to his lawyer, whose level or remuneration is contingent on the outcome of the case, Hodges, *Multi-party Actions* (n 20) 139.

[59] See also Issacharoff and Miller (n 42) 198.

[60] Recommendation (n 7) Art 29.

[61] ibid, recital 19.

[62] ibid, Art 30.

The fundamental problem with contingency and success fees in a class action context is that the class lawyer acquires a personal interest in the outcome of the litigation, which can be a breeding ground for conflicts of interest between the class and its counsel. This is the so-called agency problem,[63] which primarily derives from the fact that the class lawyer represents a large number of unknown class members rather than an individual plaintiff. This problem can lead to 'sweetheart settlements' concluded by the class lawyer and the defendant with the goal of serving their own financial interests instead of those of the class.[64] In one-on-one litigation this 'personal interest in the outcome of the litigation' might not be an argument any more because the interests of the client and the lawyer are more aligned, but in class action litigation it still is. This kind of procedure requires the mandatory intervention of a lawyer.[65] Not only because of the procedural technicality and complexity, but especially because of the interests of the class members, who are absent in the procedure but bound by its outcome.[66] Therefore, the adequacy (ie, expertise, knowledge, and financial and human resources) of the class representative, and in particular of the class lawyer, is vital. The class members are forced to almost blindly rely on the way the class lawyer administers, deals with and settles the case. The class counsel must also serve as a gatekeeper for the defendant, who has to be protected against frivolous claims and blackmail settlements. In other words, the class lawyer serves a semi-public role. A personal financial interest in the outcome of the case can hinder, and even impede, this semi-public task.

As mentioned above, the Recommendation leaves an opening for contingency fees, as long as they are nationally regulated. It is indeed imperative to create safeguards. In order to avoid abuses and conflicts of interest, there should be oversight or monitoring of the class counsel. One option is to allow European judges, just like their American counterparts, to assess and award reasonable lawyer fees and costs in collective redress procedures. Such judicial oversight and approval could prevent conflicts and abuses. However, contrary to, for example, common law judges who are regarded as flexible case managers and who have no problem in ruling on lawyer fees, judges in some civil law jurisdictions will probably be more reluctant and hesitant to delve into the lawyer fee issue. In some countries, such as Belgium, judges are already tremendously reluctant to rule on lawyer fees

[63] See NJ Moore, 'Who Should Regulate Class Action Lawyers?' (2003) 2003 *University of Illinois Law Review* 1477 and J Kalajdzic, 'Self-Interest, Public-Interest and the Interests of the Absent Client: Legal Ethics and Class Action Praxis' (2011) 49 *Osgoode Hall Law Journal* 1.

[64] Tzankova (n 21) 554.

[65] eg, Rule 23(g) US Federal Rules of Civil Procedure: 'unless a statute provides otherwise, a court that certifies a class *must* appoint class counsel' (emphasis added). See also Art 1049 Code of Civil Procedure Québec: 'the representative or member who applies to act as such *must* be represented by an attorney' (emphasis added).

[66] Issacharoff and Miller (n 42) 206.

in one-on-one disputes. In most cases, they ask the local Bar Council for advice, with which they nearly always agree. Tzankova rightly observed the following:

> Overall Dutch judges seem to feel uncomfortable and hesitate when they must invoke financial incentives and sanction parties for their conduct in the course of the litigation. Presumably, this is not an example of Dutch exceptionalism, but rather a feature of the judiciary system in civil law jurisdictions ... One could summarize the different attitudes towards costs and funding as *civil law legal idealism and dogmatism* versus *common law legal realism and pragmatism*.[67]

In that regard, it is significant that the Dutch Collective Settlements Act,[68] although inspired by the US class action settlement regime, does not allow the Amsterdam Court of Appeal that has exclusive jurisdiction in approving a collective settlement, to assess and review the lawyer fees directly. If these fees are paid out of the settlement fund, the court can review them indirectly as part of its assessment of the general fairness of the settlement agreement.[69] For example, in the *Converium* case, and to the surprise of many, the court had no problem with the contingency fee arrangement for the American lawyers, which involved up to 20 per cent of the settlement.[70] The court stated it could rely on customary US fee practices when the legal services largely took place in the US by American law firms and on US court decisions approving American settlements. If on the other hand the lawyer fees are excluded from the settlement, the court will not be able to review them, making them subject to manipulation.

When the class lawyer acquires a personal interest in the outcome of the litigation, he can also be monitored and controlled by the client. Since the client represents the absent group of class members in this setting, this task could be entrusted to the latter, in their capacity as possible objectors. However, this is not only considered to be costly and time-consuming, it is also doubtful whether individual class members are sufficiently equipped to reveal possible collusion between defendants and class counsel.[71] It seems unfeasible for individual class members to exert optimal control. Therefore, it is better to rely on governmental bodies and/or associations as class representatives to keep a watchful eye. Since they are more sophisticated interlocutors, they are in a much better position to stand up to the class counsel should a potential conflict or abuse situation arise.

[67] Tzankova (n 21) 552 and referring to a Dutch empirical study (P Sluijter, *Sturen met proceskosten: wie betaalt de prijs van storend procesgedrag* (Deventer, Kluwer, 2011)).

[68] See (n 3).

[69] Tzankova (n 21) 563.

[70] Voet, 'Cultural Dimensions of Group Litigation' (n 17) 439 and references in n 17.

[71] JD Cox and RS Thomas, 'Leaving Money on the Table: Do Institutional Investors Fail to File Claims in Securities Class Actions?' (2002) 80 *Washington University Law Quarterly* 855 and A Klement, 'Who Should Guard the Guardians? A New Approach for Monitoring Class Action Lawyers' (2002) 21 *The Review of Litigation* 25.

5. FUNDING AND FINANCING BY A THIRD PARTY

5.1 Public Funding and Legal Aid

Finally, third parties can fund and finance class action litigation. A first option is to provide public funding through a government fund.[72] The best example is the *Fonds d'aide aux recours collectifs* in Quebec.[73] Under the auspices of the Ministry of Justice, the Fund helps to finance class action suits in the first instance or on appeal. Only natural persons and specific (statutory) associations can make an application, while (general) private associations cannot.[74] The Fund does not take any particular criteria into account; it only verifies whether or not the class action would be initiated without its intervention. When the Fund grants financial aid, it sets the terms of payment and reimbursement with the applicant and the applicant's counsel. If assistance is denied, the decision may be appealed before the *Tribunal administrative du Québec*. The latest annual report reveals that in 2012–13, the Fund received 25 new applications.[75] Of the 83 decisions made that year, all the applications bar one were granted.[76] When a case the Fund has financed wins, the Fund receives the legal costs paid by the defendant and a percentage of the damages awarded to the class.

A similar fund exists in Ontario: the Class Proceedings Fund.[77] It provides financial support to approved class action plaintiffs for legal disbursements and it indemnifies plaintiffs for costs that may be awarded against them in proceedings it has funded. Just like the Quebec Fund, the Class Proceedings Fund is self-sustainable. It receives a levy amounting to 10 per cent of any awards or settlements issued in favour of the plaintiffs in funded proceedings it has funded, plus a return for any disbursements it has paid. Between 1992 and 2013, the Fund received more than 130 applications, 82 of which were approved for funding. About 30 cases have resulted in settlements or awards.[78]

Another form of public funding is through legal aid. Legal aid in a class action context is limited, since assistance is only provided to individual class members and not to entities, such as organizational plaintiffs. In EU

[72] Mulheron (n 1) 454–59 and J Kalajdzic et al, 'Canada' (2009) 622 *Annals of the American Academy of Political and Social Science* 41.

[73] See: www.farc.justice.gouv.qc.ca.

[74] Art 1048 in the Code of Civil Procedure Québec.

[75] In 2005–06 there were 31 new applications; in 2006–07: 34; in 2007–08: 19; in 2008–09: 19; in 2009–10: 14; in 2010–11: 15; and in 2011–12: 20.

[76] Fonds d'aide aux recours collectifs, *Rapport annuel 2012–2013* (Québec, Imprimerie Joseph Clermont Inc, 2013) 10–11. The report is available at: www.farc.justice.gouv.qc.ca/doc/RapportAnnuel2012-2013.pdf.

[77] See: www.lawfoundation.on.ca/class-proceedings-fund/. See Mulheron (n 1) 454–57.

[78] Class Proceedings Fund, *Class Proceedings Fund. 20 Years in Review* 13, available at: www.lawfoundation.on.ca/wp-content/uploads/CPF-Brochure-2013.pdf.

Member States legal aid is characterized by a free choice of legal counsel. Legal aid has been used in mass cases in the Netherlands, and England and Wales. For example, in the *Dexia* case, the Dutch Legal Aid Board provided support to 4,200 individual class members. Between 2002 and 2010, the Board spent about EUR 3.3 million on lawyer fees.[79] Remarkably, about half of the Dexia class members who received legal aid, opted out of the collective settlement, while the overall opt-out percentage was 10 per cent.[80] Legal aid has also been provided in England and Wales.[81] One of the conditions for providing legal aid is that a case must have the potential to produce 'real benefits' for the public at large, in addition to benefits for the applicant. The Lord Chancellor's Guidance states that such benefits may include:

> Potential financial benefit—this is usually the situation for most test cases or group actions or other cases seeking to establish a legal precedent. Success in such litigation will not usually guarantee compensation for those outside the litigation, who may still need to bring their own claims and prove their own issues on liability, causation and quantum.[82]

The European Commission does not believe in public funding as a policy option, since it considers collective redress procedures to be civil (private) procedures, with deterrence only as a side effect:

> However, given that collective redress would be a procedure arising in the context of a civil dispute between two parties, even if one of them is composed of a number of claimants, and deterrence will be a side-effect of the proceedings, the Commission does not find it necessary to recommend direct support from public funds, since if the court finds that damage has been sustained, the party suffering that damage will obtain compensation from the losing party, including their legal costs.[83]

In times when public expenditure is under intense and increasing pressure, it is highly uncertain that European governments will provide resources for a government class action fund or legal aid. If they are willing, however, this public financial intervention will again work better with a governmental body or an association as class representative than with an individual class member. As mentioned above,[84] the former does not pursue a personal interest, but instead the collective interests of the group. For a government fund or legal aid scheme, this can be a decisive and legitimizing factor in deciding whether to intervene. This intervention will have a public, and

[79] Tzankova (n 21) 580.
[80] ibid.
[81] Hodges, *Multi-party Actions* (n 20) 177–202.
[82] Lord Chancellor's Guidance under s 4 of the Legal Aid, Sentencing and Punishment of Offenders Act 2012, 11 (available at: www.justice.gov.uk/downloads/legal-aid/funding-code/lord-chancellors-guidance.pdf).
[83] Communication (n 7) 15.
[84] See above section 3.3.

therefore more acceptable, dimension. On the other hand, legal aid will only work if the principles of party autonomy, the free choice of legal counsel, and the right to determine one's litigation strategy are relaxed, or if the focus shifts to concentration:

> In the absence of a properly functioning concentration mechanism, the free choice of legal services provider that most EU Member States guarantee in mass disputes, weakens the finality of resolution and the effective use of public funds in mass claim disputes. In times of shrinking budgets for Legal Aid, it is difficult to find a convincing justification for spending disproportionate amounts of publicly available funds to resolve thousands of similar individual cases. Jointly resolving generic issues relevant for all members of the group is a more intelligent way to proceed, not only in terms of expected reductions in costs, but also in terms of improving the quality of legal representation and, therefore, outcomes. Furthermore, concentration reduces investment asymmetries between individual consumers and repeat corporate defendants. Moreover, reorganizing the Legal Aid system of mass dispute funding to facilitate concentration in dispute resolution and focus on generic, rather than individual issues, is expected to have advantages not only for individuals eligible for Legal Aid funding but for members of the group in general.[85]

5.2 Legal Expenses Insurance

In some cases, legal expenses insurance can fund class action litigation.[86] A difference is made between before- and after-the-event insurance.[87] Before-the-event insurance (BTE) is taken out by those wishing to protect themselves against potential litigation costs that could be incurred following a usually hypothetical future event. BTE insurance is generally paid on an annual basis to an insurance company. After-the-event-insurance (ATE) is taken out after an event to insure the policyholder against disbursements, as well as any costs should they lose their case. The focus in this context is on the instruction of a qualified lawyer by a legal expenses insurance when an insurance claim occurs. Another market is the 'in-kind' policies where legal services are provided by in-house lawyers of the insurance company. Legal expenses insurance in Europe is regulated by Directive 87/344/EEC.[88] The Directive aims at neutralizing agency problems, including potential

[85] Tzankova (n 21) 584.

[86] See in the US: SA Smith, 'Too Much Risk: The Impact of Class Action Lawsuits on Claims Made Insurance Policies' (2009) 74 *Missouri Law Review* 1171.

[87] M de Morpurgo, 'A Comparative Legal and Economic Approach to Third-Party Litigation Funding' (2011) 19 *Cardozo Journal of International and Comparative Law* 343, 353 and F Regan, 'The Swedish Legal Services Policy Remix: The Shift from Public Legal Aid to Private Legal Expense Insurance' (2003) 30 *Journal of Law and Society* 49, 50, fn 4 (describing the two basic forms of legal expenses insurance: before-the-event and after-the-event).

[88] Directive 87/344/EEC of 22 June 1987 on the coordination of laws, regulations and administrative provisions relating to legal expenses insurance [1987] OJ L185/77.

conflicts of interest between the insurer and the insured. It also provides an efficient settlement mechanism for these kinds of disputes.

As with legal aid, this funding mechanism will only in its present form provide assistance to individual class members with legal expenses insurance. It also adheres to the principle of free choice of legal counsel. The Court of Justice of the European Union (CJEU) ruled that where a large number of insured persons suffer a loss as a result of the same event, a legal expenses insurer cannot reserve the right to select the legal representative of all the insured persons concerned.[89] According to the CJEU, European law guarantees the policyholder the right to choose his or her own lawyer, even in a group action where several parties wish to pursue a claim against the same defendant. The policyholder has the right to instruct a legal representative of his choosing from the moment that he has a right to claim from his insurer under the policy. That right is not limited to cases where proceedings have commenced, but exists from the time the potential claim arose for which the claimant had valid cover. This decision of the CJEU implies that legal expenses insurers cannot insist that the insured be represented by a class representative on the insurer's panel.[90] Just like with the previous funding mechanism legal aid, the principles of party autonomy and the right to freely choose legal counsel thus have a negative impact on the funding of mass cases.

According to Tzankova this European case law only relates to situations where the decision to hire an external lawyer has already been taken by the insurance provider. It does not apply to 'in-kind' polices, where the provider has decided to handle the case, or when the proceedings have already been commenced by an in-house legal adviser who is not a qualified lawyer. At least according to Dutch law, the policyholder is restricted in his free choice prior to proceedings or in the context of collective settlement negotiations, allowing the legal expenses insurer to facilitate the concentration of representation to one or a limited number of lawyers.[91] In other institutional settings, such as in Germany where most disputes are resolved through litigation and lawyers have a monopoly, this European case law would cause a different litigation funding dynamic.[92]

[89] Case C-199/08 *Eschig v UNIQA Sachversicherung, AG* [2009] ECR 1-08295; EU:C:2009:538. See C Paris, 'La Cour de justice réaffirme le droit de l'assuré en protection juridique de choisir librement son avocat' (2010) 16 *Journal des Tribunaux* 272; J Rowley, 'Eschig v UNIQA Sachversicherung AG (C-199/08): Legal Expenses Insurance—Legal Expenses Insurance Regulations 1990' (2010) 1 *Journal of Personal Injury Law* C32; J Stuyck, 'Assurance-protection juridique, action de groupe et libre choix de l'avocat' (2010) 2 *Recueil Le Dalloz* 100; and PH Woolfson, 'Assurance-protection juridique et libre choix de l'avocat: une victoire à la Pyrrhus pour le consommateur?' (2009–10) 3 *Revue des affaires européennes* 605. The case concerned an interpretation of Art 4(1)(a) of Directive 87/344/EEC.

[90] Tzankova (n 21) 573.

[91] ibid, 585.

[92] ibid, 586–87.

If the class representative is an association, the insurer of the association will not cover the legal expenses of the collective redress action it initiates, for the simple reason that the association (ie, the policyholder) does not suffer personal losses that are covered. It acts on behalf of (unknown) victims who do not have a contractual relationship with the association's insurer and whose damages are not covered. When a class member requests the intervention of his or her own insurer, it will only cover the legal expenses of that member. For example, in the Dutch *Dexia* case, some legal expenses insurers reimbursed the EUR 45 contribution some of their policyholders had paid to the representing consumer association (*Consumentenbond*).[93] In other words, the success of legal expenses insurance in mass cases will depend on the number of class members that have such insurance, and on whether the legal infrastructure of the national legal system in question facilitates the concentration of measures through legal expenses insurance.[94]

5.3 Third-Party Litigation Funding

A new kind of funding that has come to the fore, in and outside the context of class actions, and especially in legal systems without contingency fees, is (after-the-event) third-party litigation funding (TPLF).[95] Third-party funders[96] are private funders that enter into an agreement with one or more potential litigants. Funders usually assess the following criteria: the chances of success of the case (including the likelihood of a settlement); the estimate of the lawyer fees and the costs the procedure will entail; and the solvability of the defendant. The agreement provides that the funder will meet

[93] ibid, 581. See above section 3.3.

[94] Tzankova (n 21) 583.

[95] de Morpurgo (n 87) 352; GL Fowler, M Shelley and S Kim, 'Emerging Trends in International Litigation: Class Actions, Litigation Funding and Punitive Damages' (2009) 3 *Dispute Resolution International* 101; Hensler, 'The Future of Mass Litigation' (n 2); J Kalajdzic, P Cashman and A Longmoore, 'Justice for Profit: A Comparative Analysis of Australian, Canadian and US Third Party Litigation Funding' (2013) 61 *American Journal of Comparative Law* 93; M Legg and L Travers, 'Necessity is the Mother of Invention: The Adoption of Third-Party Litigation Funding and the Closed Class in Australian Class Actions' (2009) 38 *Common Law World Review* 245; J Lyon, 'Revolution in Progress: Third-Party Funding of American Litigation' (2010) 58 *UCLA Law Review* 571; R Mulheron and P Cashman, 'Third Party Funding: A Changing Landscape' (2008) 27 *Civil Justice Quarterly* 312; B Murphy and C Cameron, 'Access to Justice and the Evolution of Class Action Litigation in Australia' (2006) 30 *Melbourne University Law Review* 434; and W van Boom, 'Financing Civil Litigation by the European Insurance Industry' in M Tuil and L Visscher (eds), *New Trends in Financing Civil Litigation in Europe: A Legal Empirical and Economic Analysis* (Cheltenham, Edward Elgar, 2010) 99–104.

[96] eg, Juridica Capital, Burford Capital, Rembrandt IP Management, Coller IP Management, Counsel Financial, IMF, Allianz Prozess Finanz and IM Litigation Funding. The most frequent players are incorporated companies, listed on a stock exchange, obtaining funds from debt and equity sources.

some or all of the legal fees incurred by the law firm conducting the action, meet some or all of the out of pocket expenses incurred in the litigation, indemnify the funded party with respect to any cost orders made against that party if the litigation is unsuccessful, and pay any amount required to be provided by way of a security for costs. In return the funder will receive a percentage of the amount recovered by the persons or entities that have entered into a funding agreement in the event that they are successful in the litigation either by way of settlement or judgment. The percentage is usually in the range of 25–40 per cent depending on the time taken and/or whether the case is appealed.[97]

The TPLF industry has primarily emerged in common law jurisdictions. In the US, TPLF has been used in low-value litigation, such as car accidents and personal injury cases, but is gradually shifting to complex commercial litigation,[98] pressing regulatory concerns,[99] to date to no avail. Since class actions in the US are financed by lawyers on a contingency fee basis, private funders have not penetrated the US class action market.[100] According to Hensler:

> The entrance of third-party litigation funders into the US legal marketplace (firms that we would expect to contract with class action lawyers rather than class members) might increase the number of law firms willing to prosecute class actions, increase competition among firms for class counsel appointments, and increase investment by class counsel in pretrial development of facts and law. The results might include increased numbers of class actions and higher-value settlements.[101]

In England and Wales, Lord Jackson endorsed TPLF for collective litigation along with contingency fees.[102] In November 2011, the Civil Justice Council

[97] Kalajdzic, Cashman and Longmoore (n 95) 100.

[98] Hensler, 'The Future of Mass Litigation' (n 2) 320.

[99] eg, ABA Commission on Ethics 20/20, *White Paper on Alternative Litigation Finance*, available at: www.americanbar.org/content/dam/aba/administrative/ethics_2020/20111019_draft_alf_white_paper_posting.authcheckdam.pdf and US Chamber Institute for Legal Reform, *Selling Lawsuits, Buying Trouble. Third-Party Litigation Funding in the United States* (Washington, US Chamber Institute for Legal Reform, 2009) (available at: http://legaltimes.typepad.com/files/thirdpartylitigationfinancing.pdf). See also Engstrom (n 51).

[100] Kalajdzic, Cashman and Longmoore (n 95) 127. See also S Garber, *Alternative Litigation Financing in the United States. Issues, Known, and Unknown* (Santa Monica, Rand Corporation, 2010), available at: www.rand.org/content/dam/rand/pubs/occasional_papers/2010/RAND_OP306.pdf. Class actions in the US are mainly funded by lawyers on a contingent fee basis.

[101] Hensler, 'The Future of Mass Litigation' (n 2) 322–23.

[102] Lord Justice Jackson, *Review of Civil Litigation Costs: Final Report*, December 2009, available at: www.judiciary.gov.uk/Resources/JCO/Documents/Reports/jackson-final-report-140110.pdf, 334–35. The report also recommended experimentation with a public financing scheme funded by a tax against successful class actions, modelled after the Ontario class action fund (ibid, 131).

proposed a Code of Conduct for Litigation Funders.[103] The Code sets out standards to be observed by all funders who are members of the Association of Litigation Funders of England and Wales. It largely focuses on capital adequacy, the withdrawal of funding and control over the litigation.

In Australia, all large class actions are funded by private funders, of which Bentham IMF is the largest.[104] This is mainly explained by the Australian fee shifting rules and the risk of adverse costs. If the class action is unsuccessful, class members have statutory immunity from paying any part of the costs and other expenses incurred by the winning party. These costs and expenses will have to be paid by the class representative. This creates a financial disincentive to take on this role. Therefore, and in the absence of contingency fees and lack of legal aid funding, TPLF has become the primary means of financing class action litigation in Australia.[105] However, TPLF in Australia has changed a key feature of the Australian class action rule. Because there is no certification phase, that would result in an order binding the class members to the fee agreement between the representative plaintiff and class lawyer or the funder, third-party funders require all class members to sign individual litigation funding agreements entitling the funder to a share in the proceeds of the litigation if it is successful. This has converted the Australian opt-out scheme into an opt-in scheme. The use of so-called 'closed classes' was permitted by the Full Federal Court, given that the legislation expressly provides that a class action may be brought on behalf of 'some or all' of those affected.[106] According to some scholars this undermines one of the key rationales for the class action regime: 'because "opt-in" classes restrict the ambit of beneficiaries to those who have agreed to enter into contractual litigation funding arrangements, access to justice by all those similarly affected has been curtailed'.[107]

TPLF as such is a purely contractual matter. Private third-party funders and the class members with whom they enter into an agreement are entirely free to agree on the conditions of the agreement, including the possible (partial) transferal of the strategy-making power to the funder. However,

[103] The Association of Litigation Funders of England and Wales, *Code of Conduct for Litigation Funders*, November 2011, available at: www.judiciary.gov.uk/ JCO%2fDocuments%2fCJC%2fPublications%2fCJC+papers%2fCode+of+Conduct+for+Litigation+Funders+(November+2011).pdf.

[104] See: www.imf.com.au. The company is listed on the Australian Stock Exchange.

[105] Kalajdzic, Cashman and Longmoore (n 95) 100.

[106] *Multiplex Funds Mgmt Ltd v P Dawson Nominees Pty Ltd* [2007] 244 ALR 600. In 2009, the Court held that litigation funding should be treated as a managed investment scheme (*Brookfield Multiplex Limited v International Litigation Funding Partners Pte Ltd* [2009] FCAFC 147). Since then, the Australian government has tried to regulate TPLF; Kalajdzic, Cashman and Longmoore (n 95) 109–13. See Legg, 'Reconciling Litigation Funding' (n 20).

[107] Kalajdzic, Cashman and Longmoore (n 95) 103, also pointing out other disadvantages of 'closed classes': satellite litigation, appeals, increase in transaction costs and barriers to settlement.

some poignant problems can arise in a class action context. Besides the conversion of an opt-out scheme into an opt-in scheme, the triangular structure, as mentioned above,[108] turns into a complicated quadrangular structure. In addition to the representative plaintiff, the class lawyer and the class members, a third-party funder enters the stage. From the standpoint of the class lawyer this can lead to ethical and fiduciary concerns about who the actual client is and whose instructions he has to obey. Also the agency problems in the relationship between the class lawyer and the class[109] are amplified with the presence of a third-party funder. Soft regulation,[110] judicial oversight or statutory provisions promoting transparency and good governance could tackle these problems.[111]

In its Recommendation, the Commission gives its support to TPLF as a policy option in collective redress litigation, but this support is conditional. The Commission suggests a series of safeguards if TPLF is chosen as a funding option, in order to avoid abusive litigation.[112] On the one hand, the Commission recommends that Member States should ensure that in cases where an action for collective redress is funded by a private third party, it is prohibited for the private third party:[113]

(a) to seek to influence procedural decisions of the claimant party, including on settlements;
(b) to provide financing for a collective action against a defendant who is a competitor of the fund provider or against a defendant on whom the fund provider is dependent;
(c) to charge excessive interest on the funds provided.

On the other, the Commission recommends that courts in the Member States should be allowed to stay the proceedings where the financial resources are provided by a third party:[114]

(a) there is a conflict of interest between the third party and the claimant party and its members;
(b) the third party has insufficient resources in order to meet its financial commitments to the claimant party initiating the collective redress procedure;
(c) the claimant party has insufficient resources to meet any adverse costs should the collective redress procedure fail.

108 See above section 2.
109 See above section 4.
110 'Soft regulation should at least address (1) monitoring the conduct of third-party financiers prior to and in the course of the litigation; (2) the level of involvement of the financier with the litigation strategy; (3) the fiduciary duty of the class lawyer; and (4) the award of the third-party litigation funder', Tzankova (n 21) 588.
111 Mulheron and Cashman (n 95) 312.
112 Communication (n 7) 15.
113 Recommendation (n 7) Art 16.
114 ibid, Art 15.

In addition to these general principles of funding, the Commission proposes that Member States should ensure that in cases of private third-party funding of compensatory collective redress, it is prohibited to base remuneration given to or interest charged by the fund provider on the amount of the settlement reached or the compensation awarded unless that funding arrangement is regulated by a public authority to ensure the interests of the parties.[115]

6. CONCLUSION

It is indisputable that the funding regime of a class action system, or the absence thereof, can make or break it. Fortunately, the Commission's Recommendation on common principles for injunctive and compensatory collective redress mechanisms does not overlook this issue. It proposes some key principles that could form the basis of a future normative framework: full financial disclosure for the class representative, soft rules about third-party litigation funding (in order to avoid abuses) and no contingency fees unless they are appropriately regulated. The brief overview in this chapter mapped the various funding options and assessed their pros and cons in a collective litigation context. The bottom line is that there is no clear-cut answer to the question of how collective redress actions should best be financed. The most sustainable solution seems to be a mixture of options: direct funding by a governmental body or organizational plaintiff; a governmental fund; tailor-made designed legal aid and legal expenses insurance; regulated third-party litigation funding; and one-way cost shifting.

[115] ibid, Art 32.

12

Legal Standing in Collective Redress Actions for Breach of EU Rights: Facilitating or Frustrating Common Standards and Access to Justice?

REBECCA MONEY-KYRLE*

1. INTRODUCTION

IN JUNE 2013, the European Commission published a non-binding Recommendation for collective redress, asserting that the Member States should implement collective procedures for injunctive and compensatory relief for breaches of rights arising under EU law.[1] The Recommendation aims to facilitate access to justice and collaterally to contribute to the EU's economic and social aims. The Recommendation, to minimize abusive claims, would circumscribe redress procedures to opt-in collective claims models that are deemed compatible with fundamental rights and national legal traditions.[2] The Recommendation thus includes procedural safeguards, or 'basic principles', recommending 'opt-in' models, with minimum legal standing criteria, regulation of designated representative claimants, benchmarks for litigation funding and costs, and so on. It proposes standing for 'opt-in' group collective actions, comprising two or more group claimants,[3] and for designated Representative Entities (REs) to bring collective claims.[4] Chapters in this volume by Ervo[5] and Voet[6] assess the basic principles

* Associate Research Fellow, Centre for Socio-Legal Studies, University of Oxford.
[1] Recommendation 2013/396/EU on common principles for injunctive and compensatory collective redress mechanisms in the Member States concerning violations of rights granted under Union Law [2013] OJ L201/60, para 2.
[2] ibid, Arts 1–2; Treaty on the Functioning of the European Union (consolidated version) [2010] OJ C83/49 (TFEU) Art 67.
[3] Recommendation (n 1) Arts 21–24.
[4] ibid, Arts 4–7.
[5] Chapter 10.
[6] Chapter 11.

recommending 'opt-in' models, and concerning funding and costs. From normative and comparative perspectives, this chapter evaluates the legal standing principles to ascertain whether in practice, consumers' access to justice, and wider public economic and social objectives, will likely be facilitated or frustrated. If standing is too restrictive, to protect principles of liberty and autonomy, negative effects could exacerbate economic and social barriers to justice. If, conversely, the provisions are too permissive, autonomy, due process and minority interests could be undermined; aggregated assessment of liability and quantum could become divorced from actual harm, potentially exacerbating unfair competition and market distortions.[7]

Traditional liberal approaches to legal standing, and economic and welfare justifications for collective action, prompt theoretical dilemmas. Section 2 considers contrasting conceptual approaches to legal standing and collective redress. Theoretical tensions between autonomy-predicated, and social justice and economic approaches are evident. In section 3 the Recommendation's legal standing principles are evaluated in light of those conceptual approaches, EU legal norms, and the Commission's policy objectives. Section 4 evaluates the likely impact on access to justice in Member States, through vertical comparative analysis. Drawing on examples of national approaches to standing and collective redress, that section identifies similarities and differences between the Recommendation's standing principles and national procedures, in order to ascertain the likely effect of the Recommendation on access to justice.

In conclusion, section 5 finds that the Recommendation's standing principles, contrary to the Commission's aims, are unlikely to enhance access to justice, nor prompt greater procedural uniformity. Thus, public interest economic and social objectives will not likely be achieved. Moreover, the cross-border standing provisions could prompt disputes over jurisdiction and applicable law, and discrimination between REs from different Member States, thus potentially producing unintended harmful outcomes.

2. LEGITIMACY, LEGAL STANDING AND COLLECTIVE REDRESS

Locus standi rules in public law claims function to restrict claims 'to anyone whose interests are affected by what has been done'.[8] In respect of private claims, legal standing rules similarly establish procedural barriers, restricting access to justice to legitimate claimants. Thus, the basic principles on legal

[7] R Money-Kyrle and C Hodges, 'European Collective Action: Towards Coherence?' (2012) 19 *Maastricht Journal of European and Comparative Law* 477.

[8] *R v Paddington Valuation Officer and Another* [1965] 3 WLR 426; [1966] 1 QB 380 Court of Appeal, 401.

standing will be pivotal to the realization in practice of the Commission's access to justice objectives. What constitutes 'legitimate' standing necessarily depends on theoretical, doctrinal and contextual factors.

2.1 The Autonomy Principle

National civil justice systems are grounded on political ideals of democracy, self-determination and personal autonomy, imputing a 'positive, compulsory and individualistic' conception of law, through which self-determination and individual liberty can be realized.[9] There are nuanced rule of law concepts, but liberal theorists broadly agree that individual access to independent courts is a minimal requirement.[10] From this individualist perspective, civil law defines substantive legal relations between autonomous persons, delineating their legitimate civil liberty. Civil disputes over private rights ought to be direct and personal, between morally competent autonomous persons.

Conceptually, procedural rights derive from substantive autonomy rights; legal standing ought thus, logically, be limited to persons with a direct interest in the claim (the right-bearer), with capacity to sue. Autonomous legal standing should guarantee access to the courts for effective protection of individual rights. Equally, defendants' legal obligations ought not to be judged without defensive procedural rights to appear and be heard.[11] Conceptually, capacity concerns autonomous moral agency, presupposing individuals have the will and competence to pursue legal grievances. However, if lacking adequate mental capacity, representative standing may exceptionally be necessary and justified, to secure the personal autonomy of minors and the incapacitated. The prevailing conceptual approach to legal standing is, in short, predicated on the principle of autonomy (the 'autonomy principle').

In collective injunctions and damages claims, which are the Recommendation's concern, standing rules should regulate legitimate standing to claimants acting in respect of their own and/or others' legal rights, thus requiring exception to the autonomy principle. Collective procedures, by aggregating claims, aim to improve judicial and economic efficiency, and to assist claimants who would otherwise be unable, for economic and social

[9] J Habermas, 'Constitutional Democracy: A Paradoxical Union of Contradictory Principles?' (2001) 29 *Political Theory* 766.

[10] P Craig, 'Formal and Substantive Conceptions of the Rule of Law: An Analytical Framework' [1997] *Public Law* 467, 468–86.

[11] eg, Code de procédure civile (version consolidée au 30 mai 2014) (French Civil Procedure Code) Art 14. See also European Union, Charter of Fundamental Rights of the European Union [2000] OJ C364/1, Art 47; Council of Europe, European Convention for the Protection of Human Rights and Fundamental Freedoms, 4 November 1950, ETS 5 (ECHR) Art 6.

reasons, to enforce their rights through a representative claimant. Whilst subject to numerous exceptions, the autonomy principle ignores social, cultural and economic inequalities incapacitating the disadvantaged from exercising rights of access to justice. In practice, capacity is not merely a question of mental competence. Barriers to justice are economically and socially conditioned. The reasons why individual consumers do not always pursue legal action are multifaceted.[12] Economic barriers may be identified more readily than behavioural and social factors.[13] If losses are scattered and small, individual claims will be unviable, with legal costs dwarfing claim quantum, leading consumers to take no action (the 'rational apathy' problem).[14] Trivial claims are sometimes discouraged.[15] However, wider economic and social costs can be substantial.[16] The autonomy principle, inevitably requiring individualized assessment of liability, harm and quantum, deters efficient and effective solutions. Alternative social justice and economic analyses provide different conceptual grounds for representative and collective standing.

2.2 Social Justice Approaches

Whilst the autonomy principle pervades across Member States, the rise of the welfare state and its impact on social justice must be acknowledged.[17] Since the 1970s, 'massification' (the propensity in modern societies for mass harm to arise from similar legal and factual circumstances) has been recognized.[18] Individuals face practical and economic barriers to redress in mass harm cases. Cappelletti advocated three evolutionary 'waves', to ameliorate those barriers: legal aid, class or collective actions, and alternative

[12] H Genn et al, *Paths to Justice: What People Do and Think about Going to Law* (Oxford, Hart Publishing, 1999) 250.

[13] Undoubtedly, culturally-specific perceptions of fairness (procedural justice) dramatically impact on peoples' acceptance of legal process and decisions: TR Tyler and EA Lind, 'Procedural Justice' in J Sanders and VL Hamilton (eds), *Handbook of Justice and Research in Law* (New York, Springer, 2001) 65; on procedural justice and consumer disputes see N Creutzfeldt, 'How Important is Procedural Justice for Consumer Dispute Resolution? A Case Study of an Ombudsman Model for European Consumers' (2014) 4 *Journal of Consumer Policy* 527.

[14] R Van den Bergh, 'Private Enforcement of European Competition Law and the Persisting Collective Action Problem' (2013) 20 *Maastricht Journal* 17, 20.

[15] WH van Boom, 'De Minimis Curat Praetor: Redress for Dispersed Trifle Losses' (2009) 4 *Journal of Comparative Law* 171, 171–73.

[16] ibid, 174; O Fiss, 'The Political Theory of the Class Action' (1996) 53 *Washington and Lee Law Review* 21, 22.

[17] E Storskrubb and J Ziller, 'Access to Justice in European Comparative Law' in F Francioni (ed), *Access to Justice as a Human Right* (Oxford, OUP/Oxford Scholarship Online, 2007) 179–80.

[18] M Cappelletti, 'Vindicating the Public Interest through the Courts: A Comparativist's Contribution' (1975–76) 25 *Buffalo Law Review* 643, 645.

dispute resolution (ADR).[19] These redistributive measures should function to re-balance economic and social inequalities, enabling effective and practical realization of legal rights. Positive law and rights are contextualized, accommodating economic, social, cultural and psychological realities.[20] Similarly, social justice and capabilities approaches acknowledge socio-economic impacts on autonomy and agency of disadvantaged individuals, justifying redistributive protection so that all people will in practice be capable of realizing personal freedom.[21] Social justice and development economics approaches thus seek to re-balance the collective interest of disadvantaged groups against dominant elites, through redistributive measures, including potentially collectivization of claims, to protect weaker collective interests.[22] These approaches to rights and standing are referred to as the 'social justice approaches' hereafter.

2.3 The Economic Approach

Economic analyses are similarly redistributive. Consequentialist economic approaches, aiming to optimize economic and collective outcomes, potentially accommodate subjugation of individual autonomy, justified in the interest of public norms enforcement, optimal deterrence, and cost–benefit efficiencies.[23] An economic model must be holistically designed: individual self-interest is not necessarily sufficient to promote efficacious collective action. Coercions and incentives, to control selfish motivations, may be logical. Optimizing efficiency and effective outcomes necessitates measures to mitigate the so-called 'free-rider' problem (individuals bearing no risk, who take no individual action but free-ride on the group's initiative).[24] In economic models, efficient collateral public norms enforcement, market re-balancing and deterrence become fundamental goals.[25]

[19] M Cappelletti and BG Garth (eds), *Access to Justice: A World Survey* (Leyden, Sijthoff/Giuffre, 1978); M Cappelletti, M Seccombe and J Weisner, *Access to Justice and the Welfare State* (Alphen aan den Rijn, Sijthoff, 1981); M Cappelletti, 'Alternative Dispute Resolution Processes within the Framework of the World-Wide Access-to-Justice Movement' (1993) 56 *Modern Law Review* 282.

[20] Cappelletti, 'Alternative Dispute Resolution Processes' (n 19) 283.

[21] A Sen, 'Human Rights and Capabilities' (2005) 6 *Journal of Human Development* 151, 154; M Nussbaum, 'Capabilities as Fundamental Entitlements: Sen and Social Justice' (2003) 9 *Feminist Economics* 33; E Anderson, 'Justifying the Capabilities Approach to Justice' in H Brighouse and I Robeyns (eds), *Measuring Justice: Primary Goods and Capabilities* (Cambridge, CUP/Cambridge Books Online) 2010) 81–100.

[22] H Micklitz, 'Social Justice and Access to Justice in Private Law' EUI Working Paper LAW no 2011/02, available at: SSRN: ssrn.com/abstract=1824225, 1.

[23] B Garth, 'Conflict and Dissent in Class Actions: a Suggested Perspective' (1982) 77 *Northwestern University Law Review* 492, 495.

[24] M Olson, *The Logic of Collective Action: Public Goods and the Theory of Groups* (Cambridge, MA, Harvard University Press, 1965 and 1971) 1–2, 5–52.

[25] Fiss, 'The Political Theory of the Class Action' (n 16) 21–22.

2.4 Legal Standing and Collective Action

Collective procedures, whilst challenging the autonomy principle, can maximize efficient attainment of economic and social goals, including access to justice and redress. 'Collective redress' and 'collective action' are generic terms, comprising redistributive class, group, or representative litigation and ADR procedures, enabling groups of identified or unidentified (diffuse) consumers with low-value losses to take on powerful corporate interests.[26] A utilitarian instrument, the collective action can function to overcome rational apathy and viability issues through claim aggregation.[27] There are two distinct approaches: 'opt-in' and 'opt-out'. Both necessitate some modification to the autonomy principle. Opt-in procedures require class members having legal standing in their own right, to opt in to the litigation, filing a formal claim or defence, or power of attorney, authorizing the lead litigant to act in a representative capacity. Class members have restricted rights over discrete aspects of case management, once judicially approved as a collective case. Final judgment only binds those who have opted in. Thus, individual autonomy is voluntarily, not coercively, subjugated to collective interests. However, this model lacks sufficient incentives or coercion to ensure individual self-interest does not prejudice efficient and effective public interest outcomes, and does not necessarily resolve rational apathy problems.

Opt-out procedures necessarily derogate from the autonomy principle radically. These are privately incentivized or publicly funded mechanisms that encapsulate all class claims, thus optimizing legal certainty, judicial efficiency, collateral enforcement of public norms, and deterrence.[28] Formal litigants have legal standing, on behalf of a diffuse class, or numerous absent parties having similar claims. Final judgment, binding on all class members who have not opted out, precludes future individual claims, abrogating completely legal standing and due process rights of class members. Coercive abrogation of the autonomy principle is rationalized on grounds of public interest outcomes. For example, the US class action allows one lead litigant, subject to judicial certification, to pursue a class action for injunctions and/or damages in which the final judgment will be binding on all class members who have not opted out.[29] The case proceeds on the basis of a generic description of class members, who need not be identified until after final judgment, when they can assert a claim on the class action damages fund.

[26] A Cassone and G Ramello, 'The Simple Economics of Class Action: Private Provision of Club and Public Goods' (2011) 3 *IEL Paper in Comparative Analysis of Institutions, Economics and Law* 3.

[27] H Kalven and M Rosenfield, 'The Contemporary Function of the Class Suit' (1941) 8 *University of Chicago Law Review* 684, 688, 714–15, 717; Van den Bergh (n 14) 20–21.

[28] Kalven and Rosenfield (n 27) 717.

[29] Federal Rules of Civil Procedure, Rule 23.

Opt-out models sometimes grant standing to representatives with no direct interest in the claims. The representative functions as public defender, or attorney general, protecting, through class actions, individual class members' rights, and the public interest in norms enforcement. Some public/private attorney general models focus on enforcement of public interest civil and political rights, and social and economic constitutional rights, including consumer rights.[30] Injunctive relief, historically, in common law jurisdictions, an 'individuated' private remedy, is utilized as a quasi-public remedy on behalf of diffuse interests, to control behaviour that violates constitutional rights.[31] Thus, justification for legal standing in opt-out and diffuse cases is necessarily determined contextually, depending on relevant constitutional norms. Representative standing may be designated to a public official, imbued with a *parens patriae* function.[32] With respect to 'private attorney general' models,[33] private parties may be authorized in law to bring a claim on behalf of an identifiable or diffuse class.

The functional effectiveness of opt-out models requires optimal balance between economic incentives to bring a claim (as the group size increases, the relative risk-reward ratio for the majority is enhanced), whilst minimizing detriment to minority class interests, and 'free-rider' problems.[34] Simply granting standing to a 'private attorney general' is not economically sufficient to prompt class claims. A privatized attorney general model should incentivize third-party entrepreneurial investment in the claim. For example, the US model operates in the context of permissive rules on contingency fees, and jury damages awards that may have a punitive element. Especially with respect to economic approaches, the class attorney, who stands to profit if successful, is incentivized to act entrepreneurially,[35] although conflicts with class interests are problematic.[36] In private damages claims, and 'mass tort' class actions, there are inherent conflicts with traditional concepts of autonomy and due process.[37]

The opt-in model concerns efficiency and deterrence, but its primary objective is, through claims aggregation, to enable cost-effective case management,

[30] eg, La Constitución Española 1978 (as amended) Art 51.

[31] O Fiss, *The Civil Rights Injunction* (Bloomington, IN, Indiana University Press, 1978) 12–18.

[32] J Luther, 'The Constitutional Impact of Class Actions in European Legal Systems' in JG Backhaus, Alberto Cassone and Giovanni Ramello (eds), *The Law and Economics of Class Actions in Europe* (Cheltenham, Edward Elgar, 2012) 310.

[33] Kalven and Rosenfield (n 27).

[34] Olson (n 24); Kalven and Rosenfield (n 27) 713.

[35] JC Coffee, 'Understanding the Plaintiff's Attorney: The Implications of Economic Theory for Private Enforcement of Law through Class and Derivative Actions' (1986) 86 *Columbia Law Review* 669.

[36] JC Coffee, 'Rescuing the Private Attorney General: Why the Model of Lawyer as Bounty Hunter is Not Working' (1983) 42 *Maryland Law Review* 215.

[37] S Issacharoff, 'Preclusion, Due Process, and the Right to Opt Out' (2002) 77 *Notre Dame Law Review* 1057, 1058–59.

facilitate individual access to justice, and overcome economic barriers that individuals face, especially in scattered loss cases.[38] Opt-in remains primarily process and (individual) rights oriented, whereas the predominant rationale for opt-out models is consequentialist, justified by public outcomes (enforcement, optimal deterrence, collective social welfare and justice, judicial and economic efficiency).[39]

3. EU NORMS, THE RECOMMENDATION'S OBJECTIVES AND LEGAL STANDING PRINCIPLES

Whilst the autonomy principle precludes utilitarian, economically expeditious denial of individual access to the court through restrictions on legal standing and opt-out mechanisms, public interest outcomes are emphasized in economic and social approaches. In concrete terms, neither autonomy nor economic and social objectives can be ignored in the European context.

3.1 European Norms

The EU's primordial treaty norms, within which framework the Recommendation must necessarily be understood, are economic and social, and subject to EU exclusive competence.[40] The Lisbon Strategy set goals for economic growth and social advancement.[41] Enforcement of EU consumer and competition law, out of which the policy on collective redress emerged, derives from the founding economic freedoms: movement of goods, services, workers and capital.[42] Those freedoms impute welfare protections of diffuse social interests, for example, workers and consumers. EU treaty norms thus include commitments to 'high levels of consumer protection',[43] and other collective, social and economic interests ('solidarity rights').[44] Equality under EU law is founded on economic, welfare and social justice ideals, facilitating the realization of rights and interests of disadvantaged social groups, and maximizing labour resources in the Internal Market. For example, the Charter of Fundamental Rights, 'Recognises and respects

[38] R Mulheron, 'Cultural Dimensions of Group Litigation in England and Wales' (International Association of Procedural Law Conference, Moscow, 2012) 1.

[39] Cassone and Ramello (n 26) 16.

[40] TFEU, Art 3.

[41] *Lisbon Strategy* (European Council Meeting 23–24 March 2000) (CEC 2000).

[42] eg, European Community Treaty 1957 (Rome, 25 March 1957) Art 3; Treaty of Maastricht 1992 (Treaty of the European Union (TEU)) Art B; Treaty on European Union (consolidated version) [2010] OJ C83/13 (TEU) Art 3.

[43] TFEU, Arts 4, 12, 114 and 169; Charter of Fundamental Rights (n 11) Art 38.

[44] Charter of Fundamental Rights (n 11) ch IV, Arts 27–38.

the rights of persons with disabilities to benefit from measures designed to ensure their independence, social and occupational integration and participation in the life of the community'.[45] Thus, the Recommendation, contextually understood, is a redistributive instrument, promoting access to justice for diffuse consumer interests, as an instrumental means of furthering economic and social objectives.

Indeed, European private rights, enforcement of which the Recommendation aims to facilitate, are derivative of economic and social norms. European public norms produce direct effects giving rise to individual private rights.[46] Besides consumer and competition law, derivative private rights within the Recommendation's purview arise, for example, under product liability,[47] commercial agency,[48] financial services,[49] environmental damage liability,[50] employment and discrimination,[51] and data protection laws.[52]

The EU's economic and social objectives do not necessarily justify abrogation of the autonomy principle on consequentialist grounds. Consumers are entitled to legal redress for breach of their rights, including damages.[53] The Commission and national regulatory authorities (NRAs) are responsible for public norms enforcement, but Member States must provide effective individual access to justice, subject to equivalence and effectiveness principles.[54] Individual access to justice, and the European Convention on

[45] ibid, Art 26.

[46] Case 26/62 *Van Gend en Loos v Administratie der Belastingen*, EU:C:1963:1, paras 12–13.

[47] Directive 85/374/EEC of 25 July 1985 on the approximation of the laws, regulations and administrative provisions of the Member States concerning liability for defective products (Product Liability Directive) [1985] OJ L210/29.

[48] Directive 86/653/EEC of 18 December 1986 on the coordination of the laws of the Member States relating to self-employed commercial agents (Commercial Agents Directive) [1986] OJ L382/17.

[49] eg, Directive 2002/65/EC of 23 September 2002 concerning the distance marketing of consumer financial services and amending Council Directive 90/619/EEC and Directives 97/7/EC and 98/27/EC [2002] OJ L271/16.

[50] Directive 2004/35/EC of 21 April 2004 on environmental liability with regard to the prevention and remedying of environmental damage [2004] OJ L143/56 (Environmental Liability Directive).

[51] Directive 2000/78/EC of 27 November 2000 establishing a general framework for equal treatment in employment and occupation [2000] OJ L303/16 (Employment Equality Directive); Directive 2000/43/EC of 29 June 2000 implementing the principle of equal treatment between persons irrespective of racial or ethnic origin [2000] OJ L180/22 (Racial Equality Directive).

[52] Directive 95/46/EC of 24 October 1995 on the protection of individuals with regard to the processing of personal data and on the free movement of such data [1995] OJ L281/31; Case C-131/12 *Google Spain and Google*, EU:C:2014:317.

[53] Case C-453/99 *Courage and Crehan* [2001] ECR I-6297, EU:C:2001:465, paras 21–27.

[54] Case 45-76 *Comet BV v Produktschap voor Siergewassen*, EU:C:1976:191, paras 12–13; Case 33/76 *Rewe v Landwirtschaftskammer für das Saarland*, EU: C:1976:188; [1977] 1 CMLR 533, para 5; Case C-213/89 *The Queen v Secretary of State for Transport, ex parte Factortame*, EU: C:1990:257, [1991] 1 AC 603, 643–44; Case C-432/05 *Unibet*, EU: C:2007:163, [2008] All ER (EC) 453; [2007] 2 CMLR 30, para 37.

Human Rights and Fundamental Freedoms (ECHR), must be respected.[55] Observing fundamental human rights is a judicially recognized 'condition of the lawfulness of Community acts'.[56] European measures denying the right to be heard could infringe general principles of effective judicial protection, access to justice and fair trial rights.[57] That might not exclude mandatory ADR as a means of affording effective judicial protection in individual cases, if effective safeguards exist which protect individual autonomy.[58] The Recommendation is a civil justice measure, an area of shared competence.[59] There are limits generally on EU competence in private law,[60] and in respect of its shared competencies,[61] not least due to subsidiarity and proportionality principles,[62] and respecting Member States' legal traditions.[63] That is especially pertinent in civil justice, where legislative competence is generally limited to cross-border issues.[64]

However, enforcement of public norms and private rights are not politically and functionally exclusive. Private enforcement collaterally enhances public norms enforcement.[65] Absent European rules, Member States enjoy procedural autonomy,[66] but should prescribe rules enabling effective judicial protection.[67] There are 30 EU civil jurisdictions, with different rules on enforcement and redress for violations of EU private rights.[68] Thus, some inconsistency and inequality of access to justice and redress is inevitable across the EU, with consequences for the general effectiveness of public norms enforcement, and equality of effective judicial protection of individual private rights.

[55] Charter of Fundamental Rights (n 11) Art 47; TEU, Art 6; ECHR, Arts 6 and 13. In numerous cases the Court of Justice has affirmed that effective judicial protection is a general principle of EU law, eg, Case C-222/84 *Johnston v Chief Constable of the Royal Ulster Constabulary*, EU: C:1986:206 [1987] QB 129, 147; *Unibet* (n 54) para 37; Joined Cases C-402/05 P & C-415/05 P *Kadi and Al Barakaat International Foundation v Council and Commission*, EU:C:2008:461, [2008] 3 CMLR 41, paras 331–35.

[56] *Kadi* (n 55) paras 282–84.

[57] ibid, paras 345–53.

[58] Joined Cases C-317/08, C-318/08, C-319/08, C-320/08 *Alassini and Others*, EU:C:2010:146, para 42.

[59] TFEU, Arts 4(2), 67(4) and 81.

[60] S Weatherill, 'Competence and European Private Law' in C Twigg-Flesner (ed), *The Cambridge Companion to European Private Law* (Cambridge, Cambridge University Press, 2010).

[61] TFEU, Arts 4, 67 and 81.

[62] TEU, Art 5.

[63] TFEU, Art 67.

[64] ibid, Art 81(1).

[65] *Van Gend en Loos* (n 46) paras 12–13.

[66] *Unibet* (n 54) paras 79–82; Joined Cases C-295/04 to C-298/04 *Vincenzo Manfredi v Lloyd Adriatico Assicurazioni SpA*, EU:C:2006:461, para 71.

[67] *Manfredi* (n 66), paras 71, 92–94.

[68] Twenty-eight Member States and, in the UK, three jurisdictions: England & Wales, Northern Ireland and Scotland.

3.2 Policy Objectives

Initially, enhancing public norms enforcement was the Commission's primary policy focus, with economic and social justice approaches to private claims predominating. The 'rational apathy' enforcement gap, economic harm from un-redressed aggregated losses, and social justice considerations, drove deliberations on damages and collective redress for years prior to the Recommendation.[69] The European Single Market of 500 million consumers represents a paradigm example of 'massification' potential, and barriers to justice that Cappelletti identified.[70] The 'three wave' solutions (legal aid, collective action, ADR) have all been deployed through EU measures, although representative standing in collective claims has previously been limited to injunctive proceedings.[71] The Recommendation, for the first time, proposes collective redress in private damages claims.[72]

Throughout the extended consultation prior to the Recommendation, policy initiatives pursued separately by Directorates General (DG) for Competition, Health and Consumer Affairs (SANCO), and Justice, explored collective redress and private enforcement policies from economic, social justice and individual access to justice perspectives, in respect of consumer and competition law.

First, the Commission considered collective procedures for competition damages. Economic growth was the primary driver;[73] collective redress and other redress initiatives were seen as part of the Lisbon economic development strategy.[74] *Courage and Crehan* had established private rights to competition damages.[75] DG Competition identified low levels of private enforcement, due to legal and procedural hurdles, with competition law

[69] Commission, 'Green Paper on Damages actions for breach of the EC antitrust rules' COM(2005) 672 final, para 2.5; 'White Paper on Damages Actions for Breach of EC Antitrust Rules' COM(2008) 165 final, paras 1.1–2.1; 'Green Paper on Consumer Collective Redress' COM(2008) 794 final, paras 6–9; Commission Staff Working Document Public Consultation: Towards a Coherent European Approach to Collective Redress SEC(2011) 173 final, para 4.

[70] Cappelletti and Garth (n 19).

[71] Directive 2002/8/EC 27 January 2003 to improve access to justice in cross-border disputes by establishing minimum common rules relating to legal aid for such disputes [2003] OJ L26/41; Employment Equality Directive (n 51) Art 9; Racial Equality Directive (n 51) Art 7; Directive 2009/22/EC of 23 April 2009 on injunctions for the protection of consumers' interests [2009] OJ L110/30, Art 2 (Injunctions Directive); Directive 2008/52/EC of 21 May 2008 on certain aspects of mediation in civil and commercial matters [2008] OJ L136/3 (Mediation Directive); Directive 2013/11/EU of 21 May 2013 on alternative dispute resolution for consumer disputes and amending Regulation (EC) No 2006/2004 and Directive 2009/22/EC [2013] OJ L165/63; Regulation (EU) No 524/2013 of 21 May 2013 on online dispute resolution for consumer disputes and amending Regulation (EC) No 2006/2004 and Directive 2009/22/EC [2013] OJ L165/1.

[72] ADR is encouraged but is not the primary focus: Recommendation (n 1) paras 25–27.

[73] 'Green Paper' (n 69) para 1.1; 'White Paper' (n 69) para 2.1.

[74] 'White Paper' (n 69) para 1.2.

[75] *Courage and Crehan* (n 53).

infringers retaining several billion euros per annum of illicit gains, at a direct cost to consumers and other victims of between EUR13 and EUR 37 per annum.[76] DG Competition explored policy solutions, with the public aim of improving market equilibrium through an efficient private claims mechanism that could redistribute burdens of illicit activity from consumers and SMEs to wrongdoers.[77] Collective redress was proposed, to address the 'clear need for mechanisms allowing aggregation of the individual claims of antitrust infringements'.[78] The 2008 White Paper thus proposed that, across Member States, designated representative entities should have standing to bring antitrust damages claims, with individuals having standing in group damages actions.[79] Evident in the Commission's 2005 staff working document, the Green Paper on antitrust damages, and the 2008 White Paper, are predominant policy aims of safeguarding 'undistorted competition', and promoting 'better allocation of resources, greater economic efficiency, increased innovation and lower prices',[80] consistent with the Commission's economic and deterrence enforcement strategy.[81] Separately, DG SANCO considered collective consumer redress, with economic and social objectives in relation to scattered loss claims.[82] More recently, DG Justice introduced measures to enhance individual consumers' access to justice.[83]

The Green Paper consultation 'Towards a Coherent Approach' brought together those disparate initiatives, examining collective redress as a potential mechanism to achieve economic objectives, social goals of 'high levels of consumer protection',[84] and effective access to justice for individual private rights.[85] This consultation explored whether collective redress could facilitate private enforcement and individual access to justice, particularly in cross-border claims.[86] With a complex mix of public and private, individual and collective, policy objectives, the consultation lacked coherence on what conceptual or normative approach to standing and collective redress could satisfy all those objectives. Many consultation responses submitted that an opt-out procedure could conflict with European legal traditions, contrary to Article 67.[87] The European Parliament had passed a resolution

[76] Impact Assessment Accompanying Document to the White Paper on Damages Actions for Breach of the EC Antitrust Rules SEC(2008) 405, para 42.

[77] Green Paper and White Paper (n 69).

[78] White Paper (n 69) para 2.1.

[79] ibid.

[80] ibid, paras 1.2–2.1.

[81] Guidelines on the method of setting fines imposed pursuant to Article 23(2)(a) of Regulation No 1/2003 [2006] OJ C210/02, para 4.

[82] Green Paper on Consumer Collective Redress COM(2008) 794 final, paras 6–7.

[83] The Legal Aid in Cross-border Disputes Directive 2002/8/EC [2003] OJ L26/41; Mediation Directive; The Small Claims Procedure Regulations 861/2007 [2007] OJ L199/1.

[84] TFEU, Arts 12 and 169; EU Charter of Fundamental Rights, Art 38.

[85] Charter of Fundamental Rights, Art 47.

[86] Commission Staff Working Document (n 69) paras 1–6.

[87] TFEU, Art 67; B Hess et al, *Overview of Study on Evaluation of Contributions to the Public Consultation and Hearing: 'Towards a Coherent European Approach to Collective Redress'* (Study JUST/2010/JCIV/CT/0027/A4, 2011) 10.

in February 2013. Given the incorporation of civil justice objectives into the policy discourse, the requirements of Article 67 TFEU, and the volume of consultation responses that asserted the autonomy principle, an opt-in model was almost inevitable, with restrictions on legal standing likely to be a central safeguard in any European collective redress framework.[88]

Thus, economic and social objectives remained contextually important,[89] but access to justice had emerged as the primary goal. As such, any legislative or soft law measures, necessarily, should fall within the EU's civil justice competence.[90] That would require respect for the autonomy principle.[91] What was not evident is how a procedural design would emerge that could attain wider economic and social objectives too, which evidently remain as important wider goals. The Commission's Communication, published simultaneous to the Recommendation, refers to diffuse interests, and economic objectives of legal certainty, efficiency, competition, growth, the 'Europe 2020' strategy and the Single Market Act.[92] The economy and efficiency rationale appeared to predominate in the Communication's descriptive definition of collective redress, but nevertheless emphasized that compensation was the primary goal, and deterrence and punishment ought to be retained as a separate, complementary public enforcement objective.[93]

The economic and social justice policy context suggests, on the one hand, that the Recommendation ought to be justified on the basis of exclusive economic competencies.[94] On the other hand, prioritizing individual access to justice points to civil justice competencies. The EU's civil justice competencies are explicitly conditioned by requirements to respect fundamental rights and the Member States' legal traditions; civil justice measures should predominantly be limited to cross-border issues, and mutual recognition.[95]

The Recommendation's stated aims and purpose are 'to facilitate access to justice, stop illegal practices and enable injured parties to obtain compensation in mass harm situations caused by violations of rights granted under Union law, while ensuring appropriate procedural safeguards to avoid abusive litigation'.[96] A subtle yet important distinction can be drawn with the Directive for competition damages.[97] The Directive, enacted pursuant to the EU's exclusive economic competences, aims to improve the functioning of

[88] EP Resolution of 2 February 2012 on 'Towards a Coherent European Approach to Collective Redress' (2011/2089 (INI)) para 20.

[89] ibid, recitals, para I.

[90] ibid, recitals, paras A–C; operative parts, paras 1, 15.

[91] ibid, para 20.

[92] Commission, 'Towards a European Horizontal Framework for Collective Redress' COM(2013) 401 final, para 1.1.

[93] ibid, para 3.1.

[94] TFEU, Arts 3 and 114.

[95] ibid, Arts 4, 67 and 81.

[96] Recommendation (n 1) para 1.

[97] Directive 2014/104/EU of 26 November 2014 on certain rules governing actions for damages under national law for infringements of the competition law provisions of the Member States and of the European Union [2014] OJ L349/1 (Directive on Competition Damages).

the Internal Market.[98] Under the Internal Market competencies, the Directive aims to improve and equalize the basis on which EU citizens and SMEs are able to enforce private legal rights arising under EU law, as a means of enhancing collaterally the enforcement of EU competition law and improving the functioning of the Internal Market.[99]

The Recommendation's objectives are to secure greater access to justice in private damages claims whilst mitigating the perceived risk of 'abusive' litigation.[100] The Recommendation further aims, through the basic principles, to ensure common standards across Member States, with respect to fundamental rights and Member States' legal traditions.[101]

3.3 The Legal Standing Principles

As explored above, conceptually, different justificatory restrictions on legal standing inhere from the autonomy principle, and social justice and economic approaches. The legal standing principles on the one hand seek to protect autonomy, whilst also enabling public/private attorney general standing in representative claims. Neither approach is completely reconciled with underlying theoretical and doctrinal ideas of legitimacy and standing before the courts.

The standing principles are related to the Recommendation's two-pronged definition of collective redress:

(i) injunctive collective redress, which is 'a legal mechanism that ensures a possibility to claim cessation of illegal behaviour collectively by two or more natural or legal persons or by an entity entitled to bring a representative action', and
(ii) compensatory collective redress, which is defined as 'a legal mechanism that ensures a possibility to claim compensation collectively by two or more natural or legal persons claiming to have been harmed in a mass harm situation or by an entity entitled to bring a representative action'.[102]

A 'mass harm situation' is defined as a minimum of two persons who 'claim to have suffered harm causing damage resulting from the same illegal activity of one or more natural or legal persons'.[103] Standing is provided for in respect of representative collective actions, brought by designated representative entities (REs) or public authorities, and 'collective follow-on

[98] ibid, recitals, citing TFEU Arts 103 and 114.
[99] Directive on Competition Damages (n 97) recitals, paras (1)–(3) and (8).
[100] Recommendation (n 1) para 1.
[101] ibid, para 2.
[102] ibid, para 3(a).
[103] ibid, para 3(b).

actions', that is, claims for compensation that proceed after a finding of violation by a public or regulatory authority.[104] Other types of collective claim, such as a group claim on an originating motion, are not precluded.

In respect of compensatory collective redress by group claimants (the 'claimant party'), the Recommendation anticipates individual group members ('two or more natural or legal persons claiming to have been harmed in a mass harm situation') should have standing, on an opt-in basis.[105] By necessary inference, only individuals who are class members should have standing. As all members of the group must allege actual or threatened 'harm', consistent with the autonomy principle, implicitly, all group members, including the lead claimant, will be rights-bearers with a direct, personal interest in the claim. Claim and litigant autonomy is preserved, because of the opt-in requirement. Further safeguards to autonomy include that group members should be able to join and withdraw at any time prior to judgment, thus protecting individual standing and due process rights.[106]

However, whilst Member States 'should' ensure opt-in mechanisms, with standing according with the autonomy principle as just described, exceptions might be 'duly justified by reasons of sound administration of justice'.[107] Thus, the Recommendation does not expressly preclude opt-out models. Member States might adopt a variety of approaches to legal standing, economic and social justice approaches, on redistributive welfare grounds, and the wider interest in legal certainty, economic and judicial efficiency, and optimal deterrence.

The recommended approach to representative standing is restricted to designated REs[108] and/or public authorities,[109] subject to *minimum* RE eligibility criteria. REs should have a 'non-profit making character', and there must be a direct relationship between the RE's constitutive objectives and the EU rights to which the action relates. 'Capacity' is also provided for, although not according to concepts of autonomy and moral agency, but rather, with respect to economic and resource considerations (financial, human, legal expertise), such that REs should have sufficient capacity to represent multiple claimants.[110] If these conditions are no longer met, the Recommendation suggests RE status should be withdrawn.[111] Subject to those minimum thresholds, Member States have latitude in how to implement these standing principles. Member States could, without necessarily contravening the Recommendation, implement far more designation restrictive

[104] ibid, paras 3(d)–3(e).
[105] ibid, para 21.
[106] ibid, paras 23–24.
[107] ibid, para 21.
[108] ibid, para 4.
[109] ibid, para 7.
[110] ibid, para 4.
[111] ibid, para 5.

criteria. The manner of designation is left to the Member States, with the prospect of designation, for example, by judicial process, executive order, or legislative act. Designation could occur in advance, suggesting some form of official registration and approval system, or on an ad hoc basis, the latter suggesting a judicial certification process under rules integral to the collective action procedure.

The RE standing principles depart significantly from traditional litigant and claim autonomy. Third parties with no personal interest may pursue injunctive and compensatory collective claims. Instead of being predicated on the litigant's own rights and moral agency, standing is to be legitimized through official authorization and regulation. 'Capacity' is reduced to a utilitarian calculus, in that the REs must have adequate *resources* to pursue collective claims. This public/private attorney general approach evidently draws on redistributive social justice, welfare and economic frames of reference. Unfortunately, however, the Recommendation as a whole does not provide a complete and coherent procedural model for public/private attorney general collective action. As noted above, in respect of private attorney general models, the economic approach necessitates incentives for the representative and coercive restrictions on disparate individual interests, to deliver a viable economic reward that is balanced against the litigation cost risk, and to ensure optimal collective interest outcomes.[112] It is not likely that REs will regard the prospect of collective action as viable, especially in legal cases in which there is only a small number of individuals with compensation claims, unless the procedural model strikes a viable and economically effective balance between risk and reward. Costs and funding are critical to the economic private attorney general model. As Voet notes in this volume, there is scope for a variety of funding approaches, albeit subject to regulation and control over third-party interests.[113] Thus, in terms of representing a fully developed private attorney general model, the Recommendation leaves unanswered questions. A social justice, welfare approach to representative claims looks to public funding and resources to mitigate cost and funding risks, a matter on which the Recommendation is silent.

The prospect of common standards emerging is further undermined because of the implementing latitude afforded to Member States. A similar model for legal standing was employed under the Injunctions Directive, requiring Member States to designate 'Qualified Entities' (QEs) to pursue representative claims on behalf of consumers for injunctive relief to stop illegal practices.[114] Unlike the Recommendation's access to justice rationale, the Injunctions Directive, a binding measure executed under exclusive

[112] Section 2.3 above.
[113] See chapter 11 in this volume.
[114] Injunctions Directive (n 71) para 3.

economic competencies, aimed to improve the smooth functioning of the Internal Market.[115] The Injunctions Directive's QE representative standing, to enforce public norms, in the public/private attorney general mode, is consistent with redistributive economic approaches to collective actions and legal standing. By granting standing to specialist organizations, such as consumer associations, to apply for injunctive relief, the Injunctions Directive aims to supplement regulatory enforcement of European public norms. It is not designed directly to fulfil Member States' obligations in respect of access to justice and redress for breach of private rights, thus its standing provisions do not directly confront normative commitments to autonomy and due process rights in private actions.[116] To this extent the Injunctions Directive is internally consistent, and broadly compatible with Member States' legal traditions. That is not the case in respect of the Recommendation, which is a non-harmonizing measure, and which aims to improve, through collective mechanisms, individual access to justice in respect of substantive private rights arising under European law.

Further, economic justifications for representative public or private attorney general standing necessarily demand an assessment and evaluation in terms of economic and regulatory outcomes. Unfortunately, whilst generally regarded as a useful enforcement tool, evidence indicates that the Injunctions Directive has not achieved common standards and the Commission's economic objectives. The designation rules, and the number and characteristics of QEs vary significantly across Member States. QEs have shown a reluctance to issue proceedings outside their jurisdiction, and the mechanism is rarely deployed in cross-border claims because of cost and inherent litigation risks.[117]

The cross-border standing principles raise further anomalies. As the Recommendation contemplates future legislative action if voluntary implementation does not materialize,[118] cross-border elements of the Recommendation are critically important. As noted above, the Recommendation's access to justice objectives are directed towards civil justice, an area of shared competence.[119] Future legislative action will require that the measures concern, at some level, cross-border issues, conflict of laws and recognition and enforcement of judgments.[120] The European Parliament emphasized that any harmonizing collective redress measure should make provision for jurisdiction in collective redress claims to mitigate the risk of

[115] ibid, recitals, citing TEC Art 95 (now TFEU Art 114).

[116] Similar observations have been made in respect of US injunctive class actions to enforce public and constitutional rights: Issacharoff (n 37).

[117] Report from the Commission Concerning the application of Directive 2009/22/EC on injunctions for the protection of consumers' interest COM(2012) 635 final.

[118] Recommendation (n 1) para 41.

[119] TFEU, Art 4.

[120] ibid, Arts 67(4) and 81.

'forum shopping', and should address substantive conflict of laws in cross-border collective claims.[121] Jurisdiction and conflict of laws do not feature in the Recommendation. This is a missed opportunity. Common standards will be elusive. Forum shopping, and complex, expensive, preliminary legal arguments on private international law are almost inevitable in collective redress actions under the Recommendation's model.[122] Moreover, the absence of provisions addressing jurisdiction, applicable laws, and cross-border enforcement means that the legal basis for future legislative action under the EU's civil justice competencies is unclear.

The only cross-border provisions concern legal standing. It is recommended that group claimants and REs with legal standing in one Member State should not be prevented from bringing collective claims in other Member States.[123] The potential for discrimination and inconsistency is self-evident. Inevitably, because of the implementation latitude, there will be different standards regulating legal standing of group claim and RE standing across Member States. Foreign groups and entities may have legal standing in the Member State where the claim is issued, based simply on their RE status in their home jurisdiction, whereas identical or similar domestic groups and entities may not because of more restrictive group standing and RE designation criteria in the jurisdiction where proceedings are issued.

The cross-border provisions, if observed, could potentially subvert established conflict of law principles. Legal standing is a procedural issue. Ordinarily, procedure is a matter of *lex fori*. However, designation and regulation of REs could, depending on manner of implementation in Member States, be subject to substantive public and administrative law, opening the prospect of rejection of some foreign claimants on public policy (*ordre public*) grounds.[124] Even if that is not the case, there are no European treaties or regulations on conflict of laws that would require the domestic courts to apply, on the basis of this non-binding Recommendation, foreign procedural laws on legal standing. Which law, then, should the court seised of jurisdiction apply? The Recommendation essentially anticipates that national courts will voluntarily recognize procedural standing defined according to foreign law in cross-border claims, whereas national courts, which enjoy procedural autonomy, will most likely be under a legal duty to apply the domestic procedural law. Disregarding the Recommendation's principles on

[121] EP Resolution (n 88) paras 19, 26–27.

[122] A Stadler, 'The Commission's Recommendation on common principles of collective redress and private international law' (2013) 4 *Nederlands Internationaal Privaatrecht* 483, para 3.1.

[123] Recommendation (n 1) paras 17–18.

[124] H Muir Watt, 'Evidence of an Emergent European Legal Culture: Public Policy Requirements of Procedural Fairness under the Brussels and Lugano Conventions' (2001) 36 *Texas International Law Journal* 539 542–43.

cross-border standing will stultify the Recommendation's impact on cross-border mass harm cases. On the other hand, following the non-binding Recommendation might contradict established conflict of law principles on civil procedure, undermine European principles of non-discrimination, subsidiarity, and mutual respect and sovereignty, and be contradictory to the legal tradition in that national system, contrary to TFEU Article 67. Thus, the legal standing provisions could have the adverse unintended consequence of exacerbating cross-border 'forum shopping', a risk that is already present due to the absence of substantive harmonizing standards applicable to collective actions.[125]

4. COMPARATIVE ASSESSMENT WITH LEGAL STANDING IN NATIONAL LEGAL TRADITIONS

Beyond internal coherence, the Recommendation's impact on access to justice will be conditioned by national civil procedure rules, and national approaches to implementation. A comparative analysis of existing collective procedures and standing in Member States will enable evaluation of its likely impact in practice. As Micklitz observed, nationally, concepts of substantive 'justice' are embedded through culture and tradition, but in emergent welfare and social justice fields of European private law, especially labour rights, embedded traditions are less entrenched, thus a window exists for progressive social justice transformation less in tension with existing legal traditions.[126] However, concerning procedural justice, development of social justice initiatives such as collective redress procedures are conditioned by the EU's limited competence and, specifically, fundamental rights and national legal traditions.[127] That has implications for the nature and scope of legal standing under the Recommendation, and the Directive on Competition Damages.[128] Both 'opt-out' class or collective actions and any model recognizing third-party representative standing were said in consultation responses to conflict with many Member States' legal traditions.[129] This section explores, through comparative examples of national civil procedures and collective action mechanisms, the richly divergent European procedural landscape, with evidence of autonomy-premised, and economic and social justice approaches to standing in collective redress procedures.

125 Stadler (n 122) para 3.1.

126 HW Micklitz, *The Many Concepts of Social Justice in European Private Law* (Cheltenham, Edward Elgar, 2011) 2.

127 TFEU, Art 67(1).

128 As recognized by the EP: Motion for a EP Resolution on 'Towards a Coherent Approach to Collective Redress' 12 January 2012, para 2.

129 Hess et al (n 87) 10.

4.1 Autonomy

Autonomy principles theoretically preclude generic class or representative claims for damages.[130] There are three basic standing requirements in most European justice systems: legal personality, a direct interest in the claim, and capacity to sue.[131] In most Member States, judicial review claimants should have a direct or sufficient interest in the claim; standing generally depends on personal legal rights being in issue. Exceptionally, public interest standing is acknowledged.[132] 'Legal standing' in private law claims[133] also denotes a legitimate right to appear and be heard by the court. Across Europe, standing in civil claims is generally predicated on the autonomy principle. For example, in England and Wales, natural or legal persons can sue or be sued.[134] Claimants should have an interest in the subject of the claim,[135] meaning a vested legal right, or beneficial equitable interest as trustee or beneficiary.[136] Reflecting the autonomy concept of capacity, special rules allow for representative standing for persons lacking full capacity to act on their own behalf.[137] Similar approaches are found in other Member States with common law or hybrid systems. In civil code jurisdictions, legal standing generally adheres to similar principles. Claimants should have a vested legal right and personal interest in the dispute,[138] with exceptional third-party representation for the mentally incapacitated to ensure that their autonomy can be protected.[139]

'Capacity to sue' is generally either an express requirement, or implicitly understood. Provisions are made in all European civil justice systems, to grant representative standing on grounds of incapacity of the interested party (claimant or defendant). In keeping with autonomy ideals of moral agency, typically, the notion of 'incapacity' is limited to mental impairment. The UK's Court of Protection functions to enable and control third-party

[130] M Eliantonio et al, *Standing up For Your Right(s) in Europe: A Comparative Study on Legal Standing (Locus Standi) before the EU and Member States' Courts* (Directorate General for Internal Policies, Citizens' Rights and Constitutional Affairs PE 462478 EN, 2012) 13.

[131] ibid, 6, 52–54.

[132] eg, Portuguese *actio popularis* proceedings: Constituição da República Portuguesa 1976 (VII revisão 2005) (Portuguese Constitution) Art 52(3); Direito de participação procedimental e de acção popular, Lei 83/95, de 31 Agosto 1995 (Law on Procedural Participation and Popular Action). Public Interest Standing in English Judicial Review is Exceptional: *R v Secretary of State for Foreign Affairs ex p World Development Movement Ltd* [1995] 1 All ER 611, 620, 628.

[133] Eliantonio et al (n 130) 54.

[134] *Halsbury's Laws of England: Civil Procedure* vol 11, 5th edn (2009) para 207 (albeit subject to numerous exceptions).

[135] *Clowes v Hilliard* [1876 C 206]; (1876) 4 Ch D 413, 418.

[136] *Halsbury's Laws of England: Civil Procedure* (n 134) para 208.

[137] Civil Procedure Rules 1998 (as amended) (CPR) Part 21.

[138] eg, Code Judiciaire (Belgium) Arts 17–18; French Civil Procedure Code, Art 31.

[139] eg, French Civil Procedure Code, Art 338 and Code civil (version consolidée au 5 juin 2014) (French Civil Code) Arts 388 and 389(3).

protective intervention to look after the affairs of mentally incapacitated adults. A person lacks capacity to make decisions in relation to a matter if he 'is unable to make a decision for himself ... because of an impairment of, or a disturbance in the functioning of, the mind or brain'.[140] In France, vulnerable adults (*majeurs protégés*) may be placed under judicial protection on grounds of incapacity, to protect their autonomy, individual liberty and fundamental rights.[141] Vulnerable adults are entitled to a range of protective measures, including representative protection concerning legal rights, if disability prevents expression of their will.[142]

Elsewhere, traditional requirements of claim autonomy are in many respects adhered to. For damages claims in Germany, similar claims may be joined and heard at the same time. However, the autonomy principle, read in light of German constitutional protection of the right of access to the court,[143] requires all litigants to be formal parties to the proceedings, and presumes attendance at all hearings.[144] Arguably, that model whilst highly restrictive, centred on autonomy, and unsuited to efficient and effective case management of mass scattered loss cases, would comply with the group claim standing requirements of the Recommendation. Thus, the Recommendation will not likely have any beneficial impact in facilitating access to justice for group claims in Germany.

That said autonomy is a benchmark, subject to widespread exceptions. Idiosyncratic standing rules, rooted in national legal cultures, exist in some jurisdictions. Some Member States have adapted traditional representative civil procedure rules to accommodate, on an opt-in basis, the collective management of multiple claims. Contrary to the commonly held understanding that opt-out mechanisms contradict European legal traditions, some traditional and modern rules allow identified and/or unidentified class members to be represented by a third party. In England and Wales, the Group Litigation Order (GLO) procedure represents a modern adaptation of the common law representative procedure that has its roots in nineteenth-century Chancery court rules for equitable claims. The GLO is a typical example of an opt-in collective action process.[145] The GLO procedure still requires all claimants

[140] Mental Capacity Act 2005, s 2(1).
[141] Civil Code, Art 415.
[142] ibid, Art 425.
[143] Grundgesetz für die Bundesrepublik Deutschland vom 23 Mai 1949 (BGBl S 1), zuletzt geändert durch das Gesetz vom 21 Juli 2010 (BGBl I S 944) (Constitution of the Federal Republic of Germany) Art 103.
[144] Bundesrepublik Deutschland Zivilprozessordnung (ZPO) In der Fassung der Bekanntmachung vom 05.12.2005 (BGBl I S 3202, ber 2006 I S 431, 2007 I S 1781) zuletzt geändert durch Gesetz vom 22.12.2011 (BGBl I S 3044) mWv 30.12.2011 bzw 01.01.2013 Stand: 01.01.2012 aufgrund Gesetzes vom 07.07.2009 (BGBl I S 1707) (German Civil Procedure Code) Arts 59–63.
[145] CPR, Part 19II.

or defendants in the group to be parties to the litigation.[146] Nevertheless, its precursor, which still exists today, the representative action, rooted in equity but now with more or less trans-substantive application, recognizes representative standing to bring claims on behalf of non-parties with similar claims in fact and law.[147] In limited circumstances, representatives may act on behalf of 'interested persons who cannot be ascertained', permitting claims on behalf of an absent class.[148] Whilst implicitly presumed that class interests are predicated on individual autonomy and due process rights, that long-standing traditional model nevertheless undermines claims that strict claim autonomy is always a necessary requirement in civil claims. Other jurisdictions have similar long-standing rules allowing a type of collective action in civil claims. Cyprus has no modern collective action law, but its ordinary civil procedure rules allow 'numerous' claimants or defendants to grant a power of attorney to a representative litigant to bring or defend claims on their behalf.[149]

In these examples, and others besides, 'traditional' civil procedure rules on legal standing, joinder and limited representative standing (where it exists) are not aimed at, nor do they assist much with, genuinely mass harm claims. The primary objectives are to ensure judicial efficiency with respect to a relatively small number of individual claims, and to avoid conflicting judgments in similar cases.[150] These procedural rules would broadly seem to be compatible with the Recommendation's basic principles for legal standing to bring group collective actions. Thus, taking the examples discussed here, the Recommendation will not likely facilitate existing access to justice standards for breaches of rights arising under European law.

However, other exceptions to the autonomy principle will not necessarily be consistent with the Recommendation's standing requirements because they are more permissive in some respects, and more restrictive in other respects. In German collective or representative *Verbandsklage* actions, unincorporated associations representing commercial and professional interests, trade unions and chambers of commerce have exceptional representative standing, but only for injunctive or declaratory relief.[151] Similarly, in Austria, representative test claims can seek injunctive and declaratory

[146] ibid, Part 19II.

[147] ibid, Part 19.6

[148] ibid, Part 19.7.

[149] Civil Procedure Rules (Cyprus), Rules of Court made under the Civil Procedure Law, et al. Order 9 R 9.

[150] Eliantonio et al (n 130) 116.

[151] Gesetz gegen den unlauteren Wettbewerb consolidated version of 3 March 2010 (BGBI Part I, 254) (Law against unfair competition) (Germany) (UWG); Gesetz gegen Wettbewerbsbeschränkungen in der Fassung der Bekanntmachung vom 15 Juli 2005 (BGBl I S 2114; 2009 I S 3850) das zuletzt durch Artikel 6 des Gesetzes vom 4 November 2010 (BGBl I S 1480) geändert worden ist (GWB); Gesetz Über Unterlassungsklagen bei Verbraucherrechts und anderen Verstößen Nov 26 2001/27 August 2002, BGBI I, 3422, as amended (UKlaG).

relief.[152] When compared with the group claim standing requirements of the Recommendation, the *Verbandsklage* model (in which the claimant is a representative organization, not a harmed individual group member) will fail the 'harm' test, thus, whilst a traditional, established procedure that can potentially accommodate at least injunctive mass claims, it will not automatically comply with the Recommendation's basic principles. Further legislative action will be required to officially designate those representative bodies according to the Recommendation's minimum standards for RE standing, and to enable compensation claims. However, German constitutional rights of access to the court and personal rights to appear and be heard necessarily preclude legislators from restricting personal standing in respect of such claims. At best, the representative mechanism will need to accommodate individual rights (which may not be practical or efficient in genuine mass harm cases) or maintain the representative process as a parallel, optional mechanism. In other words, the German Constitution precludes coercive restrictions on personal and claim autonomy, which is conceptually necessary to control self-interest and rational apathy if collective proceedings are to function effectively and efficiently. The German Constitution almost certainly provides an insurmountable barrier to national implementation of the non-mandatory Recommendation's RE standing principles for compensation claims. Thus, the Recommendation will most likely be ineffective in the German context and improved efficiency and effectiveness, legal certainty, access to justice and redress, deterrence and collateral public norms enforcement is a remote prospect.

4.2 The European Welfare State and Social Justice

Whilst the Recommendation's standing principles for group claims adhere to the autonomy principle, in some national jurisdictions the welfare state ideal has been manifested through constitutionalized redistributive social justice provisions, recognizing substantive and procedural social and economic rights, such as consumer rights and interests,[153] and guarantees for legal aid and assistance.[154] The global trend towards class actions as a solution has continued in the European Union to some extent.[155]

[152] Austrian Civil Procedure Code, Zivilprozessordnung Stand BGBl I Nr 7/2006 (ZPO) Art 227.

[153] eg, La Constitución Española 1978 (as amended) Art 51; Portuguese Constitution, Art 60.

[154] Storskrubb and Ziller (n 17) 180–82; eg, Portuguese Constitution, Art 20.

[155] eg, Finland Ryhmaäkannelaki (Group Action Act) 444/2007; Sweden Group Proceedings Act 2002 (as amended); Netherlands Wet collectieve afwikkeling massaschade, Staatsblad 2005, no 340 (WCAM); Group Proceedings Act 2009 (Poland) (GPA); Codice del Consumo, decreto legislativo 206/2005 (Italy); (Consumer Code) ch 5; Collective Proceedings Act, Act no VI 2012 (Chapter 520 Laws of Malta); Denmark Retsplejeloven: Consolidated Act No 1008 of 24 October 2012 (in force) (Danish Administration of Justice Act) ss 250–54; The Republic of Lithuania Civil Procedure Code (as amended by Law No. XII-771 of 13 March 2014) article 441.

Some jurisdictions have sector-specific collective litigation procedures, with distinctive procedural design and delineation of legitimate representative standing. There is a variety of approaches, some of which seek to adhere to principles of autonomy more rigidly than others. The German model is restrictive, applying to capital markets claims, and still requiring all claimants individually to issue proceedings; no one else has legal standing to bring the claim.[156] Thus, whilst informed by economic objectives,[157] the German model maintains complete adherence to autonomy with regard to standing and due process rights. It could potentially comply with the Recommendation's group claim standing requirements, but has been widely criticized for failing to deliver improved access to justice or greater efficiency because, amongst other things, of standing requirements preserving the autonomy principle and individual due process rights.[158]

Other opt-in class action laws will require amendment to achieve consistency with the Recommendation. For example, the Polish Group Proceedings Act (GPA), an opt-in model, grants standing to individual class members (for group claims), but only on the basis that the class consists of a minimum of 10 persons. Local ombudsmen have standing to bring representative actions, again on behalf of a minimum of 10 persons.[159] Thus, the Polish law's standing provisions will not accommodate group or representative claims comprising two or more persons, as set out in the Recommendation. Amendments to the GPA, to accommodate groups comprising two or more persons will have no impact whatsoever on genuinely mass harm scattered losses cases. To comply with the Recommendation's minimum designation criteria for RE standing, further legislation will be required to regulate the Consumer Ombudsman's representative status in line with the Recommendation. Those additional measures will not likely change the functional status and legal standing rights of the Ombudsman.

Bulgaria's permissive class action model introduced in 2008 grants representative standing to a wide category of natural and legal persons on an opt-in or opt-out basis.[160] Unique approaches are also found, such as the Dutch 'class action settlement' model, which recognizes the legal standing of special purpose vehicles (SPVs) to apply to the court for judicial approval of a class action settlement.[161]

[156] Gesetz Über Musterverfahren in kapitalmarktrechtlichen Streitigkeiten of 16 August 2005 BGBI 1, 2437, last amended by Art 2, para 28 of the Act of 22 December 2011 (Law on Model Proceedings in Capital Market Disputes) ('KapMuG').

[157] E Feess and A Halfmeier, 'The German Capital Markets Model Case Act (KapMuG): A European Role Model for Increasing the Efficiency of Capital Markets? Analysis and Suggestions for Reform', available at: ssrn.com/abstract=1684528, 2.

[158] ibid, 26–27.

[159] GPA (Poland) Art 4.

[160] Law on Consumer Protection promulgated SG 99/9.12.2005, effective 10.06.2006, most recently amended and supplemented, SG No 18/1.03.2011 Arts 188–89.

[161] WCAM (n 155).

In other instances, legal standing in opt-out class actions is restricted to public officials. In Spain, specified public authorities and consumer associations have standing to bring diffuse collective consumer claims.[162] The Spanish system also allows class members to bring consumer class actions and, in respect of 'diffuse' consumer interests (when the consumers are indeterminate or difficult to ascertain), consumer associations have exclusive representative standing in claims for both injunctive and compensatory relief.[163] The diffuse claim does not require class members to opt in, and necessarily precludes the possibility of opting out, because it is predicated on indeterminate consumer interests.

Danish class action laws regulating consumer claims recognize individual class members' (autonomy-based) standing in opt-in claims, restricting (social justice and economically-predicated) standing in opt-out claims to public officials. Adopting a 'public attorney general' welfare state approach, the Consumer Ombudsman has exclusive standing in opt-out consumer class claims for damages.[164]

As such, pre-existing and diverse opt-in and opt-out collective redress procedures motivated by public interest, economic and welfare state objectives in several Member States already provide greater access to justice, and more flexibility in respect of representative standing, than the Recommendation proposes.

4.3 ADR and Regulatory Models

There are examples in Member States of regulatory mechanisms that sit alongside the formal civil justice system, and have been developed to handle mass compensation claims as an aspect of the regulatory system. There is a wide array of consumer redress models across Member States, including sector-specific and regulatory complaints mechanisms, arbitration, mediation, and other forms of ADR, which function alongside civil justice systems.[165]

When integrated into regulatory systems, these types of ADR and dispute resolution models can enable private redress, enhanced public norms

[162] Real Decreto Legislativo 1/2007 de 16 de noviembre, por el que se aprueba el texto refundido de la Ley General para la Defensa de los Consumidores y Usarios y otras leyes complementarias (Royal Legislative Decree 1/2007) Art 54; Ley Enjuiciamiento Civil, ley 1/2000 (LEC 1/2000) (Law on Civil Proceedings) Art 6.

[163] La Constitución Española 1978 (as amended) Art 51; LEC 1/2000 (LEC) Arts 6(7), and 11(3); Royal Legislative Decree 1/2007, Art 37.

[164] AJA s 254(c); Consolidated Marketing Practices Act no 58 of 20 January 2012, 20.

[165] N Creutzfeldt, 'The Origins and Evolution of Consumer Dispute Resolution Systems in Europe' in C Hodges and A Stadler (eds), *Resolving Mass Disputes: ADR and Settlement of Mass Claims* (Cheltenham, Edward Elgar, 2013); for a comprehensive review, see C Hodges, I Benohr and N Creutzfeldt-Banda (eds), *Consumer ADR in Europe* (Oxford, Hart Publishing, 2012).

enforcement, and regulatory objectives of economic and market re-balancing (reallocating the cost burden of illicit behaviour from consumers to perpetrators), monitoring and behaviour control.[166]

In the Netherlands, a sophisticated, out of court, consumer ADR system operates, with multiple sector-specific complaints and dispute resolution mechanisms operating under consumer complaints board (*Geschillencommissie Stichting* (GS)) oversight.[167] The GS has support from government, consumer associations and trade associations.[168]

The Spanish consumer arbitration system, including in collective claims,[169] is far more entrenched than the Recommendation anticipates. Against the backdrop of coercive, opt-in and diffuse collective action procedures, it provides national coverage for consumer arbitration, with executive and judicial oversight, with maximum delegation to local level, consistent with EU subsidiarity norms. RD 1/2007 provides for an extrajudicial arbitration system for the resolution of disputes between consumers and corporate suppliers of goods and services. This informal resolution process applies to all types of consumer disputes, with the exception of any dispute involving intoxication, injury or death or reasonable suspicion of a crime.[170]

The Spanish system could be regarded as central to its legal tradition. The Constitution, as already noted,[171] protects consumer rights, and obliges the state to establish laws that ensure effective protection of those rights.[172] Consumer protection laws enacted in 1984 obliged the executive to establish a system for arbitration of consumer disputes.[173] The 1993 regulations, and subsequent laws, provided the basic framework for consumer arbitration,[174] establishing a National Consumer Arbitration Board (*Junta Arbitral de Consumo de ámbito nacional*), and National Consumer Institute (*Instituto Nacional del Consumo* (INC)).[175] The government established arbitration

[166] C Hodges, 'New Modes of Redress for Consumers: ADR and Regulation', Oxford Legal Studies Research Paper No 57/2012, available at: ssrn.com/abstract=2126485 or dx.doi.org/10.2139/ssrn.2126485, 5; see also Adrian Dally's remarks about the UK Financial Ombudsman Service: C Hodges and N Creutzfeldt, *The Hidden World of Consumer ADR: Redress and Behaviour* (Conference Report, The Foundation for Law Justice and Society in affiliation with the Centre for Socio-Legal Studies, University of Oxford, 28 October 2011) 9.

[167] F Weber and C Hodges, 'Netherlands' in C Hodges, I Benohr and N Creutzfeldt-Banda (eds), *Consumer ADR in Europe* (Oxford, Hart Publishing, 2012) 129–66.

[168] Hodges and Creutzfeldt (n 166) 9.

[169] Real Decreto 231/2008, de 15 febrero, por el que regula el sistema arbitral de consumo, Arts 56–62.

[170] Royal Legislative Decree 1/2007, Art 57(1).

[171] See (n 153).

[172] La Constitución Española 1978 (as amended) Art 51.

[173] Ley 26/1984 de 19 de julio, General para la defense de los consumidores Art 31.

[174] Real Decreto 636/1993, de 3 de mayo, por el que regula el Sistema Arbitral de Consumo (repealed and replaced by Real Decreto 231/2008, de 15 febrero, por el que regula el sistema arbitral de consumo).

[175] RD 636/1993, Art 2(1).

boards at municipal, provincial and regional level,[176] and executed agreements with municipal, provincial and regional bodies, establishing competence of local arbitration boards, to hear consumer disputes locally, with preference towards the most subsidiary arbitration board.[177] The Spanish consumer arbitration system is now regulated pursuant to Royal Legislative Decree 1/2007 and detailed procedural rules enacted in 2008.[178] This legislation amended Spain's consumer protection laws, to comply with the Injunctions Directive.[179]

Whilst essentially an extrajudicial process, Spain's arbitration system does not compromise individual rights of access to the court, and has extensive procedural safeguards to ensure fairness. Consumer arbitration is voluntary. Agreement to submit to arbitration must be confirmed in writing or by electronic means.[180] The Committee on Consumer Arbitration Boards is responsible for establishing uniform criteria and the determination of appeals against decisions of the Consumer Arbitration Boards.

Simultaneously, the arbitration system incorporates mechanisms to enhance regulation. The Consumer Arbitration Board can collect and disseminate technical data, issue reports and advisory opinions, and reports on issues concerning withdrawal of accreditation of arbitrators.[181] The General Council of Consumer Arbitration, a body functionally attached to the INC, comprises directors drawn from the national and territorial arbitration boards, the ministries of justice, public administration, finance, industry, tourism and trade, as well as representatives from regional consumer administrations, the Consumer Council, business and professional organizations, chambers of commerce, and the General Bar Council. The General Council is responsible for monitoring and making recommendations for improvement of the consumer arbitration system, and establishing uniform criteria for specialist and sectoral arbitration bodies.[182] The law also makes provision for the constitution of arbitration boards, consisting of accredited arbitrators, and provides grounds for disqualification if arbitrators violate the obligations of independence, impartiality and confidentiality.[183] Detailed rules prescribe the necessary form and content of arbitration agreements. These may be concluded in individual cases. However, the law also provides a mechanism for companies to make a 'public offer' to join the arbitration

176 ibid, Art 2(2).

177 ibid, Arts 2(3)–2(4).

178 Royal Legislative Decree 1/2007; Real Decreto 231/2008, de 15 febrero, por el que regula el sistema arbitral de consumo.

179 Injunctions Directive (n 71).

180 Royal Legislative Decree 1/2007, Art 58(1).

181 Real Decreto 231/2008, de 15 febrero, por el que regula el sistema arbitral de consumo Arts 9–11.

182 ibid, Arts 12–15.

183 ibid, Arts 16–23.

system. The INC administers the Consumer Arbitration System and maintains a public register of companies participating in the scheme.[184] The complaints procedure is provided for in the law.[185] Supplementary rules regulate full conduct of the arbitration via electronic means.[186]

The Danish model provides a further example of collective redress systems, integral to the regulatory and legal framework. As noted, the Consumer Ombudsman has legal standing to bring opt-out consumer class actions.[187] However, that power is rarely used, precisely because it forms part of a wider, integrated consumer redress and regulatory scheme, with hard and soft law powers to achieve both redress and wider economic objectives.[188] The Ombudsman has regulatory powers to negotiate restitution schemes to deliver compensation to consumers, which is invariably successfully deployed, thus avoiding the need for opt-out litigation. Henrik Øe, the former Danish Consumer Ombudsman, has opined that his standing to bring opt-out consumer claims before the courts provides important coercive authority to his soft law and regulatory powers, thus contributing to the effectiveness of those techniques: 'It is not necessary to resort to its use in the vast majority of circumstances, but the existence of the power constitutes important authority and deterrent'.[189]

In the UK, the Financial Conduct Authority has powers to work with regulated entities to implement consumer redress schemes, if there has been 'widespread or regular failure' by firms to comply with regulatory standards.[190] That model has delivered redress to millions of consumers who were victims of systemic and widespread mis-selling by all the major retail banks of payment protection insurance, delivering over £15 billion of consumer compensation by April 2014.[191] Recently, a similar consumer redress scheme has been applied to mis-selling of card protection and identity protection insurance.[192] The Consumer Rights Act 2015, which received Royal Assent on 26 March 2015, includes detailed provisions for judicial, regulatory and alternative dispute resolution processes for handling consumer claims. It introduced regulatory powers for consumer redress schemes to be

[184] ibid, Arts 24–32.

[185] ibid, Arts 33–50.

[186] ibid, Arts 51–55.

[187] (n 164) and main text.

[188] H Øe, 'How to Achieve Compliance: The Danish Regulatory System and the Use of Soft and Hard Law in the Enforcement of Consumer Protection Legislation' (Building Effective Markets—The Role of an Integrated Legal System, Zurich, January 2013).

[189] Hodges and Creutzfeldt (n 165) 14.

[190] Financial Services Act 2010, s 14; Financial Services and Markets Act 2000 (as amended) (FSMA) s 404.

[191] Financial Conduct Authority, 'Monthly PPI refunds and compensation' press release, 3 July 2014, available at: www.fca.org.uk/consumers/financial-services-products/insurance/payment-protection-insurance/ppi-compensation-refunds.

[192] Financial Conduct Authority, 'Redress package agreed for consumers mis-sold CPP insurance products' press release, 28 October 2010, available at: www.fca.org.uk/news/consumer-redress-agreed-for-mis-sold-cpp-insurance.

included in regulatory enforcement orders[193] and, like the Danish model in mind, backed by an opt-out claims mechanism for breaches of competition law.[194]

5. CONCLUSIONS

The aim of this chapter was to explore whether the Recommendation's access to justice and wider public goals will be facilitated or frustrated by the legal standing principles. In conclusion, the normative and comparative analysis in this chapter indicates that the Recommendation's standing principles will not likely facilitate access to justice and, in some respects, may have adverse unintended consequences that could frustrate existing collective redress procedures. Cross-border uniformity is a remote prospect; indeed the Recommendation's limited provisions on cross-border standing raise the prospect of discrimination between REs from different Member States, forum shopping, and complex legal arguments over jurisdiction and applicable law, all of which will constitute additional barriers to justice for consumers.

As section 2 explained, collective redress procedures motivated by social and economic objectives, challenge liberal concepts of justice, and legal standing predicated on the autonomy principle. Prevailing approaches to procedural legitimacy and legal standing in Europe are autonomous and individualistic, reflecting overriding political norms. Opt-in and opt-out collective redress models necessarily require departure from the autonomy principle. In contrast, social justice and economic approaches take into account social, economic and other contextual barriers to justice, and legitimize redistributive, economically efficient mechanisms that maximize collective and public interest outcomes, conceptually justifying collective and representative standing, in class/collective actions, regulatory compensation schemes and other forms of collective ADR. Opt-in and opt-out collective procedures can improve judicial efficiency, and may be more effective at delivering redress in scattered loss cases but, as both involve some repression of individual and claim autonomy, conflict conceptually with the autonomy principle. Opt-out procedures are more likely to deliver optimal public norms enforcement and deterrence, as well as maximizing public interest economic and social outcomes.

Through the standing principles, European norms, and immediate and wider policy objectives of enhanced consumer access to justice, economic efficiency, collateral public norms enforcement, and redistributive social justice, must be balanced with autonomy, due process, and individual access to justice. Doctrinally, EU legal principles include economic and social treaty

[193] Consumer Rights Bill 2014–15, sch 7.
[194] ibid, sch 8.

norms and commitments to basic human rights predicated on autonomy. That is manifested in the legal standing principles, which acknowledge both the autonomy principle, and wider economic and social justice justifications for collective standing, but do not necessarily reconcile the normative constraints of either approach. Despite the Recommendation's stated access to justice objectives, the legal standing provisions belie unresolved confusion between contrasting approaches to autonomy, procedural rights and legal standing before the civil courts, and broader economic and welfare/social objectives. This vacillation is symptomatic of wider tensions in the EU's treaty framework, between diffuse economic and social welfare objectives of the founding treaties, and principles of national autonomy, subsidiarity and individual fundamental rights. The RE cross-border standing principles, whilst admitting broad margins to Member States for designation and regulation of REs, fail to address adequately cross-border issues in collective claims. This will likely risk discrimination between national REs in cross-border claims, and exacerbate rather than remedy the lack of uniformity of access to justice and redress across Member States.

As the comparative analysis in section 4 revealed, the Recommendation's standing principles for group claims, in seeking to respect claim autonomy and national legal traditions, are largely consistent with existing models for multiparty claims in many Member States. Perversely, some traditional, entrenched national models for representative standing, including on behalf of unidentified claimants, depart from the autonomy principle more radically than the Recommendation itself.

The Recommendation's adherence to autonomy principles in group claims fails to acknowledge the evolution of the welfare and regulatory state, incorporating collective social justice measures, across Europe. As section 4 found, there have been significant procedural and regulatory innovations, to confront problems of judicial and economic efficiency in mass harm litigation, with redistributive social justice and welfare objectives in mind. Many of those innovations adopt opt-in and opt-out redress procedures, both in formal civil procedures and ADR and regulatory mechanisms, already providing greater and more flexible scope for collective redress than the Recommendation envisages. In jurisdictions such as Germany, Poland, and England and Wales, private group claims can be subjected to collective case management, but individual autonomy at a fundamental level is preserved. Broadly, subject to only minimal amendments (for example, in Poland, restricting the minimum group size to two rather than 10 claimants) it would seem that the Recommendation's standing principles with respect to group claims are largely compatible with those national approaches. Those models have been found to be largely ineffective in enhancing access to justice in mass harm cases. It follows that the Recommendation will not, even in Member States where the autonomy principle provides the fundamental benchmark for legal standing, make much if any difference to consumers' access to justice.

There is an apparent presumption by the Commission that opt-out mechanisms are alien to European legal traditions. That is not the case. As the comparative analysis in section 4 demonstrates, public/private attorney general opt-out models have evolved in several Member States, some, such as Bulgaria, with permissive rules on representative standing. The Recommendation and the opt-out national examples discussed above are, clearly, radically different in terms of procedural design and underlying conceptual approach. It is difficult to see how Member States in examples cited in section 4 could implement the Recommendation's more restrictive opt-in legal standing principles without considerably frustrating existing access to justice standards. As the non-binding Recommendation anticipates Member States in any event might depart from its basic principles on opt-in and standing, there is no realistic prospect that the Recommendation will impact at all on access to justice in relation to those examples.

As noted in section 3, the EU's legal norms include a fundamental commitment to individual rights, including the right of access to justice and effective judicial protection, but that does not preclude ADR mechanisms, so long as adequate safeguards for formal rights of access to the courts are protected.[195] In this respect, the Commission has missed an opportunity to navigate a pathway through competing public interests and private rights, and supranational and national norms. The Recommendation's basic principles on legal standing focus on formal litigation, as the primary means for attaining collective redress. ADR is encouraged but little attention is paid to developing a suitable model for collective ADR, or other regulatory mechanisms that might efficiently and effectively deliver public interest outcomes and collective redress to consumers, without necessarily undermining the autonomy principle in traditional civil procedures. The Recommendation could have built on burgeoning alternative and regulatory approaches to consumer redress that exists across Member States, through consumer ombudsmen, arbitration and mediation. Those mechanisms, in states such as the UK, Denmark, Spain and the Netherlands, have successfully delivered redress to consumers, whilst also enabling economic and regulatory re-balancing of the market.

When integrated into the formal civil law and regulatory system these collective ADR approaches can provide effective and efficient solutions to competing public and private objectives. The Recommendation's basic principles on legal standing, in failing to embrace and build on those integrated approaches, will more likely serve to exacerbate rather than ameliorate unequal access to justice, cross-border disparity, and theoretical, doctrinal and policy tensions between competing public interest and private rights enforcement across Member States.

[195] See (n 58).

Part VI

The Quest for Mutual Recognition

13

Abolition of Exequatur, *All in the Name of Mutual Trust!*

MARIE LINTON*

1. ONGOING DEVELOPMENTS

THIS CHAPTER DEALS with the cross-border enforcement of foreign judgments, or, in a European context, the free circulation of judgments in civil and commercial matters. The importance of a European scheme for the reciprocal recognition of foreign judgments has been recognised for a long time. The functioning of the European area of justice requires the free circulation of judgments as a derivative of the freedoms of persons, goods, services and capital. However, the circulation of judgments has in general been conditional on a national intermediate control system in the Member State of enforcement known as the *exequatur* procedure. This procedure involves the verification and control of the foreign judgment before it can be 'imported' into the legal system of another Member State. The procedure is found in several EU instruments in the area of private international law, viz:

— the Brussels Convention[1]
— the Insolvency Regulation[2]
— the Brussels I Regulation[3]
— the Brussels II *bis* Regulation[4]

* Associate Professor, Uppsala University, President of the Swedish Association of Comparative Law.

[1] The Convention on jurisdiction and the enforcement of judgments in civil and commercial matters [1972] OJ L299/32.

[2] Regulation (EC) No 1346/2000 of 29 May 2000 on insolvency proceedings [2000] OJ L160/1 (Insolvency Regulation).

[3] Regulation (EC) No 44/2001 of 22 December 2000 on jurisdiction and the recognition and enforcement of judgments in civil and commercial matters [2001] OJ L12/1 (Brussels I Regulation).

[4] Regulation (EC) No 2201/2003 of 27 November 2003 concerning jurisdiction and the recognition and enforcement of judgments in matrimonial matters and the matters of parental responsibility, repealing Regulation (EC) No 1347/2000 [2003] OJ L338/1 (Brussels II *bis* Regulation).

— the Mediation Directive[5]
— the Maintenance Regulation[6]
— the Succession Regulation.[7]

In the years 1999 and 2000, the European lawmaker decided to reform the European *exequatur* procedure, and to simplify and reduce the number of national intermediate measures necessary for the enforcement of foreign judgments. The ultimate aim is to abolish *exequatur* for all judgments in civil and commercial matters.[8] This quest has resulted in the adoption of several instruments which wholly or partially abolish the *exequatur*:

— the Brussels II *bis* Regulation[9]
— the European Enforcement Order (EEO) Regulation[10]
— the European Order for Payment (EOP) Regulation[11]
— the European Small Claims (ESCP) Regulation[12]
— the Mediation Directive[13]
— the Maintenance Regulation[14]
— the Brussels I recast Regulation.[15]

Some of the above-mentioned EU instruments feature in both of the above lists as including an *exequatur* procedure, as well as abolishing it. This is

[5] Directive 2008/52/EC of 21 May 2008 on certain aspects of mediation in civil and commercial matters [2008] OJ L136/3 (Mediation Directive).

[6] Regulation (EC) No 4/2009 of 18 December 2008 on jurisdiction, applicable law, recognition and enforcement of decisions and cooperation in matters relating to maintenance obligations [2009] OJ L7/1 (Maintenance Regulation). According to recital 20 of the Mediation Directive, enforcement can, for example, occur under the Brussels I Regulation or under the Brussels II *bis* Regulation (n 3) and (n 4). See also Art 6 of the Mediation Directive.

[7] Regulation (EU) No 650/2012 of 4 July 2012 on jurisdiction, applicable law, recognition and enforcement of decisions and acceptance and enforcement of authentic instruments in matters of succession and on the creation of a European Certificate of Succession [2012] OJ L201/107 (Succession Regulation).

[8] See Commission, 'Green Paper on the Review of Regulation (EC) No 44/2001 on jurisdiction and the recognition and enforcement of judgments in civil and commercial matters' COM(2009) 175 final, 2.

[9] See (n 4).

[10] Regulation (EC) No 805/2004 of 21 April 2004 creating a European Enforcement Order for uncontested claims [2004] OJ L143/15 (EEO Regulation). See also Regulation (EC) No 1869/2005 of 16 November 2005 replacing the Annexes to Regulation (EC) No 805/2004 creating a European Enforcement Order for uncontested claims [2005] OJ L300/6.

[11] Regulation (EC) No 1896/2006 of 12 December 2006 creating a European order for payment procedure [2006] OJ L399/1 (EOP Regulation).

[12] Regulation (EC) No 861/2007 of 11 July 2007 establishing a European Small Claims Procedure [2007] OJ L199/1 (ESCP Regulation).

[13] See (n 5).

[14] See (n 6).

[15] Regulation (EU) No 1215/2012 of 12 December 2012 on jurisdiction and the recognition and enforcement of judgments in civil and commercial matters (recast) [2012] OJ L351/1 (Brussels I recast Regulation). Rules on recognition and enforcement are also found in Regulation (EU) No 655/2014 of 15 May 2014 establishing a European Account Preservation Order procedure to facilitate cross-border debt recovery in civil and commercial matters [2014] OJ L189/59.

because some of the instruments contain a two-track system for enforcement: one with *exequatur* and one without for specific matters or in relation to specific proceedings.

In a European context, the *exequatur* and its elimination raises a number of problematic issues, some of which will be explored in this contribution. First, the underlying question: what is the purpose and objective of the *exequatur* procedure (section 2)? Second, what are the reasons for abolishing the *exequatur* procedure in the EU (section 3)? Third, what has been achieved regarding the quest for the free circulation of judgments so far (section 4)? How can an interested party obtain an enforceable judgment in the EU? Are fundamental rights of defence adequately protected when *exequatur* is abolished? Can a judgment, seemingly enforceable under EU law, nevertheless be unenforceable because national laws apply to the actual execution? Thereafter, some overall observations and conclusions will be made (section 5).

2. THE *EXEQUATUR* PROCEDURE

2.1 Basic Theories

The point of departure in cross-border enforcement law is the principle of territorial sovereignty. A foreign judgment cannot operate by its own force within another state's territory, without that state having agreed to it. There is no public international law duty to that end.[16]

The recognition that one Member State gives to another Member State's judgment is built on a notion of reciprocity with origins in international comity.[17] If Member State A recognises and enforces judgments from Member State B, Member State B can, in return, expect recognition and enforcement of its judgments in Member State A. The reciprocal recognition and enforcement that one Member State bestows on another Member State's judgments flows from various provisions in the EU treaties.[18]

2.2 Purposes and Objectives

At the outset, it is clear that the purpose of the *exequatur* procedure is to determine whether a judgment granted in a foreign state should be given

[16] See also M Jänterä-Jareborg, 'Foreign Law in National Courts. A Comparative Perspective' (2003) 304 *Recueil des cours* 204.

[17] TC Hartley, 'General Course on Private International Law' (2006) 319 *Recueil des cours* 9, 279–80.

[18] See, eg, Art 4(3) Treaty on European Union (TEU), and Arts 67(3) and 81 Treaty on the Functioning of the European Union (TFEU).

extraterritorial effect in another state. When a foreign judgment produces legal effects in another state, it debars re-litigation of the dispute and, moreover, the judgment can be enforced in that state. The procedure is exclusive in the sense that the judgment creditor cannot access any other way of obtaining enforcement.

The *exequatur* serves to erase any doubts about the authenticity of the foreign judgment prior to any enforcement measures in the Member State of enforcement. The aim of the *exequatur* procedure is also to ensure that the defendant is cognisant of the judgment in order to be able to contest it, before rights are irreversibly affected by enforcement measures. This matrix prevents the enforcement of foreign judgments rendered in violation of fundamental rights, such as the right to a fair trial, or judgments obtained by procedural fraud.[19]

After a foreign judgment has been verified and scrutinised, it will be declared enforceable by a national court in a declaration of enforceability. By and large, a declaration of enforceability means that the foreign judgment becomes 'equal' to a domestic judgment for enforcement purposes.[20] The basis for actual enforcement is thus the declaration of enforceability, rather than the foreign judgment itself.[21]

2.3 An Example

An example of a simplified *exequatur* procedure common to the Member States is found in the Brussels I Regulation.[22] The procedure recurs in other EU private international law instruments, too. Consider a straightforward Swedish case as an illustration of the procedure in the Brussels I Regulation.[23] A British court had ruled that two Swedish defendants were liable to pay certain amounts to an American plaintiff. As the defendants were reluctant to pay the amounts, the plaintiff wanted to enforce the British judgment against the defendants' assets in Sweden. To intervene and attach the defendants' assets, the plaintiff applied to a Swedish court to obtain the necessary declaration of enforceability.

The application initiated the first ex parte stage of the *exequatur* procedure; no arguments for or against enforcement may be submitted.[24] At this

[19] See also G Cuniberti and I Rueda, 'Abolition of Exequatur. Addressing the Commission's Concerns' (2011) 75 *Rabels Zeitschrift* 287.

[20] Case C-139/10 *Prism Investments v Jaap Anne van der Meer* [2011] ECR I-9511, EU:C:2011:653, and Case 145/86 *Horst Ludwig Martin Hoffmann v Adelheid Krieg* [1988] ECR 645, EU:C:1988:61.

[21] XE Kramer, 'Abolition of *Exequatur* under the Brussels I Regulation: Effecting and Protecting Rights in the European Judicial Area' (2011) 4 *Nederlands Internationaal Privaatrecht* 633, 635–36.

[22] See (n 3).

[23] Svea Court of Appeal decision 17 June 2004, case No Ö 498-04.

[24] See Art 41 Brussels I Regulation (n 3).

stage, the Swedish court only made a formal, summary check of the British judgment. As a consequence, an affirmative Swedish declaration of enforceability was issued and served on the Swedish defendants.[25] The ex parte character is to retain an element of surprise and to avoid delay in execution due to fact finding and legal arguments.[26]

The Swedish defendants appealed the declaration of enforceability, allowing the case to enter the second *inter partes* stage of the *exequatur* procedure.[27] The Swedish defendants claimed that the British court lacked jurisdiction, that they had not been served with the claim documents or been represented in the British proceedings. Additionally, the Swedish defendants invoked that it would be contrary to Swedish public policy to enforce the British judgment in Sweden. The plaintiff contested the appeal and sought to uphold the declaration of enforceability.

However, the Brussels I Regulation only accepts certain grounds for refusal (defences) that the reviewing court may use to deny or revoke a declaration of enforceability. These are the well-known grounds of public policy, judgments in default after lack of proper service, cases of irreconcilable judgments, and violations of designated rules of jurisdiction.[28] In the case above, the Swedish court of appeal found no reason to repeal the declaration of enforceability as none of the grounds for refusal provided by the Brussels I Regulation were present. Therefore, the British judgment was enforceable, and enforced, in Sweden.

A factor to bear in mind is that the real review of a foreign judgment takes place at the appeal stage, after a declaration of enforceability has been issued, and not at the first stage. This is a hallmark of the Brussels I Regulation so as to avoid delaying tactics, and to achieve a swift procedure. According to certain other legal instruments, the *exequatur* procedure consists only of one stage. This means that the defendant is allowed to put forward arguments regarding the application, and that the court evaluates the grounds for refusal before it issues a declaration of enforceability.[29]

2.4 Empirical Data

Empirical studies show that the *exequatur* procedure under the Brussels I Regulation operated well.[30] It has been rather simple and swift. In

[25] See Art 42(2) Brussels I Regulation. An appeal against a declaration of enforceability shall be lodged within one or two months thereof pursuant to Art 43(5) Brussels I Regulation (n 3).

[26] See W Kennett, *The Enforcement of Judgments in Europe* (Oxford, Oxford University Press, 2000) 215.

[27] See Art 43(3) Brussels I Regulation (n 3).

[28] See Arts 34 and 35 Brussels I Regulation (n 3).

[29] See, eg, Art 31(2) Brussels II *bis* Regulation (n 4).

[30] See COM(2009) 175 final (n 8).

90 per cent of the cases, an affirmative declaration of enforceability was granted. Only 1–5 per cent of the decisions on enforceability were appealed. In an ordinary case the costs for an *exequatur* procedure range from EUR 1,100 to 4,000. The duration of the procedure at the first stage, and the average time to obtain an *exequatur* decision, is rather short. In the Member States, it varies from seven days to four months. Because of the summary nature of the first stage of the *exequatur*, the outcome will rarely be anything but affirmative, provided of course that the applicant has produced the necessary documentation.[31]

If an application is incomplete, the time to reach a decision regarding enforcement is of course longer. In appellate cases, the costs will increase to an average of EUR 12,700 and the time in which a decision is affirmed or revoked ranges from one month to three years. However, these figures do not include the time the applicant needs to prepare the *exequatur* proceedings, collect the necessary documents and organise a possible translation of the judgment and the certificate.[32]

3. REASONS FOR ABOLISHING THE *EXEQUATUR* PROCEDURE

3.1 A True European Area of Justice: Mutual Recognition and Mutual Trust

The ambition to abolish *exequatur* for all judgments in civil and commercial matters is mainly promoted by political and economic considerations, which need to be further examined. Abolishing *exequatur* is part of establishing a true European area of justice. The origins of abolishing intermediate measures can be found in the multi-annual programmes of the European Council. In the 1999 Tampere Conclusions, the principle of mutual recognition of judgments was recognised as the cornerstone in the creation of a true European judicial area that needed to be enhanced.[33] In the 2005 Hague Programme, it was confirmed that borders should not be an obstacle to the enforcement of judgments.[34] The mutual recognition of judgments is believed to be an effective way of protecting rights, and

[31] See Art 53 Brussels I Regulation (n 3). The necessary documentation includes a copy of the foreign judgment so that the national court can authenticate it, and a certificate issued by the court of origin.

[32] *Report on the Application of Regulation Brussels I in the Member States* presented by B Hess, T Pfeiffer and P Schlosser (Study JLS/C4/2005/03 also referred to as the Heidelberg Report, 2007) 20–24 and 221–64.

[33] Tampere European Council 15 and 16 October 1999 Presidency Conclusions No 33 and 34, available at: www.europarl.europa.eu/summits/tam_en.htm.

[34] The Hague Programme: Strengthening freedom, security and justice in the European Union [2005] OJ C53/1. See also Draft programme of measures for implementation of the principle of mutual recognition of decisions in civil and commercial matters [2001] OJ C2/1.

securing cross-border enforcement in Europe. For mutual recognition to become effective, mutual trust needs to be improved. This was reiterated in the 2009 Stockholm Programme.[35] The importance of mutual recognition and mutual trust was again emphasised as essential components in the creation of a European judicial area in the EU Justice Agenda for 2020;[36] mutual recognition should create bonds between the legal systems of the Member States. Improved mutual trust between courts and administrations should further boost the recognition and enforcement of judgments, facilitating the access to justice on equal terms.

Mutual recognition and mutual trust are thus two core concepts in the quest for the free circulation of judgments. These are two distinct, yet closely intertwined concepts. The principle of mutual recognition as a vital component of European civil justice cooperation is firmly entrenched in the Treaty on the Functioning of the European Union (TFEU).[37] Article 67(4) provides that the Union shall facilitate access to justice through the principle of mutual recognition of judicial decisions in civil matters. Article 81(1) of the same Treaty states that the Union shall develop judicial cooperation in civil matters having cross-border implications, based on the principle of mutual recognition of judgments.

Mutual recognition suggests that irrespective of whether a judgment has been issued in Berlin, Prague or Stockholm, it should be treated equally within the EU.[38] Assuming equivalence between European judgments, mutual recognition calls for mutual trust, confidence and an understanding of diversity in different legal and administrative systems.[39] Working horizontally between courts and administrations, mutual trust ultimately requires democratic and independent judiciaries, quality and efficiency of the judicial systems and observation of the rule of law as well as fundamental rights in each Member State. Only if these conditions are met, will the purpose and objectives of *exequatur* become superfluous, and a true European area of justice will be formed.

[35] The Stockholm Programme—An Open and Secure Europe Serving and Protecting Citizens [2010] OJ C115/1.

[36] 'The EU Justice Agenda for 2020—Strengthening Trust, Mobility and Growth within the Union' COM(2014) 144 final.

[37] Mutual recognition can not only be understood as a European objective, but also as a European principle, an element in EU law. See especially R Arenas García, 'Abolition of Exequatur: Problems and Solutions. Mutual Recognition, Mutual Trust and Recognition of Foreign Judgments: Too Many Words in the Sea' (2010) XII *Yearbook of Private International Law* (Sellier European Law Publishers, 2011) 360–64.

[38] In its original meaning, mutual recognition is perceived as a prohibition to impose national controls or verifications in another Member State, if already carried out in the Member State of origin, dating back to the *Cassis de Dijon* case, Case 120/78 *Rewe-Zentral AG and Bundesmonopolverwaltung für Branntwein* [1979] ECR 649, EU:C:1979:42.

[39] M Jänterä-Jareborg, 'Harmonisering, samordning och ömsesidigt förtroende inom Europeiska unionen—utvecklingen inom familjerätt' (2005) *Svensk Juristtidning* 804, 813–14.

3.2 Effective Access to Justice

Another justification for abolishing the *exequatur* procedure concerns the economic aspects. To support this view the European Commission has explained that the procedure brings additional costs and delays in cross-border enforcement. This is true. Any judgment creditor must go through an additional procedure to obtain a declaration of enforceability, and this is of course costly and time-consuming, considering that the judgment creditor will need to spend time and resources on translations, court fees levied to process the application, expenses and delays to serve the declaration of enforceability on the defendant, legal counselling in two countries, etc. Bearing in mind that the *exequatur* procedure in most cases leads to affirmative declarations of enforceability that are rarely appealed, the European Commission concludes that there is no need for it, and especially not the costs associated with it.[40]

The economic explanation can be subject to criticism, if regarded in isolation. Measured against the costs at stake as a whole, the expenses for *exequatur* appear, in principle, to be negligible.[41] However, if this justification is coupled with the stakeholders' rightful demand for effective access to justice in the European area, it becomes more convincing. To the average European citizen or company it is difficult to explain why a judgment is directly enforceable in the Member State of origin, but not in another Member State without further ado. The free circulation of judgments without additional costs for *exequatur* may enhance the citizens' and companies' confidence and trust in the European area, in which case mutual trust would not only operate horizontally, but also vertically. In addition, the abolition of *exequatur* would harbour an essential objective of private international law—namely the protection of rights laid down in a judgment and acquired under a foreign state's system of law, ensuring the continuity of enforcement for anyone who has obtained a favourable judgment.

4. CONCERNS ARISING FROM THE QUEST FOR FREE CIRCULATION OF JUDGMENTS

4.1 Different Enforcement Schemes

From the point of view of a true area of justice, and the needs of stakeholders in this area, it is particularly relevant to call attention to certain difficulties caused by existing EU legislation. In particular four areas give rise for

40 See also Cuniberti and Rueda (n 19) 291.

41 See section 2.4 above.

concern: (i) the piecemeal schemes to obtain enforceable judgments; (ii) the tension between mutual trust and fundamental rights; (iii) the confusion that reigns over the relationship between European and national grounds for refusal; and (iv) the increased need for parallel proceedings. This section provides an illustration of five different schemes to obtain enforceable judgments in the EU as an example of how complex and worryingly fragmented the area of private international enforcement law has become.

4.1.1 The 'Exequatur *Scheme*'

First, as mentioned in section 2.3, there is the 'old traditional way' of obtaining an enforceable judgment. At the application of an interested party, a foreign judgment can be declared enforceable in another Member State after a national formal *exequatur* procedure. The decision regarding the application for a declaration may be appealed. A declaration of enforceability can only be denied or revoked after appeal, if the *exequatur* court finds that one of the defined grounds for refusal exists—the grounds for refusal are technically restricted to the rights of defence.[42]

This scheme is included in the Brussels I Regulation, the Insolvency Regulation,[43] the Brussels II *bis* Regulation (with regard to matrimonial matters and matters of parental responsibility),[44] the Mediation Directive,[45] the Maintenance Regulation (in relation to Member States not bound by The Hague Protocol)[46] and the Succession Regulation.[47] However, the Brussels II *bis* Regulation directs the court in the Member State of enforcement to examine, at its own motion, the grounds for refusal already at the first stage of the *exequatur* procedure. But at this stage the parties are barred from submitting arguments.[48]

Another aspect of this enforcement scheme is that the competent court in the Member State of origin must, at the request of an interested party, issue a

[42] See, eg, Arts 34 and 35 Brussels I Regulation (n 3), Arts 22–24 Brussels II *bis* Regulation (n 4), and Art 40 Succession Regulation (n 7).

[43] Art 25(1) Insolvency Regulation (n 2) refers to the enforcement scheme in the Brussels Convention (n 1). See also 'Proposal for a Regulation amending Regulation (EC) No 1346/2000 on insolvency proceedings' COM(2012) 744 final.

[44] See esp Arts 21–24, 28(1) and 31 Brussels II *bis* Regulation (n 4).

[45] Recital 20 of the Directive (n 5) refers to other European enforcement schemes to supplement the Directive.

[46] See Arts 23–24, 26, 30 and 32 Maintenance Regulation (n 6).

[47] See Arts 39–41 and 43–50 Succession Regulation (n 7). The question can be raised if the Brussels enforcement scheme is suited to succession matters. See especially B Hess, C Mariottini and C Camara, Note PE 462.493 from Directorate General for Internal Policies, 'Regulation (EC) No 650/2012 of July 2012 on jurisdiction, applicable law, recognition and enforcement of authentic instruments in matters of succession and on the creation of a European Certificate of Succession' (2012) 19–20.

[48] See Art 31(2) Brussels II *bis* Regulation (n 4).

certificate using assigned standard forms set out in some of the instruments.[49] Briefly, the standard forms authenticate the judgment's enforceability in the Member State of origin and provide information about the judgment, service and the parties. The certificate can also be part of the documentation that an applicant must produce in the Member State of enforcement before a declaration of enforceability can be issued.[50] The purpose of using such certificates is the same under all instruments: to streamline the procedure and to easily determine the enforceability of the judgment concerned.

It is noteworthy that several of the instruments adopted after the quest for abolishing the *exequatur* procedure began, include the procedure. The impression conveyed is that the level of mutual trust between the legal and administrative systems of the Member States has not reached a sufficient 'maturity' to eliminate the control exercised in the enforcing Member State.

4.1.2 The 'Endorsement Scheme'

Another track provides for automatic recognition and enforcement without the need for *exequatur*, or any procedure allowing the defendant to oppose recognition, provided that the judgment is accompanied by a certificate issued in accordance with a standard form. This 'endorsement scheme' is found solely in the Brussels II *bis* Regulation concerning judgments of access to and the return of children. The court of origin will certify that the judgment is enforceable if certain requirements are met, such as proper service, the hearing of the parties and the child concerned—and with reference to return orders, compliance with Article 13 of the 1980 Hague Convention on the civil aspects of international child abduction. The certification is 'automatic', as it will take place at the initiative of the court of origin. The certificate is not subject to appeal, but proceedings for rectifying the certificate can be instituted in the Member State of origin if it does not correctly reflect the judgment.[51]

The endorsement scheme in this Regulation has not only replaced the formal part of *exequatur*, but also its controlling function, as no grounds for refusal are available at all in the enforcing Member State if the judgment concerns access to or the return of a child. This Regulation was the first EU instrument to completely do away with *exequatur* for particular judgments. For other judgments covered by the Regulation, the *exequatur*

[49] The Brussels I Regulation (n 3), the Brussels II *bis* Regulation (n 4) and the Maintenance Regulation (n 6) contain annexed standard forms. *cf*, however, Arts 62–73 Succession Regulation (n 7). In addition to what has been said, the Insolvency Regulation (n 2) currently referring to the enforcement scheme of the Brussels Convention, does not contain any annexed standard forms.

[50] See Art 53(2) Brussels I Regulation (n 3), Arts 37 and 39 Brussels II *bis* Regulation (n 4) and Arts 28 and 29 Maintenance Regulation (n 6).

[51] See Arts 41–43 Brussels II *bis* Regulation (n 4).

procedure is preserved. Hence, the Regulation contains a two-track system for enforcement.

4.1.3 The 'Review Scheme'

Another enforcement scheme can be called the 'review scheme'. The abolition of *exequatur*, and the removal of grounds for refusal in the Member State of enforcement, has been made possible by the introduction of procedural safeguards and a review mechanism in the Member State of origin. This scheme is found in the EEO, EOP and ESCP Regulations. The way to obtain enforceable judgments under these Regulations is more or less similar, but each instrument deals with a different type of judgment. In general, the reason for the liberal approach to enforcement was made possible by the fact that the Regulations are limited in scope, and optional to other enforcement procedures available under European and national law.

A judgment enforceable in the Member State of origin will be enforced in another Member State without the need for a declaration of enforceability and without the possibility of opposing its recognition.[52] After a procedure, which is usually a written procedure, the court of origin endorses its judgment on a certificate.[53] A certificate can generally be issued if the court proceedings in the Member State of origin complied with certain compulsory procedural safeguards or minimum standards.[54] These procedural prerequisites aim at ensuring that the judgment debtor was informed of the proceedings and was provided with due information about the claim or the procedures to safeguard its right to a fair trial. The court in the Member State where enforcement is sought has no mandate to check that the standards have been met. That is the duty of the court of origin. If there are inconsistencies with regard to the certificate, it can be rectified or withdrawn in the Member State of origin.[55]

If a violation of rights of defence has occurred nonetheless, a review mechanism is also available to the judgment debtor in the Member State of origin. The review mechanism can be initiated under certain limited circumstances: in cases of default in service, or if the debtor was prevented from objecting to the claim by reason of *force majeure*, or due to extraordinary circumstances without any fault on his or her part.[56] In the review proceedings,

[52] Art 5 EEO Regulation (n 10), Art 19 EOP Regulation (n 11) and Art 20 ESCP Regulation (n 12).

[53] See Art 6 EEO Regulation (n 10), Art 18(1) EOP Regulation (n 11) and Art 20(2) ESCP Regulation (n 12).

[54] See Arts 12–19 EEO Regulation (n 10) and Arts 2–4, 7 and 8 EOP Regulation (n 11).

[55] See Art 10 EEO Regulation (n 10). *cf* also Art 9 EOP Regulation (n 11) and Art 4(4) ESCP Regulation (n 12), which gives the claimant the opportunity to rectify the application.

[56] See Art 19 EEO Regulation (n 10), Art 20 EOP Regulation (n 11) and Art 18 ESCP Regulation (n 12).

the court of origin can uphold or revoke its decision. The review mechanism in the Member State of origin must also be seen in the light of available grounds for refusal in the Member State of enforcement. The grounds have been narrowed down to a minimum, and cover only certain cases of irreconcilable judgments.[57] Under the existing rules, a concentration of the rights of the defence in favour of the court of origin has taken place.[58] As a consequence, the Member State of enforcement practically has no influence over the judgment's extraterritorial effects.

The EOP Regulation contains an additional defence in the Member State of enforcement: upon application of the judgment debtor it can be invoked that the amount awarded in the certificate order for payment has already been paid.[59] This defence is commonly found in the national enforcement laws of most Member States, but has not been part of the general grounds for refusal found in the EU instruments. This may of course be explained by the fact that the Regulation covers orders for payment. However, instead of invoking that a debt is settled in the course of actual enforcement, the judgment debtor must initiate proceedings in a court in the Member State of enforcement to plead compliance with the payment order. This raises questions on the relationship between European and national grounds for refusal.[60]

4.1.4 *The 'Choice-of-Law Scheme'*

A further scheme that exemplifies the differentiated approach is the 'choice-of-law scheme'; the typical feature of this scheme is that the applicable law is essential to the abolition of *exequatur* and immediate enforcement. It puts choice-of-law rules right at the centre of the circulation of judgments.[61] So far, this scheme only exists in one EU instrument: the Maintenance Regulation.[62]

[57] See Art 21 EEO Regulation (n 10), Art 22 EOP Regulation (n 11) and Art 22 ECSP Regulation (n 12).

[58] See also Á Rodríguez Vázquez, 'Review of the Brussels I Regulation: Complete Abolition of Exequatur?' in B Campuzano Díaz, M Czepelak, A Rodríguez Benot and Á Rodríguez Vázquez (eds), *Latest Developments in EU Private International Law* (Cambridge, Intersentia, 2011) 161.

[59] Art 22(2) EOP Regulation (n 11).

[60] See section 4.3 below.

[61] F Ferrand, 'The Council Regulation (EC) No 4/2009 of 18 December 2008 on Jurisdiction, Applicable Law, Recognition and Enforcement of Decisions and Cooperation in Matters Relating to Maintenance Obligations' in B Campuzano Díaz, M Czepelak, A Rodríguez Benot and Á Rodríguez Vázquez (eds), *Latest Developments in EU Private International Law* (Cambridge, Intersentia, 2011) 97.

[62] See (n 6).

The abolition of *exequatur* for maintenance decisions[63] was deemed possible primarily for two reasons. First, only judgments issued in a Member State bound by the uniform choice-of-law rules in the 2007 Hague Protocol benefit from the abolition of *exequatur*.[64] Consequently, the application of unified choice-of-law rules justifies that decisions issued in a Member State bound by the Hague Protocol are enforceable in the other Member States without the need for *exequatur*. Instead the court of origin endorses its decision, upon request, using a standard form.[65] Second, the abolition of *exequatur* is accompanied by a review mechanism in the Member State of origin so as to protect certain non-alienable rights; especially the right to be heard, proper service and sufficient time to prepare a defence. The right to apply for a review is limited in time and only available in cases where there is a lack of appropriate service or if the defendant was unable to contest a maintenance decision due to *force majeure* or extraordinary circumstances standing in the way of a timely reaction.[66] If the court in the Member State of origin decides that a review is justified, the decision is null and void. If the court rejects the application for review, the decision remains in force.

The possibility to contest the enforcement of a maintenance decision in the Member State of enforcement is reduced to situations where the decision is extinguished by the effect of time limitation, or in certain cases of irreconcilable decisions.[67] The Maintenance Regulation, furthermore, introduces the possibility to suspend enforcement in the enforcing Member State. This can occur if the court of origin has been seised of an application for review, or the enforceability of the decision has been suspended in the Member State of origin.[68]

If the judgment is not delivered in a Member State bound by the Hague Protocol (ie, Denmark and the United Kingdom), an *exequatur* procedure comparable to the one in the 2001 Brussels I Regulation applies. In that sense, the Maintenance Regulation contains a two-track system for the enforcement of foreign judgments.

63 Where private international law is concerned, maintenance decisions are regarded as ordinary judgments, although they differ from other judgments in the sense that they direct money to be paid at intervals subject to variation from time to time due to the debtor's financial situation.

64 The Protocol of 23 November 2007 on the Law Applicable to Maintenance Obligations was elaborated at The Hague Conference on Private International Law and in parallel with the making of the Maintenance Regulation. In order to stick to international developments, and to avoid incompatibilities in the choice of law, the European lawmaker decided to make use of the choice-of-law rules in The Hague Protocol. Art 15 of the Maintenance Regulation refers directly to the 2007 Hague Protocol as part of EU law (the Protocol is available at: www.hcch.net/index_en.php?act=conventions.text&cid=133).

65 Art 28 Maintenance Regulation (n 6).

66 ibid, Art 19.

67 ibid, Art 21(2).

68 ibid, Art 21(3).

The choice-of-law approach merits special reflection, as it is an odd resurrection of an old technique used in private international law.[69] Historically, the applicable law has occasionally been a necessary requirement for enforcement in some Member States. A foreign judgment would only be recognised and enforced if the foreign court applied the 'accurate' applicable law. In modern private international law, however, the connection between the applicable law and the enforceability of a judgment has faded over time.[70] One reason is that it could hamper the free circulation of judgments if choice-of-law-rules differ; if a court in state X applied a different legal order from the enforcing state Y, the X-judgment would not be enforceable in state Y. Another reason is that the applicable law, which may be foreign to the court hearing the case, has nothing to do with the quality of the judgment or the quality of the proceedings resulting in the judgment. Even when the 2001 Brussels I Regulation applied to maintenance decisions, the applicable choice-of-law rules were not a necessary requirement for enforcement.[71]

4.1.5 The 'Hybrid Scheme'

Finally, a new form of European enforcement procedure designed to further enhance mutual recognition of judgments was introduced in the Brussels I recast Regulation. The formal procedure of *exequatur* has been abolished, but the grounds for refusal in the Brussels I Regulation have been maintained. In this case, the European quest for free circulation of judgments has targeted the formal part of the *exequatur* procedure, but not the function it serves in inspecting whether the foreign judgment meets the necessary requirements for enforcement.

Under this hybrid scheme, judgments delivered in another Member State no longer need to be declared enforceable after a judicial intermediate control in the enforcing Member State.[72] The judicial control of the judgment is transferred from the Member State of enforcement to the Member State of origin. The court in the Member State of origin endorses its judgment on a specimen certificate.[73] Consequently, the enforcing Member State has no power to check the foreign judgment. The certificate verifies whether the judgment is enforceable in the Member State of origin, and it contains extracts of the judgment. It also provides information about service on the defendant, recoverable costs of the proceedings and, if appropriate, the

[69] See also Ferrand (n 61) and Kramer (n 21) 635.

[70] M Jänterä-Jareborg, *Svensk domstol och utländsk rätt. En internationellt privat- och processrättslig studie* (Uppsala, Iustus förlag, 1997) 23 and 34.

[71] See also Kramer (n 21) 635.

[72] Art 39 Brussels I recast Regulation (n 15).

[73] ibid, Art 53.

calculation of interest.[74] With a copy of the judgment and the certificate, the creditor can turn directly to local enforcement authorities in the Member State where the debtor has assets, instead of having to go through a national court for a declaration of enforceability. The certificate and, if necessary, the judgment is served on the judgment debtor prior to any enforcement measures.[75]

If the judgment debtor wants to oppose enforcement, he or she must institute new proceedings in a court of the enforcing Member State. The burden of conducting yet another procedure has, consequently, been shifted from the judgment creditor to the judgment debtor being the party opposing enforcement. Only in court proceedings for non-enforcement in the Member State of enforcement is it possible to invoke the grounds for refusal listed in Article 45, to be read in conjunction with Article 46. In fact, an analysis of the defences in the Brussels I recast Regulation confirms the fact that they are modelled on the defences in Articles 34 and 35 of the Brussels I Regulation, with only slight adjustments.[76]

Maintaining the grounds for refusal could be viewed as a response to the concerns that were raised during the revision process of the Brussels I Regulation of not going too far, too quickly. In view of the previous European developments in the area of cross-border enforcement, it may, however, be surprising that the Regulation deviates from the solutions chosen in earlier instruments. The outcome is a more narrow form of European *exequatur* consisting of a combination of approaches. Basically, additional judicial scrutiny of the judgment is available in the enforcing Member State only if the party opposing enforcement applies for it. Presumably it is the opposing party that bears the cost of initiating the non-enforcement procedure.[77] The solutions chosen in the Regulation provide European citizens and businesses with yet another enforcement regime. The question is whether the path chosen will be an improvement or a complication.

It could be argued that the Brussels I recast Regulation is an improvement as it is more efficient for stakeholders seeking transnational enforcement in the Internal Market. In a straightforward case, the abolition of intermediate measures reduces costs and delays, while it still ensures the continuity of enforcement for anyone who has obtained a favourable judgment. By contrast, the grounds for refusal are still upheld, albeit available in new proceedings in the Member State of enforcement. It could be held that some or

[74] ibid, Annex I.

[75] ibid, Art 43.

[76] See especially M Linton, 'The Brussels I *bis* Regulation—*Status Quo* or a New Order for Enforcement?' in *Essays in Honour of Michael Bogdan* (Lund, Juristförlaget i Lund, 2013) 286–90.

[77] The Brussels I recast Regulation is silent on the matter. *cf* Art 52 Brussels I Regulation (n 3).

possibly all defences included in the Regulation are not compatible with the idea of mutual trust between Member States.[78] At most, the Brussels I recast Regulation has limited the scope of the European *exequatur* by suppressing the formal function of *exequatur*, while retaining its control-function in the Member State of enforcement.

4.1.6 A Patchwork

The elimination of *exequatur* as a precondition to enforcement in European instruments does not follow a consistent pattern. A wide range of different enforcement schemes can be identified. At one end, there is the 'ordinary' procedure with *exequatur* and certain defences to enforcement. At the other, there is the total abolition of *exequatur* and no possibility of refusing enforcement or opposing recognition. A complicating aspect is that some of the instruments contain dual schemes; viz *exequatur* is abolished for certain judgments, but retained for others.

The result is a fragmented set of provisions on enforcement, which are based on different methodological approaches ranging from procedural conditions, minimum safeguards, all the way up to the applicable law.[79] The numerous schemes can properly be attributed to the different nature of the judgments covered by the concept of civil and commercial matters (for example, certain interests and considerations need to be protected in family proceedings, others in commercial proceedings). To some extent, it can also be explained by the fact that certain Member States are not part of European civil justice cooperation, and for that reason remain with the 'ordinary' *exequatur* scheme.

From the EU perspective, the varied schemes for enforcement can be an impediment to predictability for stakeholders and judiciaries concerning the applicable rules. If legislation is too complicated to reach its addressees, or judiciaries, a credibility deficit in European law will emerge. Below follows a Table to illustrate the ways of enforcing foreign judgments under the different EU instruments, all based on the premise of mutual trust.

4.2 Tension Between Mutual Trust and Fundamental Rights

4.2.1 Exequatur *as a Remedy*

There is a tension between, on the one hand, mutual trust in combination with the abolition of *exequatur* and, on the other, fundamental rights and

[78] See also A Dickinson, 'The Revision of the Brussels I Regulation. Surveying the Proposed Brussels I *bis* Regulation—Solid Foundations but Renovation Needed' (2010) XII *Yearbook of Private International Law* (Sellier European Law Publishers, 2011) 247, 254–68.

[79] Kramer (n 21) 635.

Table 1: Ways to obtain an enforceable judgment in the EU in civil and commercial matters

	Exequatur	Abolition of *exequatur*	Possible review or rectification in the Member State of origin	Ground for refusal in the Member State of enforcement: public policy	Ground for refusal in the Member State of enforcement: default judgments	Ground for refusal in the Member State of enforcement: cases of irreconcilable judgments	Additional ground for refusal in the Member State of enforcement
1. The 1968 Brussels Convention	X Article 31			X Article 27	X Article 27	X Article 27	X Articles 27(4) and 28
2. The Insolvency Regulation	X Article 25(1)			X	X	X	X Article 25(3)
3. The 2001 Brussels I Regulation	X Article 38			X Article 34(1)	X Article 34(2)	X Articles 34(3) and (4)	X Article 35
4. The Brussels II *bis* Regulation—dual scheme	X Article 28 (parental responsibility)	X Articles 41 and 42 (rights of access and return of a child)	X Article 43(1) (rights of access and return of a child)	X Article 22(a) (divorce, separation, annulment) Article 23(a) (parental responsibility)	X Article 22(b) (divorce, separation, annulment) Article 23(c) (parental responsibility)	X Articles 22(c) and (d) (divorce, separation, annulment) Articles 23(e) and (f) (parental responsibility)	X Articles 23(b), (d) and (g) (parental responsibility)

(continued)

Table 1: (*Continued*)

	Exequatur	Abolition of *exequatur*	Possible review or rectification in the Member State of origin	Ground for refusal in the Member State of enforcement: public policy	Ground for refusal in the Member State of enforcement: default judgments	Ground for refusal in the Member State of enforcement: cases of irreconcilable judgments	Additional ground for refusal in the Member State of enforcement
5. Reg No 805/2004 (European Enforcement Order)		X Article 20(1)	X Articles 10 and 19			X Article 21	
6. Reg No 1896/2006 (Payment Procedure)		X Article 19	X Article 20			X Article 22(1)	X Article 22(2)
7. Reg No 861/2007 (Small Claims)		X Article 20(1)	X Article 18			X Article 22	
8. The Maintenance Regulation—dual scheme	X Article 26 (Member State not bound by the 2007 Hague Protocol)	X Article 17 (Member State bound by the 2007 Hague Protocol)	X Article 19 (Member State bound by the 2007 Hague Protocol)	X Article 24(a) (Member State not bound by the 2007 Hague Protocol)	X Article 24(b) (Member State not bound by the 2007 Hague Protocol)	X Articles 24 (c) and (d) (Member State not bound by the 2007 Hague Protocol)	X Article 21 (Member State bound by the 2007 Hague Protocol)

(continued)

Table 1: (*Continued*)

	Exequatur	Abolition of *exequatur*	Possible review or rectification in the Member State of origin	Ground for refusal in the Member State of enforcement: public policy	Ground for refusal in the Member State of enforcement: default judgments	Ground for refusal in the Member State of enforcement: cases of irreconcilable judgments	Additional ground for refusal in the Member State of enforcement
9. The Mediation Directive—the enforceability of an agreement resulting from mediation shall be ensured by other EU enforcement schemes, ie, the Brussels I Regulation or the Brussels II *bis* Regulation							
10. The Regulation on Successions	X Article 43		X Article 71	X Article 40(a)	X Article 40(b)	X Articles 40(c) and (d)	
11. The Brussels I recast Regulation		X Article 39		X Article 45(a)	X Article 45(b)	X Articles 45(c) and (d)	X Article 45(e)

concrete interests at stake in an individual case. The abolition of *exequatur* must not jeopardise the judgment debtor's rights of defence. *Exequatur* can be seen as a remedy against violations of fundamental rights; it may prevent violations from generating effects outside the jurisdiction where they were committed. The pivotal question is whether these rights should be secured in the Member State of origin or in the Member State of enforcement—or both.

At present, a complex system protects the rights of the defendant. Some EU instruments guard these rights in the Member State of enforcement, others in the Member State of origin. Yet further instruments lay down safeguards in both the Member State of origin as well as in the Member State of enforcement. In general, EU law appears to be developing towards a Member State of origin solution. Because of mutual trust, flaws in the original proceedings to the detriment of the defendant should mainly be remedied in the Member State of origin, and not in the course of enforcement. Difficulties arise when errors are not, or cannot, be remedied in the Member State of origin.

4.2.2 Zarraga v Pelz

The problem with the Member State of origin solution is perceptible in *Zarraga v Pelz*,[80] which concerned a Spanish return order of a child wrongfully retained by the mother in Germany. The Brussels II *bis* Regulation endorsement scheme applied in the case, and as a consequence no *exequatur* took place. Instead, the Spanish court that ordered the return of the child certified its decision, but allegedly without hearing the child in accordance with Article 42 of the Brussels II *bis* Regulation. When the mother opposed the enforcement of the Spanish order in Germany, the Court of Justice of the European Union (CJEU) was asked to rule on whether a court in the Member State of enforcement exceptionally could oppose the enforcement of a certified judgment because the court of origin had infringed Article 42 of the Regulation.[81]

The argument and decision of the CJEU is adamant: the court of the Member State of enforcement must enforce a certified judgment. The CJEU held that the issue of the lawfulness of the judgment ordering the return or an action for rectification of the certificate must be raised before the courts in the Member State of origin. Article 42(2) of the Brussels II *bis* Regulation does not empower the enforcing Member State to review the conditions for the issue of that certificate, as it would undermine the effectiveness of

[80] Case C-491/10 *Joseba Andoni Aguirre Zarraga v Simone Pelz* [2010] ECR I-14247, EU:C:2010:828.

[81] For remarks see B Hess, Remarks on Case C-491/10PPU—*Andrea Aguirre Pelz*, available at: conflictoflaws.net/2010/hess-remarks-on-case-c-49110ppu-%E2%80%93-.

expeditious enforcement. The CJEU further emphasised that the system for recognition and enforcement is based on mutual trust and the 'national legal systems [of the Member States] are capable of providing an equivalent and effective protection of fundamental rights'.[82]

The case gives food for thought. If there was an infringement of fundamental rights, the CJEU has instructed Member States to enforce orders issued contrary to the right of defence. Indirectly, Germany, as the Member State of enforcement, would as a continuation of the Spanish order commit an infringement of the right to be heard as safeguarded in Article 42 if it enforced the Spanish order. In contrast, the European Court of Human Rights has stated that contracting states, before enforcing foreign judgments, should authenticate whether they comply with Article 6 of the European Convention on Human Rights and the right to a fair trial.[83] Another consequence of the *Zarraga v Pelz* decision is that the principle of territoriality has to yield to the absolute non-acceptance of unlawful removals or detentions of children. Hence, in such cases the court of origin determines the extraterritorial effects of its judgment in another Member State.

4.2.3 Salzgitter v Laminorul

Salzgitter v Laminorul[84] concerns two irreconcilable judgments issued in the same Member State, Romania. Laminorul, established in Romania, brought an action seeking payment for a delivery of steel products against Salzgitter, established in Germany. The action was dismissed because Salzgitter was not the actual party to the contract (the first judgment). Laminorul instituted new proceedings against Salzgitter before the same court for the same cause of action. Due to an alleged lack of proper service, Salzgitter did not appear, and the Romanian court delivered a default judgment ordering Salzgitter to pay a certain amount to Laminorul (the second judgment). Salzgitter appealed the second judgment, but for various formal reasons the appeals were rejected, and the Romanian legal remedies were finally exhausted. In the German enforcement proceedings, the question was raised concerning whether the defence to enforcement in Article 34(4) of the Brussels I Regulation on irreconcilable judgments delivered in different states also applied to irreconcilable judgments delivered in the same Member State.

The CJEU found that Article 34(4) does not cover irreconcilable judgments issued by courts in the same Member State. According to the CJEU, the rules on recognition and enforcement are based on mutual trust in the administration of justice. Furthermore, the CJEU held that mutual trust

[82] See *Zarraga v Pelz* (n 80) 70.
[83] See generally Cuniberti and Rueda (n 19) 293–302.
[84] Case C-157/12 *Salzgitter Mannesmann Handel v Laminorul* SA, EU:C:2013:597.

means that the courts of the Member State of origin retain jurisdiction to assess the lawfulness of the judgment to be enforced, in principle to the exclusion of the court of the Member State of enforcement. Another interpretation of Article 34(4) would, according to the CJEU, be incompatible with mutual trust as it would allow the court in the Member State of enforcement to substitute the assessment of the court of origin with its own in a review of the substance of the judgment, expressly excluded by Article 45(2). In the present case, however, the legal system of origin was not able to repair the injustice in irreconcilable judgments. The argument and decision *Salzgitter v Laminorul* indicate that the protection of the principle *ne bis in idem* had to surrender to mutual trust, at least where the judgments originate in the same Member State.

4.3 Confusion over Grounds for Refusal

4.3.1 National Enforcement Laws Govern Actual Enforcement?

It is important to distinguish between the proceedings to obtain an enforceable judgment and the subsequent executive proceedings. To add to the complexity, the EU regulations specify that the actual execution of a foreign judgment is governed by the domestic laws of the Member States if it is not covered by the Regulations.[85] For execution purposes a foreign judgment should be dealt with as a domestic judgment in the Member State of enforcement.[86]

At this point, the free circulation of judgments encounters difficulties. There may be no grounds to refuse a judgment its enforceable character under EU law, but there may be national grounds for refusing execution. This implies, for example, that a French judgment, which is enforceable in France, might be unenforceable in Sweden because a Swedish judgment cannot be executed under the same circumstances. A variety of national grounds for refusal exist. According to Swedish law, execution can, for example, be rejected if a debt is paid or because of the existence of a valid set-off.[87] In family law, for instance, execution can be barred if it is the will of a child over the age of 12, and it is not contrary to the best interests of the child, or if execution is incompatible with the best interests of the child.[88]

The relationship between, on the one hand, European grounds for refusal, and on the other, national grounds for refusal are surrounded by uncertainty.

[85] See, eg, Art 30(1) Brussels II *bis* Regulation (n 4), Art 20(1) EEO Regulation (n 10), Art 21(1) EOP Regulation (n 11), Art 21(1) ESCP Regulation (n 12), Art 41(1) Maintenance Regulation (n 6) and Art 41(1) Brussels I recast Regulation (n 15).

[86] See, eg, Art 47(2) Brussels II *bis* Regulation (n 4).

[87] See Chapter 3 § 21 of the Swedish Execution Code (*Utsökningsbalken*).

[88] See Chapter 21 § 5 of the Swedish Code on Parents and Children (*Föräldrabalken*).

What national grounds for refusal are compatible with EU law? The question is relevant as EU regulations stipulate that under no circumstances may a foreign judgment be reviewed as to its substance.[89] Are national enforcement laws left untouched by the ongoing development in this field? In addition, is it possible to reconcile diverging national defences with mutual trust and the equal treatment of judgments? Diverging national grounds for opposing execution could be viewed as incompatible with mutual trust and the free circulation of judgments. Furthermore, you could argue that it is at the actual execution stage that the issue on mutual trust will really be determined.

4.3.2 Case Law

In several cases—such as *Hoffman v Krieg*[90] and *Apostolides v Orams*[91]—the CJEU has stated that procedural rules of the Member State of enforcement may not 'impair the effectiveness' of the Brussels I scheme for enforcement. The same line of reasoning is found in the *Salzgitter* case mentioned above in section 4.2.3, where the CJEU held that the sound operation of the rules on recognition and enforcement in the Brussels I Regulation rests on mutual trust. This means that the court of origin maintains its jurisdiction to assess the lawfulness of the judgment, in principle, to the exclusion of the court in the enforcing Member State.

In *Povse v Alpago*,[92] the CJEU is even more explicit. The CJEU states that the enforcement of a foreign judgment certified under Article 42 of the Brussels II *bis* Regulation cannot be refused because of changed circumstances, in the best interests of the child. The CJEU emphasises that under no circumstances may a substantive ground of opposition to the judgment be assessed in the Member State of enforcement. Such a change must be pleaded before the court of origin.[93]

In Sweden, the ruling in *Povse* came as a surprise. It was commonly believed that national grounds for opposing execution, such as the best interests of the child, might be considered in the course of enforcement.[94] However, the CJEU has made it very clear that no grounds as to substance

[89] See, eg, Art 36 Brussels I Regulation (n 3), Art 26 Brussels II *bis* Regulation (n 4), Art 42 Maintenance Regulation (n 6) and Art 52 Brussels I recast Regulation (n 15).

[90] *Hoffmann v Krieg* (n 20).

[91] Case C-420/07 *Meletis Apostolides v David Charles Orams, Elizabeth Orams* [2009] REC I-3571, EU:C:2009:271.

[92] Case C-211/10PPU *Doris Povse v Mauro Alpago* [2010] REC I-6673, EU:C:2010:400. *cf* recital 23 Brussels II *bis* Regulation (n 4).

[93] See also M Jänterä-Jareborg, 'Barnets bästa och Sveriges ansvar för överflyttning av olovligen bortförda barn' (2014) *Svensk Juristtidning* 387, 409–11.

[94] See also M Lindqvist, 'Olovligt bortförande av barn inom EU' in M Jänterä-Jareborg (ed), *Tre aspekter av EU-IP. Studier rörande olovligt bortförande av barn, samkönade parrelationer och säkerhetsrätter i lösöre* (Uppsala, Iustus förlag, 2011) 91–92.

can be taken into account in the Member State of enforcement; only procedural grounds for opposing a judgment are allowed as a bar to enforcement if a judgment has been certified under Article 42 of the Brussels II *bis* Regulation.

This tendency to limit the scope of domestic enforcement laws is also evident in Article 41(2) of the Brussels I recast Regulation. The provision lays down that national grounds for refusal under the law of the Member State of enforcement shall only apply if they are 'not incompatible' with the European grounds listed in Article 45, ie, public policy, default judgments due to lack of proper service, and certain cases of irreconcilable judgments. The very same follows from Article 21(1) of the Maintenance Regulation. Therefore the Regulations put constraints on national enforcement laws and demand their compliance with the spirit of the grounds for refusal in the Regulations.

A decision that appears to deviate from what has just been said is the ruling in *Prism Investments v Jaap Anne van der Meer*.[95] In this case the judgment debtor claimed that he had settled the debt in the Member State of origin in compliance with the judgment. The reference made to the CJEU was whether this circumstance could be taken into account in the *exequatur* procedure in the Member State of enforcement under the Brussels I Regulation. The CJEU held that an application for enforcement could only be refused or revoked on the grounds provided for in Articles 34 and 35. That a debt was settled is not one of them. The CJEU found that such a ground may be brought before enforcement authorities in the enforcing Member State, and that 'national legislation of that Member State relating to enforcement applies in the same way as to judgments delivered by national courts'.[96]

In line with the reasoning in *Povse* among others, matters of substance (that a debt is settled) should be referred to the court of origin. By contrast, the *Prism* case gives the impression that it is an issue for the Member State of enforcement. The distinction of the roles of the two layers of grounds for refusal in EU law and national laws is not clearly settled. Greater clarification on the relationship would help to avoid confusion.

4.4 Parallel Proceedings

An additional consequence of the quest for the free circulation of judgments and abolition of *exequatur* is that parties may be forced to pursue arduous

[95] *Prism v van der Meer* (n 20).

[96] See, eg, M Bogdan, 'Svensk och EU-domstolens rättspraxis i internationell privat- och processrätt 2011–2012' (2013) *Svensk Juristtidning* 968.

parallel proceedings in different Member States. An ordinary appeal may have been lodged on the merits in the Member State of origin, and another for the refusal of enforcement in the Member State of enforcement. In addition, in the case of an appeal against any provisional measures, yet a further one may be lodged in the court of the Member State of enforcement. This entails a potential risk of contradictory judgments.

The Brussels I recast Regulation will possibly add to this problem if the grounds for refusal provided for in the Regulation and grounds for refusal available under national law cannot be invoked in the same procedure as foreseen in recital 30 of the Regulation. In Sweden, the party opposing the enforcement of a foreign judgment must institute new proceedings in a Swedish district court to access the grounds of refusal in Articles 45 and 46 of the Brussels I recast Regulation. Swedish executive authorities will not apply these grounds for refusal as these authorities are in principle not regarded as courts under the Regulation.[97] On the contrary, the available Swedish grounds for refusal will not be applied by a district court, but only by Swedish executive authorities. If the judgment debtor challenges the enforcement authorities' act with a district court there will be a situation of concurrent and parallel proceedings with the same purpose: to prevent the enforcement of a foreign judgment.[98] The difference is that the grounds for refusal originate in different sources—EU and domestic law—accessible in different proceedings. To the average person or business this must seem utterly confusing.

5. CONCLUSIONS

In general terms, the rapid abolition of *exequatur* has mainly targeted its formal function, and not the function it serves in controlling a foreign judgment. As a natural sequel to mutual trust, this control function has, in principle, been shifted to the Member State of origin. However, the Member State of enforcement may retain limited powers to refuse a foreign judgment its enforceable character depending on which instruments applies.

Considering each individual EU instrument, it is in principle possible to comprehend the various considerations behind the enforcement provisions. Practical concerns, as well as the aspiration of finding the best possible solution for each type of judgment, are the guiding principles. But if the enforcement provisions in the EU instruments are seen as a whole, a vexing picture

[97] With the exception in Art 3 of the Brussels I recast Regulation (n 15). In some Member States enforcement is carried out by non-judicial authorities or private bailiffs. See generally Kennett (n 26) 76–85.

[98] To counteract this problem somewhat, Art 51(1) Brussels I recast Regulation (n 15) allows the court in the Member State of enforcement to stay the proceedings.

of non-transparency and unpredictability emerges. The formula used is a variety of combinations in piecemeal legislation. The legal situation in the EU has plainly become too complex and complicated, where the CJEU shields a system built on efficiency and perceived mutual trust—sometimes at the expense of stakeholders' interest in the individual case.[99] To overcome the structural differences I personally would welcome a review of the EU's private international law instruments as predicted in the EU Justice Agenda for 2020.[100]

[99] It has also been described as 'sacrificing individual parties on the altar of mutual trust': P Oberhammer, 'The Abolition of Exequatur' (2010) *Praxis des internationalen Privat- und Verfahrensrechts* 201.

[100] See (n 36).

14

On the Abolition of Exequatur

MARTA REQUEJO ISIDRO*

1. INTRODUCTION

THROUGHOUT EUROPE, THE recognition and enforcement of a foreign judgment in another jurisdiction has traditionally been subject to compliance with certain requirements which need to be checked within the framework of a specific procedure—the (so-called) *exequatur*. To the extent that the *exequatur* procedure adds complexity, discomfort, and ultimately deters from entering into cross-border transactions—in the same way that language barriers or different currencies do—the final goal of the EU is to abolish such an intermediate step between the Member States, in the name of mutual trust. In the last 10 years, *exequatur* has been removed to allow for the direct enforcement of access rights, of decisions ordering the return of a child, as well as of certain decisions on money claims. These sectorial outcomes pave the way towards the unrestricted freedom of movement of Member States' decisions within the EU. However, recent developments have made it clear that the end of the *exequatur* (of the procedure and/or of the intermediate conditions) will be the fruit of a slow, piecemeal process: the Commission's proposal in 2010 aiming to remove the *exequatur* from the 'star' instrument of the European judicial area—the Brussels I Regulation—met with fierce opposition; eventually a trade-off solution had to be found (section 2). In 2011, an application against a Member State for blind compliance with Article 42 of the Brussels II *bis* Regulation was lodged before the European Court of Human Rights (ECtHR), challenging the suppression of the *exequatur* in the light of the European Convention on Human Rights and Fundamental Freedoms (ECHR) (section 3). A gradual approach allows for further deeper reflection on the best way to endorse mutual trust; conversely, it results in a complex legal scenario at the expense of easy management by stakeholders (section 4).

* Senior Research Fellow, Max Planck Institute Luxembourg for International, European and Regulatory Procedural Law.

2. FROM THE COMMISSION'S PROPOSAL TO THE FINAL TEXT

2.1 Somewhere Between Renewal and Continuity

Under the Brussels I Regulation[1] the declaration of enforceability is granted following an application before the competent body at the requested State; a purely formal check is performed on specific documents supplied by the State of origin. Although the Regulation provides for grounds to refuse the *exequatur*, they are only relevant upon the debtor's appeal against the declaration of enforceability. In the new Brussels I recast Regulation[2] the situation has been reversed: a judgment given in a Member State on the subject matter of the Regulation does not need to be declared enforceable in the other Member States. However, the person against whom enforcement is sought may apply for a refusal of enforcement.

The recast of the Brussels I Regulation rests on political and economic arguments; the reform is based on a proposal of the Commission[3] supported by various studies containing empirical data,[4] and amended by the European Parliament.[5] According to the Heidelberg Report, obtaining a decision on *exequatur* takes a matter of weeks, or even days, and only about 1–5 per cent of all cases of *exequatur* granted are appealed by the judgment debtor.[6] The Commission reading of these data led to the conclusion that the declaration of enforceability 'remains an obstacle to the free circulation of judgments which entails unnecessary costs and delays for the parties involved and deters companies and citizens from making full use of the internal market'. The Heidelberg Report also noted that the substantive public policy exception is seldom pleaded in order to refuse the declaration of enforceability;[7] from this the Commission inferred that the exception no longer serves a useful purpose. Thus, in the proposal of

[1] Regulation (EC) No 44/2001 of 22 December 2000 on jurisdiction and the recognition and enforcement of judgments in civil and commercial matters [2000] OJ L12/1.

[2] Regulation (EU) 1215/2012 of 12 December 2012 on jurisdiction and the recognition and enforcement of judgments in civil and commercial matters (recast) [2012] OJ L351/1.

[3] Commission, 'Proposal for a Regulation on jurisdiction and the recognition and enforcement of judgments in civil and commercial matters (recast) COM(2010) 748 final.

[4] For our purposes, mainly B Hess, T Pfeiffer, P Schlosser, *Application of Regulation Brussels I in the Member States*, Study JLS/C4/2005/03 (Heidelberg Report, 2007); and the Study on Data Collection and Impact Analysis of Certain Aspects of a Possible Revision of Regulation 44/2001 on Jurisdiction and the Recognition and Enforcement of Judgments in civil and commercial matters, Centre for Strategy & Evaluation Services (CSES), 2010. A Green Paper on the Review of the Regulation COM(2009) 175 final, was launched in April 2009.

[5] 'Report on the Proposal for a Regulation on jurisdiction and the recognition and enforcement of judgments in civil and commercial matters (recast)' COM(2010) 748 final.

[6] Heidelberg Report (n 4) 22 and 221.

[7] Heidelberg Report (n 4) 249–50. Along the same lines, B Hess and T Pfeiffer, *Interpretation of the Public Policy Exception as Referred to in EU Instruments of Private International and Procedural Law* (study commissioned by the European Parliament, 2011).

the Commission the *exequatur* procedure in the Regulation was replaced by a system of automatic 'import' of foreign decisions. That did not mean the complete suppression of the grounds for non-recognition/enforcement, as some procedural safeguards were still available in the State of origin. Also, an extraordinary remedy in the Member State of enforcement would enable the defendant to contest any other procedural defects which might have arisen during the proceedings before the court of origin, infringing his or her right to a fair trial. A third remedy granted the defendant the possibility to stop the enforcement of the judgment in case of inconsistency with another judgment issued in the Member State of enforcement or—provided that certain conditions were fulfilled—in another country. The substantive public policy exception did not exist any more.

The final text of the Brussels I recast Regulation does not endorse the proposal; nor does it simply reproduce the previous model. Rather, it enshrines a system already suggested in academic literature[8] of direct implementation of the decisions in all Member States, upon submission of two documents to the competent authority of the executing State.[9] The person against whom enforcement is sought is entitled to apply for a refusal of the recognition or enforcement of a judgment, if he considers one or more of the following grounds for refusal of recognition to be present (Article 45): manifest contrariety to public order of the requested Member State; absence of service of the document instituting the proceedings in sufficient time when the judgment was rendered by default; irreconcilability with an earlier decision of the Member State required; irreconcilability with an earlier judgment in another state; or breach of certain rules of jurisdiction by the courts of the State of origin.

2.2 Assessment (As Regards the Upkeep of the Public Policy Exception)

The Brussels I recast Regulation has retained a twofold ex parte public policy exception: both substantive *ordre public* and procedural *ordre public* (embedding the right to a due process beyond the issue of service of process) may be invoked under the new Regulation. It has been said that:

> If judgment debtors are hardly ever successful with a claim of violation of substantive public policy, this does not necessarily mean that the exception serves no

[8] P van der Grinten, 'Abolishing Exequatur in the European Union: an Alternative' in *Crossing Borders: Essays in Honour F van der Velden* (Deventer, Kluwer, 2006) 82.

[9] Art 42, a copy of the decision in the Member State of origin satisfying the conditions necessary to establish its authenticity, and a certificate issued by the court of origin in accordance with the form set out in Annex I of the Regulation. The certificate must be served on the person against whom enforcement is sought, together with the original decision if it has not yet been served.

> useful purpose. Instead, it may simply demonstrate that the courts of the member state understand that this is a safety valve rarely to be applied.[10]

Those who agree have surely rejoiced in the solution of the recast, which is consistent with the Parliament's Report to the Commission Proposal: 'Such an exception [the public policy exception] might be required by Member States' international obligations'.[11] Convergence between the protection of fundamental rights in the most representative document, the ECHR, and the EU, has certainly been endorsed by Articles 6(2) and 6(3) of the Treaty on European Union (TEU), as well as by Article 52(3) of the EU Charter of Fundamental Rights; but this alone does not warrant an absolute lack of diverse interpretations and dissimilar outcomes of the weighing up of values and rights against one another.[12] Moreover, such weighing up materializes in general formulae (ie, abstract formulae) in the EU cross-border procedural instruments while the ECtHR approach to fundamental rights is individual: it focuses on the single case. The public policy clause of the Regulations offers the Member States the tool to comply with their international obligations in the single case.

Further reasons speak in favour of the upkeep of the public policy exception. The contents of the *ordre public* clause originate from multiple sources. Besides an *ordre public* originating from the ECHR, from other international public law common values,[13] and from a (possibly already in force) European public policy,[14] there is an international public policy in the forum. The Parliament's Report evokes this point: 'A Member State before which proceedings are brought is entitled to preserve its fundamental values; therefore, equally, it must be the case for a Member State in

[10] SP Baumgarten, 'Changes in the European Union's Regime of Recognizing and Enforcing Foreign Judgments and Transnational Litigation in the United States' (2012) 18 *Southwestern Journal of International Law* 567, 585.

[11] Heidelberg Report (n 4) 138.

[12] Besides, some fundamental values are inherent to the EU (eg, the four essential freedoms), but do not exist elsewhere: J Kramberger Skerl, 'European Public Policy (with an Emphasis on Exequatur Proceedings)' (2011) 7 *Journal of Private International Law* 461; H Schack, 'The Misguided Abolition of Exequatur Proceedings in the European Union' in *Festschrift für T Ercinski* (Warsaw, LexisNexis Polska, 2011) 1345, 1353.

[13] See, for instance, the worldwide criminalization of bribery and corruption, leading to affirm their contrariety to 'transnational public policy'. Also XE Kramer, 'Approaches to Jurisdiction and Foreign Judgments and the International Fight against Corruption' in HG van de Bunt (ed), *International Law and the Fight against Corruption, Mededelingen van de Koninklijke Nederlandse Vereniging voor Internationaal Recht, Preadviezen* 139 (Advisory Report for the *Dutch Royal Society of International* Law, Asser Press, 2012) 99, 132: 'The situation of judicial corruption—for example, the bribing of a judge—can be regarded as a matter of procedural public policy. Where enforcement is challenged in view of corruption in the underlying relationship upon which the foreign decision based, this may be captured by the substantive procedural public policy'.

[14] Kramberger Skerl (n 12).

which the enforcement of a judgment is sought'.[15] Contracts for surrogate motherhood provide a good example of the international *ordre public* of the forum. These contracts are allowed in some Member States, whereas they are null and void and contrary to public policy in others. A problem could therefore arise if a surrogate mother tried to enforce a judgment of one Member State awarding her compensation for the expenses incurred during the pregnancy in another Member State that prohibits such contracts.[16] A second example is provided by an Auto of the *Audiencia Provincial de Madrid*, of 16 December 2011, in relation to an award made in Italy ordering the Spanish Administration, or the king, to issue a letter of peerage succession: enforcement would have been contrary to the Spanish *ordre public* as in Spain such letters are only issued 'as of grace'. Surely, under the influence of international law and of European Union law, public policy is no longer just a national concept; however, it still is a national concept, at least to a certain extent.[17]

The dynamic character of the public policy exception, along the lines of the social and economic evolution of the forum, should also be recalled. In as far as this evolution is obviously not following the same path (or rhythm) throughout the EU, keeping safeguard mechanisms makes sense. Even if it might seem paradoxical, a public policy exception looks like a useful device from the point of view of European integration. The negative perception of *ordre public*, commonly conceived as a barrier, is reversed when the exception is linked to the understanding of mutual trust as a natural result of the state of affairs rather than as an artificial outcome of a political will.[18] In this context, the clause develops a prophylactic purpose: it works to protect and to increase mutual trust.[19] Such a role for the escape mechanism is not unknown in the EU; actually, this is how the ruling in *NS v SSHD* has been explained: 'the Court implies that each Member State should cooperate with another Member State to the extent that, and *as long as*, the latter does not experience major operational problems that lead to a systemic violation

[15] Heidelberg Report (n 4) 38.

[16] The example corresponds to a first, unpublished version of JJ Kuiper, 'The Right to a Fair Trial and the Free Movement of Civil Judgments' (final version to be found in the (2010) 6 *Croatian Yearbook of European Law & Policy* 23; this will be the one quoted from now on).

[17] The relevance of this national *ordre public* which applies to the international situation is certainly limited. Still, the existence of eigenvalues, related to idiosyncratic characteristics of single States, cannot be discarded. It should also be recalled that we are living a period of social and economic crisis digging up severe differences among the Member States.

[18] See as point of departure of Kramberger Skerl's study (n 12) 462.

[19] Of course, this approach would allow for the *ordre public* control to be performed by any Member State—therefore, also in the context of an appeal in the Member State of origin. In this regard, see Hoge Raad 5 March 2002, cited by van der Grinten (n 8) 75: public policy cannot be invoked in an appeal against the granting of an *exequatur* when it could have been invoked in the proceedings in the Member State of origin if an appeal had been lodged.

of European Fundamental rights'.[20] Thus, supervision performed by one Member State in relation to another does not 'necessarily spread suspicion, caution or mistrust'; on the contrary, it 'underscores the dynamic nature of the mutual relationship among the Member States', which is 'in turn a *sine qua non* for the establishment of a genuine and sincere mutual confidence'.[21]

The proposal to abolish the public policy exception leant on a purely quantitative analysis. On this basis (ie, the number of cases where the public policy exception has been successfully invoked), the Commission carried out an operation similar to the prohibition to review the jurisdiction of the Member State of origin under the Brussels I Regulation (already under its immediate precedent, the Brussels Convention of 1968): the ban applies even if the court of origin could not have relied on common grounds of jurisdiction due to the circumstances of the case, for instance, if the defendant was not domiciled in a Member State. In this regard, the Commission implements a policy decision where the free movement of decisions as a general objective prevails over the protection of fundamental procedural rights of a particular defendant in a particular case. Surely, the actual number of cases where a genuine violation of procedural rights has occurred is likely to be rather low. However, the legitimacy of a quantitative approach is questionable when the issues at stake—whose protection is ensured thanks to the public policy exception—rank to human rights and similar core values.

In as far as substantive *ordre public* is concerned, it is largely true that the protection of substantive fundamental rights can be sought under the guise of a violation of a procedural right. This implies a shift of perspective: the question under review is no longer the correctness of a court's decision, but whether the losing party had or did not have a say in relation to that decision. However, such an approach is reductionist: the breach of the right to be heard and the violation of the substantive right to, let us say, family life, are obviously not interchangeable.

As for the procedural *ordre public* (beyond the service of process) no European regulation on procedural law sweeps away the clause without further ado. In the Brussels I Regulation, procedural rights are already embedded in the definition of a judgment: a judgment must 'emanate from a court body of a Member State deciding on its own authority on the issues between the parties'.[22] Moreover, all regulations abolishing *exequatur* require that

[20] Joined Cases C-411/10 and C-493/10 *NS v Secretary of State for Home Department and ME v Refugee Applications Commissioner* [2011] ECR I-13905, EU:C:2011:865; and I Canor, 'My Brother's Keeper? Horizontal Solange: An Ever Closer Distrust among the Peoples of Europe' (2013) 50 *Common Market Law Review* 383, 401.

[21] Canor (n 20) 402.

[22] See Case C-414/92 *Solo Kleinmotoren GmbH v Emilio Boch* [1994] ECR I-02237, EU:C:1994:221, para 17.

certain procedural rights or standards are abided by.[23] In the same vein, the Commission's proposal of 2010 preserved procedural rights as well: recognition and enforcement could be refused if contrary to the fundamental principles underlying the right to a fair trial. In fact, such an approach echoes the actual state of affairs: difficulties still exist; national practice offers examples of refusals of *exequatur* on procedural grounds.[24] The fact that the same phenomenon has been acknowledged with respect to other regulations abolishing *exequatur* has probably worked as a warning.[25]

2.3 Assessment (General)

Even after the step backwards represented by the final version of the Brussels I recast Regulation, criticism has continued as regards the abolition of the *exequatur* proceedings. The move has been qualified as 'premature' because it is supported by an unrealistic presumption—one which is contained in recital 26:[26] 'Unresolved issues in the system of allocating jurisdiction, with the practical application of the rules often leading to unpredictable consequences' still exist; there is 'a profound heterogeneity in the procedural laws of the Member States' and 'Case Law of the European Convention on Human Rights and the Court of Justice of the European Union [show] scenarios of violations of fundamental rights by Member States'.[27]

The abolition of the *exequatur* proceedings as such has been contested as well, although to a lesser extent, in relation to the regulations that entrust to the sole courts of origin the equal protection of both parties' rights.[28] Part of this criticism cannot apply to the Brussels I recast Regulation: the added value of *exequatur* proceedings, which lies in the concentration of the examination/scrutiny of all grounds for refusal before one court, has been preserved therein.

[23] See for instance Arts 12–19 of Regulation (EC) No 805/2004 of 21 April 2004 creating a European Enforcement Order for uncontested claims [2004] OJ L143/15.

[24] See examples in Schack (n 12); Kuiper (n 16) 43–44.

[25] Particularly in the field of family law: see ECtHR decision in *Sneersone and Kampanella v Italia* App no 14737/09 (ECtHR, 12 July 2011); or the saga leading to the CJEU decision in Case C-491/10 PPU *Joseba Andoni Aguirre Zarraga v Simone Pelz* [2010] ECR I-14247, EU:C:2010:828, where the Spanish and the German courts displayed different understandings of the right of a child to be heard.

[26] 'Mutual trust in the administration of justice in the Union justifies the principle that judgments given in a Member State should be recognised in all Member States without the need for any special procedure. In addition, the aim of making cross-border litigation less time-consuming and costly justifies the abolition of the declaration of enforceability prior to enforcement in the Member State addressed. As a result, a judgment given by the courts of a Member State should be treated as if it had been given in the Member State addressed'.

[27] LJ Timmer, 'Abolition of *Exequatur* under the Brussels I Regulation: Ill Conceived and Premature?' (2013) 5 *Journal of Private International Law* 129, 136.

[28] Schack (n 12) 1357–58.

However, the new scheme is not without flaws. Whether the reversal of the roles played so far by claimant and defendant (under the new regulation it is up to the defendant to lodge an application for a refusal of the recognition or enforcement of a judgment, if he or she considers one of the grounds for a refusal of recognition to be present), will really result in the saving of money or time remains to be seen. In contrast, the debtor's position has been worsened, in the sense that any reaction against the foreign decision rests upon his shoulders.[29]

The new Brussels I Regulation presents some weaknesses, which of course are not insurmountable, but did not exist before: namely, how and who should proceed to adapt the foreign decision to a local equivalent, as required by Article 54(1). Under the Brussels I Regulation, the *exequatur* proceedings facilitated such adaptation.[30] The new regulation's scheme may be more vulnerable to fraud. Under the recast, the assessment of the civil or commercial character of the subject matter, as well as the authenticity of the foreign judgment and of the documents to be provided under Article 42(1), rests on the enforcement authorities. It remains to be seen whether they are always equipped to take on that responsibility.[31]

3. THE ABOLITION OF *EXEQUATUR* IN THE BRUSSELS II *BIS* REGULATION

3.1 Introduction

The failure of the project to completely abolish the *exequatur* in the new Brussels I recast Regulation, entails that the Brussels II *bis* Regulation remains as the 'leading representative' of the Commission's policy regarding the free movement of decisions. However, the application of the Brussels II *bis* model is not always a smooth, easy one: for example, due to the limited types of decisions entitled to an automatic declaration of enforceability, an

[29] Although arguably the change is not as great as it may seem at first sight, as under the Brussels I Regulation the debtor has to contest the declaration of enforceability—which is also granted almost automatically. Still, a better balance between claimant and defendant may be identified under this model, as a judgment given in a Member State and which is enforceable in that State needs the exequatur in another Member State to enjoy enforceability there, and this requires the application of the interested party.

[30] A Nuyts, 'La refonte du reglèment Bruxelles I' (2013) 102 *Revue critique de droit international privé* 1, 25–26 ; Timmer (n 27) 137–38.

[31] Timmer (n 27) 140. A similar mistrust of the domestic enforcement bodies was expressed by AG J Kokkot in Case C-92/12 PPU *Health Service Executive v SC and AC*, EU:C:2012:255, View delivered on 28 March 2012, EU:C:2012:177, paras 68–75: they 'would not really be in a position to undertake any assessment of a foreign judgment submitted to them, in particular to examine the conditions governing the enforceability of the judgment and to infer from it the nature and extent of the enforcement to be effected'.

accurate interpretation of Article 40 is needed all the more. However, the proper delimitation of the scope is not as simple as it may seem at first sight.[32]

The enlargement of the scope of the Regulation as regards decisions exempted from *exequatur* has been proposed *de lege ferenda*.[33] The opportunity of such a move has been contested;[34] it may also be disputed in the light of situations such as the one underlying the *Aguirre Pelz* saga,[35] or leading to the application before the ECtHR in the *Povse* affair:[36] a case that draws attention to the edgy relationship between the Brussels II Regulation and the ECHR.

3.2 *Povse v Austria*

3.2.1 The Facts

Ms Povse and Mr Alpago lived together as an unmarried couple in Italy with their daughter Sofia, of whom they had joint custody. When Sofia was two years old, her mother left her father and took Sofia with her to Austria, where they lived from then on, without contact with her father. This was the starting point of a series of court proceedings and judgments in Italy and in Austria. In the end, the Italian court granted the father sole custody and ordered the immediate return of the child to Italy. Following Article 42 of the Brussels II *bis* Regulation the return order was enforced in Austria. The applicants complained under Article 8 ECHR that the Austrian courts'

[32] For instance, whether Art 40 comprises all decisions on the right of access, or just those related to the parents of the child: MC Baruffi, 'Osservazioni sul Regolamento Bruxelles II-*bis*' in S Bariatti (ed), *La famiglia nel diritto internazionale privato comunitario* (Milan, Giuffrè, 2007) 175, 205.

[33] K Boele-Woelki and M Jänterä-Jareborg, 'Protecting Children Against Detrimental Family Environments under the 1996 Hague Convention and the Brussels II-*bis* Regulation' in *Convergence and Divergence in Private International Law—Liber Amicorum Kurt Siehr* (The Hague, Asser Press, 2010) 125, 156. See also *Health Service* (n 31) para 121: 'without prejudice to any amendments which the EU legislature might, where appropriate, decide to make to the Regulation in order to meet the concerns expressed by several of the parties who made submissions at the hearings in relation to the loss of time inherent in the pursuit of enforcement proceedings'.

[34] See AG Kokkot in *Health Service* (n 31) paras 79–86, against the abolition of the *exequatur* (or its replacement by an application for a declaration of non-enforceability made by the affected child). The severity of the action taken, depriving the child, temporarily or permanently, of his or her family environment, requires a high level of protection; according to Art 20 UN Convention on the Rights of the Child, he or she is entitled to special protection and assistance provided by the State; to comply with this mandate every domestic court must be able to examine on its own motion the possible grounds for refusal of the decision of the Member State of origin, including public policy with express reference to the interests of the child.

[35] Which ended up before the CJEU, *Aguirre Pelz* (n 25).

[36] *Povse v Austria* App no 3890/11 (ECtHR, 18 June 2013).

decisions had violated their right to respect for their family life. In particular, they argued that the Austrian courts had limited themselves to ordering the enforcement of the Italian court's return order and had not examined their argument that the first applicant's return to Italy would constitute a serious danger to Sofia's well-being and lead to the permanent separation of mother and child.

The ECtHR applied the so-called 'Bosphorus test'. The doctrine, named after the ECtHR decision in *Bosphorus v Ireland*[37] is based on the following premise: contracting States transferring sovereign powers to an international organization retain responsibility for the acts of their bodies, 'regardless whether the act or omission was a consequence of domestic law or of the necessity to comply with international obligations'. However, in as far as the international organization 'is considered to protect fundamental rights … in a manner which can be considered at least equivalent to that for which the Convention provides', a presumption that the contracting State has complied with the ECHR enters into play, if it lacked discretion in relation to the obligations derived from its membership of the international organization. Therefore, a three-step examination is needed in order to determine whether there is equivalence between the protection offered by the Convention and the international organization in question, as regards both the substantive guarantees offered and the mechanisms controlling their observance (Step 1), and the degree of freedom of the State concerned (Step 2); finally, the arguments against the presumption of equivalence in the specific case must be discarded (Step 3). The examination led the ECtHR to declare the *Povse* application inadmissible.

3.2.2 The Bosphorus Test as Applied to Povse

Step 1 in *Povse*: Whether the relevant organization is understood to protect fundamental rights in a manner. In the *Povse* decision this point is dealt with exclusively in paragraph 77, in such a manner that it is not just superficial: it is non-existent.[38] This is a little bit disappointing, because as of today, ie, at the time of the analysis, the existence of truly 'substantive guarantees' offered by the EU as a unit (instead of as a group of diverse systems striving for coherence), in the field covered by Article 8 ECHR, is not self-evident.[39] However, the absence of further studies is consistent with the

[37] *Bosphorus v Ireland* App no 45036/98 (ECtHR, 20 June 2005).

[38] Para 77 is a mere reminder of a general finding of the ECtHR, not linked to any particular subject matter. It is justified to regret such a broad, vague point of departure.

[39] See the facts underlying the CJEU's decision in *Aguirre Pelz* (n 25), showing different ways of understanding the child's right to be heard. Although this does not in itself bear witness of a systemic deficit of protection in the EU, it challenges the lightness of the assessment made by the ECtHR in para 77.

previous practice of the ECtHR when applying the Bosphorus test, and also with the logic underlying a rebuttable presumption (ie, the major discussion takes place under Step 3).[40]

Step 2 in *Povse*: Discretion. There was no discussion as regards Austria's lack of discretion under Article 42 of the Brussels II *bis* Regulation. Step 3: Whether the presumption has been rebutted in the present case. In contrast to Step 1, the analysis here was extensive. Two elements seem to be essential: the role of the CJEU defining the applicability and interpretation of the relevant legal provisions (paragraph 85); and the status quo before the court of origin (the opportunity open to the applicants to still rely on their Convention rights there: paragraph 86). The importance given to these issues warrants further questions. To start, what would happen in a hypothetical future case in the absence of consultation with the CJEU? On the one hand, the stress/emphasis placed by the ECtHR on the role of the CJEU suggests that the answer would have been different in the absence of a preliminary ruling.[41] On the other hand, the CJEU's ruling in Case C-211/10 PPU *Povse v Alpago*, stating that any change in the situation of the abducted child with consequences on the return order must be pleaded before the competent court in the Member State of origin, creates a legal precedent for all Member States, thus exempting them from referring new queries on the same subject.

As for the second element retained by the ECtHR (the status quo in Italy), would its decision have been the same had the applicants exhausted their resources before the Italian courts without success? In the light of paragraphs 85 and 86, the answer could be positive. However, the decision is not conclusive in this respect. This is to be regretted: it would have given a hint of the opinion of the ECtHR as to the legislative decision to restrict the safeguards related to fundamental rights to the State of origin. A question that not only affects the Brussels II *bis* Regulation, but also those following the same mechanism—even if the answer does not have to be the same for all of them.

[40] Actually, the case law shows the different degrees of depth in the ECtHR's examination in order to affirm or to deny the equivalence of the protection offered by the international organization under review: T Lock, 'Beyond Bosphorus: The European Court of Human Rights' Case Law on the Responsibility of Member States of International Organizations under the European Convention on Human Rights' (2010) 10 Human Rights Law Review 529. Another example in the domain of EU PIL is provided by the recent ECtHR decision Avotiņš v Latvia App no 17502/07 (ECtHR, 25 February 2014) focusing on Art 34.2 Brussels I Regulation. For a comment on the decision and references see M Requejo Isidro, 'On Exequatur and the ECHR: Brussels I Regulation before the ECtHR' (2015) 2 *Praxis des Internationalen Privat- und Verfahrensrechts* 69.

[41] No matter whether due to a lack of a request to refer the matter to the Court of Justice for a preliminary ruling, or of an actual referral by the national court: see *Michaud v France* App no 12323/11 (ECtHR, 6 December 2012).

3.3 Consequences

A question arises as to the analysis performed by the ECtHR in *Povse*, and also as to its likely consequences for other EU regulations, as well as for a general suppression of the *exequatur* proceedings.[42]

3.3.1 On Other EU Regulations

What would be the likely outcome of the Bosphorus test if applied to other EU private international law instruments, such as the Brussels I Regulation or its recast?[43] According to both instruments (albeit in different ways) the requested State is allowed to refuse the declaration of enforceability if specific restricted grounds provided by the Regulations themselves are presented; in particular, if such a declaration is manifestly contrary to public policy. Thus, at first glance, the answer is that these cases are not eligible for the *Bosphorus* presumption, as the requested State enjoys a certain degree of discretion.[44] However, this conclusion may not survive the following clarifications: first, it should be recalled that the public policy exception does not work ex officio, but ex parte—'hence, the absence of an active defence by the debtor places the enforcement court in the same position of no discretion that exists in regulations with no public policy exception'.[45] Second, whether the States really have discretion as regards public policy when implementing the legal obligations stemming from their membership can be discussed in the light of the CJEU case law, namely *Krombach, Renault* and *Gambazzi*.[46]

[42] The accession of the EU to the ECHR casts doubt on the future of the Bosphorus test. Admittedly, the equivalence presumption in favour of the EU itself is no longer justified. However, it is worth considering whether it should not survive in the context of the analysis of a Member State's compliance with the Convention, if it had to blindly obey a mandate of the EU; indeed, the presumption of equivalence makes more sense because of the EU's accession to the ECHR. In this context, provided that no ECtHR decision has yet been pronounced against the EU, maintaining a rebuttable presumption of equivalence would simplify the applicant's choice of the correct respondent.

[43] The ECtHR has now also delivered its decision *Avotiņš v Latvia*, on Art 34(2) of the Brussels I Regulation, thus on the right to a due process as an obstacle to *exequatur*. The ECtHR concluded there had been no violation of Art 6 ECHR; the decision, however, was adopted by a slim majority of four judges against three. One of the reasons why the three dissenting judges contest the decision is the 'discretion' prong of the Bosphorus test in the context of Art 34(2) Brussels I Regulation.

[44] See ibid, on discretion within the framework of Art 34(2) Brussels I Regulation (right to a due process).

[45] F Gascón Inchausti, 'Gascón on Povse: A Presumption of ECHR Compliance when Applying the European Civil Procedure Rules?' contribution to www.conflictoflaws.net, 7 October 2013.

[46] Case C-7/98 *Dieter Krombach v André Bamberski* [2000] ECR I-01935, EU:C:2000:164; Case C-38/98 *Régie nationale des usines Renault SA v Maxicar SpA and Orazio Formento* [2000] ECR I-02973, EU:C:2000:225; Case C-394/07 *Marco Gambazzi v Daimler Chrysler Canada Inc and CIBC Mellon Trust Company* [2009] ECR I-02563, EU:C:2009:219, respectively.

3.3.2 For the Abolition of Exequatur

Before the Bosphorus test, academic opinion had contested the abolition of *exequatur* in the light of ECtHR case law, mainly the *Pellegrini* decision,[47] where *exequatur* had been considered as an intermediate stage requiring a separate assessment. What is the importance of *Povse* for a system opting for no *exequatur*—and also suppressing any control of grounds for refusal such as incompatibility with the *ordre public*?

There is no easy answer to this question. As expected,[48] the ECtHR has not expressed a general opinion on the guarantee system designed by the Brussels II *bis* Regulation—a system where the protection of the fundamental rights rests exclusively on the Member State of origin; paragraph 85 suggests an implicit approval of the mechanism, but *within* the framework of the *Bosphorus* presumption. The few academic views so far published also seem to believe that there has been no general endorsement of the abolition of *exequatur*: 'according to the *Bosphorus* line of reasoning, there is an exhaustion of local remedies condition, that does not of course preclude a challenge to the return order at the place of enforcement, *if all else fails*';[49] 'There is ... no control in the State of enforcement, and no further control can either be expected to be made by the ECtHR over the requested State, since the latter could benefit from the presumption of compliance doctrine'.[50]

4. A PLURAL, COMPLEX SCENARIO

4.1 Introduction

In the last 10 years, several regulations have been adopted providing for the suppression of the intermediate procedure of *exequatur*: besides the Brussels II *bis* Regulation, this is the situation regarding the European Enforcement Order (EEO) Regulation (Regulation (EC) No 805/2004); the European Small Claims Procedure (ESCP) Regulation (Regulation (EC) No 861/2007); the European Order for Payment Procedure (EOP) Regulation (Regulation (EC) No 1896/2006); and the Maintenance Regulation (Regulation (EC) No 4/2009) (for Member States also parties to the 2007 Hague Protocol). These Regulations allow the creditor (or the interested party) to apply directly for the enforcement of a Member State's decision in another Member State. On the other hand, other recent regulations have remained faithful to the

[47] *Pellegrini v Italy* App no 30882/96 (ECtHR, 20 July 2001).

[48] The ECtHR's approach is restricted to the specific case.

[49] H Muir Watt, 'On Abolition of Exequatur and Human Rights' contribution to www.conflictoflaws.net, 5 October 2013.

[50] Gascón Inchausti (n 45).

traditional solution consecrated by the Brussels I Regulation, therefore providing for an intermediate procedure in the requested State. Such is the case of the Succession Regulation (Regulation (EU) No 650/2012).[51]

Lack of uniformity hampers the easy management of the European network of regulations. The situation is further complicated by the relevant differences among the instruments that share the common feature of the absence of *exequatur*. Such differences concern important points: for instance the scope of the regulations or the rationale underlying the abolition of the *exequatur* procedure.[52] We will just explain some of them, as examples of a heterogeneous situation where the final outcome is complexity: the precise opposite to the purpose originally sought.[53]

4.2 Scope of the Regulations

In some regulations, *exequatur* has been abolished for all the subject matters within the material scope of application, but not for all the countries (Member States) to which the regulation applies (see the Maintenance Regulation). In some regulations, *exequatur* has been eradicated only for some subject matters or types of decisions within the material scope (see the Brussels II *bis* Regulation). The EEO, EOP and the ESCP Regulations aim to create a European Enforcement Order. However, although they apply to civil and commercial matters as defined in the Brussels I Regulation, some matters excluded from the scope of each regulation differ. The EOP Regulation is applicable to arbitration but not to claims arising from non-contractual obligations. As for the ESCP Regulation, it shall not apply to matters concerning employment law; tenancies of immovable property, with the exception of actions on monetary claims; or violations of privacy and of rights relating to personality including defamation.

[51] The 'Proposal for a Regulation on jurisdiction, applicable law and the recognition and enforcement of decisions in matters of matrimonial property regimes' COM(2011) 126 final, also provides for an intermediate procedure. So does the 'Proposal for a Regulation on jurisdiction, applicable law and the recognition and enforcement of decisions regarding the property consequences of registered partnerships' COM(2011) 127 final.

[52] See for the EEO, EOP and ESCP Regulations, E D'Alessandro, 'Choosing Among the Three Regulations Creating a European Enforcement Order (EEO Regulation, EOP Regulation, ESCP Regulation): Practical Guidelines' (2009–2010) 9 *Rivista di diritto processuale internazionale e arbitrato internazionale* 39.

[53] Doubts have been raised as well as to the appropriateness of the formulae to attain the objective sought. By way of example, if the EEO may be seen at first glance as a step forward, it has nevertheless also been qualified as 'a step in the wrong direction'. See van der Grinten (n 8) 79–80: 'especially if an EEO application is made after the judgment, the procedure is more cumbersome for the creditor and the court than the "rubber-stamp judgment of Art 41 Brussels I"; it offers less legal certainty for the creditor since the well-defined grounds for refusal of Art 34 Brussels I have been replaced by the more vague wording of Art 10 EEO Regulation with regard to withdrawal of an EEO'.

Still regarding the scope, it is worth mentioning that some regulations create a completely new procedure which does not supersede the national one, but coexists with it. Thus, there is a dual set of procedural rules: this is the case with the EOP Regulation. Given the differences between the European scheme and the existing national procedures, confusion of the domestic courts facing 'double-tracked systems of civil procedure in which domestic and European procedures essentially serving the same purpose existed alongside each other'[54] would not come as a surprise.

4.3 Rationale

The rationale underlying the abolition of *exequatur* is also different. In the Brussels II *bis* Regulation the decision to entrust all safeguards to the court of origin is justified because of the need to effectively combat international child abduction within the EU. In a similar vein, the need to enhance the protection of the creditor explains the solution in the Maintenance Regulation. In the remaining three regulations, the rationale is simply mutual trust, accompanied by the respect of detailed minimum standards, in the EEO Regulation, and the harmonization of procedural rules in the EOP and ESCP Regulations.

5. CONCLUSION

The complete, total abolition of the *exequatur* proceedings in all European civil procedural regulations would certainly simplify a much too complex situation. However, even if the Brussels I recast Regulation may be seen as a move in this direction, it could also be understood as endorsing the opposite view. The large number of opinions expressed against the abolition prior to the adoption of the Regulation indicates that the time is not yet ripe. As regards the Brussels II *bis* Regulation, some academics have raised their voices in favour of extending the system of direct enforcement to the whole material scope of the Regulation; the difficulties experienced in the practice of Article 42 cast doubt on the timeliness of such a proposal.

Albeit more the result of intuition rather than of scientific conviction, we hereby claim that as of today, in the light of the strong political will of the Commission, the real question is no longer whether the *exequatur* should be abolished or not, but rather when this will occur. In the meantime, the real question is to what extent the *exequatur* (and the conditions traditionally associated with the procedure) can be removed, or at least, softened.

[54] G Wagner, 'Harmonisation of Civil Procedure: Policy Perspectives' in XE Kramer and CH van Rhee, *Civil Litigation in a Globalising World* (The Hague, TMC Asser Press, 2012) 93, 100.

So far, some degree of caution has prevailed. At a sensitive time when the role of the ECJ as a constitutional court is under discussion, and uncertainty about the system of fundamental rights within the EU has to be eradicated, this seems the likeliest outcome. A complete deletion, or even a severe restriction, of the basic conditions so far linked to the *exequatur* would mean an assessment as to the lower status of certain rights listed in the European Charter:[55] their violation would never lead to the setting aside of cooperation among Member States. The *ordre public* exception, which has worked its way into the final text of the Brussels I recast Regulation, makes it possible to put off that decision, at least for the foreseeable future. In the meantime, there is room to elaborate the elements that form the basis of real mutual trust.

Decisions of a foreign Member State will not be treated as domestic ones as a matter of course. Like many other steps taken on the road to a European Union the goal of an equal treatment for national and foreign decisions could be attained 'by sheer force': that is, be imposed on the Member States. However, for it to meet with the least resistance as possible real trust is essential. There is nothing wrong with the Commission's political willingness to create a truly unique area of justice; the discussion is rather on the best strategy to use to make it real. In this regard, we believe that at the end of the day, allowing for differences in the understanding of fundamental rights and principles between the Member States to come to light, so that they can be adequately addressed before moving forward, is in the best interest of mutual trust between the Member States.

[55] A kind of 'second-class' right.

15

Mutual Recognition as a Governance Strategy for Civil Justice

EVA STORSKRUBB*

1. INTRODUCTION

'MUTUAL RECOGNITION' HAS been a central concept in EU integration since the famous and seminal *Cassis de Dijon* case.[1] But what is mutual recognition? According to commentators 'it is generally acknowledged that mutual recognition entails a governance strategy and embodies choices as how to achieve market integration'.[2] The purpose of this chapter is to conduct an initial review of mutual recognition as a regulatory or governance strategy for the policy area 'judicial cooperation in civil matters'[3] that falls within the broader EU policy of creating an Area of Freedom, Security and Justice (AFSJ).[4] The shortened name of 'civil justice' is used in this chapter for the policy area.

The aim of this chapter is to present some thoughts on the viability of transporting the general market integration strategy of mutual integration into the field of civil justice.[5] To this end a glimpse will be first cast at the historic developments of mutual recognition (section 2). Thereafter, certain doctrinal contributions on the functioning of mutual recognition as a governance strategy will be presented in order to identify relevant themes and critical issues for consideration (section 3). Finally, drawing upon those contributions and identified critical issues some conclusions will be drawn from the particular perspective of civil justice (section 4).

* Marie Curie Research Fellow, Uppsala University.

[1] Case 120/78 *Rewe-Zentral AG v Bundesmonopolverwaltung für Branntwein*, EU:C:1979:42; but see C Janssens, *The Principle of Mutual Recognition* (Oxford, Oxford University Press, 2013) 11–13.

[2] P Craig and G de Búrca, *EU Law—Text, Cases and Materials*, 5th edn (Oxford, Oxford University Press, 2011) 594.

[3] Art 81 Treaty on the Functioning of the European Union (TFEU).

[4] Title IV TFEU

[5] For an analysis of the criminal justice policy area see, inter alia, the work of Janssens (n 1) and A Suominen, *The Principle of Mutual Recognition in Cooperation in Criminal Matters: A Study of the Principles in Four Framework Decisions and in the Implementation Legislation in the Nordic Member States* (Cambridge, Intersentia, 2011).

2. BACKGROUND

2.1 The Internal Market Origins of Mutual Recognition

There are numerous sources outlining the role that mutual recognition has played in the creation of the Internal Market, depicting the historic development of this dramatic judicial contribution to market integration and setting it in context.[6] Mutual recognition was first introduced in the context of free movement, ie, the four fundamental market freedoms of the EU.[7] At a concise and simplified level, the development in relation to the free movement of goods can be explained as follows. In the 1970s and 1980s, market integration was based on a combination of, on the one hand, prohibition of quantitative restrictions and other discriminative national rules and, on the other, legislative harmonisation. In the absence of harmonisation, Member States were thus free to impose market restrictions, ie, to enact rules that set product standards for goods, as long these rules were applied both to domestic goods and goods from other Member States.[8] In addition, restrictions on imports could be justified on grounds of, inter alia, public morality, security and health. Harmonisation was considered important for integration, because otherwise actors that wished to operate cross-border on the market still had to fulfil diverging domestic product standards. However, harmonisation was tedious and during this period mired by the requirement of unanimity and political discord. Thus, at a stage when there was a legislative impasse, the European Court of Justice (CJEU) stepped in and with its *Cassis* ruling fundamentally changed the regulatory framework by setting a requirement of mutual recognition.[9] The requirement entailed that Member States could no longer impose their domestic rules on foreign goods, but had to 'recognise', ie, accept the importation of foreign goods. Thus, the Member States had to accept the product standards of the other Member States and also trust the other Member States in this respect.[10]

It is important to note that mutual recognition came with a caveat and restrictions. In the *Cassis* case itself, the CJEU introduced the concept of mandatory requirements and conceded that there may sometimes be a need for derogation from mutual recognition. Member States may refuse an

[6] See, inter alia, Craig and de Búrca (n 2) 583, 594–600; J Snell, 'The Internal Market and Philosophies of Integration' in C Barnard and S Peers (eds), *European Union Law* (Oxford, Oxford University Press, 2014) 307–23.

[7] The free movement of goods, services, persons and capital, see, inter alia, Arts 28, 45, 56 and 63 TFEU.

[8] Based on Art 34 TFEU (ex Art 28 EC) and in particular *Dassonville*, Case 8/74 *Procureur du Roi v Benoît and Gustave Dassonville*, EU:C:1974:82.

[9] Craig and de Búrca (n 2) 583.

[10] D Chalmers, G Davies and G Monti, *European Union Law*, 3rd edn (Cambridge, Cambridge University Press, 2014) 775.

import to protect mandatory requirements, in other words to protect important public interests such as consumer protection or public health, if it can be shown that the prohibition was necessary. Thus, the derogations or limitations of free movement must be justifiable and proportionate on a case-by-case basis.[11] Therefore, mutual recognition with mandatory requirements may often bring to the fore and highlight the need for harmonisation to replace the multitude of potential national protective derogations. As an adjunct to mutual recognition, minimum harmonisation is thus foreseen as necessary in certain fields to fill in gaps.[12] In its so-called new approach to harmonisation and push to complete the Internal Market launched by the Commission in the wake of the *Cassis* ruling and the Single European Act of 1986, the harmonisation project in relation to product standards was indeed recalibrated in the form of limiting it to ancillary minimum mutual standards for essential health and safety matters.[13]

Mutual recognition in its 'pure form' may be considered as being deregulatory and as embodying negative rather than positive harmonisation. The harmonisation pressures mentioned above, however, negate the picture of 'pure' mutual recognition. In addition, aside from formal harmonisation, legislative and administrative attention is shifted to other types of 'flanking measures' that support mutual recognition as a regulatory method. These may, for example, be cooperation and communication structures between the relevant government bodies and other actors, such as standardisation organisations in the Internal Market context.[14] Therefore, 'pure' mutual recognition is rare, and as one commentator notes, mutual recognition is generally applied in a restricted way mediating its consequences, or in other words, because it is often applied in combination with other regulatory principles, its impact is modified.[15]

2.2 Mutual Recognition: A 'Cornerstone' of Civil Justice

Mutual recognition was formally introduced as a regulatory method for civil justice in the Tampere European Council Conclusions in 1999.[16] Ten years later, in 2009, when the Lisbon Treaty entered into force it was

[11] ibid, 775–76. See also Art 36 TFEU.

[12] Chalmers, Davies and Monti (n 10) 778.

[13] Snell (n 6) 310.

[14] E Storskrubb, *Civil Procedure and EU Law—A Policy Area Uncovered* (Oxford, Oxford University Press, 2008) 277.

[15] SK Schmidt, 'Mutual Recognition as a New Mode of Governance' (2007) 14 *Journal of European Public Policy* 5, 667, 675–76.

[16] European Council Conclusions No 200/1/99, para 33, available at: www.consilium.europa.eu/uedocs/cms_data/docs/pressdata/en/ec/00200-r1.en9.htma and www.europarl.europa.eu/summits/tam_en.htm.

even enshrined in the treaties: 'The Union shall facilitate access to justice, in particular through the *principle of mutual recognition* or judicial and extra-judicial decisions in civil matters'[17] and 'The Union shall develop judicial cooperation in civil matters having cross-border implications, based on *the principle of mutual recognition* of judgements and of decisions in extra judicial cases'[18] (italics added). Below a review of the policy documents for civil justice spanning the relevant decade and beyond outlines what can be gleaned from the professed policy objectives and perspectives of the EU institutions in relation to mutual recognition in the civil justice context.

The Tampere Conclusions of the European Council drew up specific objectives in order to develop the AFSJ in the same year that the Treaty of Amsterdam entered into force and which introduced the political vision of the AFSJ.[19] The Tampere Conclusions state that:

> Enhanced mutual recognition of judicial decisions and judgments and the necessary approximation of legislation would facilitate co-operation between authorities and the judicial protection of individual rights. The European Council *therefore endorses the principle of mutual recognition* which, in its view, should *become the cornerstone of judicial co-operation* in both civil and criminal matters within the Union (italics added).[20]

It is notable that mutual recognition is not only 'endorsed' as a regulatory method; it is even elevated to the level of a 'principle' for civil justice. In addition, it is billed to become the 'cornerstone' of the policy area. Thereby, it is evident that mutual recognition is seen as an important tool for the future development of the policy area.

After the Tampere Conclusions, the Council published a specific programme for the implementation of the principle of mutual recognition of decisions in civil matters.[21] The programme contended that the principle was not new in the context of cross-border procedural regulation, referring back to the Brussels Convention of 1968, being the first measure to deal with recognition and enforcement of judgments in the Community.[22] However, the programme argued that the principle had not yet had full effect in the field of civil justice since barriers to free movement still existed and mentioned as an example the too restrictive intermediate enforcement

[17] Art 67(4) TFEU.

[18] Art 81(1) TFEU.

[19] Art 2 of the Treaty of the European Union (as it then was) and Art 61 of the Treaty on the European Community (as it then was).

[20] The Tampere Conclusions (n 16).

[21] 'Draft programme of measures for implementation of the principle of mutual recognition of decisions in civil and commercial matters' [2001] OJ C12/1, 1.

[22] ibid, 2. The Brussels Convention was entered into on the basis of Art 220 of the Treaty on the European Community (as it then was). For a discussion on the evolution of a legal basis for civil justice see, inter alia, Storskrubb, *Civil Procedure and EU Law* (n 14) 33–43, and P-E Partsch, *Le Droit International Privé Européen—De Rome à Nice* (Brussels, Larcier, 2003).

(*exequatur*) procedures.[23] Free movement refers to the free movement of judgments, which can be held to be the 'fifth freedom'. The programme outlines the state of play and also puts forward proposals to achieve further levels of mutual recognition with a tentative timetable.

The programme uses the same regulatory language or terms common from the Internal Market and free movement of goods context when it also focuses on 'ancillary measures'. As regards ancillary measures, the programme first notes that in some cases, safeguards or minimum standards will have to be laid down for procedural rules in order to strengthen mutual trust and ensure the requirements of a fair trial. Further, it is noted that where the establishment of minimum standards appears to be insufficient 'discussions should be directed towards a certain degree of harmonisation of the procedures'.[24] Second, the programme refers to measures supporting the efficiency of mutual recognition as ancillary measures. In this respect, addressing adjacent issues such as enforcement or execution proper, information on the debtor's assets or conflict of law rules may, according to the programme, facilitate mutual recognition. In addition, general measures to improve judicial cooperation in civil matters such as networks, providing general information to the public and cross-border legal aid would be conducive to the implementation of the principle of mutual trust according to the programme.[25]

Further, subsequent to the Tampere Conclusions, two additional European Council multi-annual programmes for the AFSJ followed with five-year intervals; the Hague Programme[26] and the Stockholm Programme respectively.[27] In the Hague Programme 'strengthening justice' to ensure among other things the full employment of mutual recognition is emphasised. At the more general level, 'mutual trust' and the development of common judicial culture are held to be important to enhance the policy area. The evaluation of the implementation of the policies in the field of justice is held to be important to facilitate mutual recognition.[28] According to the Programme, the effectiveness of mutual recognition should also be increased by standardising procedures and documents as well as by developing minimum standards for aspects of procedural law such as the service of documents.[29]

[23] 'Draft programme' (n 21) 2. M Linton, chapter 13, and M Requejo Isidro, chapter 14, in this volume deal with the abolition of the *exequatur* procedure.

[24] 'Draft programme' (n 21) 5–6.

[25] ibid, 6. See also H Hartnell, 'EUstitia: Institutionalizing Justice in the European Union' (2002) 23 *Northwestern Journal of International Law & Business* 65, in relation to the use of networks and other structures to support civil justice.

[26] 'The Hague Programme: Strengthening freedom, security and justice in the European Union' [2005] OJ C53/1.

[27] 'The Stockholm Programme: An open and secure Europe serving and protecting citizens' [2010] OJ C115/1.

[28] 'The Hague Programme' (n 26) 11.

[29] ibid, 13.

In the Stockholm Programme, the professed link between mutual trust as well as the development of the judicial culture and the implementation of mutual recognition is again emphasised. Therefore, the Programme focuses both on furthering mutual recognition and on various means of strengthening mutual trust. To ensure minimum rights is considered important to both enhance mutual trust and develop mutual recognition.[30] Specifically, in the field of civil justice, the focus is on continuing the abolishment of all intermediate measures and equally on introducing safeguards to support this.[31] To support mutual trust, a number of practical support tools and measures are seen as relevant in relation to, for example, judicial training, developing networks and enhancing operational capabilities such as electronic tools.[32]

Following the end of the five-year time period for the Stockholm Programme, no new multi-annual programme has been launched for the development of the AFSJ. Instead, the European Council has defined more streamlined 'strategic guidelines' for legislative and operational planning for the AFSJ in coming years.[33] These very brief guidelines note as a general programmatic statement that:

> The smooth functioning of a true European area of justice with respect for the different legal systems and traditions is vital for the EU. In this regard, *mutual trust* in one another's justice systems should be further enhanced (italics added).[34]

Further, as one of the listed action points mutual recognition of judgments is specifically mentioned to 'enhance *mutual recognition* of decisions and judgments in civil and criminal matters' (italics added).[35]

In all of these policy programmes and strategic guidelines, it is possible to note a very strong commitment to mutual recognition as a regulatory strategy. However, the interesting question is whether mutual recognition is perceived as a 'pure' regulatory technique or whether it is to be used together with supporting harmonisation and flanking measures to mediate its consequences as in the Internal Market context. In these policy documents, it is possible to note, albeit sometimes in fairly veiled or general terms, an understanding that ancillary and flanking measures are required. The need for minimum standards or harmonisation is mentioned but often not elaborated upon. The need to create a mutual judicial culture and judicial training as well as networks and electronic tools are mentioned as flanking measures. It is also apparent that mutual trust is held to be an important

30 'The Stockholm Programme' (n 27) 11–12.

31 ibid, 13 and 15.

32 ibid, 13–14.

33 European Council Conclusions of 27 June 2014 (EUCO 79/14) 1–6. Note that the European Council is obliged to provide strategic guidelines, see Art 68 TFEU for the legislative and operational planning of the AFSJ.

34 ibid, 5.

35 ibid, 6.

adjunct to or support for mutual recognition, in order perhaps to mediate or avoid negative consequences of mutual recognition. However, practical proposals to support mutual trust (and thereby mutual regulation) have not been developed further than the above-mentioned flanking measures and the most recent guidelines merely state that mutual trust should be 'enhanced'. Therefore, the question to which I will revert below (see section 4) is: how far have we actually come in the debate on shaping a functional regulatory strategy for civil justice?

Finally, it should be noted the mutual recognition is also specifically mentioned in the legislative measures of civil justice, one example being the fairly recent Brussels I recast Regulation that is considered to be the flagship regulation of the policy area and the central one for the 'fifth freedom':[36]

> The Union has set itself the objective of maintaining and developing an area of freedom, security and justice, inter alia, by facilitating access to justice, in particular through the *principle of mutual recognition* of judicial and extra- judicial decisions in civil matters.

And:

> Certain differences between national rules governing jurisdiction and recognition of judgments *hamper the sound operation of the internal market*. Provisions to unify the rules of conflict of jurisdiction in civil and commercial matters, and to ensure rapid and simple recognition and enforcement of judgments given in a Member State, *are essential* (italics added).[37]

These statements in the recitals to the Regulation show that mutual recognition as a regulatory choice behind the free movement of judgments in the civil justice context is meant to facilitate access to justice as well as improve the sound operation of the Internal Market. There are potential tensions between these goals; the efficiency of the market and the protection of fundamental procedural rights, which arguably should influence how mutual recognition is used and moderated as a regulatory strategy.

Such tensions may have had an impact on the fact that mutual recognition was not fully or 'purely' implemented in the recast of the Brussels I Regulation. The legislative process demonstrated clearly that the Member States in the Council supported by the European Parliament were not prepared to completely remove *exequatur*, and in particular that they were in favour of the limited grounds for refusal of enforcement being retained.[38] The *exequatur* has, however, been 'reshuffled' in the recast of the Brussels I

[36] Regulation (EU) No 1215/2012 of 12 December 2012 on jurisdiction and the recognition and enforcement of judgments in civil and commercial matters (recast) [2012] OJ L351/1.

[37] ibid, recitals 3–4.

[38] See E Storskrubb, 'Civil Justice—The Contested Nature of the Scope of EU legislation' in F Trauner and A Ripoli Servent (eds), *Policy Change in the Area of Freedom Security and Justice* (Abingdon, Routledge, 2014) 208f.

Regulation and has been removed to varying degrees in various other civil justice measures together with a fragmented set of safeguards and minimum standards.[39] However, a number of cases have already shown that such safeguards or standards may not be enough.[40] These cases are proof of the difficult tension that exists in mutual recognition between the goals of free movement—simplification and efficiency—and the goal of protecting the fundamental rights of both litigating parties. Coupled with the different standards in practice of the procedural systems in the Member States that have also occasioned problems in mutual recognition, these cases show, at a broader level, that mutual trust cannot be presumed in EU civil justice.[41] Logically, mutual trust as a political wish cannot be a panacea to support mutual recognition and solve difficult regulatory questions. These are issues that I will also revert to below (section 4).

In sum, in the civil justice context, mutual recognition has first been introduced in policy programmes and thereafter formally been referred to in secondary legislation and case law, as well as enshrined in primary treaty provisions. In addition, it is not only a mode of governance but rather the 'cornerstone' of the regulatory strategy. Further, it is held to be a principle to which the adjunct concept of mutual trust is linked. However, regardless of the strong support for mutual recognition in overarching policy documents, there are tensions occasioned by the choice of regulatory method. Before further analysing these regulatory choices with respect to civil justice, it is pertinent to step back and understand the broader regulatory debate that has taken place so far on mutual recognition (section 3). Certain contributions to that debate will be presented below in order to provide useful tools for comparison with the particular civil justice context. In addition, the broader debate may help us identify relevant themes and critical issues for the civil justice context.

3. REGULATORY DEBATE ON MUTUAL RECOGNITION

3.1 General Theoretical Background

In looking at mutual recognition as a regulatory mode of governance, it is beneficial to consider what the underlying issue is as well as what the potential alternative solutions are to deal with the issue. Traditionally,

[39] See M Linton, chapter 13 in this volume for an overview.

[40] See M Linton, chapter 13, and M Requejo Isidro, chapter 14 in this volume.

[41] See XE Kramer, 'Cross-Border Enforcement and the Brussels I-Bis Regulation. Towards A New Balance Between Mutual Trust and National Control over Fundamental Rights' (2006) *NILR* 60, 3643–67, mentioning also the cases on *lis pendens*. See also G Cuniberti, chapter 2 in this volume.

mutual recognition offers a regulatory or governance solution to the diversity of distinct markets when the desire is to integrate these markets. As a first step, it should be noted that there has to be a political will for integration, and logically also a political vision that integration is paramount to diversity. Having decided in favour of the integration of the distinct markets this can be accomplished in different ways: (i) national treatment (host-country rules); (ii) harmonisation (similar rules); or (iii) mutual recognition (home-state rules).[42]

There are certain advantages and disadvantages with these three alternatives in classic market discourse, and they are different depending on the perspective taken. Under the first alternative, national treatment, the burden on the market participants is high because they have to adapt to different national rules, but the host country keeps its rules and does not have to relinquish sovereignty. It only has to open up its market to participants willing to enter and follow its rules (non- discrimination). With the second and opposite alternative, harmonisation, market participants wishing to enter other markets do not face additional costs but the states have to relinquish sovereignty vertically to the supranational level and may face considerable negotiating costs. Finally, the third option, mutual recognition, may be seen as an ostensibly benign and easy middle ground. The countries do not need to face negotiation costs and companies do not have to face adaptation costs as home-state control means that fulfilling one set of national rules suffices.[43]

Nevertheless, what is sometimes overlooked is that mutual recognition as a mode of governance means that states relinquish sovereignty albeit horizontally.[44] In addition, the national regulator can no longer ensure the same level of regulation to users within its territory when new and foreign participants enter the market based on their own (foreign) home-state regulation. This means that although mutual recognition may be a simple solution for states and market participants, the end-users, buyers or consumers may face information and other costs due to the diversity. In addition, diversity may fuel regulatory competition, even creating a risk of a race to the bottom. If diversity is perceived to cause unwanted risks, the legitimacy of the system may be questioned by the users and states held politically accountable.[45] Therefore, there is often a combination of governance mechanisms, a combination of approximation (or harmonisation) and mutual recognition, and these mechanisms are in reality often complementary rather than strict alternatives. As we saw above in section 2, in the

[42] Schmidt (n 15) 671.

[43] ibid, 672.

[44] K Nicolaïdis, 'Trusting the Poles? Constructing Europe through Mutual Recognition' (2007) 14 *Journal of European Public Policy* 685.

[45] Schmidt (n 15) 672.

Internal Market context, harmonisation, ancillary measures and individual derogations are used to 'mediate' the consequences of mutual recognition. Therefore, mutual recognition has also been called 'managed', meaning that it does not operate in a void but is always related 'formally' to other forms of integration and 'informally' to societal prerequisites such as acceptance and trust.[46]

Even in the Internal Market context the principle has led to political legitimacy and regulatory challenges because of the way in which it divides authority over regulation and relies on mutual trust.[47] Thus, as one observer notes, it may be particularly difficult to apply this mode of governance beyond the context of the trade in goods. In addition, she observes that the kinds of rules, which are being mutually recognised matters and that the democratic legitimation may be different for different policy areas. For certain fields it may be more difficult to delegate the responsibility of setting the standard to another state.[48]

3.2 Debate on Mutual Recognition in JHA

Concerning the policy areas of immigration, asylum and criminal cooperation (what has been called the Justice and Home Affairs (JHA) part of AFSJ) and mutual recognition as a regulatory strategy, central contributions in the field of political science were published in 2007 in the *Journal of European Public Policy*.[49] It is not possible to fully present and review these contributions in this chapter. However, some of the strands of analysis of selected contributors will be described below in order to provide a backdrop for further discussions. It is perhaps natural that political scientists rather than legal scholars have focused more on understanding the complex regulatory issues inherent in and underlying mutual recognition. However, there is certainly a natural interdisciplinary overlap in this respect and some of the contributors to the particular articles reviewed are also lawyers. I posit that these contributions and the interdisciplinary perspective are valuable for us as lawyers trying to understand and analyse the regulatory issues and governance developments in relation to a policy area. Notably these contributions do not raise the particular perspective of civil justice, but deal with other policy areas under the umbrella of the same political project of creating an AFSJ. It is apparent that the policy areas related to national security and immigration issues have been of more direct interest in the

[46] S Lavenex, 'Mutual Recognition and the Monopoly of Force: Limits of the Single Market Analogy' (2007) 14 *Journal of European Public Policy* 767. See also Nicolaïdis (n 44).

[47] Schmidt (n 15) 675.

[48] ibid, 675–76.

[49] (2007) 14 *Journal of European Public Policy*.

political research arena. This leaves open a lacuna that I hope to address in this chapter and in future work. The contributions may, nevertheless, be of generic use and contrasting their findings to the field civil justice may help identify mutual or diverging issues and trends.

In her central contribution, Lavenex argues that there are limits to the use of the Internal Market analogy in the JHA context.[50] She notes that the adoption of mutual recognition in these fields is a typical case of institutional isomorphism where a policy concept that has been useful for the integration of a certain policy field is borrowed to realise integration in another field.[51] She argues that if you ask the basic questions 'who benefits' and 'what is being mutually recognised'? it will emerge that there is a fundamental difference between cross-border trade in goods and the cross-border movement of sovereign acts (eg, judgments). Underlying such sovereign acts is de facto another state's procedural and legal system. Thus, underlying mutual recognition is de facto an assumption that judgments are legal and legitimate based on a shared standard of human rights and procedural safeguards.[52]

Lavenex further notes that a major political driver for introducing mutual recognition as a regulatory strategy for AFSJ matters at the Tampere European Council summit in 1999 was the fact that this meant that national sovereignty was preserved. Mutual recognition and cooperation were perceived as politically more realistic and achievable than other governance modes (eg, harmonisation) because the Member States could retain sovereignty in the policy fields of the AFSJ. She calls this the 'lure of sovereignty'. However, what has apparently been ignored, at least in the political rhetoric, is the fact that sovereignty was only ostensibly preserved and the fact that mutual recognition actually entails relinquishing sovereignty—not vertically to the supranational regulator but horizontally to the other national regulators.[53]

Lavenex also describes how, together with embedded transgovernmentalism, mutual recognition has led to limited results and difficulties encountered in harmonisation in the field of criminal cooperation. Despite the fact that harmonisation has been perceived as necessary to counter the effects of unbalanced mutual recognition.[54] In addition, the necessary mutual trust cannot be presupposed. In the field of asylum, she posits that the implementation of mutual recognition has entailed the prevalence of visible mutual distrust.[55] Her overall conclusion is that the Internal Market analogy in relation to mutual recognition as a strategy for integration of JHA policies has its limits and mutual recognition has deep implications

[50] Lavenex (n 46), she uses the term 'Single Market' instead of 'Internal Market'.
[51] ibid, 762.
[52] ibid, 764–66.
[53] ibid, referring to Nicolaïdis.
[54] ibid, 768–71.
[55] ibid, 772.

for the transfer of sovereignty. In terms of costs for individual freedoms and human rights, she notes that ancillary measures to support trust, learning and adaptation may be questioned. She argues for more supranational structures and harmonisation to overcome the problems encountered.[56]

Nicolaïdis has identified that it took a long time even in the Internal Market context for regulators and others to realise that mutual recognition could not deal with everything and that it constitutes a surrender of control (and of sovereignty). According to her, the conflictual nature of mutual recognition should, however, come as no surprise because a horizontal transfer of sovereignty is both about respecting sovereignty and radically reconfiguring it. It is reconfigured in the sense that authority to prescribe laws and enforce them is dislocated from the territory (ie, from the host state) and allocated reciprocally (ie, to any relevant home state).[57] She has noted that in implementing mutual recognition, a fine-tuned balance must be struck between recognition and the constraints that must be attached to it. Thus, mutual recognition is not 'pure' but 'managed'.[58]

She further posits that there is a difference between blind and binding trust; the first being predicated upon separateness and potentially even mutual ignorance, whilst the latter requires prior and continued knowledge about the other.[59] Using the Internal Market example of the debate on the free movement of services and the 'Polish plumber', she notes that recognition, if it is managed, is not based only on blind trust but on binding trust that includes a consensual choice of the limits of that trust. According to Nicolaïdis, mutual recognition is a Janus-faced norm, considered as the 'easy option' but in reality the hardest of all. She finds it surprising that visible political conflict in relation to mutual recognition came so late in the Internal Market and notes that the conflict in the field of services highlighted the instability of the bargains struck based on mutual recognition, bargains that, for example, highlight the social differences between old and new Member States.[60]

She notes that the systematic extension of the principle of mutual recognition to the JHA realm testifies to its strength as a political paradigm.[61] She further notes that in both the traditional market context as well as in new fields, mutual recognition is not a liberal principle as such and since it involves state power, individual rights may be needed to counterbalance that power. However, she also notes that harmonising rights may run counter to subsidiarity.[62] Mutual recognition and harmonisation/convergence are not

[56] ibid, 775–76.
[57] Nicolaïdis (n 44) 684–85.
[58] ibid, 683–84.
[59] ibid, 684.
[60] ibid, 685–86.
[61] ibid, 689.
[62] ibid, 689–90.

pure alternatives but predicated on one another. Taking an example from the Internal Market context, the recognition of professional standards is predicated upon trust in mutually compatible standards that will result in mutually compatible decisions. In the new JHA context, for example, in immigration, there should be some inherent level of mutually compatible standards in order to ensure tolerance for recognition.[63] Finally, among the criteria for mutual recognition there should be critical safeguards, in other words, that it is possible for local rules to prevail in some instances if necessary and proportionate.[64]

Finally, Poiares Maduro notes that all contributions stress the connection between mutual recognition and questions of mutual identity and trust.[65] This leads him to ask whether mutual recognition de facto depends on a certain degree of identity between the participants and whether it depends on the pre-existence of mutual trust. Referring to Lavenex he notes that in the field of JHA, mutual recognition is more difficult, adding that it is broader in this context, broader than specific economic or market norms because it involves mutual trust in the entire system of law in another state.[66] He also notes that it is a problem when the same variable (lack of consensus or trust) encourages the use of mutual recognition as a regulatory choice, making it difficult to actually enforce mutual recognition.[67] Referring to Nicolaïdis and Schmidt, he further asks whether mutual recognition needs to be grounded in political commitment 'entailing some degree of solidarity between the participants'.[68] In addition, he notes that the EU form of 'managed' mutual recognition with minimum standards or references to general clauses or principles, delegates the final responsibility for the application of the principle to the judicial process. This may, according to Poiares Maduro, be problematic since it places a high burden on the courts in these politically sensitive areas and therefore, ideally and for the sake of legitimacy, they should be supported by the political process.[69]

4. A FUNCTIONAL REGULATORY STRATEGY FOR CIVIL JUSTICE?

4.1 Searching Questions

The theoretical debate above shows that mutual recognition is strong as a political paradigm although it in practice entails an idealised European

[63] ibid, 691.
[64] ibid, 695.
[65] M Poiares Maduro, 'So Close and Yet So Far: The Paradoxes of Mutual Recognition' (2007) 14 *Journal of European Public Policy* 822.
[66] ibid, 823.
[67] ibid.
[68] ibid, 824.
[69] ibid.

vision. This vision means that we live with our differences and seek to harmonise only if such differences are illegitimate in the eyes of others. As Nicolaïdis notes, this is a tough political call in an ever more differentiated world.[70] In addition, mutual recognition can be described as a principle of tolerance, similar to multiculturalism, embodying the idea of 'all different—all equal'.[71] However, is this tough political call suitable for matters related to justice? Was there de facto an awareness at Tampere that mutual recognition actually radically configures sovereignty, and cedes horizontal sovereignty, in the sovereignty sensitive policy fields of the AFSJ? Have we fallen into a reality of blind trust (based on mutual ignorance) without having binding trust, ie, without having had the difficult discussions on what the limits of that trust are? Did we have the necessary level of mutual identity and pre-existing mutual trust when the choice was made to adopt mutual recognition as the guiding principle and regulatory method? These are questions that we may never receive answers to and it may be naive or simplistic to put the questions in these terms, as there were most certainly a multitude of considerations and factors involved in the negotiations and compromises reached among the relevant Member State actors at that point in time.

Nevertheless, it is arguably useful to ask these questions now framed in these structured terms because they may help us to improve our understanding of the current situation as well as to discern the future challenges with more clarity. The current reality is that mutual recognition is the chosen regulatory strategy. Thus, a more functional question to ask is whether we can now make mutual recognition work, even if it was rather the lack of consensus or lack of trust that originally lay behind the choice of mutual recognition as a regulatory method—as the ostensible 'easy option'. The even more pressing question is by what means we can try to make mutual recognition work. What are the suitable tools to support mutual recognition and appropriate means to modify any undesired impact? Do we agree with Lavenex when she finds that in terms of costs for individual freedoms and human rights, ancillary measures to support mutual trust, learning and adaptation may not be enough? Do we agree when she calls for more supranational structures and harmonisation to overcome the problems encountered with mutual recognition? In addition, in relation to civil justice we may ask whether we are arriving 'late to the game'. Why is it that there was a debate as early as 2007 focusing on the limits of mutual recognition in relation to criminal cooperation and immigration? Has there been no similar awareness in the civil justice arena?

[70] Nicolaïdis (n 44) 695–96.
[71] Chalmers, Davies and Monti (n 10) 777.

4.2 Tough Answers

4.2.1 Awareness and Current Status

Taking the last question first, there has been awareness also in the field of civil justice of the potentially conflictual nature of mutual recognition and that mutual recognition may be a tough call. As Andersson noted in 2005: 'the big problem ... with the principle of mutual recognition or the idea of recognition is that is requires mutual trust' and 'A principle of recognition ... requires in its extreme, that a domestic legal system allows for enforcement of judgments based on procedural rules and ideological values over which the Member State has no influence and very little knowledge'.[72] However, as Andersson notes, the intermediary *exequatur* procedure was traditionally the general safeguard against unwanted effects of mutual recognition. At the time of his statement above, many of the civil justice measures that abolish or modify the *exequatur* procedure such as the EEO, EOP and ESCP Regulations[73] were not yet in force or applicable. In addition, subsequent to entering into force, many of them have had a low or slow progress in take-up in the Member States.[74]

However, with some delay, cases are emerging and reaching the CJEU that are in practice proof of the difficult nature of questions of mutual trust and mutual recognition also in the field of civil justice. The cases that have been dealt with in the preceding chapters have so far mainly fallen under the Brussels II *bis* Regulation in the field of family law.[75] This does not necessarily mean that there are no other difficult cases or problems identified in the safeguards or the minimum standards introduced in the other regulations to support mutual recognition. As an example, Oro Martinez notes in this volume that there is a discrepancy in the ESCP Regulation in relation to the right to appeal and perceives a need for a harmonised approach.[76] It is also notable that in the recast of the flagship regulation, the Brussel I Regulation, the *exequatur* has only been 'reshuffled', not completely removed, and the grounds for refusal remain as mentioned above. Thus, it is evident that the Member States were not yet prepared for full or 'pure' mutual recognition

[72] T Andersson, 'Harmonization and Mutual Recognition: How to Handle Mutual Distrust' in M Andenas, B Hess and P Oberhammer (eds), *Enforcement Agency Practice in Europe* (British Institute of International and Comparative Law, 2005) 247.

[73] Regulation (EC) No 805/2004 of 21 April 2004 creating a European Enforcement Order for uncontested claims [2004] OJ L143/15; Regulation (EC) No 1896/2006 of 12 December 2006 creating a European order for payment procedure [2006] OJ L399/1; and Regulation (EC) No 861/2007 of 11 July 2007 establishing a European Small Claims Procedure [2007] OJ L199/1.

[74] See C Crifò, XE Kramer and C Oro Martinez in this volume, chapters 5–7.

[75] See M Linton, chapter 13 and M Requejo Isidro, chapter 14 in this volume.

[76] See C Oro Martinez, chapter 7 in this volume.

and perhaps even wanted to retain protection against enforcement in certain limited circumstances to actually promote and ensure mutual trust. Thus, not imposing blind trust but rather basing mutual recognition on some form of limited or binding trust. Adopting an analogy and the terminology from the Internal Market context, it has been found essential to place a caveat on mutual recognition and allow for certain limited derogations when necessary to protect certain fundamental values and when it is proportionate.

To my mind this is a sound approach. It is essential to realise that mutual recognition should never be introduced in a void, but rather forms part of a complex regulatory strategy, coupled with other tools and support structures. The Internal Market and in particular the classic story of the free movement of goods is instructive in this sense, showing also that the regulatory strategy is honed, revised and supplemented over time with both the legislator and the CJEU contributing to this development. The picture painted above (section 2.1) would not be complete without the *Keck*[77] ruling that came after *Cassis* and limited its impact. The CJEU held in *Keck* that certain types of rules, selling arrangements, fall outside mutual recognition. Thus, Member States can still require that foreign goods that are imported into their market follow the local rules on selling arrangements as long as these rules are not discriminatory; the logic being that selling arrangements have less of an impact on free trade.[78] Although it has been the subject of much criticism, the *Keck* ruling can for our purposes add another layer to the regulatory matrix.[79] Namely, it reminds us that aside from harmonisation and mutual recognition there is also a regulatory option which allows local diversity or host-state control, and in the Internal Market context all three options coexist in practice.[80] The result can also be likened to the principle of subsidiarity that should be taken seriously not least in the current political climate.[81] Even if you consider that civil justice integration is positive or necessary, as the Commission often argues that it is, the question is whether EU action is always the best way forward and more fittingly to what extent and in what manner that action should have an impact on and interact with the relevant domestic rules. It is instructive that the European Parliament, in its report on the recast of the Brussels I Regulation, held that it would be necessary to retain public policy and noted that: 'A Member State before which proceedings are brought is entitled to preserve its fundamental

[77] Joined Cases C-267/91 and C-268/91 *Bernard Keck v Daniel Mithouard* [1993] ECR I-06097, EU:C:1993:905.

[78] Chalmers, Davies and Monti (n 10).

[79] ibid.

[80] Snell (n 6).

[81] See E Storskrubb, 'Civil Justice—Constitutional and Regulatory Issues Revisited' in M Fletcher, E Herlin-Karnell and C Matera (eds), *The EU as an Area of Freedom, Security and Justice* (Abingdon, Routledge, 2016, forthcoming).

values; therefore, equally, it must be the case for a Member State in which the enforcement of a judgment is sought'.[82]

4.2.2 Means and Methods

If it is acknowledged that mutual recognition needs to be supported by a broader regulatory strategy and analysis, the next question to address is: what are the suitable tools to support mutual recognition and the appropriate means to modify any undesired impact? First, it should be noted that the debate on and identification of the difficult issues in implementing mutual recognition is important in itself as a starting point. In the Internal Market, the appropriate level of regulation has at times even been fiercely debated and contested.[83] Many of the chapters in this volume are a testament to the fact that such a debate has started and should continue. In addition, empirical work and the follow-up of the practical functioning of all measures are vital and should also continue. As Kramer notes, it is important that our research agendas include empirical research and that we understand what is going on in domestic courts on a day to day basis.[84] It is also essential to identify the difficult cases, the ones where the minimum standards are perhaps not enough. Moreover, it is crucial that we continually critically examine and re-evaluate the EU measures that often represent the fruit of complex compromises between, or concessions to, divergent procedural rules and systems.

In the sphere of justice, a 'race to the bottom' type of situation resulting from mutual recognition would naturally be undesirable. If the safeguards and minimum standards introduced in civil justice measures are in practice not enough to support both efficient mutual recognition and fundamental procedural guarantees, they need to be reconsidered and revised. There is no 'easy way out' and to simply say that mutual trust (imposed or simply presumed) will solve the problem is arguably an unsatisfactory way forward to achieving binding trust. The observations of Poiares Maduro are insightful in this respect when he observes that mutual recognition may be problematic if it places a high burden on the courts in these politically sensitive policy areas and that a true political process is needed in order to achieve legitimacy.[85] The CJEU has considered itself and the Member States bound by a presumption of mutual trust in the cases that have emerged so far in civil justice in which the requirements of mutual recognition have

[82] A7-320/2012.

[83] Chalmers, Davies and Monti (n 10) 667–77 and 687–702.

[84] XE Kramer, 'Procedure Matters: Construction and Deconstructivism in European Civil Procedure' *Erasmus Law Lectures 33* (The Hague, Eleven International Publishing, 2013) 27.

[85] See (n 69).

been challenged from a fundamental rights perspective.[86] Thus, to leave the matter entirely for the courts to resolve does not appear to be a satisfactory solution.

This leaves us with the question of whether to agree with Lavenex or not. Are ancillary measures to support mutual recognition and mutual trust such as learning and adaptation not enough? Are more supranational structures and harmonisation indeed called for to overcome the problems encountered with mutual recognition? The impact of the existing ancillary or flanking measures of an overarching nature such as judicial training, networks and e-justice certainly deserve more attention in our empirical and other research.[87] I aim to devote more time to these aspects in my current research project and work. The Stockholm Programme has placed the most emphasis on such measures among the policy programmes, and this is likely the result of the progressing maturity of the policy area and the progression of legislative measures to abolish *exequatur*.[88] However, it will take time for such measures to have an impact and the impact will most likely not be possible to observe or be apparent from the start. There also needs to be a true political commitment to these measures, for example, to judicial training on EU civil justice and other measures. In addition, a means in favour of and efforts made in relation to dissemination of information are required, for example, to ensure that the information on the e-justice portal reaches the users. Finally, logically, the impact of these measures may go deeper and have more effect if the relevant stakeholders are engaged and involved; both relevant civil servants but also first instance judges, members of the Bar, bailiffs and others who work with civil justice on a daily basis. In order for networks and other governance mechanisms to work, there needs to be a successful horizontal culture and environment.

Finally, on the question of more supranational harmonisation, there may indeed be a need for further harmonisation to support mutual recognition in certain respects. As Hess has mentioned, there are trends such as constitutionalisation and the development of self-standing EU procedures that

[86] See, inter alia, C-491/10 *Joseba Andoni Aguirre Zarraga v Simone Pelz* [2010] ECR I-14247, EU:C:2010:828. The blind trust has also been called the systematic approach to mutual trust, see V Mitsilegas, 'The Limits of Mutual Trust in Europe's Area of Freedom, Security and Justice: From Automatic Inter-State Cooperation to the Slow Emergence of the Individual' (2012) 31 *Yearbook of European Law* 337.

[87] Hartnell (n 25) was one of the first contributions to realise their impact on civil justice. See also E Storskrubb, *Civil Procedure and EU Law* (n 14) 233–58. For a more general presentation of the current networks and support structures, see A Molitorisová, 'On Some Aspects of the Current State of Horizontal Judicial Cooperation in the European Union with Special Regard to EU Law Development' (2014) *Europarättslig Tidskrift* 85. See also as an example the work being done by the Centre for Judicial Cooperation at the European University Institute, available at: www.eui.eu/Projects/CentreForJudicialCooperation/Home.aspx.

[88] See E Storskrubb, 'Civil Justice—A Newcomer and an Unstoppable Wave?' in P Craig and G de Búrca (eds), *The Evolution of EU Law*, 2nd edn (Oxford, Oxford University Press, 2011) 316–17.

highlight the need for a more systematised approach.[89] However, to simply latch onto the promise of harmonisation may not lead us to a functional regulatory strategy either. To simply harmonise rules may not succeed if procedural systems and structures remain diverse and if the vision of justice is idiosyncratic.[90] Therefore, at present we need to deepen our understanding and be aware of the fact that regulatory options interact. To find the correct mix, a working balance, more work needs to be done at a multitude of levels.[91] As commentators and academics we have a special role to play hopefully in interaction and in tandem with the institutions, practitioners and users.

[89] See B Hess in this volume, chapter 1. See also Storskrubb (n 81).

[90] Storskrubb (n 81).

[91] The project started by the European Law Institute (ELI) and Unidroit on European Principles of Civil Procedure is an example of a project that can provide the platform for such debate among experts across Europe to truly identify best practices and provide a solid basis and inspiration for future reform. See project description, available at: www.europeanlawinstitute.eu/projects.

16

Mutual Recognition in Civil and Criminal Justice: Towards Order and Method?

MARIA BERGSTRÖM*

1. INTRODUCTION

THE ARGUMENT THAT there are limits to the analogy of mutual recognition beyond the Internal Market is well founded.[1] These spring in particular from 'a fundamental difference between the cross-border trade in goods and the cross-border movement of sovereign acts (eg judgments)'.[2] Nevertheless, as pointed out by Storskrubb in the previous chapter of this volume, the starting point must be that there is de facto an assumption underlying mutual recognition that judgments are legal and legitimate based on a shared standard of human rights and procedural safeguards. However, this assumption needs to be verified and possibly developed.

As the principle of mutual recognition has been transplanted and given a central role also within the Area of Freedom Security and Justice (AFSJ), EU criminal and civil law have been brought together. This volume, along with many other publications including a previous volume in this series on European Police and Criminal Law Co-operation,[3] identifies some of the benefits and shortcomings inextricably linked with the principle of mutual

* Associate Professor in European Law and Senior Lecturer in EU Law, Faculty of Law, Uppsala University.

[1] E Storskrubb, chapter 15 in this volume with further references to M Poiares Maduro, 'So Close and Yet So Far: The Paradoxes of Mutual Recognition' (2007) 14 *Journal of European Public Policy* 822.

[2] Storskrubb (n 1) with further references to S Lavenex, 'Mutual Recognition and the Monopoly of Force: Limits of the Single Market Analogy' (2007) 14 *Journal of European Public Policy* 762.

[3] M Bergström and A Jonsson Cornell (eds), *European Police and Criminal Law Co-operation* (Oxford, Hart Publishing, 2014).

recognition.[4] The primary purpose of this chapter is, however, not to add to the long list of such publications. Instead, while drawing on some of them as illustrative examples, the aim of this chapter is rather to emphasise the need for methodological awareness. Thereby, it is argued that it might in fact be beneficial to transplant not only the principle of mutual recognition, but also the methodological considerations so inextricably linked with this cornerstone of judicial cooperation in civil and criminal matters. The Internal Market method could possibly be developed also for AFSJ purposes, thereby striking a balance between mutual recognition and the protection of fundamental rights while taking the proportionality principle into consideration. In particular, this chapter concludes that a developed methodological awareness may help to balance and protect the sensitive issues of proportionality and fundamental rights protection within the AFSJ.

2. THE PRINCIPLE OF MUTUAL RECOGNITION AND THE AFSJ

As the previous chapter by Storskrubb explains, the principle of mutual recognition emerged in the case law of the Court of Justice of the European Union (CJEU) within the context of the Internal Market. When the AFSJ was created, the principle of mutual recognition was transplanted and given a central role.[5] Following the 1995 European Legal Area Project, the Corpus Juris proposal,[6] although not realised as such, laid one of the foundation

[4] See in particular, C Jansens, *The Principle of Mutual Recognition in EU Law* (Oxford: Oxford Studies in European Law, Oxford University Press, 2013); V Mitsilegas, *EU Criminal Law* (Oxford, Hart Publishing, 2009); A Suominen, *The Principle of Mutual Recognition in Cooperation in Criminal Matters: A Study of the Principles in Four Framework Decisions and in the Implementation Legislation in the Nordic Member States* (Cambridge, Intersentia, 2011); M Thunberg Schunke, *Whose Responsibility? A Study of Transnational Defence Rights and Mutual Recognition of Judicial Decisions within the EU* (Cambridge, Intersentia, 2013); and the European Criminal Policy Initiative, *A Manifesto on European Criminal Procedural Law* (Stockholm, Skrifter utgivna av Juridiska fakulteten vid Stockholms universitet nr 82, 2014). See also MJ Borgers, 'Mutual Recognition and the European Court of Justice: The Meaning of Consistent Interpretation and Autonomous and Uniform Interpretation of Union Law for the Development of the Principle of Mutual Recognition in Criminal Matters (2010) 18 *European Journal of Crime, Criminal Law and Criminal Justice* 99; and S Peers, 'Mutual Recognition and Criminal Law in the European Union: Has the Council Got it Wrong?' (2004) 41 *Common Market Law Review* 5.

[5] In particular V Mitsilegas, 'The Constitutional Implications of Mutual Recognition in Criminal Matters in the EU' (2006) 43 *Common Market Law Review* 1277.

[6] In 1995, the European Commission launched the European Legal Area Project, resulting in the proposal called Corpus Juris. This was primarily aimed at the adoption of a number of penal provisions in order to protect the financial interests of the European Union, accompanied by procedural provisions for their effective enforcement. See, eg, PO Träskman, 'Mutual Trust and Political Intensions: The European Arrest Warrant and the Nordic Arrest Warrant' in M Bergström and A Jonsson Cornell (eds), *European Police and Criminal Law Co-operation* (Oxford, Hart Publishing, 2014) 127 with further references.

stones for future European cooperation. Later, the conception of the whole European Area as one single jurisdiction has mainly been realised through the provisions on mutual recognition of judgments and judicial decisions.

Mutual recognition of judicial decisions came into focus at the meeting of the European Council in Cardiff in June 1998 and later that year it was 'accentuated as a basic principle for European cooperation'[7] in the Action Plan adopted by the European Council in Vienna. The importance of the concept of mutual recognition was further emphasised as the cornerstone of judicial cooperation in both civil and criminal matters at the Tampere Summit in 1999.[8] Thus, as observed by Storskrubb, mutual recognition was not formally introduced as a regulatory method for civil justice until 1999:

> Enhanced mutual recognition of judicial decisions and judgments and the necessary approximation of legislation would facilitate co-operation between authorities and the judicial protection of individual rights. The European Council therefore endorses the principle of mutual recognition which, in its view, should become the cornerstone of judicial co-operation in both civil and criminal matters within the Union. The principle should apply both to judgements and to other decisions of judicial authorities.[9]

In the 2005 Hague Programme,[10] it was confirmed that borders should not be an obstacle to the enforcement of judgments.[11] The 2009 Stockholm Programme however emphasised that mutual trust needs to be improved in order for mutual recognition to become effective.[12] In the same year, when the Lisbon Treaty entered into force, the principle of mutual recognition was enshrined in the treaties.

The Lisbon Treaty changes have brought about and built on the principle of mutual recognition, applied and administered both in the fields of civil justice and EU criminal law. According to Article 3(2) TEU:

> The Union shall offer its citizens an area of freedom, security and justice without internal frontiers, in which the free movement of persons is ensured in conjunction with appropriate measures with respect to external border controls, asylum, immigration and the prevention and combating of crime.

After the changes made by the Lisbon Treaty in 2009, the provisions on EU criminal law and police cooperation can be found in Part three,

[7] Träskman (n 6) 128.

[8] Tampere European Council 15 and 16 October 1999 Presidency Conclusions No 33 and 34, available at: www.europarl.europa.eu/summits/tam_en.htm.

[9] European Council Conclusions No 200/1/99 para 33, available at: www.europarl.europa.eu/summits/tam_en.htm.

[10] 'The Hague Programme: Strengthening freedom, security and justice in the European Union' [2005] OJ C53/1. See also 'Draft programme of measures for implementation of the principle of mutual recognition of decisions in civil and commercial matters' [2001] OJ C2/1.

[11] See further M Linton, chapter 13 in this volume.

[12] 'The Stockholm Programme—An Open and Secure Europe Serving and Protecting Citizens' [2010] OJ C115/1.

Title V of the TFEU, regulating the AFSJ. The more specific provisions on judicial cooperation in criminal matters are found in Chapter 4. According to Article 82 TFEU, judicial cooperation in criminal matters in the EU shall be based on the principle of mutual recognition of judgments and judicial decisions and shall include an approximation of the laws and regulations of the Member States in certain specific areas. The provisions on police cooperation are inserted in Chapter 5. These provisions have again been brought together with the provisions on policies on border checks, asylum and immigration that can now be found in Chapter 2.[13]

The provisions on judicial cooperation in civil matters have a chapter of their own under the same Title (Chapter 3). Article 81(1) TFEU states that the Union shall develop judicial cooperation in civil matters having cross-border implications, based on the principle of mutual recognition of judgments.

The more general provisions can be found in Chapter 1, where Article 67(3) TFEU states that the Union shall

> endeavour to ensure a high level of security through measures to prevent and combat crime, racism and xenophobia, and through measures for coordination and cooperation between police and judicial authorities and other competent authorities, as well as through the mutual recognition of judgements in criminal matters and, if necessary, through the approximation of criminal laws.

Then Article 67(4) TFEU provides that the Union shall facilitate access to justice through the principle of mutual recognition of judicial decisions in civil matters. As a result, the principle of mutual recognition 'as a vital component of European civil justice cooperation is firmly entrenched in the Treaty on the Functioning of the European Union'.[14]

Any interpretation of the principle of mutual recognition must consider this overall legal framework in which it is set to operate. As pointed out by Kargopoulos, in the field of cooperation in criminal matters and, in particular, in the regulation of conflicts of jurisdiction between the Member States, harmonisation is subordinate to mutual recognition.[15] Hence, he argues that: 'Harmonisation should be used only as a means for the facilitation of mutual recognition of judgements and only through the enactment of secondary legislation'.[16]

[13] See further M Bergström and A Jonsson Cornell, 'Introduction' in M Bergström and A Jonsson Cornell (eds), *European Police and Criminal Law Co-operation* (Oxford, Hart Publishing, 2014).

[14] M Linton, chapter 13 in this volume.

[15] A Kargopoulos, 'Ne Bis in Idem in Criminal Proceedings' in M Bergström and A Jonsson Cornell (eds), *European Police and Criminal Law Co-operation* (Oxford, Hart Publishing, 2014) 110.

[16] ibid, 109.

Thus, interestingly, the overarching principle of mutual recognition of judgments and judicial decisions can be found both in Chapter 3 and Chapter 4 thereby emphasising its importance in both civil and criminal law matters. As a result, after Lisbon, there may now be similarities between the applicable EU rules on mutual recognition between such diverse areas of law as those of civil and criminal law respectively.

As observed by Linton, the importance of mutual recognition and mutual trust are again highlighted as essential components in the creation of a European judicial area in the EU Justice Agenda for 2020;[17] 'mutual recognition should create bonds between the legal systems of the Member States. Improved mutual trust between courts and administrations should further boost the recognition and enforcement of judgments, facilitating the access to justice on equal terms'.[18] Thus, mutual recognition and mutual trust are continuously core concepts in the quest for the free circulation of judgments. These concepts are distinct, yet closely intertwined.

3. POTENTIAL PROBLEMS FOR THE AFSJ

The AFSJ includes policies and legislation for cross-border criminal matters but also cross-border civil and commercial matters, including the principle of mutual recognition of judgments and other decisions in criminal and civil matters. Arguably, EU legislative action in these fields poses significant challenges to the legal orders of the Member States because the policy fields have a direct impact on the protection of fundamental rights and on the relationship between the individual and the state. In addition, the development of EU law in these fields poses challenges to state sovereignty and the relationship between the EU and its Member States.[19]

To give an example, there have been developments in relation to the *ne bis in idem* principle. This principle, which is typically associated with the free movement of persons, has also been identified with the principles of mutual trust and mutual recognition. In this respect, mutual recognition forces 'the acceptance of criminal judgements issued in other Member States, even when the outcome would be different under the law of the recognising state'.[20]

Put differently, the principle of mutual recognition requires the acceptance of foreign judgments regardless of their outcome,[21] ie, even if the

[17] 'The EU Justice Agenda for 2020—Strengthening Trust, Mobility and Growth within the Union' COM(2014) 144 final.

[18] M Linton, chapter 13 in this volume.

[19] Mitsilegas, *EU Criminal Law* (n 4).

[20] A Kargopoulos (n 15) 92 with reference to relevant case law of the CJEU.

[21] ibid, with further references to Case C-467/04 *Giuseppe Francesco Gasparini*, Judgment of 28 September 2006, [2006] ECR I-09199; EU:C:2006:610, paras 29–30.

outcome would be different under internal national legislation, 'in light also of the lack of harmonisation in the respective field which necessitates such an approach'.[22]

Although the EU principle of mutual recognition does not create common substantive rules, it reduces the demand for harmonising measures. As pointed out by Storskrubb, there is, however, often a combination of governance mechanisms, ie, approximation (or harmonisation) and mutual recognition. In reality, these mechanisms are often complementary rather than strict alternatives. In comparison to approximation or harmonisation, the principle of mutual recognition constitutes 'the least contentious method for integration'.[23] Yet, as pointed out by Storskrubb, mutual recognition as a mode of governance, entails that 'states relinquish sovereignty albeit horizontally'.[24]

Nevertheless, according to Mitsilegas, it is handy as it can provide 'results for judges and prosecutors when cooperating across borders ... while *prima facie* Member States do not have to change their domestic criminal law to implement EU standards'.[25] Hence, the principle of mutual recognition although not creating common substantive rules, is rather dependent on the tolerance of the Member States with regard to the diversity characterising national legal systems. In this respect, it 'encourages cooperation between the Member States through mutual trust and recognition of each other's practices'.[26] To give an example, the abolishment of the requirement of double criminality in the relations between different Member States, which is founded on the principle of mutual trust, seems very logical if you are serious about the principle of mutual recognition of judgments and judicial decisions.[27]

Still, it has been questioned whether the timing was right. Accordingly, Träskman amongst others has asked whether the time is really ripe enough for this step to be taken within the European Union: 'Is the common feeling of trust between the Member States as regards each other's criminal systems strong enough?'[28]

In stark contrast, at the beginning of November 2014, a group of British academics, senior lawyers and judges warned that the UK would be more at

[22] Kargopoulos (n 15) 98 with further references to CJEU Case C-436/04 *Léopold Henri van Esbroeck* [2006] ECR I-02333; EU:C:2006:165, paras 31–32, 35–36 and operative part, Case C-150/05 *Jean Leon Van Straaten* [2006] ECR I-09327; EU:C:2006:614, paras 44 and 47.

[23] T Konstadinides, 'The Europeanisation of Extradition: How Many Light Years Away to Mutual Confidence?' in C Eckes and T Konstadinides (eds), *Crime within the Area of Freedom, Security and Justice: A European Public Order* (Cambridge, Cambridge University Press, 2011) 194.

[24] E Storskrubb, chapter 15 in this volume referring to K Nicolaïdis, 'Trusting the Poles? Constructing Europe through Mutual Recognition' (2007) 14 *Journal of European Public Policy* 685.

[25] Mitsilegas, 'The Constitutional Implications' (n 5) 1280.

[26] Konstadinides, 'The Europeanisation of Extradition' (n 23) 194.

[27] Träskman (n 6) 133.

[28] ibid.

risk from foreign criminals 'unless the Government opts back into the controversial European Arrest Warrant',[29] (EAW). In their view, there was no credible alternative available at the national level. In comparison, according to Swedish academics, the mechanism instituted by the EAW, which is based on mutual trust and mutual recognition, have had a negative impact on the quality of legislation regulating cooperation amongst the Nordic States, bringing to an end the 'Golden Age of Nordic Cooperation'[30] within this field. According to Träskman, it was decisive that Nordic legislation was firmly based on an existing and solid trust. He further claims that 'the introduction of the system with mutual recognition and the adoption of the European Arrest Warrant were political means used to shape and construct a common European sense of trust',[31] where all criticism against the EAW is proof of this.

Similarly, in the field of EU cooperation in family and succession law, Sweden and Finland have been referred to as 'backseat drivers'; although not entrusted with driving, as pointed out by Jänterä-Jareborg in this volume, they have felt the need to intervene, often 'irritating the driver'.[32] It is likely that their repeated request to apply an inter-Nordic convention in their mutual relations, for example, in place of the EU enhanced cooperation measure in the area of divorce and legal separation,[33] has contributed to this reputation.[34] In this respect, the Nordic countries 'have mutually achieved what the EU is aspiring to achieve, namely the direct recognition and enforcement of the other states' judgments due to the long since prevailing mutual trust'.[35]

In both cases, the interplay between EU-based instruments and the Swedish legal system triggered frictions, and the influence of EU law on the pre-existing Nordic system was regarded as a negative phenomenon. Nevertheless, as legal issues increasingly imply a high level of interdependency both horizontally and vertically, any solution adopted, including regional solutions such as the Nordic one, need to be analysed and compared with the wider European (if not global) framework in order to identify best practices and further challenges.

The previous examples show that the UK and Sweden, that have often taken a similar stance on many EU law related matters, have opted for different opt-out alternatives in relation to AFSJ matters. Faced with European

[29] 'Britain needs the European Arrest Warrant, senior legal figures say' *Telegraph* (5 November 2014).

[30] Träskman (n 6) 143.

[31] ibid, 142.

[32] M Jänterä-Jareborg', chapter 8 in this volume.

[33] Regulation (EU) No 1259/2010 of 20 December 2010 implementing enhanced cooperation in the area of the law applicable to divorce and legal separation [2010] OJ L343/10.

[34] M Jänterä-Jareborg, chapter 8 in this volume.

[35] ibid.

and global challenges of cross-border movement, the similarly praised and controversial European law principle of mutual recognition entails both solutions and further problems.

At the Tampere Summit in 1999, the concept of mutual recognition was already linked to judicial protection of individual rights. The need to respect fundamental rights within the AFSJ implies, in particular, that proper attention is given to the protection and observance of the due process rights extending beyond the first pillar where they first appeared on the EU scene, towards EU civil and criminal law, and the area of internal and external security.[36] Within the EU system, to give an example concerning persons listed as suspected terrorists, due process rights have been given considerable attention with the rulings of the CJEU.[37] According to the Council, listing and de-listing procedures pursuant to Regulation 2580/2001 and Common Position 2001/931/CFSP have been improved in accordance with these rulings.[38] Accordingly, the EU judicature 'has carefully and respectfully motivated the Council to improve the legal rights of targeted parties by enforcing customary standards of human rights and the rule of law'.[39] Many academics have, however, generally remained more critical.[40] Nevertheless, after the changes made by the Lisbon Treaty, fundamental rights protection has been improved by the now legally binding effect of the Charter of Fundamental Rights (the EU Charter) and by allowing for judicial review even of lists of terrorist suspects 'adopted with a view to imposing economic sanctions'.[41]

Hence, in the AFSJ, where the principle of mutual recognition is the guiding principle of integration, there are in particular potential problems of fundamental rights violations for victims. The principle, therefore, poses

[36] This paragraph is partly taken from M Bergström, 'The Dynamic Evolution of EU Criminal Law' in M Bergström and A Jonsson Cornell (eds), *European Police and Criminal Law Co-operation* (Oxford, Hart Publishing, 2014) 195.

[37] The CJEU thereby including its General Court. Considerable attention has been paid to this case law where almost every EU Law scholar, international law scholars and many penal law and procedural law scholars have published at least one article on this subject, in particular following Joined Cases C-402/05 P & C-415/05 P *Kadi and Al Barakaat* [2008] ECR I-6351.

[38] Council of the European Union, Revised Strategy on Terrorist Financing, 17 July 2008, 8.

[39] J Vestergaard, 'Terror Financing—Asset Freezing, Human Rights and the European Legal Order' (2011) 2 *New Journal of European Criminal Law* 175, 198.

[40] CC Murphy, *EU Counter-Terrorism Law: Pre-Emption and the Rule of Law* (Oxford, Hart Publishing, 2012). See also I Cameron, T Andersson and K Norback, 'EU Blacklisting: The Renaissance of Imperial Power, but on a Global Scale' (2003) 14(2) *European Business LawReview* 111; I Cameron, *The European Convention on European Rights, Due Process and United Nations Security Council Counter-Terrorism Sanctions* (Strasbourg, Council of Europe, 2006); and P Eeckhout, 'Community Terrorism Listings, Fundamental Rights, and UN Security Council Resolutions. In Search of a New Fit' (2007) 3(2) *European Constitutional Law Review* 183.

[41] C Eckes, 'The Legal Framework of the European Union's Counter Terrorism Policies' in C Eckes and T Konstadinides (eds), *Crime within the Area of Freedom, Security and Justice: A European Public Order* (Cambridge, Cambridge University Press, 2011) 127, 158.

significant challenges to the legal orders of the Member States and it may undermine sufficient judicial protection, notably from the viewpoint of the individuals that are the primary addressees of AFSJ law. The principle of mutual recognition may lower the standard of protection,[42] and it may lead to the presumption that the Member States should provide an equivalent and effective protection of the fundamental rights granted by the EU Charter of Fundamental Rights.[43]

More specifically, in the AFSJ context, the principle of mutual recognition may entail a number of shortcomings, not only, but most notably in relation to the protection of fundamental rights. Shortcomings in relation to the principle of mutual recognition may therefore impede upon the Union's objective to offer its citizens an AFSJ where fundamental rights and the different legal traditions and systems of the Member States are respected (*cf* Article 3(2) TFEU).

Accordingly, and as pointed out by Hans G Nilsson in the foreword to a previous volume of this series on European Police and Criminal Law Co-operation, the sensitive issues of proportionality and fundamental rights protection will no doubt be raised in the important area of mutual recognition. Nilsson argues that the question of whether the necessary mutual trust exists will become 'a Litmus test in the negotiations between the Council and the European Parliament'.[44] Thus, there is an ongoing political debate on important issues relevant to the application of the principle of mutual recognition in two topical fields within the AFSJ, ie, cross-border civil and criminal justice, which both have a strong impact on citizens' rights.

Against this background, the question posed in this chapter is how and to what extent the sensitive issues of proportionality and fundamental rights protection have been or could be balanced or protected, within two of the areas embracing the principle of mutual recognition within the AFSJ, ie civil and criminal matters respectively.[45]

4. MUTUAL RECOGNITION IN CRIMINAL MATTERS

After the adoption of the first concrete measure implementing the principle of mutual recognition of judicial decisions in European Union criminal law, ie, the European Arrest Warrant, several measures implementing the

[42] Case C-399/11 *Melloni*, EU:C:2013:107.

[43] Case C-491/10 *Joseba Andoni Aguirre Zarraga v Simone Pelz*, EU:C:2010:828.

[44] HG Nilsson, 'Foreword' in M Bergström and A Jonsson Cornell (eds), *European Police and Criminal Law Co-operation* (Oxford, Hart Publishing, 2014) vii.

[45] Concerning immigration see, eg, K Lenaerts, 'The Contribution of the European Court of Justice to the Area of Freedom, Security and Justice' (2013) 59(2) *International and Comparative Quarterly* 255, 301.

principle have followed.[46] According to Träskman, the problems that have arisen in conjunction with an EAW are mainly twofold.[47]

First, the practice by certain Member States to use the system in cases concerning relatively minor offences[48] may undermine the confidence in the application of the EAW. In this respect, a proportionality check may be necessary including issues such as the seriousness of the offence, the length of the sentence, the existence of an alternative and less cumbersome approach, etc. In this respect, Träskman argues that there is a disproportionate effect on the liberty and freedom of requested persons when EAWs are issued 'concerning cases for which (pre-trial) detention would otherwise be felt inappropriate'.[49]

Second, and more relevant for the purposes of this chapter, the procedural rights of an accused person have not been sufficiently protected.[50] This second problem is closely connected to mutual trust or rather lack of trust, as the principle of mutual recognition rests on the idea of mutual trust between Member States. In other words, if mutual trust is lacking, such trust must be ensured in order for mutual recognition instruments to function. It is partly in this light that you should view the Commission's activities to strengthen the procedural rights of suspected and accused persons through a set of minimum guarantees for a fair trial.

Accordingly, the 2009 Roadmap for strengthening procedural rights of a suspected person stated:

> Discussions on procedural rights within the context of the European Union over the last few years have not led to any concrete results. However, a lot of progress has been made in the area of judicial and police cooperation on measures that facilitate prosecution. It is now time to take action to improve the balance between these measures and the protection of procedural rights of the individual.[51]

Hence, it was deemed necessary to correct the distortion between the possibilities of initiating EU criminal procedures and 'the legal possibilities for suspected and accused persons to defend themselves against accusations'.[52] As a result, the EU has become increasingly active in the field of procedural

[46] See, eg, Directive 2011/99/EU of 13 December 2011 on the European Protection Order [2011] OJ L338/2; and Directive 2014/41/EU of 3 April 2014 regarding the European Investigation Order in criminal matters [2014] OJ L130/1.

[47] Träskman (n 6) 134.

[48] eg, in relation to Poland. See also Konstadinides, 'The Europeanisation of Extradition' (n 23).

[49] Träskman (n 6) 137.

[50] ibid, 134, pointing out that these problems are mentioned in the 2011 report from the European Commission to both the European Parliament and the Council about the implementation from 2007 of the Council Framework Decision of 13 June 2002 on the European arrest warrant and the surrender procedures between Member States, COM(2011) 175 final, 6.

[51] Resolution of the Council of 30 November 2009 on a Roadmap for strengthening procedural rights of suspected or accused persons in criminal proceedings (2009/C 295/01).

[52] Träskman (n 6) 134.

protection, which is also a direct consequence of the extended competences granted by the Lisbon Treaty.[53]

In this respect, these initiatives that follow the Roadmap for the strengthening of procedural rights of suspects and accused persons aim to promote mutual trust in cross-border cases, and

> represent an example of the EU's emphasis on the procedural rights side of the coin instead of (as previously) having mostly focused on the question of enforcement of coercive measures. The proposed instruments are based on Article 82(2) in order to facilitate mutual recognition in criminal matters.[54]

According to Herlin-Karnell, the Directive on the right of access to a lawyer in criminal proceedings and on the right to communicate upon arrest[55] is the most far-reaching piece of EU criminal law legislation in procedural criminal law so far.[56] Still, it only lays down minimum requirements at the EU level, promotes the application of the Charter, ie, Articles 6, 47 and 48, and builds upon Article 6 of the European Convention on Human Rights (ECHR) and the notion of a fair trial.[57] In respect of derogations, the EU principle of proportionality and the case law of the European Court of Human Rights (ECtHR) must be complied with. Yet, as pointed out by Herlin-Karnell, the EU Charter also grants exceptions to the rule of fundamental rights protection.[58] According to Article 52 of the EU Charter, Member States can derogate from Charter obligations on the basis of what is proportionate.[59] It is exactly in relation to the expanding area of EU procedural criminal law that there is reason to believe that the EU Charter and the ECHR will be particularly important.[60] Yet, as pointed out by Herlin-Karnell, the added value of the EU Charter 'will largely depend on the willingness of the Court

[53] Directive 2010/64/EU of 20 October 2010 on the right to interpretation and translation in criminal proceedings [2010] OJ L280/1; Directive 2012/13/EU of 22 May 2012 on the right to information in criminal proceedings [2012] OJ L142/1; and Directive 2013/48/EU of 22 October 2013 on the right of access to a lawyer in criminal proceedings and in European arrest warrant proceedings, and on the right to have a third party informed upon deprivation of liberty and to communicate with third persons and with consular authorities while deprived of liberty [2013] OJ L294/1.

[54] E Herlin-Karnell, 'Recent Developments in the Field of Substantive and Procedural EU Criminal Law—Challenges and Opportunities' in M Bergström and A Jonsson Cornell (eds), *European Police and Criminal Law Co-operation* (Oxford, Hart Publishing, 2014) 27.

[55] Commission, 'Proposal for a Directive on the right of access to a lawyer in criminal proceedings and on the right to communicate upon arrest' COM (2001) 326, *cf* Directive 2013/48/EU (n 53).

[56] Herlin-Karnell (n 54) 27, with further references to the discussion in European Union Committee, 30th Report of Session 2010–2012 *The European Union's Policy on Criminal Procedure* (HL 2010–12, 288).

[57] ibid.

[58] ibid.

[59] *cf* the Annex to the manual of the European Arrest Warrant ('Staff Working Document') where the Commission has included a part containing 'proportionality'.

[60] Herlin-Karnell (n 54) 34.

of Justice to interpret the wording "implementation of EU Law" in a liberal fashion'.[61]

Yet, the CJEU in the first national challenge against the EAW Framework Decision explored the practical consequences stemming from the application of the principle of mutual recognition in criminal matters.[62] The Court ruled on the conformity of the abolition of the principle of double criminality with the principle of legality. In short, the CJEU held that the EAW was compatible with fundamental rights in this respect.[63] According to Konstadinides, the aftermath of this case suggested

> a certain inconsistency deriving from the hesitation on the part of the EU institutions to address issues that are not raised in secondary legislation. It also unveiled the national courts' disinclination to question the protection of fundamental rights in EU law beyond a selfish critique related to the constitutional safeguards against the application of EU legislation upon their own nationals.[64]

Yet, in Klimek's view, the EAW is not only the most successful mutual recognition instrument of the EU, it might, 'in the area of European Union Criminal law—or more precisely—in the area of judicial co-operation in criminal matters, be the most successful mutual recognition instrument ever'.[65] This may well be the case, but found in a volume on civil justice, the imminent question is what relevance this argument might have for the field of study of this volume.

5. MUTUAL RECOGNITION IN CIVIL MATTERS

Against the background of the previous sections of this chapter, this section is drawing entirely on the previous chapters of this volume on civil justice. As pointed out in the foreword to this volume, mutual trust is a central issue for the development of civil justice and it runs as a thread throughout the chapters in this volume, being raised both explicitly and implicitly in many contributions. Mutual trust also forms part of the final specific theme on mutual recognition, in these final contributions. In her conclusions, Requejo-Isidro, for example, notes that differences in understanding between Member States on fundamental rights should be addressed in the interest of mutual trust.[66] Likewise, Storskrubb questions whether the concept should be imported into civil justice without safeguards.[67]

[61] ibid.

[62] Case C-303/05 *Advocaten voor de Wereld*, EU:C:2007:261.

[63] See further the analyses by T Konstadinides, 'Mass Surveillance and Data Protection in EU Law—The Data Retention Directive Saga' in M Bergström and A Jonsson Cornell (eds), *European Police and Criminal Law Co-operation* (Oxford, Hart Publishing, 2014) 77.

[64] ibid.

[65] L Klimek, *European Arrest Warrant* (Cham, Springer, 2015) 1.

[66] M Requejo-Isidro, chapter 14 in this volume.

[67] E Storskrubb, chapter 15 in this volume.

Yet, the EU's civil justice competencies are explicitly conditioned by requirements to respect fundamental rights as well as the legal traditions of the Member States; civil justice measures should predominantly be limited to cross-border issues and mutual recognition.[68] In this respect, and from the point of view of 'a true area of justice', Linton identifies four main areas of concern in existing EU legislation: (i) The piecemeal schemes to obtain enforceable judgments; (ii) the tension between mutual trust and fundamental rights; (iii) the confusion that reigns over the relationship between European and national grounds for refusal; and (iv) the increased need for parallel proceedings.[69] Thus, mainly agreeing with Träskman with regard to the criminal justice area, Linton finds it noteworthy that several of the instruments adopted after the quest for the abolishment of the *exequatur* procedure began, include the procedure. The impression conveyed is that the level of mutual trust between the legal and administrative systems of the Member States has not reached a sufficient 'maturity' to eliminate the control exercised in the enforcing Member State. This impression corresponds to a large extent with the legislative evolution of the field in general.

Comparing legislative techniques, Hess in the first chapter of this volume distinguishes between several different generations of legal instruments. The first generation including, for example, the Brussels I Regulation, mainly coordinates the national procedures in cross-border situations by providing for common rules on jurisdiction, pendency and recognition, and enforcement. Under the Brussels I Regulation, judgments and settlements are recognised automatically according to the principle of mutual trust.[70] The second generation aims at 'the abolition of *exequatur* proceedings and is based on the overarching principle of mutual recognition'.[71] In relation to this second generation, Hess argues that the framework of European procedural law encourages the growing competition between the national adjudicative systems. Within this second generation focusing on procedural law, Hess further comments upon several sectorial instruments adopted after 2004 that provide for minimum standards and rules and for an automatic recognition of judicial decisions in other Member States. Amongst third generation instruments, Hess places instruments focusing on private international law and more recently also combining private international law with international procedural law.

According to Hess, the law-making process has slowed down in recent years due to

> political resistance in the Member States and the European Parliament with regard to underlying regulatory concepts such as mutual trust, the abolition of the public

[68] ibid, Arts 4, 67 and 81. See further R Money-Kyrle, chapter 12 in this volume.

[69] M Linton, chapter 13 in this volume.

[70] B Hess, chapter 1 in this volume with further reference to B Hess, *Europäisches Zivilprozessrecht* (Heidelberg, CF Müller, 2010) § 3, paras 22ff.

[71] B Hess, chapter 1 in this volume.

policy clause and the growing empowerment of the CJEU as a consequence of the communitarization of procedural (and substantive) law.[72]

Thereby, European law does not provide for a set of minimum standards of domestic civil procedures. Instead, 'the pertinent standards are not found in EU instruments, they were developed by the case law of the CJEU'.[73] According to Hess,[74]

> several principles can be detected: first, Union law provides for procedural guarantees such as the principle of access to justice, fair trial and also mutual trust. These principles are derived from human rights law, which entails a growing constitutionalization of the procedural laws at the EU level (reinforced by the Charter of Fundamental Rights and the European Convention on Human Rights). Second, the principles of effectiveness and equivalence influence the national adjudication systems.[75] In practice, however, these principles are applied according to the circumstances of a specific case,[76] and it seems to be difficult to elaborate a comprehensive line in the case law. Nevertheless, it might be advisable to elaborate a set of common principles of European and Constitutional law to be applied in domestic proceedings.

These standards can certainly be further improved and developed. Highly interesting in this respect are the conclusions drawn by Linton in her chapter of this volume. While analysing the various legal instruments in the area that protects the rights of the defendant, she observes that some EU instruments guard these rights in the Member State of enforcement, others specify the Member State of origin, while a further set of instruments lay down safeguards in both the Member State of origin and the Member State of enforcement. Linton concludes that, in general, EU law appears to be developing towards a Member State of origin solution. She then argues that because of mutual trust, flaws in the original proceedings to the detriment of the defendant should mainly be remedied in the Member State of origin, and not in the course of enforcement. She rightly points out that difficulties arise when errors are not, or cannot, be remedied in the Member State of origin.[77]

The following quotation,[78] from a 2011 joint proposal by Finland and Sweden to the EU working party in charge of the drafting of the Succession Regulation, captures the concerns of the two countries about changes for

[72] ibid.

[73] ibid. For a critical assessment *cf* J Schmidt, *Rechtssicherheit im Europäischen Zivilverfahrensrecht* (Tübingen, Mohr Siebeck, 2015) 260ff.

[74] B Hess, chapter 1 in this volume.

[75] Hess, *Europäisches Zivilprozessrecht* (n 70) § 11, paras 4ff.

[76] Conclusions AG Jääskinen in Case C-352/13 *CDC*, EU:C:2014:2443 paras 119ff, on the restrictive interpretation of arbitration and jurisdiction clauses according to the principle of effectiveness in order to guarantee the efficient enforcement of EU cartel law.

[77] M Linton, chapter 13 in this volume.

[78] Brussels, 4 November 2011, 16386/11, LIMITE, JUSTCIV 290, CODEC 1893.

the worse, if Sweden and Finland in their mutual relations were to be covered by Union rules:

> Having to introduce less flexible rules and, not least, rules on *exequatur* after more than 70 years without such provisions would send the wrong message to our citizens on the benefits of further EU integration, and we are strongly opposed to this.

Generally, the main concerns have been elegantly summarised by Linton in this volume:

> Mutual recognition suggests that irrespective of whether a judgment has been issued in Berlin, Prague or Stockholm, it should be treated equally within the EU.[79] Assuming equivalence between European judgments, mutual recognition calls for mutual trust, confidence and an understanding of diversity in different legal and administrative systems.[80] Working horizontally between courts and administrations, mutual trust ultimately requires democratic and independent judiciaries, quality and efficiency of the judicial systems and observation of the rule of law as well as fundamental rights in each Member State. Only if these conditions are met, will the purpose and objectives of *exequatur* become superfluous, and a true European area of justice will be formed.

In relation to grounds for refusal, a new form of European enforcement procedure designed to further enhance mutual recognition of judgments was introduced in the Brussels I recast Regulation. Although the formal procedure of *exequatur* has been abolished, the grounds for refusal in the Brussels I Regulation have instead been maintained. As Linton puts it, 'the European quest for free circulation of judgments has targeted the formal part of the *exequatur* procedure, but not the function it serves in inspecting whether the foreign judgment meets the necessary requirements for enforcement'.[81] As a result, the Brussels I recast Regulation has limited the scope of the European *exequatur* by suppressing the formal function of *exequatur*, while retaining its control function in the Member State of enforcement. Arguably and as Linton states, it could be held that some or possibly all defences included in the Regulation are not compatible with the idea of mutual trust between Member States.[82] Linton further argues that, 'the varied schemes for enforcement can be an impediment to predictability for stakeholders and judiciaries concerning the applicable rules. If legislation is

[79] In its original meaning, mutual recognition is perceived as a prohibition to impose national controls or verifications in another Member State, if already carried out in the Member State of origin, dating back to the *Cassis de Dijon* case, Case 120/78 *Rewe-Zentral AG and Bundesmonopolverwaltung für Branntwein* [1979] ECR 649, EU:C:1979:42.

[80] M Jänterä-Jareborg, 'Harmonisering, samordning och ömsesidigt förtroende inom Europeiska unionen—utvecklingen inom familjerätt' (2005) *Svensk Juristtidning* 804, 813–14.

[81] ibid.

[82] See also A Dickinson, 'The Revision of the Brussels I Regulation. Surveying the Proposed Brussels I *bis* Regulation—Solid Foundations but Renovation Needed' (2010) XII *Yearbook of Private International Law* (Sellier European Law Publishers, 2011) 247, 254–68.

too complicated to reach its addressees, or judiciaries, a credibility deficit in European law will emerge'.[83]

6. MUTUAL RECOGNITION AND GROUNDS FOR REFUSAL

In the Internal Market context, where the principle of mutual recognition was first set in operation, there are legitimate derogations from mutual recognition. As stressed by Storskrubb, this was introduced in the *Cassis* case itself with the concept of mandatory requirements,[84] ie, to legitimately protect important public interests such as consumer protection or public health, if it can be shown that the prohibition and limitation to free movement was proportional.[85] Arguably, this Internal Market method could possibly also be developed for the AFSJ purposes, thereby striking a balance between mutual recognition and the protection of fundamental rights while taking the proportionality principle into consideration.

Notwithstanding, minimum harmonisation is often deemed necessary in order to complement mutual recognition that may otherwise lead to too much fragmentation.[86] In the AFSJ context, minimum harmonisation can generally be found in the EU Charter and to some extent also in the ECHR. Still, as referred to by Storskrubb, Poires Maduro notes that falling back on the general clauses or principles entails a less beneficial delegation of responsibility 'for the application of the principle to the judicial process'.[87] Further, as pointed out by Storskrubb, the CJEU 'has considered itself and the Member States bound by a presumption of mutual trust in the cases that have emerged so far in civil justice in which the requirements of mutual recognition have been challenged from a fundamental rights perspective'.[88] Minimum harmonisation might therefore be necessary beyond the EU Charter and the ECHR possibly addressing specific issues that have been identified as particularly problematic.

For example, Linton argues that the relationship between, on the one hand, European grounds for refusal, and on the other, national grounds for refusal are surrounded by uncertainty.[89] In this respect, Linton argues that diverging national grounds for opposing execution could be viewed as incompatible with mutual trust and the free circulation of judgments.

[83] M Linton, chapter 13 in this volume.

[84] Case 120/78 *Rewe-Zentral AG v Bundesmonopolverwaltung für Branntwein*, EU:C:1979:42.

[85] E Storskrubb, chapter 15 in this volume.

[86] A balance need to be struck between recognition and the constraints attached to it. See further E Storskrubb, chapter 15 in this volume with further references to Nicolaïdis 'Trusting the Poles?' (n 24).

[87] E Storskrubb, chapter 15 in this volume with further references to M Poiares Maduro (n 1).

[88] E Storskrubb, chapter 15 in this volume.

[89] M Linton, chapter 13 in this volume.

Instead, whereas initial control should be moved to the Member State of origin, Member States may retain limited powers to refuse a foreign judgment depending on which instrument applies.

As a result, Linton argues that the legal situation in the EU has plainly become too complex and complicated. In order to overcome structural differences, she would welcome a review of the EU's private international law instruments as predicted in the EU Justice Agenda for 2020.[90] The added value, in general European terms, would be an increased predictability and legal certainty, due to the achieved unity of approach. This argument is equally relevant for the criminal justice field, where a more coherent legislative plan could be equally beneficial.

Generally, a system based on initial control in the Member State of origin, coupled with limited powers to refuse a foreign judgment beyond a certain level of minimum harmonisation, with due respect for the proportionality principle, both within civil and criminal justice would, as Linton has pointed out, greatly benefit predictability and legal certainty. Arguably, judicial control could then follow the same methodological considerations developed in the Internal Market context where the protection of fundamental rights could be legitimately upheld by the enforcing state beyond the minimum harmonisation level if applied in a proportionate way.

Mutual recognition and trust must thereby be based on a realistic examination of the concrete circumstances thereby involving a wider scope for taking human rights considerations into the mutual recognition procedures. In this respect, the new configurations of crime fighting need to be viewed and interpreted through a methodological and theoretical lens, in order to address the problems identified and meet wider challenges,[91] for example, that fundamental rights are respected in relation to the development of closer judicial cooperation and coordination in Europe.[92] Within the wider AFSJ, Vice-President Lenaerts has already argued that, as the ECJ's contribution to the AFSJ develops, 'an unprecedented level of coordination between quite different areas of EU law on both the procedural and substantive levels is to take place. Respect for fundamental rights will definitely be a unifying factor binding them all together'.[93]

[90] COM(2014) 144 final.

[91] B Wennström, 'In Search of a New Lens' in M Bergström and A Jonsson Cornell (eds), *European Police and Criminal Law Co-operation* (Oxford, Hart Publishing, 2014).

[92] K Lenaerts and JA Gutierrez-Fons, 'To Say What the Law of the EU Is: Methods of Interpretation and the European Court of Justice (Academy of European Law, Distinguished Lectures of the Academy, AEL 2013/9).

[93] K Lenaerts, 'The Contribution of the European Court of Justice to the Area of Freedom, Security and Justice' (2013) 59(2) *International and Comparative Quarterly* 255, 301. See also V Mitsilegas, 'Mutual Recognition, Mutual Trust and Fundamental Rights After Lisbon' in V Mitsilegas, M Bergström and T Konstadinides (eds), *Research Handbook on EU Criminal Law* (Cheltenham, Edward Elgar Publishing, forthcoming 2015).

Index